# UNITED STATES AND INTERNATIONAL SALES, LEASE, AND LICENSING LAW

ASPEN CASEBOOK SERIES

# UNITED STATES AND INTERNATIONAL SALES, LEASE, AND LICENSING LAW

## CASES AND PROBLEMS

**Second Edition**

**Bryan D. Hull**
*Professor of Law*
*Loyola Law School, Los Angeles*

Wolters Kluwer
Law & Business

Published by Wolters Kluwer Law & Business in New York.

Wolters Kluwer Law & Business serves customers worldwide
with CCH, Aspen Publishers, and Kluwer Law International
products. (www.wolterskluwerlb.com)



To contact Customer Service, e-mail customer.service@wolterskluwer.com, call 1-800-234-1660, fax 1-800-901-9075, or mail correspondence to:

Wolters Kluwer Law & Business
Attn: Order Department
PO Box 990
Frederick, MD 21705

Printed in the United States of America.

1 2 3 4 5 6 7 8 9 0

ISBN 978-0-7355-0714-2

Library of Congress Cataloging-in-Publication Data

Hull, Bryan, 1957-
United States and international sales, lease, and licensing law : cases and problems / Bryan D. Hull. — 2nd ed.
p. cm.
— (Aspen casebook series)
ISBN 978-0-7355-0714-2
1. Export sales contracts — United States. 2. Sales — United States. 3. Licenses — United States. 4. Casebooks. I. Title.

KF915.H85 2012
346.7307'2—dc23

2012001059

# About Wolters Kluwer Law & Business

Wolters Kluwer Law & Business is a leading global provider of intelligent information and digital solutions for legal and business professionals in key specialty areas and respected educational resources for professors and law students. Wolters Kluwer Law & Business connects legal and business professionals as well as those in the education market with timely, specialized authoritative content and information-enabled solutions to support success through productivity, accuracy, and mobility.

Serving customers worldwide, Wolters Kluwer Law & Business products include those under the Aspen Publishers, CCH, Kluwer Law International, Loislaw, Best Case, ftwilliam.com, and MediRegs family of products.

**CCH** products have been a trusted resource since 1913 and are highly regarded resources for legal, securities, antitrust and trade regulation, government contracting, banking, pension, payroll, employment and labor, and healthcare reimbursement and compliance professionals.

**Aspen Publishers** products provide essential information to attorneys, business professionals, and law students. Written by preeminent authorities, the product line offers analytical and practical information in a range of specialty practice areas from securities law and intellectual property to mergers and acquisitions and pension/benefits. Aspen's trusted legal education resources provide professors and students with high-quality, up-to-date, and effective resources for successful instruction and study in all areas of the law.

**Kluwer Law International** products provide the global business community with reliable international legal information in English. Legal practitioners, corporate counsel, and business executives around the world rely on Kluwer Law journals, looseleafs, books, and electronic products for comprehensive information in many areas of international legal practice.

**Loislaw** is a comprehensive online legal research product providing legal content to law firm practitioners of various specializations. Loislaw provides attorneys with the ability to quickly and efficiently find the necessary legal information they need, when and where they need it, by facilitating access to primary law as well as state-specific law, records, forms, and treatises.

**Best Case Solutions** is the leading bankruptcy software product to the bankruptcy industry. It provides software and workflow tools to flawlessly streamline petition preparation and the electronic filing process, while timely incorporating ever-changing court requirements.

**ftwilliam.com** offers employee benefits professionals the highest quality plan documents (retirement, welfare, and non-qualified) and government forms (5500/PBGC, 1099 and IRS) software at highly competitive prices.

**MediRegs** products provide integrated health care compliance content and software solutions for professionals in healthcare, higher education, and life sciences, including professionals in accounting, law, and consulting.

Wolters Kluwer Law & Business, a division of Wolters Kluwer, is headquartered in New York. Wolters Kluwer is a market-leading global information services company focused on professionals.

*To my niece and nephew, Lisa and Ben Kellerman.*

*May they experience much happiness in their lives.*

*Love, Uncle Bryan*

# *SUMMARY OF CONTENTS*

# CONTENTS

# PREFACE TO SECOND EDITION

I read somewhere that "the only reason to teach a class once is to teach it twice." I believe there is a lot of truth in that statement. Much time and effort goes into the preparation of a class, and it may not be worth it if you teach the class only once. In addition, I know I made a fair number of mistakes the first time I taught a class and know that I did a much better job the second time.

I think one could also say that "the only reason to write a casebook is to write a second edition." As I used the first edition of this book and heard from others who had also used it, I realized that there were certainly areas for improvement in a second edition. So, here it is, and I hope that it is indeed an improvement.

Of course, one reason to write a second edition is to update the first edition. Since the last edition was written, new editions of the INCOTERMS and Uniform Customs and Practice for Documentary Credits have been released by the International Chamber of Commerce. The Uniform Law Commission (National Conference of Commissioners on Uniform State Laws) and American Law Institute decided to drop the 2003 amendments to UCC Article 2 because they were not being adopted by state legislatures. More state legislatures adopted the 2001 revision of Article 1. The second edition of this book discusses these changes, among other things.

Because of the decision to drop the 2003 amendments to Article 2, I have decided to drop references to them in the second edition. I have also decided to cite only the 2001 revision of Article 1 (including the change to UCC 1-301 that was made in 2008) because most states have now adopted the revised Article 1. I hope this makes things less complicated for the students and for the professors teaching the course.

In response to some helpful suggestions by professors who have used the book, I have added more explanatory material in some areas. I have also changed some of the cases. It is my hope that the new cases do a better job of exploring the relevant concepts than the cases they replaced in the prior edition.

I want to give special thanks to my colleague at Loyola Law School, Associate Dean Sean Scott, for taking the time to give me many thoughtful suggestions on improvements for the book. I also want to thank Professor Richard Hyland of Rutgers Law School in Camden, New Jersey, for his kind comments and helpful suggestions. I haven't necessarily had time to implement all of the excellent suggestions I have received, but perhaps by the third edition I'll get things right! Any errors or omissions in the text are obviously my own.

*Bryan D. Hull*
Loyola Law School
Los Angeles, California
January 2012

# ACKNOWLEDGMENTS

I would first like to thank my employer, Loyola Law School, Los Angeles, for its financial support in helping me write this book. Second, thanks to my colleague Professor Lary Lawrence, for his encouragement and his willingness to serve as a "guinea pig" in using the manuscript in his classes. Lary has also given me many useful comments that have assisted me in improving the product. Of course, any remaining errors are my own! Also, thanks to my colleague, Dean Emeritus Gerald T. McLaughlin, for sharing with me his materials on letters of credit. He has forgotten more on this subject than I will ever know.

I want to thank Professor Eric Bergsten for putting on the Willem C. Vis International Arbitration Moot Competition the last fourteen years in Vienna, Austria. It was our school's involvement in that competition that motivated us to offer the comparative sales law class that gave rise to this book. Some of the problems in the book are inspired by issues that were considered in prior Vis competitions.

Thanks go to the editors and reviewers of Aspen Publishers. Their hard work and helpful comments have made this a better product.

Over the years I have been aided by a number of student research assistants and proofreaders and am grateful to all of them. In chronological order in which they worked on the book, they are: Samir Sheth, Mark Murad, Jason Rothman, Alexis Endsley, Michael Coker, Mike Lavaee, and Jeff Payne. I also want to thank all of the students who have taken my class during the time that I have been working on this book. My experience in using the manuscript with them has been invaluable.

Finally, anyone who writes a casebook in an established area owes a debt to those who have previously written casebooks in the area. I have learned a lot from those books, both from my days as a student and now as a professor who has reviewed them and taught out of them. My first exposure to many of the problems and cases that are in this book came when I used or reviewed those casebooks.

*Bryan D. Hull*
Loyola Law School
Los Angeles, California
January 2012

# *UNITED STATES AND INTERNATIONAL SALES, LEASE, AND LICENSING LAW*

CHAPTER 1

# INTRODUCTION

## A. THE SALES TRANSACTION

The primary focus of this book is on domestic and international laws governing contracts for the sale of goods. Assume, for example, that Pronto Printer Company, located in Texas, agrees to sell a printing press that it has manufactured to Paula's Print Shop, located in California. Numerous legal questions might arise concerning this transaction. For example, has an enforceable contract been formed? Do the goods conform to warranties given by the seller? In the event of breach, which remedies are available to the injured party? These questions would be covered by the Uniform Commercial Code ("UCC") as enacted in Texas and California.

Assume instead that Paula's Print Shop is located in California but that Pronto Printer Company is located in Mexico. Now the UCC may not apply, but instead the Convention on Contracts for the International Sale of Goods ("CISG") may govern much of the transaction. Some of the legal questions raised in the transaction may be covered by the domestic sales law of California and Mexico, which will fill gaps left by the CISG. As we will see, difficult choice-of-law questions are sometimes raised when sales transactions are conducted across national borders.

A long-distance sales transaction may also include third parties, such as carriers (e.g., truckers or airlines) that transport the goods from seller to buyer, and banks that agree to pay the seller via a letter of credit upon proof that the goods have been shipped. This book covers laws governing the duties of carriers and banks involved in sales transactions.

This book does not cover real estate transactions or service contracts, which are the subject of myriad nonuniform laws (and which are covered in other law school courses). Difficult questions may exist, however, in mixed goods-and-services transactions as to whether the law governing sales or the law governing services applies. These "scope" questions will be considered in the next chapter.

## B. LEASES AND LICENSES

In Part II of this book are materials dealing with transactions that in some ways are similar to sales of goods; that is, leases of goods and licenses of information (including software). You may have been involved in lease and license transactions yourself. For example, you may have leased a car. When you purchase software for your computer, you are not really "buying" the software, you are obtaining a license to use it. Lease and license transactions are sufficiently similar to sales that courts have sometimes applied sales law in resolving disputes involving leases of goods or licenses of software. The transactions are sufficiently dissimilar, however, that uniform laws have been developed that would apply to leases and licenses instead of sales law. In Chapters 10 and 11, *infra*, the similarities and differences of lease and license law to sales law are considered.

## C. PRACTICAL IMPORTANCE OF THE SUBJECT MATTER

Students may ask whether it is important for them to take a course covering the topics that are considered in this book. If the student is interested in going into transactional business law or commercial litigation, it is worth noting that in 2010 the value of goods exported from the United States was over $1.2 trillion while the value of goods imported was over $1.9 trillion.[1] The sheer volume of transactions indicates the need for lawyers to deal with the legal issues that arise from them. The import/export data also underscores the need for the business lawyer to understand not only domestic law covering sales of goods, but also international law. The student may have been exposed to domestic and international sales law in the first-year course in contracts, but perhaps additional study would be useful.

With regard to leases of goods and licenses of information, these types of transactions are becoming increasingly important in both the United States and international economies. In 2010, the value of transactions within the information sector of the United States economy, which includes software, publishing, motion pictures, and data processing, was over $670 billion. Transactions in these areas generally involve licenses rather than sales; for example, software from Microsoft is obtained via license, not sale. Leases of non–real property assets in 2009 accounted for over $182 billion.[2] The law in this area, especially regarding licensing of information, is not as well-developed as the law covering sales of goods and is typically not covered in first-year contracts courses. A student going into transactional business law or commercial litigation might find it useful to study it here.

---

1. U.S. Dep't of Commerce Web site, *http://tse.export.gov* (accessed Oct. 2011).

2. U.S. Dep't of Commerce, Bureau of Economic Analysis Web site, *www.bea.gov* (accessed Oct. 2011).

# D. SOURCES OF LAW

## 1. THE UNIFORM COMMERCIAL CODE—SALES AND LEASES

### (a) Background and Content

The Uniform Commercial Code ("UCC"), in particular Article 2, will cover most (if not all) of the aspects of a sale-of-goods transaction if the buyer and the seller are located in the United States (other than Louisiana). Likewise, the UCC, in particular Article 2A, will cover most (if not all) of any transaction involving leases of goods. The UCC was first promulgated in the 1940s by the American Law Institute ("ALI") and the National Conference of Commissioners on Uniform State Laws ("NCCUSL"), also known as the Uniform Law Commission ("ULC"). ALI and NCCUSL are organizations dedicated to law reform efforts; their members consist of lawyers, judges, law professors, and other public officials. When ALI and NCCUSL draft model legislation, they then encourage the states to enact it. The UCC was enacted by all states except Louisiana during the 1950s and 1960s.[3]

The chief architect of the UCC was Professor Karl Llewellyn, one of the leaders of the legal realism movement. Professor Llewellyn's goal was to provide uniform and certain rules to govern commercial transactions throughout the United States, thus reducing the costs of transacting business across state boundaries. He sought to make the UCC flexible, rejecting formalistic mechanical application of rules, so that courts would be able to react to changing business practices. He was not so much interested in drafting rules that would cause businesspeople to conform their business practices to the rules, but instead sought to draft rules that reflected the way that people transacted business.[4]

As an example of what Llewellyn was trying to accomplish, UCC Article 2 rejects the notion of "title" as being important in terms of allocating risk of loss when goods are destroyed.[5] This was a large change from prior law, the old Uniform Sales Act, which generally imposed loss on the party who had title. Much litigation had arisen under prior law over the question of who had "title" to goods, and the law was uncertain. The rules in Article 2, sections 2-509 and 2-510, are based on the way that parties allocated risk themselves by contract; for example, by use of a C.I.F. contract (price includes "Cost, Insurance, and Freight"). C.I.F. contracts (covered in UCC section 2-320) and sections 2-509 and 2-510 allocate risk of loss based on the occurrence of certain defined events, for example whether the goods have been handed over to the carrier, rather than on the murky concept of title. More certain results are achieved, reflecting the way that people actually do business.[6] The UCC risk allocation rules are discussed further on pages 113-117, *infra*.

---

3. Louisiana has subsequently adopted many provisions of the UCC, but not Article 2.
4. See G. Gilmore, *The Ages of American Law* 85 (1977).
5. See UCC §2-401.
6. Testimony of Professor Karl Llewellyn, 1 N.Y. State Law Revision Commn. 1954 Report 160-61 (1954).

The UCC replaced some prior uniform laws, such as the Uniform Sales Act and Negotiable Instruments Law, and other nonuniform state laws. Originally, the UCC covered sales of goods (Article 2), negotiable instruments (Article 3), bank collections (Article 4), letters of credit (Article 5), bulk sales (Article 6), documents of title (Article 7), investment securities (Article 8), and secured transactions in personal property (Article 9). Subsequently, articles were added covering leases of goods (Article 2A) and wire transfers of funds (Article 4A). Article 1 of the UCC contains general provisions applicable to the other articles.

The UCC is a "living organism" in that it is constantly subject to study and revision by its sponsors. All of the articles have been the subject of significant revisions over the past 20 years or have been first added to the Code during that time (Articles 2A and 4A). Once the ALI and NCCUSL agree on changes to the UCC, they are submitted to the states for adoption. Unless otherwise indicated, citations in this book are to the official text of the UCC as of 2011, including the 2001 and 2008 approved revisions to UCC Article 1.[7]

### (b) Using the UCC

#### i. Does the UCC Apply?

In using the UCC, the first question that a practitioner must ask is whether it applies to a given transaction. While the UCC is a very comprehensive statute, it does not cover all contractual relationships. For instance, it does not cover real estate transactions or service transactions. Those types of transactions are left to other contract law. In this book, we will primarily study sales transactions, which are covered by Article 2 of the UCC. We will also cover leases of goods, which are covered by Article 2A of the UCC. The scope of UCC Article 2 will be considered in more detail in the next chapter.

#### ii. Which State's Version of the Code Applies?

Once it is determined that the contract is within the scope of the UCC, the practitioner must consider which state's version of the UCC is applicable. While the UCC purports to be a "uniform" code, all states have adopted their own versions of the Code with varying degrees of nonuniformity. In addition, the courts in the various states have given their own interpretations of the law. How courts deal with choice-of-law problems is considered in the next chapter. Once the practitioner has determined the appropriate state, the practitioner must consult that state's version of the UCC and its court decisions to see if the law in that state is different from that adopted in other states.

---

7. In 2003, a number of amendments to UCC Articles 2 and 2A were approved by the ALI and NCCUSL. These amendments proved to be quite controversial and were not adopted by state legislatures. In 2011, the ALI and NCCUSL decided to drop the proposed amendments from the official text of the UCC; thus, they are not considered in this book. For a discussion of the contentious Article 2 revision process by one of the reporters, see Speidel, *Revising UCC Article 2: A View from the Trenches*, 52 Hastings L.J. 607 (2001).

### iii. The Role of Article 1

The practitioner must be aware that Article 1 of the UCC will apply together with the specific UCC Article covering the transaction. For example, in a sale of goods case, Article 1 will apply along with Article 2. Article 1 contains the general provisions that apply to all of the UCC articles. The practitioner should first look to the specific article of the UCC for the applicable rule and then should also consider the rules in Article 1. In case of conflict, the rule from the specific article controls.

### iv. Defined Terms

In using the UCC, the practitioner must not assume that words used have the meaning that would be attached by a layperson. The UCC is full of special definitions for terms. Each article of the UCC contains its own set of definitions; for example, the definitions for Article 2 are contained in Part 1 of that Article. Section 1-201 contains general definitions that are applicable to all articles (unless the specific article has a more specialized definition that trumps it). At the end of many of the UCC sections, there is a cross-reference table for definitions. While this is useful, the practitioner must be careful because not all defined terms are cross-referenced! When in doubt, a reader of the UCC should check to see if a particular term is defined.

### v. Official Comments

Another useful tool in interpreting the UCC is its official commentary. The comments provide insight as to the intent of the drafters of the Code. It must be kept in mind, however, that the comments do not carry the same weight as the statutes themselves; state legislatures enact the statutes, not the comments. Nevertheless, because the comments are often easier to read than the statutes, practitioners and courts may be tempted to put greater weight on them than the statutes. An example of a discrepancy between the comments and the statutes can be found in UCC section 2-207. Subsection (2) indicates that terms in an acceptance that are additional to those in the offer should be considered for inclusion in the contract under that subsection. Official Comment 3 to 2-207 indicates that both additional *and different* terms should be considered (emphasis added). Some courts choose to follow the comment, and consider different terms under subsection (2).[8]

### vi. Case Law

As it has been more than 40 years since the UCC was enacted, there is a large body of case law interpreting it. Lower courts in a particular jurisdiction are bound by interpretations of the UCC from higher courts in that jurisdiction. Since the enactments of the UCC are largely uniform, decisions by a court

8. *See, e.g., Steiner v. Mobil Oil Corp.*, 20 Cal. 3d 90, 141 Cal. Rptr. 157, 569 P.2d 751 (1977).

in one state interpreting a section of the UCC will be influential on courts of another state interpreting the identical section.

### vii. Other Applicable State and Federal Laws

The practitioner must realize, however, that the UCC will not necessarily answer all questions in cases that are within its scope. First of all, applicable federal statutes will govern to the extent that they are inconsistent with the UCC by virtue of the Supremacy Clause of the U.S. Constitution.[9] In the sales area, examples of federal statutes that apply are the Magnuson-Moss Consumer Warranty Act[10] and the Federal Bills of Lading Act.[11] Both of these federal laws will be discussed later in the book.

In addition, the UCC does not supply all of the state law that might apply to a transaction. Section 2-102 states that the UCC does not impair or repeal state consumer protection statutes. An example of state consumer protection law is the "lemon law" that many states have adopted, permitting consumers to return defective automobiles after the seller has had a specified number of opportunities to repair defects. See the discussion of lemon laws at page 111, *infra*.

UCC section 1-103 indicates that certain general principles of law and equity "supplement" the provisions of the Code. This provision can be viewed as a bit of a "wild card" provision in that it gives license to courts to look outside the UCC to resolve disputes. It should be noted, however, that general principles of law and equity are not to be used if displaced by a particular provision of the UCC. The official comments to UCC section 1-103 indicate that general principles of law and equity should not be used if they are inconsistent with the purposes and policies of the applicable provisions of the Code.

## 2. LICENSING LAW

As noted above, the law governing licenses of information is not as well-developed as the law governing sales and leases of goods. There is not a widely adopted uniform code like the UCC covering the topic. Courts have thus sometimes used UCC Article 2 to resolve disputes involving licenses, believing that the rules governing sales also make sense in a license transaction.

Believing that it is inappropriate to apply Article 2 to licensing transactions, NCCUSL sponsored the Uniform Computer Information Transactions Act ("UCITA"). UCITA has been criticized as being unduly favorable to software providers and has thus not been widely adopted. The reasons for this are discussed more fully in Chapter 11, *infra*. Nevertheless, UCITA may yet be influential to courts as persuasive authority as to what the law ought to be, and its provisions may also be included in licensing contracts. It is therefore useful for students to learn at least some of its provisions.

---

9. U.S. Const. art. VI, ¶ 2.
10. 15 U.S.C. §§2301-2312.
11. 49 U.S.C. 80101, *et seq.*

Courts dealing with licensing issues involving software may also be persuaded by the *Principles of the Law of Software Contracts* promulgated by the ALI in 2010. These principles were developed by experts in contract law and are designed to give guidance to judges dealing with issues posed by new technology. Because the law is undeveloped, the principles are not a *restatement* of the law, but rather suggestions as to how the law should develop. Only time will tell as to whether they indeed prove to be influential.

Since licenses of information involve permission granted to use copyrighted or patented materials, federal law covering copyrights and patents are also important. An in-depth study of those areas of the law is beyond the scope of this book.

## 3. TORT LAW

Sometimes a dispute involving a sale, lease, or license may also involve a possible tort. For example, a defective product might cause severe injury to the purchaser. This might give rise to both a breach of warranty action under UCC Article 2 and also an action for strict tort products liability. Sometimes representations may be made by a seller, lessor, or licensor that prove to be false. These representations may be warranties and may also be actionable fraud. The practitioner must decide whether the case can proceed on a contract theory, tort theory, or both. There are advantages and disadvantages to proceeding on a contract versus a tort theory, and vice versa. For example, a tort cause of action may permit punitive damage recovery, while a contract cause of action generally does not. A tort action sometimes requires a showing of negligence or intentional wrongdoing, while a contract action does not. The practitioner must then keep tort law in mind when considering cases involving sales, leases, or licenses. This issue is discussed more fully on pages 72-78 and 209-218, *infra*.

## 4. THE CONVENTION ON CONTRACTS FOR THE INTERNATIONAL SALE OF GOODS (CISG)

In this book, we will also study the United Nations Convention on Contracts for the International Sale of Goods ("CISG"). In its most basic application, the CISG will apply to a sale-of-goods transaction if the buyer is located in a nation that has adopted the CISG, the seller is located in another nation that has adopted the CISG, and the parties have not opted out of the CISG in their contract. We will study the scope of the CISG in more detail in the next chapter.

### (a) Background

The CISG was promulgated by the United Nations through its Commission on International Trade Law ("UNCITRAL") in 1980. It came into force on January 1, 1988, following adoption by 11 states. As of fall 2011, the

CISG was in force in 77 nations, including the United States. Noteworthy among those nations that have *not* adopted the CISG is the United Kingdom. For a complete listing of those nations that have adopted the CISG, see the UNCITRAL Web site, *www.uncitral.org.*

The CISG is part of an overall effort by UNCITRAL and other international organizations, such as the International Institute for the Unification of Private Law ("UNIDROIT") and the Hague Conference on Private International Law (the Hague Conference), to provide international commercial law covering many of the same areas that are covered by the UCC in the United States. The purpose of these organizations is similar to the purpose of the original drafters of the UCC, namely to provide uniformity and certainty to law governing commercial transactions. Without a unifying international convention in place, an international commercial transaction would be subject to the myriad nonuniform laws of the nations involved in the transaction. From time to time, the book will refer to other international commercial laws.[12]

### (b) Interpreting the CISG

In comparing the UCC to the CISG, a couple of differences may be particularly obvious to the reader. One difference is that the UCC is a much more detailed set of rules. Another difference is that the CISG has few defined terms. The CISG had to be drafted in a way that is acceptable to many different nations and understood by people who speak many different languages. At times, the CISG is written in a broad, vague way, leaving implementation to courts and arbitral tribunals.

One area of ambiguity is whether there exists an implied covenant of good faith and fair dealing in international contracts for the sale of goods. CISG Article 7 states that judges and arbitrators should have regard for the CISG's "international character and to the need to promote uniformity in its application and the observance of good faith in international trade." Unlike the UCC, the CISG does not provide that there is an implied covenant of good faith and fair dealing in sales contracts. Because of disagreement among nations as to the role of good faith in sales contracts, Article 7 was drafted ambiguously. Taken literally, it appears that Article 7 brings good faith into play only in the interpretation of the CISG: When in doubt regarding the meaning of a provision, the judge or arbitrator should adopt the meaning that promotes good faith in international trade. On the other hand, the provision could be read broadly to imply an obligation on the part of parties to a sales contract to act in good faith.

Another command of Article 7 is that decision makers should have regard for the CISG's "international character and the need to promote uniformity." Decisions by tribunals in one nation should thus be influential on decisions made by tribunals in other nations. CISG case law can be found on a Web site maintained by Pace University School of Law, *www.cisg.law.pace.edu* (referred

12. For a list of the laws promulgated by UNCITRAL, see *www.uncitral.org*. See also *www.unidroit.org* and *www.hcch.net* for other international laws (all sites accessed Oct. 2011).

to as the Pace Web site). Likewise, international commentary on the CISG by scholars should be influential, as shall be discussed more fully below.

CISG Article 7 also notes that if the CISG does not decide an issue within its scope, it should be settled in conformity with the general principles on which it is based (e.g., the desire to promote good faith in international trade). In trying to determine these principles, one might refer to the UNIDROIT Principles of International Commercial Contracts, which can be viewed at *www.unidroit.org*. The UNIDROIT Principles were most recently revised in 2010. The UNIDROIT Principles can be likened to an international restatement of contract law. They are more detailed than the CISG, and were promulgated after the CISG. Many of the same people who drafted the CISG were also prominent in the drafting of the UNIDROIT Principles. The UNIDROIT Principles may thus be helpful in filling in the blanks of the CISG. For a discussion of when it is appropriate to use the UNIDROIT Principles, see *www.cisg.law.pace.edu/cisg/text/matchup/general-observations.html* (accessed Oct. 2011).

According to CISG Article 7, if no such principle can be determined that helps to fill the gap, then recourse is made to the law applicable by virtue of the rules of private international law. The "rules of private international law" are choice-of-law rules. This rule means that it may at times be necessary to do choice-of-law analysis to determine which domestic law is applicable to resolve a dispute that is otherwise within the scope of the CISG. The CISG also limits itself to issues involving contract formation and the rights and obligations of the seller and buyer arising out of the contract. CISG Article 4. This means that other law will resolve issues such as those involving title to the goods sold. The limits of the CISG and choice-of-law analysis will be discussed more fully in the next chapter.

In doing research on the CISG, the practitioner should be aware of the existence of a number of documents that were prepared during the drafting of the CISG and that provide its legislative history. A useful source containing these documents is J. Honnold, *Documentary History of the Uniform Law for International Sales* (1989). The Pace Web site is also a useful source.

Of the legislative history, the closest thing to the UCC official comments is the Secretariat Commentary on the 1978 draft of the CISG. In using the Secretariat Commentary, it is important to note changes that were made to the CISG after the 1978 draft. Among other things, the numbers of the articles were changed. The Pace Web site correlates the Secretariat Commentary to the relevant current CISG section and shows the changes that were made after 1978 to the section.

Perhaps more useful in interpreting the CISG than in interpreting U.S. domestic law are commentaries written by legal scholars. Because of the international character of the CISG, courts and arbitrators may be more impressed by a thoughtful commentary written by an internationally renowned expert on the CISG than by a single court decision handed down in one nation. Among the most important commentaries are J. Honnold, *Uniform Law for International Sales Under the 1980 United Nations Convention* (3d ed. 1999); P. Schlectriem (ed.), *Commentary on the UN Convention on the International Sale of Goods* (2d ed. 1998); C. M. Bianca and M. J. Bonell (eds.), *Commentary on the International Sales Law* (1987). There are also numerous law review articles, citations to which can be found on the Pace Web site.

### 5. ARBITRATION RULES

Arbitration has become an increasingly popular way of resolving disputes, both domestic and international. Arbitration is a means of alternate dispute resolution where the parties to a contract decide that disputes between them should be settled by the decision of a private individual or individuals rather than by the courts. The private individuals are normally lawyers, but they don't have to be. The arbitration process tends to be less formal than a judicial process.

In an international transaction, parties may prefer to settle a dispute by arbitration rather than through the national courts of one of the parties. The reasons for this can include a lack of knowledge of the civil procedure of foreign nations, a fear of favoritism for the party that resides in the nation where the matter is being adjudicated, and general preference for the flexible arbitration format over the more rigid procedures of national courts. Parties may prefer the expertise of professional arbitrators over the lack of expertise of juries or judges who are more familiar with criminal law. If parties desire arbitration, they must agree to it either in the sales contract or subsequently. They will typically opt to have the arbitration conducted according to the rules of an organization such as the American Arbitration Association or the International Chamber of Commerce. Through the course, we will study some arbitration awards, which are sometimes published. The Pace Web site is a good source of published arbitral awards. Arbitral awards are not binding precedent on courts or on other arbitration tribunals, but they may be influential, especially given the mandate of CISG Article 7 to try to bring about uniformity in rules governing international trade.

## E. THIS BOOK'S METHODOLOGY

This book attempts to focus the reader on a sales, lease, or license transaction in the manner in which a practitioner would (or, in the opinion of the author, should) focus on it. A client will show up in the office of the practitioner and explain the problem. First, the practitioner should focus on the applicable law that should apply. For example, should the law governing sales apply, or the law governing service contracts? Should international law apply, or should domestic law? Next, the practitioner should note if a contract has actually been formed, and should then focus on the terms of the contract. Once that has been determined, performance must be studied. Has there been a breach of contract? If there has been a breach, and it hasn't been excused, what are the injured party's remedies?

Cases are provided to show the student how courts use the applicable statutes in the particular area being studied. The cases have been edited in order to highlight the issue being considered and to lighten the reading load. Most of the citations within the case have also been omitted. Problems are provided to help the student learn how to apply the statutes. Many of the problems are based on actual cases and citations are provided to those cases. The student should try, however, to analyze the problem by reference only to the cited statutory material before looking up any cases that are cited. Keep in mind, by the way, that just because a court came to a different conclusion from that of the student does not mean that the court is "right" and the student is "wrong." Courts are fallible, and ultimately it is the statute that is the authority.

# PART 1
# *SALES OF GOODS*

CHAPTER 2

# CHOICE OF LAW

## A. IS THE CONTRACT FOR THE SALE OF GOODS?

Any contractual dispute raises a choice-of-law question regarding which set of rules govern the contract. Different types of contracts are governed by different rules. For example, real estate contracts are governed by the rules governing real estate contracts, while contracts for services are governed by their own rules (depending on the type of service). Contracts for the sale of goods are covered by UCC Article 2 if it has been enacted in the relevant jurisdiction. In an international sale, they may be covered instead by the CISG. If the contract is not for the sale of goods, it is outside the scope of this part of the book.

So, our first inquiry will be whether the contract in question is for the sale of goods. If not, our inquiry has ended. If it is, we move on to whether the UCC, the CISG, or some other law applies. UCC section 2-102 states that Article 2 applies to "transactions in goods." Look at the definition of "goods" in UCC section 2-105(1). Note that goods are defined as things that are movable at the time of identification to the contract, with some exceptions. Section 2-106 limits the scope of Article 2 by indicating that "contract" and "agreement" refer only to contracts or agreements to sell goods. By these definitions we then see that Article 2 applies only to sales of tangible personal property.

The CISG, in Article 1, states that it applies to contracts for the sale of goods, provided that the internationality component is met, as discussed later in this chapter. It does not contain a definition of "goods." CISG Article 2 provides for some specific exclusions. Please look to CISG Article 2.

Many times it will be abundantly clear as to whether the contract is for a sale of goods. For example, the purchase of a hammer at the local hardware store is clearly a sale of goods. Likewise, it will often be abundantly clear that a contract is not for the sale of goods. When you enter into a contract to represent your first client, that attorney-client contract is not a sale-of-goods contract and will not be subject to the UCC or CISG. A contract for the sale of a 50-story office building is also not a contract for the sale of goods.

The issue can become less clear in hybrid real estate/sales transactions and hybrid service/sales transactions. See the following two cases in which two courts differ over the application of UCC Article 2 to the same type of transaction.

### Epstein v. Giannattasio

Court of Common Pleas of Connecticut

197 A.2d 342, 25 Conn. Supp. 109, 1 UCC Rep. Serv. 114 (1963)

On or about October 5, 1962, the plaintiff visited a beauty parlor, conducted by the defendant Giannattasio, for the purpose of receiving a beauty treatment. During the course of that treatment, Giannattasio used a product called "Zotos 30-day Color," manufactured by defendant Sales Affiliates, Inc., and a prebleach manufactured by defendant Clairol, Inc. The plaintiff claims that as a result of the treatment she suffered acute dermatitis, disfigurement resulting from loss of hair, and other injuries and damages.

The complaint sets forth two causes of action against each defendant, the first sounding in negligence and the second in breach of warranty. Each of the defendants demurs to the second cause of action on the ground that the transaction does not amount to a contract for the sale of goods.

UCC section 2-102 provides: "[T]his article [Sales] applies to transactions in goods . . . ." The word "transaction" is not defined in the act. "Goods" is defined in section 2-105 as follows: " 'Goods' means all things, including specially manufactured goods, which are movable at the time of identification to the contract for sale . . . ." Section 2-106 limits the words "contract" and "agreement," as used in the Article, to the present or future sale of goods. "Contract for sale" includes a present sale of goods. UCC §2-106. "A 'sale' consists in the passing of title from the seller to the buyer for a price as provided by section 2-401." UCC §2-106.

There is a dearth of case law construing the statutes so far as concerns the claims made by the plaintiff. In Connecticut, only those cases which deal with the sale of food under the former Sales Act are relevant. It has been held repeatedly that in Connecticut the service of food in a restaurant for immediate consumption on the premises does not constitute a sale. The only thing that is "sold" is the personal service rendered in the preparation and presentation of the food, the various essentials to its comfortable consumption or other facilities provided, and the privilege of consuming so much of the meal ordered as the guest may desire. Service is the predominant feature of the transaction. If there is a transfer of title to the food actually consumed, it is merely incidental and does not constitute a sale of goods and there is therefore no implied warranty of its quality under the law of sales.

Whether a contract is for services or for sale of tangible personal property is to be found in the intention of the parties to the contract. That intention is to be ascertained from the language used, interpreted in the light of the situation of the parties and the circumstances surrounding them.

As the complaint alleges, the plaintiff asked Giannattasio for a beauty treatment, and not for the purchase of goods. From such language, it could not be inferred that it was the intention of either party that the transaction be a transaction in goods within the meaning of the code. This claim of the plaintiff is hence distinguished more by the ingenuity of its conception than by the strength of its persuasion.

There is another line of cases which involves blood transfusions received by patients in the course of medical care and treatment in hospitals. These concern the claim that injuries caused by such transfusions ground a recovery under the Sales Act. This claim has been universally rejected. Such a contract is clearly one for services, and, just as clearly, it is not divisible. It has long been recognized that, when service predominates, and transfer of personal property is but an incidental feature of the transaction, the transaction is not deemed a sale within the Sales Act. Building and construction transactions which include materials to be incorporated into the structure are not agreements of sale.

When this plaintiff made her arrangement with the beauty parlor, she did so as the complaint sets forth: "for the purpose of receiving a beauty treatment." Obviously, the subject of the contract was not a sale of goods but the rendition of services. The materials used in the performance of those services were patently incidental to that subject, which was a treatment and not the purchase of an article.

## Newmark v. Gimbel's Inc.

Supreme Court of New Jersey

258 A.2d 697, 54 N.J. 585, 6 UCC Rep. Serv. 1205 (1969)

This appeal involves the liability of a beauty parlor operator for injury to a patron's hair and scalp allegedly resulting from a product used in the giving of a permanent wave. The action was predicated upon charges of negligence and breach of express and implied warranty. Trial was had before the county district court and a jury. At the close of the proof, the court ruled as a matter of law that the warranty theory of liability was not maintainable because in giving a permanent wave a beauty parlor is engaged in rendering a service and not a sale; hence responsibility for injurious results could arise only from negligence. Consequently the court dismissed the warranty counts and submitted the issue of negligence for the jury's determination. Upon the return of a verdict for defendants, plaintiffs appealed. The appellate division reversed, holding that a fact issue existed requiring jury decision as to whether there was an implied warranty of fitness of the lotion applied to Mrs. Newmark's hair and scalp for the purpose of producing the permanent wave. Thereafter we granted defendants' petition for certification.

The defendants operated a number of beauty parlors where permanent waves were offered to the public for a consideration. For about a year and a half prior to the incident in question, Mrs. Newmark had been a patron of one of defendants' shops where she had a standing appointment every week to have her hair washed and set. She was usually attended by the same operator, one William Valante. During that period, plaintiffs' brief asserts and defendants do not deny that she had purchased permanent waves there, at least one having been given by Valante, and she had not experienced any untoward results.

On November 16, 1963, pursuant to an appointment, Mrs. Newmark went to the beauty parlor where she inquired of Valante about a permanent wave that was on special sale. He told her that her fine hair was not right for the special permanent and that she needed a "good" permanent wave. She agreed to accept the wave suggested by him. Valante conceded that the wave she received was given at his suggestion and that in accepting it she relied on his judgment as to what was good for her hair. Both Valante and Mrs. Newmark testified there was nothing wrong with her hair or scalp before the wave was given.

Valante proceeded to cut and wash her hair, after which he put her head under a dryer for about ten minutes. The hair was then sectioned off, a permanent wave solution marketed under the name "Helene Curtis Candle Wave" was applied with cotton, and the hair was rolled section by section. Following this, more of the waving solution was put on by an applicator bottle. Then a cream was placed along the hairline and covered with cotton. About three to five minutes after the last of the waving solution had been applied, Mrs. Newmark experienced a burning sensation on the front part of her head. She complained to Valante, who added more cream along the hairline. This gave some relief, but after a few minutes she told him that it was burning again. The burning sensation continued but was alleviated when Valante brought Mrs. Newmark to a basin and rinsed her hair in lukewarm water. The curlers were then removed, a neutralizing solution was applied and allowed to remain for about seven minutes, and her hair was again rinsed. After this Valante set her hair and again put her under the dryer, where she remained for about 25 minutes. The burning sensation returned and she promptly informed Valante, who reduced the heat of the dryer, thereby giving her partial relief. When the dryer operation was completed, Mrs. Newmark's hair was combed, and she left the parlor.

That evening Mrs. Newmark's head reddened, and during the following day her entire forehead was red and blistered. A large amount of hair fell out when it was combed. On November 19, she returned to defendants' place of business where Valante gave her, without charge, a conditioning treatment, which he told her is given when the hair is dry. Mrs. Newmark testified that it made her hair feel singed at the hairline.

Six days after the permanent wave Mrs. Newmark consulted a dermatologist who diagnosed her condition as contract (sic) dermatitis[1] of the scalp and loss of hair resulting therefrom. On the basis of his experience, he concluded that the sole cause of her condition was the permanent wave solution. The redness and tenderness of the scalp diminished under his treatment. When he last saw Mrs. Newmark, on December 13, 1963, the loss of hair on the top of her head was still present and he could not estimate the time it would take for replacement.

In dismissing the cause of action based on warranty, the trial court expressed the view that the transaction with Mrs. Newmark was not a sale within the contemplation of the Uniform Commercial Code, UCC section 2-106(1), but rather an agreement for the rendition of services. Therefore, it

1. After taking Contracts, some of you might have suffered from this disease! —Ed.

was not accompanied by any warranty of fitness of products used in rendering the services, and the liability of the beauty parlor was limited to the claim of negligence. Having in mind the nature of a permanent wave operation, we find that the distinction between a sale and the rendition of services is a highly artificial one. If the permanent wave lotion were sold to Mrs. Newmark by defendants for home consumption or application, or to enable her to give herself the permanent wave, unquestionably an implied warranty of fitness for that purpose would have been an integral incident of the sale. Basically defendants argue that if, in addition to recommending the use of a lotion or other product and supplying it for use, they applied it, such fact (the application) would have the effect of lessening their liability to the patron by eliminating warranty and by limiting their responsibility to the issue of negligence. There is no just reason why it should. On the contrary, by taking on the administration of the product in addition to recommending and supplying it, they might increase the scope of their liability if the method of administration were improper (a result not suggested on this appeal because the jury found no negligence).

The transaction, in our judgment, is a hybrid partaking of incidents of a sale and a service. It is really partly the rendering of service, and partly the supplying of goods for a consideration. Accordingly, we agree with the appellate division that an implied warranty of fitness of the products used in giving the permanent wave exists with no less force than it would have in the case of a simple sale.

The oft-quoted statement that in the modern commercial world the liability of a manufacturer or a retail seller of a product should not be made to depend strictly upon the intricacies of the law of sales is most pertinent here. It was not the intention of the framers of the Uniform Commercial Code to limit the birth of implied warranties to transactions which technically meet its definition of a sale. The comment to UCC section 2-313 makes this clear by saying:

> Although this section is limited in its scope and direct purpose to warranties made by the seller to the buyer as part of a contract for sale, the warranty sections of this Article are not designed in any way to disturb those lines of case law growth which have recognized that warranties need not be confined either to sales contracts or to the direct parties to such a contract. They may arise in other appropriate circumstances such as in the case of bailments for hire, whether such bailment is itself the main contract or is merely a supplying of containers under a contract for the sale of their contents.

This court has already said there is no sound reason for restricting implied warranties of fitness to conventional sales of goods, treating as a sale the serving of food for value by a restaurateur for consumption on or off the premises, and subjecting the transaction to an implied warranty of fitness. It seems to us that the policy reasons for imposing warranty liability in the case of ordinary sales are equally applicable to a commercial transaction such as that existing in this case between a beauty parlor operator and a patron.

Defendants claim that to hold them to strict liability would be contrary to *Magrine v. Krasnica*, 94 N.J. Super. 228, 227 A.2d 539 (Cty. Ct. 1967), *aff'd sub nom. Magrine v. Spector*, 100 N.J. Super. 223, 241 A.2d 637 (App. Div.1968), *aff'd*

53 N.J. 259, 250 A.2d 129 (1969). We cannot agree. Magrine, a patient of the defendant-dentist, was injured when a hypodermic needle being used, concededly with due care, to administer a local anesthetic broke off in his gum or jaw. The parties agreed that the break resulted from a latent defect in the needle. It was held that the strict liability in tort doctrine was not applicable to the professional man, such as a dentist, because the essence of the relationship with his patient was the furnishing of professional skill and services. We accepted the view that a dentist's bill for services should be considered as representing pay for that alone. The use of instruments, or the administration of medicines or the providing of medicines for the patient's home consumption cannot give the ministrations the cast of a commercial transaction. Accordingly the liability of the dentist in cases involving the ordinary relationship of doctor and patient must be tested by principles of negligence; that is, lack of due care and not by application of the doctrine of strict liability in tort.

Defendants suggest that there is no doctrinal basis for distinguishing the services rendered by a beauty parlor operator from those rendered by a dentist or a doctor, and that consequently the liability of all three should be tested by the same principles. On the contrary, there is a vast difference in the relationships. The beautician is engaged in a commercial enterprise; the dentist and doctor in a profession. The former caters publicly not to a need but to a form of aesthetic convenience or luxury, involving the rendition of nonprofessional services and the application of products for which a charge is made. The dentist or doctor does not and cannot advertise for patients; the demand for his services stems from a felt necessity of the patient. In response to such a call, the doctor, and to a somewhat lesser degree the dentist, exercises his best judgment in diagnosing the patient's ailment or disability, prescribing and sometimes furnishing medicines or other methods of treatment which he believes, and in some measure hopes, will relieve or cure the condition. His performance is not mechanical or routine, because each patient requires individual study and formulation of an informed judgment as to the physical or mental disability or condition presented and the course of treatment needed. Neither medicine nor dentistry is an exact science; there is no implied warranty of cure or relief. There is no representation of infallibility and such professional men should not be held to such a degree of perfection. There is no guaranty that the diagnosis is correct. Such men are not producers or sellers of property in any reasonably acceptable sense of the term. In a primary sense they furnish services in the form of an opinion of the patient's condition based upon their experienced analysis of the objective and subjective complaints, and in the form of recommended and, at times, personally administered medicines and treatment. Practitioners of such callings, licensed by the state to practice after years of study and preparation, must be deemed to have a special and essential role in our society—that of studying our physical and mental ills and ways to alleviate or cure them, and that of applying their knowledge, empirical judgment, and skill in an effort to diagnose and then to relieve or cure the ailment of a particular patient. Thus their paramount function—the essence of their function—ought to be regarded as the furnishing of opinions and services. Their unique status and the rendition of these sui generis services bear such a necessary and intimate relationship to public health and welfare that their obligation ought to be grounded and expressed in a duty to exercise reasonable competence and care toward their patients. In our judgment, the nature of the services, the utility of, and the need for them, involving as they do the health and even survival of many people, are so important to the general welfare as to outweigh in the policy scale any need for the imposition on dentists and doctors of the rules of strict liability in tort.

## NOTES, QUESTIONS, AND PROBLEMS

1. Why did it matter whether Article 2 applied in these two cases?
2. If the transaction were international in the last two cases, would the CISG apply? See CISG Articles 2, 3, and 5.
3. In *Epstein*, the court analogized the hair treatment to the serving of food in a restaurant, and noted that under the old Uniform Sales Act, which was the predecessor law to Article 2, the serving of food in a restaurant was *not* considered a sale. Please look at UCC section 2-314. In light of the position taken by that section on the issue of whether the serving of food in a restaurant is a sale, did the *Epstein* court err in finding that Article 2 applied? Or is the hair treatment not analogous to the serving of food in a restaurant?
4. As the foregoing two cases illustrate, the UCC does not provide much guidance to courts on how to handle mixed goods/services situations. In *Epstein*, the court seems to follow what is referred to as the "predominant factor" test and asks whether the contract was predominantly for the hairstyling service or for the good. It is probably fair to say that the predominant factor test is the one that is most frequently used by courts, and the CISG is clearer than the UCC in directly stating that it does not apply if the contract is predominantly for labor or other services. CISG Article 3.

How do we tell if a contract is predominantly for goods or for services? In *Epstein*, the court focuses on the intent of the parties. Do you think the person seeking a hair treatment gives much thought to whether the contract is for the hair product or for the service? Courts might look at things such as the language of the contract itself (does it call itself a "service" contract?), the value of the goods provided as compared to the value of the service, and public policy considerations of applying the UCC or other law.

Another approach that some courts take is to look at whether the problem is with the goods or with the service. This approach, credited by many to the late Chancellor William Hawkland, a noted commentator on the UCC, is often referred to as the "gravamen" test, as it asks whether the gravamen of the claim involves the goods or the service.[2] For example, a contract may call for goods to be installed by the seller. The installation is a service. If the installation was proper, but the goods do not work very well, the problem is with the goods and the UCC applies. If the installation is the problem, then the UCC should not apply under the gravamen test. In the *Newmark* case, is the court looking at the predominant factor of the contract or is it looking more at the gravamen of the claim?

2. See 1 Hawkland, *Uniform Commercial Code Series* §2-102:4.

***Problem 2-1.*** If a doctor or hospital supplies a drug to a patient that results in an adverse reaction, should the patient be able to sue under UCC Article 2? *See Batiste v. American Home Products Corp.*, 32 N.C. App. 1, 231 S.E.2d 269 (1977).

***Problem 2-2.*** Assume a contract to build a swimming pool. The contractor provides labor and parts, including a diving board. In christening the new pool, the owner holds a pool party and is injured when he slips off the diving board and hits the side of the pool. The owner complains that the board did not have a proper surface that would prevent slipping. Would the lawsuit against the pool builder be covered by Article 2? *See Anthony Pools v. Sheehan*, 295 Md. 285, 455 A.2d 434, 35 UCC Rep. Serv. 408 (1983).

***Problem 2-3.*** If a power surge through an electric utility line causes damage to one of the utility customer's computers, should the customer be able to sue the utility under UCC Article 2? *Compare Cincinnati Gas & Electric Co. v. Goebel*, 28 Ohio Misc. 2d 4, 502 N.E.2d 713, 2 UCC Rep. Serv. 2d 1187 (1986), *with New Balance Athletic Shoe, Inc. v. Boston Edison Co.*, 29 UCC Rep. Serv. 2d 397 (Mass. Super. Ct. 1996). Would the CISG ever apply to a sale of electricity? See CISG Article 2. If a customer of the local water company gets sick from consuming tainted water, should the customer be able to sue the water company? *Compare Zepp v. Mayor & Council of Athens*, 180 Ga. App. 72, 348 S.E.2d 673, 2 UCC Rep. Serv. 2d 1179 (1986), *with Mattoon v. City of Pittsfield*, 56 Mass. App. Ct. 124, 775 N.E.2d 770, 49 UCC Rep. Serv. 2d 52 (2002).

***Problem 2-4.*** When consumers "purchase" computer software, most of the time they are not acquiring title to the software but are instead obtaining a "license" to use it, subject to the restrictions contained in the license. You have probably been required to click "I accept" when shown terms of the license when you have loaded software on a computer. If you do not accept, you cannot use the software. Should computer software transactions of the type described be subject to UCC Article 2? Should it matter if you acquire the software on a disk or download it over the Internet? For an argument that UCC Article 2 should *not* apply to these transactions and a discussion of cases in which courts have nevertheless applied it to software transactions, see Lorin Brennan, *Why Article 2 Cannot Apply to Software Transactions*, 38 Duq. L. Rev. 459 (2000).

One reason why courts might be tempted to apply the UCC to software licenses is the absence of other law that is specifically applicable. The Uniform Computer Information Transactions Act ("UCITA") has been promulgated by the National Conference of Commissioners on Uniform State Laws to apply to software licenses. UCITA has been a very controversial proposal, and at the time of this writing (Fall 2011), versions of it have been adopted by only Maryland and Virginia. For more discussion of UCITA and licensing transactions, see Chapter 11, *infra*.

Courts may also be influenced in the future by the *Principles of the Law of Software Contracts*, which have been recently promulgated by the American Law Institute. The *Principles* are not "law" but are designed to give guidance to judges deciding cases that involve software licenses because the law in the area is not well developed. Only time will tell whether courts give much weight to the *Principles* as compared to using the UCC.

***Problem 2-5.*** Should a contract to write a book be subject to UCC Article 2? A contract to paint a painting? *See National Historic Shrines Foundation v. Dali*, 4 UCC Rep. Serv. 71 (N.Y. Sup. Ct. 1967). A contract to specially manufacture a chair? Should it matter if the chair is to be designed and manufactured by a world-renowned architect like Frank Gehry?

***Problem 2-6.*** Buyer agrees to purchase Seller's hardware store. Included in the sale is the name of the store, the store inventory and equipment, and an assignment of the lease for the store. Does Article 2 play any role in the transaction? *See Miller v. Belk*, 23 N.C. App. 1, 207 S.E.2d 792, 15 UCC Rep. Serv. 627 (1974).

***Problem 2-7.*** Should a contract for the sale of minerals from land be subject to UCC Article 2? See UCC §2-107(1). How about a contract for the sale of crops or timber? See UCC §2-107(2).

## B. DOES THE CISG APPLY?

Assuming that we have a contract for the sale of goods and assuming that the sale is international, meaning that the seller is located in one nation and the buyer in another, the next issue that must be analyzed is the choice of applicable sales law. Will the CISG, the UCC, some combination of the UCC and CISG, or some other law apply to all or part of the transaction?

### 1. IS THE TRANSACTION "INTERNATIONAL" AS DEFINED BY THE CISG?

The CISG applies to sale of goods contracts between parties whose places of business are in different nations (called "States" in the CISG) where each nation has agreed to the application of the CISG (called a "Contracting State"). CISG Article 1(1)(a). The classic case would be if a business in the United States knowingly contracts to purchase goods from a French seller. Because both France and the United States are CISG contracting states, the international requirement of the CISG would be met.

Of course, some sellers and buyers of goods have places of business in more than one nation. In such a situation, the relevant place of business is the one that has the closest relationship to the contract. CISG Article 10(a). For example, if a buyer in France purchases from the French office of a German company, the transaction would *not* be covered by the CISG, even though both France and Germany are contracting states because the relevant places of business are both in France.

Even if the parties' relevant places of business are in different nations, the CISG will *not* apply if "this fact does not appear either from the contract or from any dealings between, or from information disclosed by, the parties at any time before or at the conclusion of the contract." CISG Article 1(2). Let's assume again that the buyer is in France but this time is contracting with the German office of a German seller. The agent of the German seller, a French national, is the one conducting the transaction, and there is nothing in the contract or the surrounding facts that would cause the French buyer to believe that the seller is located in Germany. The CISG would not apply in such a case.

The CISG will also apply to a contract for the sale of goods between parties whose places of business are in different nations "when the rules of private international law lead to the application of the law of a Contracting State." CISG Article 1(1)(b). The "rules of private international law" are choice-of-law rules. As a generalization, choice-of-law rules typically lead to application of the law where the seller is located because the seller typically agrees to the contract in its home country and ships the goods from there.[3] As an example, assume that the seller is located in a nation that has adopted the CISG but the buyer is located in a nation that has not adopted it. The choice-of-law rule would probably indicate that the seller's nation's law would govern, and thus the CISG would apply under Article 1(1)(b).

Nations acceding to the CISG are allowed to opt out of Article 1(1)(b) by making a declaration under CISG Article 95. Such nations may take the position that choice-of-law analysis is too complicated and uncertain or they may only wish to subject their citizens to the CISG if the other nation involved has also agreed to subject their citizens to it. In such cases, the CISG will only apply if it has been adopted in both the seller's country and the buyer's country. The United States has made such a declaration, although few other nations have done so.[4] Assume that one party resides in the United States and the other resides in the United Kingdom, which has not adopted the CISG. In such a case, the CISG will not apply. Either U.K. sales law or the UCC will apply, depending on applicable choice-of-law rules.

## 2. IS THE TRANSACTION INCLUDED WITHIN THE CISG?

We have talked already about how the CISG applies to transactions that are predominantly for the sale of goods and that the CISG does not define "goods." We have also noted that some transactions are excluded. CISG Article 2 excludes goods bought for personal, family, or household use, unless the seller at any time before the contract was formed neither knew nor ought to have known that the goods were being bought for such use. CISG Article 2 also excludes auction sales; sales conducted under authority of law (such as an execution sale); sales of investment securities such as stocks and bonds; sales of negotiable instruments or money; sales of ships, vessels, hovercraft, or

---

3. For example, see the Rome I Regulation dealing with choice of law, acceded to by members of the European Union. *http://eur-lex.europa.eu/LexUriServ/LexUriServ.do?uri=OJ:L:2008:177:0006:0016:en:PDF* (accessed Oct. 2011).

Article 4.1(a) provides the default rule that normally the law is that of the country where the seller has "his habitual residence." Exceptions may apply where everything is done in another country or where a consumer buyer is involved.

4. As of July 2011, China, the Czech Republic, Saint Vincent and the Grenadines, Singapore, Slovakia, and the United States had made Article 95 declarations. *See www.uncitral.org/uncitral/en/uncitral_texts/sale_goods/1980CISG_status.html* (accessed Oct. 2011).

aircraft; and sales of electricity. Contracts for the special manufacture of goods are included unless the buyer undertakes to supply a substantial part of the materials necessary for manufacture. CISG Article 3(1).

## 3. IS THE RELEVANT ISSUE COVERED BY THE CISG?

Even if the internationality requirement of the CISG is satisfied and the transaction is within its scope, the CISG does not purport to cover all issues that might come up. As noted in the last section of this book, the CISG does not deal with the liability of the seller for death or personal injury caused by the goods. CISG Article 5. CISG Article 4 states that it governs "only the formation of the contract of sale and the rights and obligations of the seller and the buyer arising from such a contract." CISG Article 4(a) indicates that it does not deal with the validity of the contract or the effect that the contract may have on the property in the goods sold. Issues of "validity" would include such things as whether the contract was illegal (for example, a sale of recreational drugs) or whether a provision was so unduly harsh as to be unconscionable or violative of public policy. "The effect which the contract may have on the property in the goods sold" has to do with whether the seller is in position to give good title to the buyer. The CISG does not deal with questions of title (i.e. whether the seller has the legal right to sell the goods in question).

For issues that are excluded by the CISG, courts or arbitral tribunals will have to do a choice-of-law analysis to determine the relevant law that decides the issue. For example, if there is a question as to whether a contractual provision is invalid, the law of the seller's nation might be used to make that determination.

## 4. HAVE THE PARTIES OPTED OUT OF THE CISG IN WHOLE OR IN PART?

Article 6 of the CISG allows parties to opt out of its provisions in whole or in part. So, even if the CISG would otherwise apply, the parties may designate some other law or simply say that the CISG does not apply. The parties may also agree, with few exceptions, that some parts of the CISG apply but not others. Parties will frequently indicate in their contract which law applies, and are given a lot of leeway to do so, at least as long as the law chosen has some reasonable relationship to the transaction.[5] Many parties decide to exclude the CISG, opting instead for one of the parties' nation's domestic sales law—the devil they know. After you have learned more about the CISG, you might want to ask yourself whether you would counsel your client to opt out of the CISG or whether you would counsel them to use it, perhaps with some variations.

Parties are generally also free to opt in to the CISG in a commercial, international sales transaction. This does not seem to happen very frequently.

5. See, e.g., UCC §1-301.

## PROBLEMS

Assume in all of the following hypotheticals that there is no choice-of-law provision in the contract, unless otherwise stated. All contracts are commercial sales of goods (not consumer sales). The contracts are not exempt from application of the CISG under CISG Articles 2, 3, or 5. Each party is aware of the other party's location.

***Problem 2-8.*** Buyer is located in France, which has adopted the CISG. Seller is located in the United States, which also has adopted the CISG. Does the CISG apply to the transaction? See CISG Article 1(1)(a).

***Problem 2-9.*** Buyer is located in the United Kingdom, which has not adopted the CISG. Seller is located in France, which has adopted the CISG. The purchase order was received by Seller in France and the goods are shipped from France. Does the CISG apply to the transaction? See CISG Article 1(1)(b).

***Problem 2-10.*** Buyer is located in the United Kingdom, which has not adopted the CISG. Seller is located in California. The goods were shipped from California and the purchase order was received by Seller in California. California has adopted UCC section 1-301. The United States has made a declaration under CISG Article 95. The case is litigated in California. Does the CISG apply? Does the California version of the UCC apply?

***Problem 2-11.*** Buyer is located in the United Kingdom, which has not adopted the CISG. Seller is located in Canada, which has adopted the CISG and which has not made a declaration under CISG Article 95. The contract has a provision indicating that in the event of a dispute, the law of Canada would apply. Does the CISG apply? See CISG Article 6 and ICC Case No. 6653 of 1993, *www.cisg.law.pace.edu/cisg/wais/db/cases2/936653i1.html* (accessed Oct. 2011). See also *Asante Technologies v. PMC-Sierra, Inc.*, 164 F. Supp. 2d 1142 (ND Cal. 2001). How would you draft a contractual provision to make certain that the CISG does *not* apply to the transaction?

## CHAPTER TWO REVIEW PROBLEM

Buyer and Seller contract for Seller to specially design and manufacture a computer system for Buyer's business. Seller is to provide both hardware and software. The price is 100,000 euros. Seller is located in France, which has adopted the CISG and has not made an Article 95 declaration, while Buyer is in the United Kingdom (U.K.), which has not adopted the CISG. The computer system is to be designed and manufactured in France, and the contract calls for delivery to a shipping company in France that will then transport the system to Buyer in the U.K. The contract does not have a choice-of-law provision. Will the CISG apply? CISG Articles 1 and 3. Assuming the CISG applies, will U.K. or French law fill gaps in the CISG under Article 7?

# CHAPTER 3
# CONTRACT FORMATION

Assuming that we have been able to determine the applicable law, the next question is whether an enforceable contract has been formed. This issue is considered in Part 2 of UCC Article 2 and is also considered in Part II of the CISG. The CISG permits nations to opt out of Part II by making a declaration under CISG Article 92.[1] If a nation makes an Article 92 declaration, it is considered not to be a contracting state with respect to issues governed by Part II. That means that domestic law will govern formational issues if choice-of-law rules point to the law of the nation making the Article 92 declaration. The next set of questions and cases are designed to explore contract formation under both the UCC and the CISG.

## A. OFFER AND ACCEPTANCE

### 1. BASIC FORMATIONAL ISSUES

Both the CISG and the UCC contain rules on basic contract formation that differ from U.S. common law. On some issues, however, the UCC does not provide a rule and thus the common law must be consulted according to UCC section 1-103. One such area involves the definition of "offer." The UCC does not provide a definition. The *Restatement (Second) of Contracts* section 24 defines an "offer" as "the manifestation of willingness to enter into a contract so made as to justify another person in understanding that his assent to that bargain is invited and will conclude it." The *Restatement* further suggests that in determining whether an offer has been made, courts should look at the terms of any previous inquiry, the completeness of the terms of the suggested bargain, and the number of persons to whom a communication is addressed. Communications to the general public, such as advertisements, as well as price quotes are generally not considered to be offers, but are instead invitations to bargain. See *Restatement (Second) of Contracts* §26. Unlike the UCC, the CISG

1. At the time of this writing (fall 2011), Denmark, Finland, Norway, and Sweden have opted out of Part II of the CISG. See *www.uncitral.org* (accessed Oct. 2011).

defines "offer" in Article 14. It provides that an offer has been made if "it indicates the goods and expressly or implicitly fixes or makes provision for determining the quantity and the price." It also provides that communications to the general public are not considered offers.

You may remember from your contracts class that an offer is generally revocable before acceptance unless it is an option contract supported by consideration. Both the UCC and the CISG differ from that rule. The UCC has a "firm offer" rule, UCC section 2-205, providing that offers made by merchants in signed writings stating that they are "firm" or irrevocable cannot be revoked during the time stated, or, if no time is stated, for a reasonable time. The outside period for irrevocability under section 2-205 is three months. The CISG is broader than the UCC in this regard, stating simply that an offer can by its terms be made irrevocable—there are no formal requirements and no outside time limit.

The basic UCC rule regarding acceptance is section 2-206. It states that unless it is clear from the offer or the circumstances, an acceptance can be made in any way reasonable, including by shipping the goods. So, if a buyer orders goods for prompt or current shipment and does not clearly express that a promissory acceptance is required, the seller may accept by simply shipping the goods. In a case in which the seller accepts by shipping the goods, the seller must ship conforming goods unless the seller indicates that the goods are being shipped as "an accommodation." UCC §2-206(1)(b). In such a case, the shipment is not an "acceptance" but rather a counteroffer. For example, if a buyer orders computer model #XYZ and seller is out of stock on that item, the seller might instead ship #ABC as "an accommodation," thinking that it might be acceptable to the buyer. At this point, the buyer can decide whether to keep #ABC and form the contract or reject it. On the other hand, if the seller simply shipped #ABC without informing the buyer that it was an accommodation, the seller is both accepting the buyer's offer and breaching the contract at the same time, as even the shipment of nonconforming goods can be an acceptance of the offer! The buyer must be put on notice if the seller wishes to accept in this way.

CISG Article 18 indicates that an acceptance may be by statement or other conduct. If the offer permits it or if industry practices or prior dealings between the parties allow it, the seller may accept by shipping the goods without otherwise giving notice.

The following problems explore the similarities and differences between the CISG in simple offer and acceptance situations.

## PROBLEMS

The following questions are based on these facts: On May 15, Buyer Department Store sent a purchase order to Seller Clothing Manufacturer ordering 500 dresses at $100 per dress. No date for delivery was specified. The type of dress was designated by order number from Seller's catalog (which Seller had widely distributed). The purchase order stated, "We expect to hear from you by June 5."

***Problem 3-1.*** Is Buyer's purchase order an "offer" under the UCC? See UCC §§1-103, 2-204, and 2-205. Is the purchase order an offer under the CISG? See CISG Article 14. Of what significance is the lack of a delivery date? See UCC §2-309 and CISG Article 33. Would Seller's catalog be considered an "offer" if it contained listed prices next to its description of the goods for sale?

***Problem 3-2.*** Could Buyer revoke the purchase order after it was received by Seller and before June 5? Is Buyer a "merchant"? See UCC §§2-104, 2-205, and CISG Article 16. Would it be relevant that Seller is from a country where offers are irrevocable until the date stated, but Buyer is from a country where offers are generally revocable even before the time stated (such as the United States)? See CISG Article 8 and Secretariat Commentary to Article 14 of 1978 CISG draft, *www.cisg.law.pace.edu/cisg/text/secomm/secomm-16.html* (accessed Oct. 2011). See also Schlectriem, *Uniform Sales Law—The UN-Convention on Contracts for the International Sale of Goods* 51-53 (1986) (reproduced at *www.cisg.law.pace.edu/cisg/biblio/schlechtriem-16.html* (accessed Oct. 2011)).

***Problem 3-3.*** Assume that Buyer did not revoke its offer before June 5 and that the CISG applies. Could Seller accept by dispatching an acceptance on June 4, even though the acceptance is not received by Buyer until June 6? You may remember the "mailbox rule" from your contracts class, which states that a mailed acceptance is effective upon dispatch. Does the mailbox rule apply under the CISG? See CISG Article 18(2) and Article 21. If Seller simply shipped the goods to Buyer such that they were received by Buyer before June 5, would a contract have been formed? *Compare* CISG Article 18 *with* UCC §2-206.

## 2. "BATTLE OF THE FORMS"

### (a) UCC Treatment

One of the more perplexing issues faced by students in the basic contracts course is how to deal with the "battle of the forms." It is sufficiently perplexing that some time will be spent on it in the next few pages. We will also compare the CISG treatment of the issue to the UCC treatment.

The "battle of the forms" exists when terms in documents exchanged by the parties vary in some way. The documents involved are typically preprinted forms that have a lot of fine print boilerplate terms that are not changed from transaction to transaction. The only blanks in the documents are for things like price, description of the goods, quantity of goods sold, and delivery date. Typically, there are some variations between the forms used by the parties—they are not identical. For example, a buyer may issue a purchase order to the seller that says nothing about how disputes will be resolved, and the seller may respond with a "confirmation" that is generally in agreement with the buyer's purchase order except that it states that all disputes will be resolved through binding arbitration. The legal issues raised are (1) whether there is a contract formed at all and (2) if so, whether disputes will be resolved by arbitration.

The statute in the UCC designed to deal with the battle of the forms is UCC section 2-207. You may remember from your contracts class that section 2-207 was designed to replace the old common law "mirror image" rule and "last shot" doctrine. Under the mirror image rule, a purported "acceptance" of an offer had to be the mirror image of the offer in order to be effective. If there were variations between the offer and acceptance, the acceptance was not operative as such and was instead a rejection and counteroffer. Under the last shot doctrine, if the parties performed following the counteroffer without further communications, the original offeror was deemed to have accepted the counteroffer by performance. Thus the terms of the counteroffer, the "last shot," were included in the contract.

This traditional approach may have made sense when parties were negotiating face to face, or were at the least carefully reading the forms sent by each party. The drafters of the UCC thought that the approach led to arbitrary and sometimes unfair results in situations in which neither party was paying much attention to the standard forms of the other party aside from the so-called dickered terms of price and quantity.

### i. Do We Have a Contract?

Section 2-207 was drafted to make clear that a contract would nevertheless exist even if there were different or additional terms in the acceptance, unless the party sending the purported acceptance indicated that acceptance was expressly conditional on the offeror's assent to the additional or different terms. UCC §2-207(1). A provision making the "acceptance" expressly conditional on assent to additional or different terms is sometimes referred to as a "proviso" clause. If there is a proviso clause, the purported acceptance is not really an acceptance; it is a rejection and counteroffer. Thus, no contract is formed by the exchange of the writings.

If a purported acceptance is unconditional and the different or additional terms are relatively minor, there is a contract formed by the writings. One question that comes up under section 2-207 is how significant the different or additional terms can be before we say that the purported "acceptance" isn't really an acceptance. If a buyer orders 1,000 vials of a vaccine and a seller "confirms" at 50 vials, has the seller really accepted the buyer's offer? Commentators have suggested that a contract should be formed under section 2-207(1) only where there is a fundamental agreement on dickered terms. The dickered terms, or those over which the parties typically negotiate, would include things such as quantity and description of goods, price, and delivery date. Official Comment 1 to section 2-207 indicates that it is designed to deal with situations in which there are *minor* variations between the offer and the acceptance, not major ones (emphasis supplied). Section 2-207 is *not* designed to force parties into a contract where there is a significant disagreement. Think about it. Would it be fair to bind a buyer to a 50 vial contract if it ordered 1,000 vials or bind a seller to a 1,000 vial contract when it only agreed to send 50?

There are a couple of other ways that a contract can be formed under section 2-207. Official Comment 1 discusses situations in which parties have an informal agreement, followed by one or both parties sending written confirmations that add terms. The other is through performance.

Remember that under UCC section 2-204, the parties can have an enforceable agreement even if they haven't agreed on all terms as long as there is an intent to be bound and there is a reasonably certain basis for giving an appropriate remedy. The buyer and seller might have a verbal agreement on price, quantity, and description of the goods sold, and the buyer might send out a confirmatory memorandum that fleshes out the details of the contract. There is an enforceable contract in such a situation.

In terms of contracts formed by performance, assume that a buyer orders goods and the seller sends a purported acceptance that is in agreement on the dickered terms but contains an arbitration clause. The purported acceptance has a "proviso" clause, conditioning acceptance on assent to the additional term. Because of the proviso clause, there is no contract formed by the writings. Nevertheless, the parties go ahead and perform, with the seller shipping the goods to the buyer, who accepts and pays for them. In such a situation, there is clearly some kind of contract between the parties, and section 2-207 recognizes that a contract can be formed by performance.

### ii. If There Is a Contract, What Are the Terms?

Assuming that there is a contract, we must then determine the terms of the agreement because there is variation between the offer and acceptance. Subsection (2) of 2-207 indicates that additional terms in an acceptance or confirmation are to be considered proposals for addition to the contract. Between merchants, they automatically become part of the contract unless the offer is expressly limited to its terms, the terms materially alter the offer, or the terms are objected to within a reasonable time after they have been received. It is thus important to determine whether both of the parties are "merchants" as defined in section 2-104. Are they experienced businesspeople who should be expected to pay more attention to the form than would a consumer? If a consumer is involved, the consumer must assent to the additional terms in the form in order for them to become part of the contract.

Assuming both parties are merchants, one of the most difficult issues to analyze under section 2-207 is when a term "materially alters" the offer. Official Comment 4 to section 2-207 indicates that terms "materially alter" the offer if they cause a "surprise or hardship." Both Official Comments 4 and 5 provide examples of clauses that the drafters believe materially alter the offer and clauses that do not.

One way to look at this question is whether the terms are consistent with industry practices or course of dealing between the parties. Unless otherwise agreed, industry practice, or trade usage, and course of dealing are considered part of the contract. "Course of dealing" is how the parties have conducted business on prior contracts. See UCC §1-303. If a clause is an unusual one or imposes a risk on one of the parties that is out of the norm, then it is probably fair to say that it is a "surprise" or "hardship" or both. It is inappropriate to include the term unless the other side expressly agrees. The next case, *Dorton v. Collins & Aikman Corp.*, addresses the question of whether an arbitration clause is a "surprise or hardship" and thus material.

With regard to confirmations sent after informal agreements, it is important to distinguish between confirmations that flesh out the terms of the deal and proposals for modification that change the terms of the deal. For a confirmation to be considered under 2-207, it must be sent "within a reasonable time." Forms that are sent to the buyer after the goods have already been paid for and received should probably be considered as proposals for modification, requiring express assent by both parties. Also, terms in a confirmation that contradict terms that were expressly agreed to during formation of the informal agreement should be considered as proposals for modification, again requiring express assent by both parties. If each party sends a "confirmation" and terms conflict, they should be considered to cancel each other out, the so-called "knock out" doctrine. See UCC §2-207(3), Official Comment 6.

For contracts that are formed by performance, UCC section 2-207(3) states that the terms of the contract are those on which the parties agree along with terms provided by the UCC. If terms conflict, the knock out doctrine should again apply. How does the UCC supply terms? As just noted, the UCC indicates that usage of trade and course of dealing are part of the contract. Also, if the contract calls for repeated performances between the parties, the way the parties actually perform, called "course of performance," will provide the terms. UCC §1-303(d). If there is no trade usage, course of dealing, or course of performance, the UCC provides "gap filler" terms that will be discussed later in the book. For example, if the parties do not agree on a delivery date, the UCC provides that delivery shall be in a "reasonable time." UCC §2-309. Additional terms in the form sent by the offeree are also to be considered under UCC section 2-207(2), according to Comment 6.

One question is whether section 2-207(3) should apply at all when the offeree responds to the offer with something that is in fundamental disagreement with the offer. Going back to the hypothetical where the buyer orders 1,000 vials of vaccine and the seller responds with a "confirmation" of an order for 50 vials, assume that the seller then sends 50 vials, which the buyer receives and pays for. As noted above, section 2-207 is not really designed to deal with cases like this. The case should be viewed as one where the seller is actually making a counteroffer to the buyer, and if the buyer accepts and pays for the 50 vials, that constitutes an acceptance of the seller's counteroffer under UCC section 2-206. Parties should be expected to at least pay attention to the important "dicker" terms of the contract, such as the quantity that the seller is agreeing to sell. Section 2-207(3) should be applicable only in situations in which the writings fail to form a contract because of the existence of a proviso clause but where there is otherwise a fundamental agreement.

If you find section 2-207 confusing and difficult to apply, you can take comfort that you are not alone! Reasonable people can disagree regarding its application in a given case. The next cases demonstrate a couple of different ways of analyzing whether an arbitration clause in one of the party's forms should be included in the contract—whether it should be included under section 2-207(2) or whether section 2-207 should be applied at all.

## Dorton v. Collins & Aikman Corp.

United States Court of Appeals, Sixth Circuit

453 F.2d 1161, 10 UCC Rep. Serv. 585 (1972)

The primary question before us on appeal is whether the district court, in denying Collins & Aikman's motion for a stay pending arbitration, erred in holding that The Carpet Mart was not bound by the arbitration agreement appearing on the back of Collins & Aikman's acknowledgment forms. In reviewing the district court's determination, we must look closely at the procedures followed in the sales transactions that gave rise to the present dispute over the arbitration agreement.

In each of the more than 55 transactions, one of the partners in The Carpet Mart, or, on some occasions, Collins & Aikman's visiting salesman, telephoned Collins & Aikman's order department in Dalton, Georgia, and ordered certain quantities of carpets listed in Collins & Aikman's catalogue. There is some dispute as to what, if any, agreements were reached through the telephone calls and through the visits by Collins & Aikman's salesman. After each oral order was placed, the price, if any, quoted by the buyer was checked against Collins & Aikman's price list, and the credit department was consulted to determine whether The Carpet Mart had paid for all previous shipments. After it was found that everything was in order, Collins & Aikman's order department typed the information concerning the particular order on one of its printed acknowledgment forms. Each acknowledgment form bore one of three legends: "Acknowledgment," "Customer Acknowledgment," or "Sales Contract." The following provision was printed on the face of the forms bearing the "Acknowledgment" legend:

> The acceptance of your order is subject to all of the terms and conditions on the face and reverse side hereof, including arbitration, all of which are accepted by buyer; it supersedes buyer's order form, if any. It shall become a contract either (a) when signed and delivered by buyer to seller and accepted in writing by seller, or (b) at Seller's option, when buyer shall have given to seller specification of assortments, delivery dates, shipping instructions, or instructions to bill and hold as to all or any part of the merchandise herein described, or when buyer has received delivery of the whole or any part thereof, or when buyer has otherwise assented to the terms and conditions hereof.

Similarly, on the face of the forms bearing the "Customer Acknowledgment" or "Sales Contract" legends the following provision appeared:

> This order is given subject to all of the terms and conditions on the face and reverse side hereof, including the provisions for arbitration and the exclusion of warranties, all of which are accepted by Buyer, supersede Buyer's order form, if any, and constitute the entire contract between Buyer and Seller. This order shall become a contract as to the entire quantity specified either (a) when signed and delivered by Buyer to Seller and accepted in writing by Seller, or (b) when Buyer has received and retained this order for ten days without objection, or (c) when Buyer has accepted delivery of any part of the merchandise specified herein or has furnished to Seller specifications or assortments, delivery dates, shipping instructions, or instructions to bill and hold, or when Buyer has otherwise indicated acceptance of the terms hereof.

The small print on the reverse side of the forms provided, among other things, that all claims arising out of the contract would be submitted to arbitration in New York City. Each acknowledgment form was signed by an employee of Collins & Aikman's order department and mailed to The Carpet Mart on the day the telephone order was received or, at the latest, on the following day. The carpets were thereafter shipped to The Carpet Mart, with the interval between the mailing of the acknowledgment form and shipment of the carpets varying from a brief interval to a period of several weeks or months. Absent a delay in the mails, however, The Carpet Mart always received the acknowledgment forms prior to receiving the carpets. In all cases The Carpet Mart took delivery of and paid for the carpets without objecting to any terms contained in the acknowledgment form.

The district court found that subsection 2-207(3) controlled the instant case, quoting the following passage from 1 W. Hawkland, *A Transactional Guide to the Uniform Commercial Code* §1.090303 at 19-20 (1964):

> If the seller . . . ships the goods and the buyer accepts them, a contract is formed under subsection (3). The terms of this contract are those on which the purchase order and acknowledgment agree, and the additional terms needed for a contract are to be found throughout the U.C.C. . . . [T]he U.C.C. does not impose an arbitration term on the parties where their contract is silent on the matter. Hence, a conflict between an arbitration and a no-arbitration clause would result in the no-arbitration clause becoming effective.

Under this authority alone the district court concluded that the arbitration clause on the back of Collins & Aikman's sales acknowledgment had not become a binding term in the 50-odd transactions with The Carpet Mart.

In reviewing this determination by the district court, we are aware of the problems that courts have had in interpreting section 2-207. This section of the UCC has been described as a "murky bit of prose," *Southwest Engineering Co. v. Martin Tractor Co.*, 205 Kan. 684, 694, 473 P.2d 18, 25 (1970), as "not too happily drafted," *Roto-Lith Ltd. v. F. P. Bartlett & Co.*, 297 F.2d 497, 500 (1st Cir. 1962), and as "one of the most important, subtle, and difficult in the entire Code, and well it may be said that the product as it finally reads is not altogether satisfactory," Duesenberg & King, *Sales and Bulk Transfers under the Uniform Commercial Code, Vol. 3, Bender's Uniform Commercial Code Service*, §3.03 at 3-12 (1969). Despite the lack of clarity in its language, section 2-207 manifests definite objectives which are significant in the present case.

As Official Comment No. 1 indicates, UCC section 2-207 was intended to apply to two situations:

> The one is where an agreement has been reached either orally or by informal correspondence between the parties and is followed by one or both of the parties sending formal acknowledgments or memoranda embodying the terms so far as agreed upon and adding terms not discussed. The other situation is one in which a wire or letter expressed and intended as the closing or confirmation of an agreement adds further minor suggestions or proposals such as "ship by Tuesday," "rush," "ship draft against bill of lading inspection allowed," or the like. [UCC § 2-207], Official Comment 1.

Although Comment No. 1 is itself somewhat ambiguous, it is clear that section 2-207, and specifically subsection 2-207(1), was intended to alter the "ribbon matching" or "mirror image" rule of common law, under which the terms of an acceptance or confirmation were required to be identical to the terms of the offer or oral agreement, respectively. 1 W. Hawkland, *supra,* at 16; R. Nordstrom, *Handbook of the Law of Sales*, §37 at 99-100 (1970). Under the common law, an acceptance or a confirmation that contained terms additional to or different from those of the offer or oral agreement constituted a rejection of the offer or agreement and thus became a counteroffer. The terms of the counteroffer were said to have been accepted by the original offeror when he proceeded to perform under the contract without objecting to the counteroffer. Thus, a buyer was deemed to have accepted the seller's counteroffer if he took receipt of the goods and paid for them without objection.

Under section 2-207 the result is different. This section of the Code recognizes that in current commercial transactions, the terms of the offer and those of the acceptance will seldom be identical. Rather, under the current "battle of the forms," each party typically has a printed form drafted by his attorney and containing as many terms as could be envisioned to favor that party in his sales transactions. Whereas under common law the disparity between the fine-print terms in the parties' forms would have prevented the consummation of a contract when these forms are exchanged, section 2-207 recognizes that in many, but not all, cases the parties do not impart such significance to the terms on the printed forms. See 1 W. Hawkland, *supra*, §1.0903 at 14, §1.090301 at 16. Subsection 2-207(1) therefore provides that "[a] definite and seasonable expression of acceptance or a written confirmation . . . operates as an acceptance even though it states terms additional to or different from those offered or agreed upon, unless acceptance is expressly made conditional on assent to the additional or different terms." Thus, under subsection (1), a contract is recognized notwithstanding the fact that an acceptance or confirmation contains terms additional to or different from those of the offer or prior agreement, provided that the offeree's intent to accept the offer is definitely expressed (see sections 2-204 and 2-206), and provided that the offeree's acceptance is not expressly conditioned on the offeror's assent to the additional or different terms. When a contract is recognized under subsection (1), the additional terms are treated as "proposals for addition to the contract" under subsection (2), which contains special provisions under which such additional terms are deemed to have been accepted when the transaction is between merchants. Conversely, when no contract is recognized under subsection 2-207(1)—either because no definite expression of acceptance exists or, more specifically, because the offeree's acceptance is expressly conditioned on the offeror's assent to the additional or different terms—the entire transaction aborts at this point. If, however, the subsequent conduct of the parties—particularly, performance by both parties under what they apparently believe to be a contract—recognizes the existence of a contract, under subsection 2-207(3) such conduct by both parties is sufficient to establish a contract, notwithstanding the fact that no contract would have been recognized on the basis of their writings alone. Subsection 2-207(3) further provides how the terms of contracts recognized thereunder shall be determined.

With the above analysis and purposes of section 2-207 in mind, we turn to their application in the present case. We initially observe that the affidavits and the acknowledgment forms themselves raise the question of whether Collins & Aikman's forms constituted acceptances or confirmations under section 2-207. The language of some of the acknowledgment forms ("The acceptance of your order is subject to . . .") and the affidavit of Mr. William T. Hester, Collins & Aikman's marketing operations manager, suggest that the forms were the only acceptances issued in response to The Carpet Mart's oral offers. However, in his affidavit Mr. J. A. Castle, a partner in The Carpet Mart, asserted that when he personally called Collins & Aikman to order carpets, someone from the latter's order department would agree to sell the requested carpets, or, alternatively, when Collins & Aikman's visiting salesman took the order, he would agree to the sale, on some occasions after he had used The

Carpet Mart's telephone to call Collins & Aikman's order department. Absent the district court's determination of whether Collins & Aikman's acknowledgment forms were acceptances or, alternatively, confirmations of prior oral agreements, we will consider the application of section 2-207 to both situations for the guidance of the district court on remand.

Viewing Collins & Aikman's acknowledgment forms as acceptances under subsection 2-207(1), we are initially faced with the question of whether the arbitration provision in Collins & Aikman's acknowledgment forms were in fact "additional to or different from" the terms of The Carpet Mart's oral offers. In the typical case under section 2-207, there exist both a written purchase order and a written acknowledgment, and this determination can be readily made by comparing the two forms. In the present case, where the only written forms were Collins & Aikman's sales acknowledgments, we believe that such a comparison must be made between the oral offers and the written acceptances.[2] Although the district court apparently assumed that The Carpet Mart's oral orders did not include in their terms the arbitration provision that appeared in Collins & Aikman's acknowledgment forms, we believe that a specific finding on this point will be required on remand.

Assuming, for purposes of analysis, that the arbitration provision was an addition to the terms of The Carpet Mart's oral offers, we must next determine whether or not Collins & Aikman's acceptances were "expressly made conditional on assent to the additional . . . terms" therein, within the proviso of subsection 2-207(1). As set forth in full above, the provision appearing on the face of Collins & Aikman's acknowledgment forms stated that the acceptances (or orders) were "subject to all of the terms and conditions on the face and reverse side hereof, including arbitration, all of which are accepted by buyer." The provision on the "Acknowledgment" forms further stated that Collins & Aikman's terms would become the basis of the contract between the parties

> either (a) when signed and delivered by buyer to seller and accepted in writing by seller, or (b) at Seller's option, when buyer shall have given to seller specification of assortments, delivery dates, shipping instructions, or instructions to bill and hold as to all or any part of the merchandise herein described, or when buyer has received delivery of the whole or any part thereof, or when buyer has otherwise assented to the terms and conditions hereof.

Similarly, the provision on the "Customer Acknowledgment" and "Sales Contract" forms stated that the terms therein would become the basis of the contract

> either (a) when signed and delivered by Buyer to Seller and accepted in writing by Seller, or (b) when Buyer has received and retained this order for ten days without objection, or (c) when Buyer has accepted delivery of any part of the merchandise specified herein or has furnished to Seller specifications or

2. In describing the second (offer-acceptance) situation to which §2-207 was intended to apply, Official Comment No. 1 describes the acceptance as a "wire or letter," but makes no such reference to a written offer. As in the situation where there is but one written confirmation sent subsequent to an oral agreement—which is expressly referred to in Comment No. 1—we believe the drafters anticipated cases, such as the present one, where a written acceptance would be sent in response to an oral offer.

> assortments, delivery dates, shipping instructions to bill and hold, or when Buyer has otherwise indicated acceptance of the terms hereof.

Although Collins & Aikman's use of the words "subject to" suggests that the acceptances were conditional to some extent, we do not believe the acceptances were "expressly made conditional on [the buyer's] assent to the additional or different terms," as specifically required under the subsection 2-207(1) proviso. In order to fall within this proviso, it is not enough that an acceptance is expressly conditional on additional or different terms; rather, an acceptance must be *expressly* conditional on the offeror's *assent* to those terms. Viewing the subsection (1) proviso within the context of the rest of that subsection and within the policies of section 2-207 itself, we believe that it was intended to apply only to an acceptance that clearly reveals that the offeree is unwilling to proceed with the transaction unless he is assured of the offeror's assent to the additional or different terms therein.

Although the UCC does not provide a definition of "assent," it is significant that Collins & Aikman's printed acknowledgment forms specified at least seven types of action or inaction on the part of the buyer which—sometimes at Collins & Aikman's option—would be deemed to bind the buyer to the terms therein. These ranged from the buyer's signing and delivering the acknowledgment to the seller—which indeed could have been recognized as the buyer's assent to Collins & Aikman's terms—to the buyer's retention of the acknowledgment for ten days without objection, which could never have been recognized as the buyer's assent to the additional or different terms where acceptance is expressly conditional on that assent.

To recognize Collins & Aikman's acceptances as "expressly conditional on [the buyer's] assent to the additional . . . terms" therein, within the proviso of subsection 2-207(1), would thus require us to ignore the specific language of that provision. Such an interpretation is not justified in view of the fact that subsection 2-207(1) is clearly designed to give legal recognition to many contracts where the variance between the offer and acceptance would have precluded such recognition at common law.

Because Collins & Aikman's acceptances were not expressly conditional on the buyer's assent to the additional terms within the proviso of subsection 2-207(1), a contract is recognized under subsection (1), and the additional terms are treated as "proposals" for addition to the contract under subsection 2-207(2).[6] Since both Collins & Aikman and The Carpet Mart are clearly

6. Apparently believing that Collins & Aikman's acknowledgments were acceptances "expressly . . . conditional on assent to the additional or different terms" under the subsection 2-207(1) proviso, the district court recognized contracts between the parties under subsection 2-207(3) because the subsequent performance by both parties clearly recognized the existence of a contract. Absent our conclusion that Collins & Aikman's acknowledgments do not fall within the subsection 2-207(1) proviso, we believe that the district court correctly applied subsection 2-207(3) to Collins & Aikman's "acceptances," notwithstanding the fact that some of the language of that subsection appears to refer to the typical situation under §2-207 where there exist both a written offer and a written acceptance. Although we recognize the value that writings by both parties serve in sales transactions, where subsection 2-207(3) is otherwise applicable we do not believe the purposes of that subsection should be abandoned simply because the offeror chose to rely on his oral offer. In such a case, we believe that the district court's comparison of the terms of the oral offer and the written acceptance under subsection (3) would have been correct.

"merchants" as that term is defined in subsection 2-104(1), the arbitration provision will be deemed to have been accepted by The Carpet Mart under subsection 2-207(2) unless it materially altered the terms of The Carpet Mart's oral offers [UCC §2-207(2)(b)]. We believe that the question of whether the arbitration provision materially altered the oral offer under subsection 2-207(2)(b) is one which can be resolved only by the district court on further findings of fact in the present case.[8] If the arbitration provision did in fact materially alter The Carpet Mart's offer, it could not become a part of the contract "unless expressly agreed to" by The Carpet Mart. UCC §2-207, Official Comment No. 3.

We therefore conclude that if on remand the district court finds that Collins & Aikman's acknowledgments were in fact acceptances and that the arbitration provision was additional to the terms of The Carpet Mart's oral orders, contracts will be recognized under subsection 2-207(1). The arbitration clause will then be viewed as a "proposal" under subsection 2-207(2), which will be deemed to have been accepted by The Carpet Mart unless it materially altered the oral offers.

If the District Court finds that Collins & Aikman's acknowledgment forms were not acceptances but rather were confirmations of prior oral agreements between the parties, an application of section 2-207 similar to that above will be required. Subsection 2-207(1) will require an initial determination of whether the arbitration provision in the confirmations was "additional to or different from" the terms orally agreed upon. Assuming that the district court finds that the arbitration provision was not a term of the oral agreements between the parties, the arbitration clause will be treated as a "proposal" for addition to the contract under subsection 2-207(2), as was the case when Collins & Aikman's acknowledgments were viewed as acceptances above. The provision for arbitration will be deemed to have been accepted by The Carpet Mart unless the district court finds that it materially altered the prior oral agreements, in which case The Carpet Mart could not become bound thereby absent an express agreement to that effect.

As a result of the above application of section 2-207 to the limited facts before us in the present case, we find it necessary to remand the case to the district court for the following findings: (1) whether oral agreements were reached between the parties prior to the sending of Collins & Aikman's acknowledgment forms; if there were no such oral agreements, (2) whether the arbitration provision appearing in Collins & Aikman's "acceptances" was additional to the terms of The Carpet Mart's oral offers; and, if so, (3) whether the arbitration provision materially altered the terms of The Carpet Mart's oral offers. Alternatively, if the district court does find that oral agreements were reached between the parties before Collins & Aikman's acknowledgment forms were

---

8. While UCC §2-207, Official Comment Nos. 4 and 5 provide examples of terms that would and would not materially alter a contract, an arbitration clause is listed under neither. Although we recognize the rule "that the agreement to arbitrate must be direct and the intention made clear, without implication, inveiglement or subtlety," *Matter of Doughboy Industries, Inc., and Pantasote Co.*, 17 A.D.2d 216, 218, 233 N.Y.S.2d 488, 492 (1962) (indicating in dictum that an arbitration clause would materially alter a contract under 2-207(2)(b)), we believe the question of material alteration necessarily rests on the facts of each case. *See American Parts Co. v. American Arbitration Ass'n*, 8 Mich. App. 156, 171, 154 N.W.2d 5, 14 (1967).

sent in each instance, it will be necessary for the district court to make the following findings: (1) whether the prior oral agreements embodied the arbitration provision appearing in Collins & Aikman's "confirmations"; and, if not, (2) whether the arbitration provision materially altered the prior oral agreements. Regardless of whether the district court finds Collins & Aikman's acknowledgment forms to have been acceptances or confirmations, if the arbitration provision was additional to, and a material alteration of, the offers or prior oral agreements, The Carpet Mart will not be bound to that provision absent a finding that it expressly agreed to be bound thereby.

## NOTES, QUESTIONS, AND PROBLEMS

The court quotes several commentators' dissatisfaction with UCC section 2-207. Professors White and Summers also refer to section 2-207 as being "like an amphibious tank that was originally designed to fight in the swamps, but was sent to fight in the desert." White & Summers, *Uniform Commercial Code* §1.3 (5th ed. 2000). In their view, section 2-207 was designed to deal with the situation where minor discrepancies between offer and acceptance previously prevented contract formation. Unscrupulous parties would take advantage of the technical variance to get out of a deal because it had become less favorable. Where section 2-207 has problems is in determining the terms of the contract where there are significant variations between the forms. Perhaps no contract should be found at all in those cases.

On remand, what kind of evidence would be useful in determining whether the arbitration provision materially altered the contract? Should arbitration clauses be considered "per se" material? For a discussion of some of the problems posed by arbitration, see *Armendariz v. Foundation Health Psychcare Services, Inc.*, 24 Cal. 4th 83, 6 P.3d 669, 99 Cal. Rptr. 2d 745 (2000).

***Problem 3-4.*** Buyer sends an offer to Seller, seeking to purchase 2,000 bushels of wheat. Seller sends an "order confirmation" stating, "We agree to ship you 1,500 bushels of wheat." The forms are in agreement on price. Is there a contract? If there is a contract, how much wheat is the seller required to ship and the buyer required to accept? See UCC §2-207(1). How are different terms in an acceptance to be treated? Compare UCC §2-207(2) with its Official Comment 3. Would you advise your client to draft order forms stating, "This order is expressly limited to its terms"? Would you advise your client to draft acknowledgment forms stating, "This acknowledgment is expressly conditioned on assent to its terms"? What are the drawbacks of such provisions, if any?

***Problem 3-5.*** Seller is a manufacturer of steel tubing while Buyer is a manufacturer of cooling units. Buyer purchases steel tubing for use in the cooling units from Seller. The parties did business for a number of years. Buyer would send Seller a purchase order for the amount of steel tubing it needed, and Seller would send a "confirmation" to buyer that was in agreement with the price and quantity ordered. The confirmation clearly indicated that the acceptance of Buyer's order was expressly conditional on Buyer's assent to the additional terms on the form. One of the terms limited the Seller's liability to a refund of the purchase price or repair or replacement of the tubing if it proved to be defective. Buyer was aware of this term and had complained to Seller about it, but Seller never changed the term. Buyer never expressly agreed to the term, but continued to order tubing from Seller, which Seller shipped and Buyer then accepted and paid for. One shipment of tubing proved to be defective, causing one of Buyer's cooling units to fail. This caused damage to one of Buyer's customers, for which Buyer was responsible. Buyer would like to hold Seller responsible, but will be unable to do so if the limited liability term in Seller's confirmation is effective. First, at what point is a contract formed between the parties? Second, is the Seller's limitation on liability part of the contract? See UCC §2-207(1) & (3). *Diamond Fruit Growers v. Krack Corp.*, 794 F.2d 1440, 1 U.C.C. Rep. Serv. 2d 1073 (9th Cir. 1986).

## HILL V. GATEWAY 2000, INC.

United States Court of Appeals, Seventh Circuit

105 F.2d 1147, 33 UCC Rep. Serv. 2d 303 (1997)
EASTERBROOK, Circuit Judge.

A customer picks up the phone, orders a computer, and gives a credit card number. Presently a box arrives, containing the computer and a list of terms said to govern unless the customer returns the computer within 30 days. Are these terms effective as the parties' contract, or is the contract term-free because the order-taker did not read any terms over the phone and elicit the customer's assent?

One of the terms in the box containing a Gateway 2000 system was an arbitration clause. Rich and Enza Hill, the customers, kept the computer more than 30 days before complaining about its components and performance. They filed suit in federal court arguing, among other things, that the product's shortcomings make Gateway a racketeer (mail and wire fraud are said to be the predicate offenses), leading to treble damages under RICO for the Hills and a class of all other purchasers. Gateway asked the district court to enforce the arbitration clause; the judge refused, writing that "the present record is insufficient to support a finding of a valid arbitration agreement between the parties or that the plaintiffs were given adequate notice of the arbitration clause." Gateway took an immediate appeal, as is its right.

The Hills say that the arbitration clause did not stand out. They concede noticing the statement of terms but deny reading it closely enough to discover the agreement to arbitrate, and they ask us to conclude that they therefore may go to court. Yet an agreement to arbitrate must be enforced "save upon such grounds as exist at law or in equity for the revocation of any contract." 9 U.S.C. §2. *Doctor's Associates, Inc. v. Casarotto*, 134 L. Ed. 2d 902, 116 S. Ct. 1652 (1996), holds that this provision of the Federal Arbitration Act is inconsistent with any requirement that an arbitration clause be prominent. A contract need not be read to be effective; people who accept take the risk that the unread terms may in retrospect prove unwelcome. Terms inside Gateway's box stand or fall together. If they constitute the parties' contract because the Hills had an opportunity to return the computer after reading them, then all must be enforced.

*ProCD, Inc. v. Zeidenberg*, 86 F.3d 1447 (7th Cir. 1996), holds that terms inside a box of software bind consumers who use the software after an opportunity to read the terms and to reject them by returning the product. Likewise, *Carnival Cruise Lines, Inc. v. Shute*, 499 U.S. 585, 113 L. Ed. 2d 622, 111 S. Ct. 1522 (1991), enforces a forum-selection clause that was included among three pages of terms attached to a cruise ship ticket. *ProCD* and *Carnival Cruise Lines* exemplify the many commercial transactions in which people pay for products with terms to follow; *ProCD* discusses others. 86 F.3d at 1451-1452. The district court concluded in *ProCD* that the contract is formed when the consumer pays for the software; as a result, the court held, only terms known to the consumer at that moment are part of the contract, and provisos inside the box do not count. Although this is one way a contract could be formed, it is not the only way: "A vendor, as master of the offer, may invite acceptance by conduct, and may propose limitations on the kind of conduct that constitutes acceptance. A buyer may accept by performing the acts the vendor proposes to treat as acceptance." *Id.* at 1452. Gateway shipped computers with the same sort of accept-or-return offer ProCD made to users of its software. *ProCD* relied on the Uniform Commercial Code rather than any peculiarities of Wisconsin law; both Illinois and South Dakota, the two states whose law might govern relations between Gateway and the Hills, have adopted the UCC; neither side has pointed us to any atypical doctrines in those states that might be pertinent; *ProCD* therefore applies to this dispute.

Plaintiffs ask us to limit *ProCD* to software, but where's the sense in that? *ProCD* is about the law of contract, not the law of software. Payment preceding the revelation of full terms is common for air transportation, insurance, and many other endeavors. Practical considerations support allowing vendors to enclose the full legal terms with their products. Cashiers cannot be expected to read legal documents to customers before ringing up sales. If the staff at the other end of the phone for direct-sales operations such as Gateway's had to read the four-page statement of terms before taking the buyer's credit card number, the droning voice would anesthetize rather than enlighten many potential buyers. Others would hang up in a rage over the waste of their time. And oral recitation would not avoid customers' assertions (whether true or feigned) that the clerk did not read term *X* to them, or that they did not remember or understand it. Writing provides benefits for both sides of commercial transactions. Customers as a group are better off when vendors skip costly and ineffectual steps such as telephonic recitation, and use instead a simple approve-or-return device. Competent adults are bound by such documents, read or unread. For what little it is worth, we add that the box from Gateway was crammed with software. The computer came with an operating system, without which it was useful only as a boat anchor. Gateway also included many application programs. So the Hills' effort to limit *ProCD* to software would not avail them factually, even if it were sound legally—which it is not.

Next, the Hills insist that *ProCD* is irrelevant because Zeidenberg was a "merchant" and they are not. Section 2-207(2) of the UCC, the infamous battle-of-the-forms section, states that "additional terms [following acceptance of an offer] are to be construed as proposals for addition to a contract. Between merchants such terms become part of the contract unless. . . ." Plaintiffs tell us that *ProCD* came out as it did only because Zeidenberg was a "merchant" and the terms inside ProCD's box were not excluded by the "unless" clause. This argument pays scant attention to the opinion in *ProCD*, which concluded that, when there is only one form, "section 2-207 is irrelevant." 86 F.3d at 1452. The question in *ProCD* was not whether terms were added to a contract after its formation, but how and when the contract was formed—in particular, whether a vendor may propose that a contract of sale be formed, not in the store (or over the phone) with the payment of money or a general "send me the product," but after the customer has had a chance to inspect both the item and the terms. *ProCD* answers yes, for merchants and consumers alike. Yet again, for what little it is worth, we observe that the Hills' misunderstand the setting of *ProCD*. A "merchant" under the UCC "means a person who deals in goods of the kind or otherwise by his occupation holds himself out as having knowledge or skill peculiar to the practices or goods involved in the transaction." UCC §2-104(1). Zeidenberg bought the product at a retail store, an uncommon place for merchants to acquire inventory. His corporation put ProCD's database on the Internet for anyone to browse, which led to the litigation but did not make Zeidenberg a software merchant.

At oral argument the Hills propounded still another distinction: The box containing ProCD's software displayed a notice that additional terms were within, while the box containing Gateway's computer did not. The difference is functional, not legal. Consumers browsing the aisles of a store can look at the box, and if they are unwilling to deal with the prospect of additional terms can leave the box alone, avoiding the transactions costs of returning the package after reviewing its contents. Gateway's box, by contrast, is just a shipping carton; it is not on display anywhere. Its function is to protect the product during transit, and the information on its sides is for the use of handlers ("Fragile!" "This Side Up!") rather than would-be purchasers.

Perhaps the Hills would have had a better argument if they were first alerted to the bundling of hardware and legal-ware after opening the box and wanted to return the computer in order to avoid disagreeable terms, but were dissuaded by the expense of shipping. What the remedy would be in such a case—could it exceed the shipping charges?—is an interesting question, but one that need not detain us because the Hills knew before they ordered the computer that the carton would include *some* important terms, and they did not seek to discover these in advance. Gateway's ads state that their products come with limited warranties and lifetime support. How limited was the warranty—30 days, with service contingent on shipping the computer back, or five years, with free on-site service? What sort of support was offered? Shoppers have three principal ways to discover these things. First, they can ask the vendor to send a copy before deciding whether to buy. The Magnuson-Moss Warranty Act requires firms to distribute their warranty terms on request. 15 U.S.C. §2302(b)(1)(A). The Hills do not contend that Gateway would have refused to enclose the remaining terms, too. Concealment would be bad for business, scaring some customers away and leading to excess returns from others. Second, shoppers can consult public sources (computer magazines, the Web sites of vendors) that may contain this information. Third, they may inspect the documents after the product's delivery. Like Zeidenberg, the Hills took the third option.

By keeping the computer beyond 30 days, the Hills accepted Gateway's offer, including the arbitration clause.

## NOTES, QUESTIONS, AND PROBLEMS

1. The preceding case and *ProCD, Inc. v. Zeidenberg*, 86 F.3d 1447 (7th Cir. 1996), which is cited in the opinion, are both authored by Judge Easterbrook and are controversial. Not all courts nor do all commentators agree with the approach taken in these cases, which hold that UCC section 2-207 should not be used when the seller discloses terms after the buyer has already paid for the goods. *See Klocek v. Gateway, Inc.*, 104 F. Supp. 2d 1332 (D. Kan. 2000) (holding on similar facts to *Hill v. Gateway* that the arbitration clause should not be included in the contract under section 2-207(2) and expressly disagreeing with the reasoning in *Hill v. Gateway*). The approach taken by Judge Easterbrook is sometimes referred to as a "rolling contract" analysis because the contract is formed over time, and is also sometimes referred to as "money now, terms later." Under this approach, the seller arguably has a better chance of having its terms included in the contract since the buyer will probably not pay much attention to the terms that are included in the box containing the product. The buyer will keep the goods and then be bound by the terms, except for terms that are considered unconscionable. See Pitet, *The Problem with "Money Now, Terms Later":* ProCD, Inc. v. Zeidenberg *and the Enforceability of "Shrinkwrap" Software Licenses*, 31 Loy. L.A. L. Rev. 325 (1997).
2. Note the court's assertion that UCC section 2-207 only applies when there is more than one form involved. Is that consistent with the holding in *Dorton v. Collins & Aikman*? Is it consistent with Official Comment 1 of section 2-207?
3. Note that in *Dorton* the court holds that a merchant may not be bound by an arbitration clause if it is determined that the clause materially altered the contract, while in *Hill* the court holds that a consumer is bound to the arbitration clause. Are the results of the two cases backward? Should the salesperson either be required to read all of the terms of the contract to the consumer over the phone, or tell the consumer that important terms will be included in the box containing the product? If the salesperson were to do that, would the consumer pay more attention to the terms in the box?

If section 2-207 were applied to this case, would the arbitration clause be effective?

***Problem 3-6.*** Assume that a contract was formed when the goods were ordered over the phone and the buyer made payment. Could it be argued that by retaining the goods the buyer had agreed to modify the contract to include the arbitration provision? See UCC §2-209. See also CISG Article 29.

### (b) CISG Treatment

The CISG treatment of the "battle of the forms" is in some ways more straightforward and clear than the UCC and in some ways more vague. The

CISG article that most directly deals with discrepancies between the offer and acceptance is Article 19. It starts in the first paragraph by stating a "mirror image" rule that a purported acceptance containing varying terms is not an operative acceptance, but is instead a rejection and a counteroffer. Paragraph 2 modifies the mirror image rule somewhat by stating that an acceptance may contain immaterial additional or different terms, provided that the offeror does not timely object. If the offeror objects, then no contract is formed by the writings as the purported acceptance is deemed a counteroffer.

One area where the CISG is more clear than the UCC is on the definition of material terms. Article 19(3) provides some terms that will be considered material, including terms relating to settlement of disputes. As noted previously, there is a question under the UCC as to whether a provision relating to settlement of disputes, such as an arbitration clause, is material.

Unlike UCC section 2-207, the CISG does not have any provision dealing with confirmations that are sent following the formation of an informal contract. The following case deals with the issue of how such post-contract terms should be handled.

The CISG also does not have any provision comparable to UCC section 2-207(3) dealing with contracts formed by performance. This issue is considered in Problem 3-7, following the next case.

## Chateau des Charmes v. Sabate USA Inc.

United States Court of Appeals, Ninth Circuit

328 F.3d 528 (9th Cir. 2003)

Chateau des Charmes Wines, Ltd. ("Chateau des Charmes"), a Canadian company, appeals the dismissal of its action for breach of contract and related claims arising out of its purchase of wine corks from Sabaté, S.A. ("Sabaté France"), a French company, and Sabaté USA, Inc. ("Sabaté USA"), a wholly owned California subsidiary. The district court held that forum selection clauses in the invoices that Sabaté France sent to Chateau des Charmes were part of the contract between the parties and dismissed the case in favor of adjudication in France. Because we conclude that the forum selection clauses in question were not part of any agreement between the parties, we reverse.

### Factual Background and Procedural History

The material facts pertinent to this appeal are not disputed. Sabaté France manufactures and sells special wine corks that it claims will not cause wines to be spoiled by "cork taint," a distasteful flavor that some corks produce. It sells these corks through a wholly owned California subsidiary, Sabaté USA.

In February 2000, after some preliminary discussions about the characteristics of Sabaté's corks, Chateau des Charmes, a winery from Ontario, Canada, agreed by telephone with Sabaté USA to purchase a certain number of corks at a specific price. The parties agreed on payment and shipping terms. No other terms were discussed, nor did the parties have any history of prior dealings. Later that year, Chateau des Charmes placed a second telephone order for corks on the same terms. In total, Chateau des Charmes ordered 1.2 million corks.

Sabaté France shipped the corks to Canada in 11 shipments. For each shipment, Sabaté France also sent an invoice. Some of the invoices arrived before the shipments, some with the shipments, and some after the shipments. On the face of each invoice was a paragraph in French that specified, "Any dispute arising under the present contract is under the sole jurisdiction of the Court of Commerce of the City of Perpignan." On the back of each invoice a number of provisions were printed in French, including a clause that specified, "[A]ny disputes arising out of this agreement shall be brought before the court with jurisdiction to try the matter in the judicial district where Seller's registered office is located." Chateau des Charmes duly took delivery and paid for each shipment of corks. The corks were then used to bottle Chateau des Charmes' wines.

Chateau des Charmes claims that, in 2001, it noticed that the wine bottled with Sabaté's corks was tainted by cork flavors. Chateau des Charmes filed suit in federal district court in California against Sabaté France and Sabaté USA alleging claims for breach of contract, strict liability, breach of warranty, false advertising, and unfair competition. Sabaté France and Sabaté USA filed a motion to dismiss based on the forum selection clauses. The district court held that the forum selection clauses were valid and enforceable and dismissed the action. This appeal ensued.

**Discussion**

I.

The question before us is whether the forum selection clauses in Sabaté France's invoices were part of any agreement between the parties. The disputes in this case arise out of an agreement for a sale of goods from a French party and a United States party to a Canadian party. Such international sales contracts are ordinarily governed by a multilateral treaty, the United Nations Convention on Contracts for the International Sale of Goods ("CISG"), which applies to "contracts of sale of goods between parties whose places of business are in different States . . . when the States are Contracting States." CISG Article 1(1)(a). The United States, Canada, and France are all contracting states to the CISG. Accordingly, the Convention governs the substantive question of contract formation as to the forum selection clauses.

II.

Under the CISG, it is plain that the forum selection clauses were not part of any agreement between the parties. The Convention sets out a clear regime for analyzing international contracts for the sale of goods: A proposal is an offer if it is sufficiently definite to "indicate[] the goods and expressly or implicitly fix[] or make[] provision for determining the quantity and the price" (CISG Article 14), and it demonstrates an intention by the offeror to be bound if the proposal is accepted. *Id.* In turn, an offer is accepted if the offeree makes a "statement . . . or other conduct . . . indicating assent to an offer." *Id.,* art. 18. Further, "A contract is concluded at the moment when an acceptance of an offer becomes effective." *Id.,* Article 23. Within such a framework, the oral agreements between Sabaté USA and Chateau des Charmes as to the kind of cork, the quantity, and the price were sufficient to create complete and binding contracts.

The terms of those agreements did not include any forum selection clause. Indeed, Sabaté France and Sabaté USA do not contend that a forum selection clause was part of their oral agreements, but merely that the clauses in the invoices became part of a binding agreement. The logic of this contention is defective. Under the Convention, a "contract may be modified or terminated by the mere agreement of the parties." *Id.,* Article 29(1). However, the Convention clearly states that "[a]dditional or different terms relating, among other things, to . . . the settlement of disputes are considered to alter the terms of the offer materially." *Id.,* Article 19(3). There is no indication that Chateau des Charmes conducted itself in a manner that evidenced any affirmative assent to the forum selection clauses in the invoices. Rather, Chateau des Charmes merely performed its obligations under the oral contract.

Nothing in the Convention suggests that the failure to object to a party's unilateral attempt to alter materially the terms of an otherwise valid agreement is an "agreement" within the terms of Article 29. *Cf.* CISG Article 8(3) ("In determining the intent of a party or the understanding a reasonable person would have had, due consideration is to be given to all relevant circumstances of the case including the negotiations, any practices which the parties have established between themselves, usages and any subsequent conduct of the parties."). Here, no circumstances exist to conclude that Chateau des Charmes's conduct evidenced an "agreement." We reject the contention that because Sabaté France sent multiple invoices it created an agreement as to the proper forum with Chateau des Charmes. The parties agreed in two telephone calls to a purchase of corks to be shipped in 11 batches. In such circumstances, a party's multiple attempts to alter an agreement unilaterally do not so effect.

**Conclusion**

Because the contract for the sale of corks did not contain the forum selection clauses in Sabaté France's invoices, there was nothing for the district court to enforce, and its dismissal of this action was an abuse of discretion. The action is reinstated.

REVERSED and REMANDED.

## QUESTIONS, NOTE, AND PROBLEM

1. Would it make a difference if the provision in the invoices called for arbitration rather than litigation in France? Would this case be decided the same way under UCC section 2-207?
2. The UNIDROIT Principles of International Commercial Contracts contain more precise rules dealing with the use of standard terms in contracting. UNIDROIT Principles Articles 2.1.19-2.1.22. Standard terms are defined in Article 2.1.19 as being those that are prepared in advance for repeated use and which are not subject to negotiation. Article 2.1.20 indicates that a standard term is not enforceable if the other party could not have reasonably expected it, unless it is expressly agreed to. Article 2.1.22 indicates that where the parties use standard terms and reach agreement except on those

terms, the contract consists of the agreed terms only. Standard terms are not included. If a party wishes to insist on its standard terms, it must clearly indicate that intent to the other side. Is this approach preferable to UCC section 2-207?

***Problem 3-7.*** Buyer, a French company, sends a purchase order to seller containing a provision calling for resolution of any disputes in a French court. Seller, a German company, responds with a confirmation indicating that any disputes will be resolved in a German court. Under applicable jurisdictional rules, in absence of a contractual provision to the contrary, any disputes over the quality of the goods would be litigated in Germany since the goods are being shipped from there. The goods are shipped and accepted. The buyer claims that the goods do not conform to the contract and files an action in France. Should the French court decide the matter? Is there a contract? See CISG Article 19(3). Does the CISG use the "last shot" doctrine? Should the conflicting terms in the parties' forms cancel out? See CISG Article 18(1). Cour de Cassation (Supreme Court of France) July 16, 1998, *Les Verreries de Saint Gobain, SA v. Martinswerk GmbH*, CLOUT abstract no. 242, *http://cisgw3.law.pace.edu/cases/980716f1.html* (accessed Oct. 2011). See Vergne, *The "Battle of the Forms" Under the 1980 United Nations Convention on the International Sale of Goods*, 33 Am. J. Comp. L. 233 (1985), *www.cisg.law.pace.edu/cisg/biblio/vergne.html* (accessed Oct. 2011). What is the proper role of the UNIDROIT Principles discussed in the preceding note in a case like this? CISG Article 7. See *www.cisg.law.pace.edu/cisg/text/matchup/general-observations.html* (accessed Oct. 2011)

## B. MUST THE CONTRACT BE IN WRITING? THE STATUTE OF FRAUDS

### 1. THE BASIC REQUIREMENTS

In your contracts class you probably spent some time studying the Statute of Frauds, which requires some contracts to be evidenced by a writing. You may have learned that, under UCC section 2-201, contracts for the sale of goods of $500 or more must be evidenced by a writing signed by the party to be charged that evidences the existence of a contract. There are some exceptions to the rule, as will be explored in the problems following the next case.

By comparison, CISG Article 11 states that no writing is generally required. The drafters of the CISG recognized, however, that in some nations there is a strong public policy favoring the requirement that contracts be in writing. Thus, nations are permitted to "opt out" of Article 11 by making a declaration under CISG Article 96.[2] If a contract for sale involves a party that has its place

2. At the time of this writing (August 2011) the following nations have either made a declaration under Article 96 or otherwise stated that they are not bound by Article 11: Argentina, Armenia, Belarus, Chile, China, Hungary, Latvia, Lithuania, Paraguay, Russian Federation, and the Ukraine. See *www.uncitral.org/uncitral/en/uncitral_texts/sale_goods/1980CISG_status.html.*

of business in a nation that has made an Article 96 declaration, Article 11 does not apply to the contract. CISG Article 12. This does not necessarily mean that the contract must be in writing—it simply means that the CISG is silent on the question of whether a writing is required, leaving the matter to other law. This issue will be explored further in an upcoming problem.

The next case deals with the requirements for a necessary writing under UCC section 2-201.

## COHN V. FISHER

New Jersey Superior Court

118 N.J. Super. 286, 287 A.2d 222, 10 UCC Rep. Serv. 372 (1972)

Plaintiff Albert L. Cohn (hereinafter Cohn) moves for summary judgment against defendant Donal L. Fisher (hereinafter Fisher). The controversy concerns an alleged breach of contract for the sale of Cohn's boat by Fisher.

On Sunday, May 19, 1968, Fisher inquired of Cohn's advertisement in the *New York Times* for the sale of his 30-foot auxiliary sloop. Upon learning the location of the sailboat, Fisher proceeded to the boatyard and inspected the sloop. Fisher then phoned Cohn and submitted an offer of $4,650, which Cohn accepted. Both agreed to meet the next day at Cohn's office in Paterson, New Jersey. At the meeting on Monday, May 20, Fisher gave Cohn a check for $2,325 and affixed on same: "deposit on aux. sloop, D'Arc Wind, full amount $4,650." Both parties agreed to meet on Saturday, May 25, when Fisher would pay the remaining half of the purchase price and Cohn would presumably transfer title.

A few days later Fisher informed Cohn that he would not close the deal on the weekend because a survey of the boat could not be conducted that soon. Cohn notified Fisher that he would hold him to his agreement to pay the full purchase price by Saturday. At this point relations between the parties broke down. Fisher stopped payment on the check he had given as a deposit and failed to close the deal on Saturday.

Cohn then readvertised the boat and sold it for the highest offer of $3,000. In his suit for breach of contract Cohn is seeking damages of $1,679.50, representing the difference between the contract price with Fisher and the final sales price together with the costs incurred in reselling the boat.

Defendant contends in his answer that there was no breach of contract since the agreement of sale was conditional upon a survey inspection of the boat. However, in his depositions defendant candidly admits that neither at the time the offer to purchase was verbally conveyed and accepted nor on the following day when he placed a deposit on the boat did he make the sale contingent upon a survey.

The essentials of a valid contract are: mutual assent, consideration, legality of object, capacity of the parties, and formality of memorialization. In the present litigation, dispute arises only to the elements of mutual assent and formality of memorialization.

UCC section 2-204 states, "A contract for sale of goods may be made in any manner sufficient to show agreement, including conduct by both parties which recognizes the existence of such a contract." Although defendant has admitted to the court that at no time did he condition his offer to purchase the boat upon a survey inspection, he still asserts that the survey was a condition precedent to the performance of the contract. Thus, the issue arises as to the nature of the bargain agreed upon by the parties. UCC section 1-201(b)(3) defines "agreement" as meaning

> the bargain of the parties in fact as found in their language or by implication from other circumstances including course of dealing or usage of trade or course of performance as provided in this Act (§1-303). Whether an agreement has legal consequences is determined by the provisions of this Act, if applicable; otherwise by the law of contracts (§1-103).

Under the objective theory of mutual assent followed in all jurisdictions, a contracting party is bound by the apparent intention he outwardly manifests to the other contracting party. To the extent that his real, secret intention differs therefrom, it is entirely immaterial.

The express language of the contract, failing to manifest an intention to make the sale of the boat conditioned on a survey, and defendant failing to present evidence that the condition of a survey was implied under any section of the Uniform Commercial Code or in the general law of contracts, this court concludes that the agreement between the parties was exclusive of a condition precedent for a survey of the boat.

As to the element of formality of memorialization, UCC section 2-201 requires that a contract for the sale of goods for the price of $500 or more, to be enforceable, must comply with the statute of frauds.

Thus in the present case, there are three alternatives by which the contract could be held enforceable: (1) under section 2-201(1) the check may constitute a sufficient written memorandum; (2) under section 2-201(3)(b) defendant's testimony in depositions and his answers to demands for admission may constitute an admission of the contract; or (3) under section 2-201(3)(c) payment and acceptance of the check may constitute partial performance.

The above issues, arising under the Uniform Commercial Code adopted by this state on January 1, 1963, are novel to the courts of New Jersey. For such reason this court will determine the enforceability of the contract under each of the alternatives. Ample authority for resolving the issues is found in the notes provided by the framers of the Code and in the decisions of our sister states.

With regard to the question of whether the check satisfies the statute of frauds as a written memorandum, section 2-201(1) requires (1) a writing indicating a contract for sale, (2) signed by the party to be charged, and (3) the quantity term must be expressly stated. The back of the check in question bore the legend "deposit on aux. sloop, D'Arc Wind, full amount $4,650." Thus the check seems to prima facie satisfy the requirements in that: It is a writing which indicates a contract for sale by stating the subject matter of the sale (aux. sloop, D'Arc Wind), the price ($4,650), part of the purchase terms—50 percent down (deposit of $2,325), and by inferentially identifying the seller (Albert Cohn, payee) and the purchaser (Donal Fisher, drawer); it is signed by the party against whom enforcement is sought (Donal Fisher); and it expressly states the quantity term (the D'Arc Wind). Thus the check, although not a sales contract, would comply with the requirements of the statute of frauds under section 2-201(1).

Had the check not satisfied the requirements of section 2-201(1), the check, together with defendant's admission of a contract in his depositions and demands for admission, may satisfy section 2-201(3)(b). This subsection states, in effect, that where the requirements of section 2-201(1) have not been satisfied, an otherwise valid contract will be held enforceable if the party charged admits that a contract was made. Such a contract would be enforceable only with respect to the quantity of goods admitted.

This court is of the opinion that if a party admits an oral contract, he should be held bound to his bargain. The statute of frauds was not designed to protect a party who made an oral contract, but rather to aid a party who did not make a contract, though one is claimed to have been made orally with him. This court would therefore hold that the check, together with defendant's admission of an oral contract, would constitute an enforceable contract under section 2-201(3)(b).

Finally, under UCC section 2-201(3)(c) the check may constitute partial performance of the contract in that payment for goods was made and accepted, and, as such, the contract would be held enforceable under the statute of frauds.

## QUESTIONS AND PROBLEMS

1. Is the court correct in holding that section 2-201(3)(c) is applicable? Should the boat be sawed in two? See §2-201, Official Comment 2.
2. The Uniform Electronic Transactions Act ("UETA") and the federal Electronic Signatures in Global and National Commerce Act (sometimes referred to as the "E-Sign Act"), 15 USC section 7001, et seq, provide rules governing electronic contracting. If a state has adopted the uniform version of UETA, it supercedes E-Sign regarding matters of state law to the extent it is inconsistent.[3] UETA will apply only if parties have agreed to contract electronically. Such an agreement can be implied from the facts of the case.[4] Both UETA and E-Sign indicate that contracts are not to be considered unenforceable simply because they are in electronic form and contain electronic signatures.[5] Arguably, e-mails and other electronic records satisfy the statute of frauds in any event. In *Cloud Corporation v. Hasbro, Inc.*, 314 F.3d 289, 49 UCC Serv. 2d 413 (7th Cir. 2002), the court held that under Illinois law predating E-Sign and UETA, an e-mail satisfied the UCC section 2-201 statute of frauds. The sender's name in the e-mail satisfied the signature requirement. For more on how the statute of frauds impacts on electronic contracting, see Problem 3-11, *infra*.

***Problem 3-8.*** In *Cohn*, what if the seller held on to the check for 15 days after receipt and then returned the check to the buyer without signing it? Would the statute of frauds be satisfied if the buyer then decided to sue the seller? Are the

3. 15 U.S.C. §7002(2)(A)(i).
4. UETA §5(b).
5. 15 U.S.C. §7001(a); UETA §7(a)

parties "merchants"? See UCC §§2-104, 2-201(2). Would the advertisement containing the printed name of the seller satisfy the statute of frauds? Is it "signed"? See UCC §1-201(37) and Official Comment 37. Does it evidence a contract? *See Donovan v. RRL Corp.*, 26 Cal. 4th 261, 27 P.2d 702, 109 Cal. Rptr. 807 (2001).

***Problem 3-9.*** Assume an oral contract for the sale of grapes. Seller relies on the contract by getting another of its purchasers to agree not to take delivery under a preexisting contract so that this deal can be made. When the time for delivery comes, Buyer defaults, and Seller is unable to resell the grapes for anything close to the contract price. Does Seller have an argument under any of the exceptions in section 2-201? Can any other argument be made? See UCC §1-103; *Allied Grape Growers v. Bronco Wine Co.*, 203 Cal. App. 3d 432, 249 Cal. Rptr. 872 (1988).

***Problem 3-10.*** It is unethical to raise a frivolous defense or to knowingly make a false statement of material fact to a third party. ABA Model Rules of Professional Conduct Rule 4.1. The ABA Model Rules also require a lawyer to notify the court if the lawyer knows of a "fraudulent act by the client" that is material. See Rule 3.3(a)(2). If your client tells you the story that Fisher told to the court, would it be unethical for you to raise the statute of frauds as a defense? What kind of advice should you give the client in such a case? See Gillette & Walt, *Sales Law—Domestic and International* 153-155 (Rev. ed.).

***Problem 3-11.*** Assume that the complaint alleges an oral contract for the sale of goods and does not allege any exception to the statute of frauds. Can the defendant have the case dismissed on demurrer? Should the plaintiff have an opportunity to get the defendant to admit under oath that a contract existed? Must the case be allowed to go to trial for that purpose? *See DF Activities Corp. v. Brown*, 851 F.2d 920 (7th Cir. 1988).

***Problem 3-12.*** Company *A* has programmed its computers to automatically order additional inventory from Company *B* every time that *A*'s inventory falls to a certain level. When the inventory reaches that level, *A*'s computer sends an electronic message to Company *B*'s computer indicating the amount of goods that *A* wishes to order. The message contains the name of Company *A*. The electronic message contains the standard terms and conditions for purchasing goods of Company *A*. The amount ordered is always over $5,000. When the message is received, Company *B*'s computer responds with an electronic acknowledgment, indicating that the goods will be shipped. The message sent by *B*'s computers contains the name of Company *B* and also contains the standard terms and conditions of Company *B* that differ somewhat from those of Company *A*. Is there an enforceable contract? What happens to the varying terms in the electronic forms? See UETA §14; UCC §§2-204, 2-207. At what point are electronic messages deemed to have been sent and received? UETA §15.

***Problem 3-13.*** Assume that in an international sale of goods, Seller is located in Country *A*, which does not have a statute of frauds and which has adopted the CISG but has not made an Article 96 declaration. Buyer is located in Country *B*, which has a statute of frauds, has adopted the CISG, and has made an Article 96 declaration. Does the contract between the parties need to be evidenced by a writing? See CISG Articles 7, 11, and 12. See Gillette and Walt, *Sales Law—Domestic and International* 155-160.

## 2. MODIFICATIONS

UCC section 2-209(2) largely validates "no oral modification" clauses, meaning that parties by agreement may require that any modification of a contract be in writing. Section 2-209(3) states that if a contract as modified is within the statute of frauds, the provisions of section 2-201 must be satisfied. Does this mean that every modification of such a contract, no matter how insignificant, needs to be evidenced by a writing? Or does it simply mean that if the quantity is increased, the modification must be evidenced by a writing?

More confusion arises when subsections 2-209(4) and (5) are considered. Subsection 4 indicates that even if a modification is made that does not satisfy a "no oral modification" clause or the statute of frauds, it may nevertheless serve as a waiver. A waiver of what? A provision of the contract, perhaps including the "no oral modification" provision? A waiver of the statute of frauds? Subsection 5 indicates that the waiver may be retracted upon reasonable notice, but not if it would be unjust in view of material reliance. The next two cases explore these issues.

### WIXON JEWELERS, INC. V. DI-STAR, LTD.

United States Court of Appeals, Eighth Circuit

218 F.3d 913 (2000)

Di-Star is a wholesaler of ideal-cut diamonds,* which are sold under the Hearts on Fire brand. On May 30, 1997, Wixon and Di-Star entered into a distribution agreement, which provided: (1) Wixon would be the sole retailer of Hearts on Fire diamonds in the Minneapolis/Saint Paul area, (2) Wixon would initially purchase six Hearts on Fire diamonds, and (3) Wixon would order a minimum of $2,500 worth of Hearts on Fire diamonds per month from Di-Star in order to maintain the exclusive right to distribute Hearts on Fire diamonds in the Minneapolis/Saint Paul area. The agreement had no fixed end date. Between May 1997 and March 1998, Wixon only twice made the required minimum purchase, in November 1997 and December 1997. In early 1998, Di-Star notified Wixon that another Minneapolis/Saint Paul jeweler would be added as an authorized retailer of Hearts on Fire diamonds. Wixon then canceled the agreement with Di-Star and filed suit alleging it would lose profits in excess of $1,000,000 over the coming ten years.

Wixon argues that although the original distribution agreement required the purchase of $2,500 worth of diamonds per month, the agreement was orally modified to require the purchase of $30,000 worth of diamonds per year. If the

*The facets of ideal-cut diamonds are cut to provide maximum brilliance at the expense of size and strength. At the time of the original contract, ideal-cut diamonds appear to have been relatively rare in the United States.

oral modification is valid, then Di-Star was in breach of the exclusivity clause. Conversely, if the modification was not valid, then Wixon was in breach and the contract could be voided by Di-Star at any time.

A modification to a contract must, itself, satisfy the statute of frauds if it would be subject to the statute of frauds were it a separate contract. See UCC §2-209(3). The Minnesota statute of frauds requires a contract for the sale of goods in the amount of $500 or more to be evidenced by a writing. Here the diamonds are valued at $2,500 per month under the old contract and $30,000 under the purported modification. The minimum dollar amount that requires a writing is clearly met regardless of which dollar amount is considered to be the amount of the modification. It is equally clear that diamonds are goods. Thus, the modification must conform with the statute of frauds. Wixon admits there is no writing evidencing the modification. The district court correctly determined the statute of frauds required a writing and absent such writing the modification was not valid. Thus, under the original contract, Wixon was in breach because it did not meet the monthly minimum purchase. Because of this breach, Di-Star did not have to honor the exclusivity agreement and was not itself in breach. The district court's grant of summary judgment on the breach of contract is affirmed.

## QUESTIONS

Is the reading of section 2-209(3) by the court overly simplistic? Does section 2-201 require all of the terms in the writing to accurately reflect the parties' agreement? *Compare Costco Wholesale Corporation v. World Wide Licensing Corporation,* 898 P.2d 347 (Wash. App. 1995).

### Wisconsin Knife Works v. National Metal Crafters

United States Court of Appeals, Seventh Circuit

781 F.2d 1280 (1986)

POSNER, Circuit Judge.

Wisconsin Knife Works, having some unused manufacturing capacity, decided to try to manufacture spade bits for sale to its parent, Black & Decker, a large producer of tools, including drills. A spade bit is made out of a chunk of metal called a spade bit blank; and Wisconsin Knife Works had to find a source of supply for these blanks. National Metal Crafters was eager to be that source. After some negotiating, Wisconsin Knife Works sent National Metal Crafters a series of purchase orders on the back of each of which was printed, "Acceptance of this Order, either by acknowledgment or performance, constitutes an unqualified agreement to the following." A list of "Conditions of Purchase" follows, of which the first is, "No modification of this contract, shall be binding upon Buyer [Wisconsin Knife Works] unless made in writing and signed by Buyer's authorized representative. Buyer shall have the right to make changes in the Order by a notice, in writing, to Seller." There were six purchase orders in all, each with the identical conditions. National Metal Crafters acknowledged the first two orders (which had been placed on August 21,

1981) by letters that said, "Please accept this as our acknowledgment covering the above subject order," followed by a list of delivery dates. The purchase orders had left those dates blank. Wisconsin Knife Works filled them in, after receiving the acknowledgments, with the dates that National Metal Crafters had supplied in the acknowledgments. There were no written acknowledgments of the last four orders (placed several weeks later, on September 10, 1981). Wisconsin Knife Works wrote in the delivery dates that National Metal Crafters orally supplied after receiving purchase orders in which the space for the date of delivery had again been left blank.

Delivery was due in October and November 1981. National Metal Crafters missed the deadlines. But Wisconsin Knife Works did not immediately declare a breach, cancel the contract, or seek damages for late delivery. Indeed, on July 1, 1982, it issued a new batch of purchase orders (later rescinded). By December 1982 National Metal Crafters was producing spade bit blanks for Wisconsin Knife Works under the original set of purchase orders in adequate quantities, though this was more than a year after the delivery dates in the orders. But on January 13, 1983, Wisconsin Knife Works notified National Metal Crafters that the contract was terminated. By that date only 144,000 of the more than 281,000 spade bit blanks that Wisconsin Knife Works had ordered in the six purchase orders had been delivered.

Wisconsin Knife Works brought this breach of contract suit, charging that National Metal Crafters had violated the terms of delivery in the contract that was formed by the acceptance of the six purchase orders. National Metal Crafters replied that the delivery dates had not been intended as firm dates. It also counterclaimed for damages for (among other things) the breach of an alleged oral agreement by Wisconsin Knife Works to pay the expenses of maintaining machinery used by National Metal Crafters to fulfill the contract. The parties later stipulated that the amount of these damages was $30,000.

The judge ruled that there had been a contract but left to the jury to decide whether the contract had been modified and, if so, whether the modified contract had been broken. The jury found that the contract had been modified and not broken. Judgment was entered dismissing Wisconsin Knife Works's suit and awarding National Metal Crafters $30,000 on its counterclaim. Wisconsin Knife Works has appealed from the dismissal of its suit. The appeal papers do not discuss the counterclaim, and the effect on it of our remanding the case for further proceedings on Wisconsin Knife Works's claim will have to be resolved on remand.

The principal issue is the effect of the provision in the purchase orders that forbids the contract to be modified other than by a writing signed by an authorized representative of the buyer. The theory on which the judge sent the issue of modification to the jury was that the contract could be modified orally or by conduct as well as by a signed writing. National Metal Crafters had presented evidence that Wisconsin Knife Works had accepted late delivery of the spade bit blanks and had cancelled the contract not because of the delays in delivery but because it could not produce spade bits at a price acceptable to Black & Decker.

We conclude that the clause forbidding modifications other than in writing was valid and applicable and that the jury should not have been allowed to consider whether the contract had been modified in some other way. This may, however, have been a harmless error. Section 2-209(4) of the Uniform Commercial Code provides that an "attempt at modification" that does not satisfy a contractual requirement that modifications be in writing nevertheless "can operate as a waiver."

Because the performance of the parties to a contract is typically not simultaneous, one party may find himself at the mercy of the other unless the law of contracts protects him. Indeed, the most important thing which that law does is to facilitate exchanges that are not simultaneous by preventing either party from taking advantage of the vulnerabilities to which sequential performance may give rise. If *A* contracts to build a highly idiosyncratic gazebo for *B*, payment due on completion, and when *A* completes the gazebo *B* refuses to pay, *A* may be in a bind—because the resale value of the gazebo may be much less than *A*'s cost—except for his right to sue *B* for the price. Even then, a right to sue for breach of contract, being costly to enforce, is not a completely adequate remedy. *B* might therefore go to *A* and say, "If you don't reduce your price I'll refuse to pay and put you to the expense of suit"; and *A* might knuckle under. If such modifications are allowed, people in *B*'s position will find it harder to make such contracts in the future, and everyone will be worse off.

The common law dealt with this problem by refusing to enforce modifications unsupported by fresh consideration. Thus in the hypothetical case just put *B* could not have enforced *A*'s promise to accept a lower price. But this solution is at once overinclusive and underinclusive—the former because most modifications are not coercive and should be enforceable whether or not there is fresh consideration, the latter because, since common law courts inquire into only the existence and not the adequacy of consideration, a requirement of fresh consideration has little bite. *B* might give *A* a peppercorn, a kitten, or a robe in exchange for *A*'s agreeing to reduce the contract price, and then the modification would be enforceable and *A* could no longer sue for the original price.

The drafters of the Uniform Commercial Code took a fresh approach, by making modifications enforceable even if not supported by consideration (see section 2-209(1)) and looking to the doctrines of duress and bad faith for the main protection against exploitive or opportunistic attempts at modification, as in our hypothetical case. See UCC §2-209, Official Comment 2. But they did another thing as well. In section 2-209(2) they allowed the parties to exclude oral modifications. National Metal Crafters argues that two subsections later they took back this grant of power by allowing an unwritten modification to operate as a waiver.

The common law did not enforce agreements such as section 2-209(2) authorizes. The "reasoning" was that the parties were always free to agree orally to cancel their contract and the clause forbidding modifications not in writing would disappear with the rest of the contract when it was cancelled. "The most ironclad written contract can always be cut into by the acetylene torch of parol modification supported by adequate proof." *Wagner v. Graziano Construction Co.*, 390 Pa. 445, 448, 136 A.2d 82, 83-84 (1957). This is not reasoning; it is a conclusion disguised as a metaphor. It may have reflected a fear that such clauses, buried in the fine print of form contracts, were traps for the unwary; a sense that they were unnecessary because only modifications supported by consideration were enforceable; and a disinclination to allow parties in effect to extend the reach of the Statute of Frauds, which requires only some types of contract to be in writing. But the framers of the Uniform Commercial Code, as part and parcel of rejecting the requirement of consideration for modifications, must have rejected the traditional view; must have believed that the protection which the doctrines of duress and bad faith give against extortionate modifications might need reinforcement—if not from a requirement of consideration, which had proved ineffective, then from a grant of power to include a clause requiring modifications to be in writing and signed. An equally important point is that with consideration no longer required for modification, it was natural to give the parties some means of providing a substitute for the cautionary and evidentiary function that the requirement of consideration provides; and the means chosen was to allow them to exclude oral modifications.

If section 2-209(4), which as we said provides that an attempted modification which does not comply with subsection (2) can nevertheless operate as a "waiver," is interpreted so broadly that *any* oral modification is effective as a waiver notwithstanding section 2-209(2), both provisions become superfluous and we are back in the common law—only with not even a requirement of consideration to reduce the likelihood of fabricated or unintended oral modifications.

The path of reconciliation with subsection (4) is found by attending to its precise wording. Subsection (4) does not say that an attempted modification "is" a waiver; it says that "it can operate as a waiver." It does not say in what circumstances it can operate as a waiver; but if an attempted modification is effective as a waiver only if there is reliance, then both sections 2-209(2) and 2-209(4) can be given effect. Reliance, if reasonably induced and reasonable in extent, is a common substitute for consideration in making a promise legally enforceable, in part because it adds something in the way of credibility to the mere say-so of one party. The main purpose of forbidding oral modifications is to prevent the promisor from fabricating a modification that will let him escape his obligations under the contract; and the danger of successful fabrication is less if the promisor has actually incurred a cost, has relied.

Our approach is not inconsistent with section 2-209(5), which allows a waiver to be withdrawn while the contract is executory, provided there is no "material change of position in reliance on the waiver." Granted, in subsection (5) there can be no tincture of reliance; the whole point of the section is that a waiver may be withdrawn unless there is reliance. But the section has a different domain from section 2-209(4). It is not limited to attempted modifications invalid under subsections (2) or (3); it applies, for example, to an express written and signed waiver, provided only that the contract is still executory. Suppose that while the contract is still executory the buyer writes the seller a signed letter waiving some term in the contract and then, the next day, before the seller has relied, retracts it in writing; we have no reason to think that such a retraction would not satisfy section 2-209(5), though this is not an issue we need definitively resolve today. In any event we are not suggesting that "waiver" means different things in subsections (4) and (5); it means the same thing; but the *effect* of an attempted modification as a waiver under (4) depends in part on subsection (2), which (4) (but not 5) qualifies. Waiver and estoppel (which requires reliance to be effective) are frequently bracketed.

We know that the drafters of section 2-209 wanted to make it possible for parties to exclude oral modifications. They did not just want to give "modification" another name— "waiver." Our interpretation gives effect to this purpose. It is also consistent with though not compelled by the case law. There are no Wisconsin cases on point. Cases from other jurisdictions are diverse in outlook. Some take a very hard line against allowing an oral waiver to undo a clause forbidding oral modification. Others allow oral waivers to override such clauses, but in most of these cases it is clear that the party claiming waiver had relied to his detriment.

Missing from the jury instruction on "modification" in this case is any reference to reliance, that is, to the incurring of costs by National Metal Crafters in reasonable reliance on assurances by Wisconsin Knife Works that late delivery would be acceptable. And although there is evidence of such reliance, it naturally was not a focus of the case, since the issue was cast as one of completed (not attempted) modification, which does not require reliance to be enforceable. National Metal Crafters must have incurred expenses in producing spade bit blanks after the original delivery dates, but whether these were *reliance* expenses is a separate question. Maybe National Metal Crafters would have continued to manufacture spade bit blanks anyway, in the hope of selling them to someone else. It may be significant that the stipulated counterclaim damages seem limited to the damages from the breach of a separate oral agreement regarding the maintenance of equipment used by National Metal Crafters in fulfilling the contract. The question of reliance cannot be considered so open and shut as to justify our concluding that the judge would have had to direct a verdict for National Metal Crafters, the party with the burden of proof on the issue. Nor, indeed, does National Metal Crafters argue that reliance was shown as a matter of law.

REVERSED AND REMANDED.

EASTERBROOK, Circuit Judge, dissenting.

The majority demonstrates that the clause of the contract requiring all modifications to be in writing is enforceable against National Metal Crafters. There was no modification by a "signed writing." Yet section 2-209(4) of the Uniform Commercial Code, which Wisconsin has adopted, provides that "an attempt at modification" that is ineffective because of a modification-only-in-writing clause "can operate as a waiver." The majority holds that no "attempt at modification" may be a "waiver" within the meaning of section 2-209(4) unless the party seeking to enforce the waiver has relied to its detriment. I do not think that detrimental reliance is an essential element of waiver under section 2-209(4).

"Waiver" is not a term the UCC defines. At common law "waiver" means an intentional relinquishment of a known right. A person may relinquish a right by engaging in conduct inconsistent with the right or by a verbal or written declaration. I do not know of any branch of the law—common, statutory, or constitutional—in which a renunciation of a legal entitlement is effective only if the other party relies to his detriment.

[Subsections 2-209(4) and (5)] read well together if waiver means "intentional relinquishment of a known right" in both. Section 2-209(4) says that a failed attempt at modification may be a waiver and so relinquish a legal entitlement (such as the entitlement to timely delivery); section 2-209(5) adds that a waiver cannot affect the executory portion of the contract (the time of future deliveries, for example) if the waiving party retracts, unless there is also detrimental reliance. But for section 2-209(2) the oral waiver could affect the executory portion of the contract even without reliance. It is not necessary to vary the meaning of the word to make sense of each portion of the statute.

The majority makes reliance an ingredient of waiver not because the structure of the UCC demands this reading, but because it believes that otherwise the UCC would not deal adequately with the threat of opportunistic conduct. The drafters of the UCC chose to deal with opportunism not through a strict reading of waiver, however, but through a statutory requirement of commercial good faith. See §2-103 and Comment 2 to §2-209. The modification-only-in-writing clause has nothing to do with opportunism. A person who has his contracting partner over a barrel, and therefore is able to obtain a concession, can get the concession in writing. The writing will be the least of his worries. In almost all of the famous cases of modification the parties reduced the new agreement to writing.

A modification-only-in-writing clause may permit the parties to strengthen the requirement of commercial good faith against the careless opportunist, but its principal function is to make it easier for business to protect their agreement against casual subsequent remarks and manufactured assertions of alteration. It strengthens the Statute of Frauds. Even so, the Code does not allow the clause to be airtight. Comment 4 to section 2-209 states: "Subsection (4) is intended, despite the provisions of subsections (2) and (3), to prevent contractual provisions excluding modification except by a signed writing from limiting in other respects the legal effect of the parties' actual later conduct. The effect of such conduct as a waiver is further regulated in subsection (5)." In other words, the UCC made modification-only-in-writing clauses effective for the first time, but the drafters meant to leave loopholes. The majority's observation that waiver under section 2-209(4) could nullify some benefits of clauses permitted under section 2-209(2) is true, but it is not a reason for adding novel elements to "waiver." It might be sensible to treat claims of oral waiver with suspicion and insist on waiver by course of performance; for example, accepting belated deliveries without protest, or issuing new orders (or changing the specifications of old orders) while existing ones are in default. Waiver implied from performance is less prone to manipulation. This method of protecting modification-only-in-writing clauses gives waiver the same meaning throughout the statute, but it does not help Wisconsin Knife, for the claim of waiver here is largely based on the course of performance.

The jury's finding that Wisconsin Knife Works and National Metal Crafters modified their contract—in the words of the instruction, that Wisconsin Knife Works "by conduct or other means of expression induced a reasonable belief by [National Metal Crafters] that strict enforcement was not insisted upon, but that the modified performance was satisfactory and acceptable as equivalent"—was supported by the evidence. We are left with "an attempt at modification" that may operate as a waiver, which Wisconsin Knife Works may and did revoke.

If National Metal Crafters were claiming damages for lost profits, it would be necessary to determine whether National Metal Crafters detrimentally relied on Wisconsin Knife Works's waiver. But National Metal Crafters does not want damages for work to be performed after January 1983. It simply wants to defeat Wisconsin Knife Works's claim for damages for belated delivery. The jury, although improperly instructed, has found enough to support a judgment discharging National Metal Crafters from liability to Wisconsin Knife Works. This requires us to affirm the judgment.

## PROBLEM

***Problem 3-14.*** A sale-of-goods contract covered by the CISG has a provision indicating that all modifications to the contract must be evidenced by a signed writing. Subsequently, the parties orally agree to a change in the design of the goods. The seller makes the design change, and then ships the goods to the buyer. The buyer has subsequently changed its mind and prefers the original design. Can the buyer reject the goods on the grounds that the modification needed to be evidenced by a writing and that the goods are thus nonconforming? Could the buyer insist that for future deliveries, the original design must be used? See CISG Article 29, Secretariat Commentary on Article 27 of the 1978 Draft [draft counterpart to Article 29], *www.cisg.law.pace.edu/cisg/text/secomm/secomm-29.html* (accessed Oct. 2011).

## CHAPTER 3 REVIEW PROBLEM

Buyer Department Store received a catalog from Seller Dress Manufacturing Co. advertising various clothing items available for purchase. Buyer sent its form purchase order to Seller indicating the types of dresses, ordered by catalog number, and the quantity of dresses that it wished to purchase. The total price of dresses ordered was $10,000. The purchase order indicated that Buyer wanted "prompt shipment." Buyer's form purchase order conspicuously indicated "this purchase order is limited to its terms." The purchase order was signed by Buyer's duly authorized agent. Seller responded shortly thereafter with an "order acknowledgment" that confirmed Buyer's order in terms of the quantity and type of dresses and the price. The "order acknowledgment" stated in conspicuous terms that it was "conditional upon Buyer's assent to all of the terms contained in this acknowledgment." The order acknowledgment indicated that shipment would be in two weeks. It also contained an arbitration clause and a provision stating that there could be no oral modifications of any of the terms of the form. It was signed by a duly authorized agent of Seller. One week after the acknowledgment was sent, Buyer's agent called Seller's agent and asked if the shipment could be delayed for two months. Seller's agent orally agreed. At what point, if any, has an enforceable contract been formed? Is the arbitration provision included in the contract? What is the delivery date? Please analyze these questions under both the UCC and the CISG. Assume under the CISG that the relevant nations have made no declarations. The relevant UCC sections are 2-201, 2-207, and 2-209. The relevant CISG articles are 11, 14, 18, 19, and 29.

CHAPTER 4

# CONTRACT TERMS— WARRANTIES OF TITLE AND QUALITY

## A. THE SIGNIFICANCE OF CONTRACT TERMS

In the next two chapters we explore important terms of the contract. Why is it important to understand the terms? As we will see when we get to the question of performance and breach, we need to know the terms to see whether the seller and buyer have properly performed. There probably have been times when you purchased a good and were dissatisfied with it. That does not mean that you could make the seller give you your money back or sue the seller for damages. Your right to do that depends on whether the seller performed according to the terms of the contract. Did the goods breach a warranty given by the seller? Were they delivered on time? We begin our discussion of terms with the warranty of title.

## B. TITLE

### 1. THE WARRANTY OF TITLE AND WHEN A SELLER CAN CONVEY GOOD TITLE

The definition of "sale" under UCC section 2-106(1) is "the passing of title from the seller to the buyer for a price." Official Comment 1 to section 2-312 indicates what a buyer would typically expect: "that he receive a good, clean title transferred to him also in a rightful manner so that he will not be exposed to a lawsuit in order to protect it." UCC section 2-312 provides a warranty to a buyer (unless disclaimed) that the seller has good title to the goods being sold to the buyer, that the transfer is rightful, and that the goods are free from liens and encumbrances of which the buyer at the time of contracting has no knowledge. See UCC §2-312. CISG Article 41 requires that the seller deliver goods that are free from any right or claim of a third party, unless the buyer agreed to take the goods subject to that right or claim.

The UCC has sections dealing with when title passes and when it is that a seller has the ability to convey good title to the buyer. See UCC §§2-401, 2-403. The CISG, on the other hand, does not address questions of title. See CISG Article 4. This means that questions of title in international sales will have to be dealt with by other law determined by choice-of-law principles.

Under the UCC, a seller can have (a) good title to goods, meaning that no one has paramount rights to ownership; (b) no title to goods (also referred to as void title); or (c) voidable title. The concept of voidable title is a somewhat murky one, but basically it means that the person with such title can be dispossessed of the goods by someone with a superior ownership interest. UCC section 2-403 does not give an exhaustive definition of when someone has "voidable title," but it does give some examples, including when someone purchases goods with a bad check. UCC §2-403(1)(b). In such a case, the person who sold the goods has a right to reclaim them from the person who bought them, hence the "voidable" aspect of the title.

UCC section 2-403(1) provides that a purchaser of goods "acquires all title which his transferor had or had power to transfer except that a purchaser of a limited interest acquires rights only to the extent of the interest purchased." This means that a seller with good title transfers good title to the buyer. The converse is that a seller with no title transfers no title to the buyer (and thus breaches the warranty of title, unless disclaimed). There is an exception, however, for someone with voidable title. That person can transfer good title to a good faith purchaser for value.

The following case illustrates the application of section 2-403.

### Suburban Motors Inc. v. State Farm Mutual Automobile Insurance Co.

California Court of Appeal

218 Cal. App. 3d. 1354, 268 Cal. Rptr. 16 (1990)

PUGLIA, Presiding Justice.

Defendant State Farm Mutual Automobile Insurance Company (State Farm) appeals from a summary judgment declaring plaintiff, Suburban Motors, Inc., has valid title to an automobile. State Farm contends its title, obtained directly from the lawful owner whom it insured and from whom the vehicle was stolen, is superior to the claim of Suburban Motors, a bona fide purchaser for value under a "chain of title" traceable to the thief. We agree and shall reverse the judgment.

The summary judgment motion was submitted to the trial court on stipulated facts. Richard Kirschner was the lawful owner of a 1981 Mercedes Benz bearing Vehicle Identification Number WDBBA45A6BB006051. Kirschner was the named insured under State Farm's policy insuring the vehicle against theft. Sometime prior to November 27, 1985, the Mercedes was stolen by a thief or thieves unknown. State Farm paid Kirschner the approximate sum of $41,000 under its policy of insurance for the loss of the Mercedes in consideration for which Kirschner transferred title to State Farm.

On or about November 27, 1985, Steven Taglianetti, a licensed wholesale automobile dealer, presented the stolen Mercedes to an auction operated by California Auto Dealers Exchange (CADE). Taglianetti knew or should have known the Mercedes was stolen. CADE had no knowledge the vehicle was stolen. The original Vehicle Identification Number (VIN) on the Mercedes had been changed to WDBBA45A5BB007904. Sometime before November 27, 1985, the California Department of Motor Vehicles (DMV) had issued documents of title for the Mercedes under the altered VIN based upon a certificate of title from Louisiana.[1] Suburban Motors eventually acquired the Mercedes after it had passed from CADE through a succession of "owners" who, like Suburban Motors, had purchased the vehicle without knowledge it had been stolen.

Suburban Motors leased the Mercedes to an individual named Sergeant. On or about April 4, 1986, the California Highway Patrol (CHP) discovered that the Mercedes was a stolen automobile. Sergeant voluntarily relinquished possession of the vehicle to the CHP, who subsequently turned it over to State Farm.

Thereafter Suburban Motors filed a "complaint for possession of personal property or its value, for declaratory relief, and for damages," naming several defendants including State Farm. Cross-complaints were filed bringing into the action CADE and CADE's surety, Aetna Life and Casualty Company (Aetna).

CADE and Aetna moved for summary judgment, requesting the trial court declare and adjudge that Suburban Motors "has the right to possession, title and control" of the Mercedes. State Farm countered with its own motion for a summary judgment declaring it has valid title to and the right to possession of the Mercedes. The trial court granted the motion of CADE and Aetna and denied State Farm's motion. Judgment was entered declaring that Suburban Motors has the right to possession, title, and control of the Mercedes, and ordering State Farm to transfer possession and control to Suburban Motors. This appeal followed.

State Farm contends its title should prevail over the claim of Suburban Motors which, although a bona fide purchaser for value, claims under a title "laundered" through another state by the thief or a successor to the thief; that title, State Farm asserts, is not merely voidable, but void notwithstanding that the documents of title issued by DMV appear facially valid.

In support of its claim of title, Suburban Motors advances two arguments: First, the California Uniform Commercial Code has altered the common law rule that good title cannot pass from a thief; second, California is a "full title" state in respect to vehicles and therefore its reliance on apparently valid title documents cannot be defeated.

Although section 2-403 may enlarge the circumstances in which, at common law, a good faith purchaser for value can take good title, there is no authority for Suburban Motors's contention that section 2-403 validates a second chain of title to an automobile spuriously created after it has been stolen. Indeed, the language of section 2-403 itself, the decisions in jurisdictions

---

1. Presumably DMV received notice of the theft. (*See* Veh. Code, §§10500, 10503). On receiving notice, DMV is required to "place an appropriate notice in the electronic file system which will identify such vehicles during the processing of new certificates of registration, ownership, or registration and ownership." (Veh. Code, §10504.) This safeguard operates to prevent creation of a second chain of title for a stolen vehicle under its authentic VIN. Obviously, it is not proof against registration of a stolen vehicle under the VIN assigned to a similar car not registered in California. Although the stipulated facts do not explain the origin of the spurious VIN used here, one can speculate that it came from a heavily damaged Mercedes registered in Louisiana, probably acquired from a wrecking yard by the thief or an accomplice at the cost of its salvage value and then falsely presented to the Louisiana vehicle registration authority as "rebuilt."

construing cognate statutes, and authoritative comment on the Uniform Commercial Code belie the notion that by a process of "laundering" a thief or his successors can generate a second chain of valid title to a stolen vehicle no matter how facially credible the product of these efforts.

Section 2-403 does not in terms restrict the creation of voidable title to the four circumstances expressly identified [in subsection 1]. However, each of the four listed circumstances involves the "voluntary" transfer of goods and title, not the "involuntary" transfer as by larceny. Moreover, the statute limits the power to pass good title to one who has obtained the goods through delivery as part of a "transaction of purchase." UCC §2-403(1). Although there may be no moral distinction between larceny and theft by false pretenses (see §2-403(1)(d)), the larcenist here obviously did not obtain the vehicle through a "transaction of purchase" and therefore acquired no title that could be transferred to his successors in the chain of possession.

The consequences of the creation of a whole new title to a vehicle through "laundering" are not specifically addressed in the California Uniform Commercial Code. Nor have California appellate courts dealt with the issue. However, appellate courts of other states, applying section 2-403, have rejected the notion that title to a stolen vehicle, good as against that of the owner or his successor in interest, can be created by the process of "laundering" as employed here. For example, in *Inmi-Etti v. Aluisi* (1985), 63 Md. App. 293, 492 A.2d 917 a person who purchased an automobile from a thief bearing apparently valid title documents claimed to have passed title good as against the owner. The court rejected the claim under section 2-403 of the Uniform Commercial Code because "voidable title under the Code can only arise from a voluntary transfer or delivery of the goods by the owner. If the goods are stolen or otherwise obtained against the will of the owner, only void title can result." *Id.* at p. 923.

Applying the foregoing principles to the instant facts, it is apparent Taglianetti's title to the Mercedes was void, not merely voidable. Thus on November 27, 1985, CADE, Suburban Motors's predecessor, did not acquire valid title although a good faith purchaser for value.

We recognize that neither Suburban Motors nor State Farm share any legal or moral blame for the illegal conduct that created this impasse. We agree with Suburban Motors that many automobile owners have insurance and therefore can shift the risk of theft to an insurer that accepts premium payments in contemplation of precisely that contingency. However, not all vehicle owners have or can afford theft insurance. And if insurers are unable to recoup their costs through recovery of stolen vehicles, it will inevitably drive the rates still higher and increase the numbers who cannot afford insurance.

The judgment is reversed and the trial court is directed to enter judgment in favor of State Farm. State Farm is to recover its costs.

## NOTES, QUESTIONS, AND PROBLEMS

The case involves a Mercedes Benz automobile. Kirschner indisputably had good title at the time the good was stolen from him. Once the automobile was stolen, that broke the chain of title. The thief in possession of the automobile had void title and could not convey good title to anyone else, no matter how innocent that person was and no matter how much value was given. That the thief was able to obtain a seemingly legitimate certificate of title was of no consequence.

On the other hand, the fact that the automobile was stolen from Kirschner did not affect his good title to it. When he was paid off by State Farm, he was fully capable of transferring good title to them, which he did. Thus, State Farm had good title to the Mercedes, and Suburban Motors had no title.

What is Suburban Motors's recourse in this case? There is a clear breach of the warranty of title. The facts of the case indicate that the California Auto Dealer Exchange ("CADE") was the predecessor in title to Suburban Motors and that the latter purchased it at auction held by CADE. CADE, in turn, obtained the automobile from Steven Taglianetti, who the court indicates "knew or should have known" that the automobile was stolen. Assuming that everyone is solvent, the loss eventually falls on the thief. But if the thief is insolvent or cannot be found, the solvent person nearest to the thief will take the loss.

In another part of the opinion that has been omitted here, the court noted that the California certificate of title law was not conclusive on the issue of title. Doesn't this decision undermine the utility of the certificate of title law? Note the discussion of the competing equities of the claimants to the car near the end of the opinion. Should the law make certificates of title conclusive on the issue of rightful ownership?

***Problem 4-1.*** Assume that rather than having the car stolen, Kirschner sold his Mercedes to a car dealership in return for a check that was subsequently dishonored. The dealership immediately sold the car to one of its customers, who had no idea where or how the dealership obtained the car. Would Kirschner be entitled to get the car back? See UCC §2-403(1)(b), §2-507, Official Comment 3. Why distinguish the bounced check case from the theft case?

***Problem 4-2.*** Assume that you bring your expensive gold watch to a local jeweler for repair. The jeweler sells the watch to one of its customers who walks into the jewelry store. Besides repairing watches, the jewelry store is in the business of selling watches. The customer had no idea how or where the store got the watch and paid a fair price for it. Obviously, you could sue the jewelry store. But if the store is insolvent, could you get the watch back from the person who bought it? See UCC §§2-403(2),(3).

## 2. THE SCOPE OF THE WARRANTY OF TITLE

### Colton v. Decker

Supreme Court of South Dakota

540 N.W.2d 172 (1995)

#### Facts

Lee Decker, an over-the-road trucker, purchased a repossessed 1975 Peterbilt truck, model 359, from a Minnesota bank in 1984. The truck's history is not completely known, but its rails or frame had apparently been extended from its original length to accommodate a double sleeper, and it had also been wrecked at one time. The vehicle identification number (VIN) listed on the Minnesota title was 60596P. Decker transferred the truck's title to South Dakota. Although he claims not to have made any major structural changes, on several occasions Decker had acknowledged he rebuilt the truck "from the frame up."

Over a nine-month period in 1989, John Colton, who worked as a driver for Decker, drove the 1975 Peterbilt nearly 100,000 miles. In late December of that year, he offered to purchase the truck for $22,000. Assured of the truck's good condition, Marquette Bank of Sioux Falls financed Colton's purchase. On March 8, 1990, Decker's South Dakota truck title was transferred to Colton.

On August 22, 1991, Colton was stopped by the Wyoming Highway Patrol near Rock Springs, Wyoming, and cited for speeding. After noting discrepancies in his logbook, the trooper inspected the rig and discovered that the VIN stamped on the right frame rail did not match the VIN listed on the registration. Conflicting VINs commonly indicate a stolen vehicle or stolen parts. The truck, but not the loaded trailer, was then impounded. Colton hired another trucker to haul the cargo in his trailer to Salt Lake City and retained a Wyoming attorney, but the attorney could not obtain immediate release of his truck. Colton returned to South Dakota. During the months waiting to recover his vehicle, he found some work driving trucks for other companies.

Upon completing their nine-month investigation, Wyoming authorities determined Colton was indeed the true owner. A Wyoming court ordered a new Wyoming title to be issued, clarifying the conflicting serial numbers. The truck would then be released upon payment of a $1,000 storage fee. Colton, who was now behind on loan payments, borrowed the money from Marquette Bank, traveled to Wyoming, and paid it. Unfortunately, the truck was inoperable because, while in Wyoming's possession, it had remained dismantled and unsheltered throughout the winter. On April 11, 1992, Colton towed the truck from Wyoming back to Sioux Falls.

Once home, Colton placed the truck in storage until he could raise the money to repair it. Despite the court order, Colton was unable to obtain a new title in Wyoming because Marquette Bank refused to surrender the South Dakota title—its collateral—to Wyoming authorities. The bank also refused to exchange the faulty title for a new South Dakota "rebuilder's" title. Colton filed suit against Decker alleging breaches of warranty of title, warranty of merchantability, and express warranty of description. He also sent Decker a notice of intent to rescind the sale of the truck.

**Decision**

Wyoming authorities challenged the authenticity of Colton's title as the truck had three different VINs engraved at various points. Under these circumstances, Colton averred Decker breached the warranty of title under UCC §2-312.

Comment 1 to UCC § 2-312 states a buyer is entitled to "receive a good, clear title transferred . . . in a rightful manner so [the buyer] will not be exposed to a lawsuit in order to protect it." A split of authority persists on the scope of §2-312. Decker relies on those cases which hold that a breach of warranty of title occurs only when an outstanding superior title exists.[1] See, e.g., *C.F. Sales, Inc. v. Amfert, Inc.*, 344 N.W.2d 543 (Iowa 1983); *Johnston v. Simpson,* 621 P.2d 688 (Utah 1980). Other courts hold that under §2-312 mere initiation of a colorable challenge, one that is not spurious, regardless of the outcome, is sufficient to violate the warranty of title. *Jefferson v. Jones,* 286 Md. 544, 408 A.2d 1036, 1042 (1979) (law enforcement seizure of motorcycle when its VIN did not correspond to the VIN on the title document was colorable claim; thus seller breached title warranty); *American Container Corp. v. Hanley Trucking Corp.,* 111 N.J. Super. 322, 268 A.2d 313 (1970) (law enforcement seizure of semi-trailer as stolen was sufficient to cast substantial shadow, thus violating warranty of good title). "Good title" typically means "the title which the seller gives to the buyer is 'free from reasonable doubt, that is, not only a valid title in fact, but [also] one that can again be sold to a reasonable purchaser . . ..' " *Jefferson,* 408 A.2d at 1040 (quoting *Langford v. Berry,* 68 Ga. App. 193, 22 S.E.2d 349, 351 (1942)). We find the latter to be the better rule.

Wyoming Highway Patrol officials questioned Colton's ownership due to contradictory VINs, thus casting a colorable challenge to its title. This was sufficient for a breach of title warranty claim. Indeed, the majority view holds that a purchaser can recover for a breach of warranty of title by merely showing the existence of a cloud on the title. Once breach of good title is established, good faith is not a defense, nor is a lack of knowledge of the defect. James A. White and Robert S. Summers, *Uniform Commercial Code* §9-12 (3d ed. rev. 1993). Purchasers should not be required to enter into a contest on the validity of ownership over a titled motor vehicle. As the undisputed facts reveal, Colton was forced into a contest over ownership because of conflicting VINs and an improper title. Thus, we uphold the circuit court's ruling that Decker breached the warranty of title.

## NOTES AND PROBLEMS

How would the case be decided under CISG Article 41? Does Article 41 provide even broader protection to buyers than this court's interpretation of UCC section 2-312? See the U.N. Secretariat Commentary to Article 41, *www.cisg.law .pace.edu/cisg/text/secomm/secomm-41.html* (accessed Oct. 2011).

***Problem 4-3.*** You purchase goods from a retailer and are told that the goods are sold "as is." Does this disclaim the implied warranty of title? UCC §§2-312(2), Comment 6, and §2-316. If you purchase a diamond necklace for a bargain price out of the trunk of the seller's car in a parking lot, do you receive a warranty of title? See UCC §2-312, Official Comment 5.

***Problem 4-4.*** Buyer in Country *A* purchases goods for resale from Seller in Country *B*. Seller is aware that Buyer intends to resell the goods in Country *A*. When Buyer begins to resell the goods, a third party complains that the

1. [fn.3] Indeed, the UCC drafters flatly stated "The warranty of quiet possession is abolished." Comment 1 UCC §2-312. Yet the same comment states, "Disturbance of quiet possession, although not mentioned specifically, is one way, among many, in which the breach of the warranty of title may be established."

goods violate a patent that third party has on the goods in Country *A* and demands that Buyer cease selling the goods. Country *A* has a patent registry in which the patent could be found, although there is some question about whether the goods in question infringe on the patent. If the CISG applies to the transaction, would the Seller be liable? See CISG Article 42. See also the Secretariat Commentary to Article 40 (the precursor to Article 42), *www.cisg.law.pace.edu/cisg/text/secomm/secomm-42.html* (accessed Oct. 2011). See also Schlechtriem, *Uniform Sales Law—The UN Convention on Contracts for the International Sale of Goods* 72-75 (1986), reproduced at *www.cisg.law.pace.edu/cisg/biblio/schlechtriem-42.html* (accessed Oct. 2011). If the UCC applies, same analysis? Does "rightful claim" mean that there must actually be a violation of the patent? See UCC §2-312(3) and Official Comment 3; *Pacific Sunwear v. Olaes Enterprises*, 167 Cal. App. 4th 466, 84 Cal. Rptr. 3d 182, 67 UCC Rep. Serv. 2d 62 (2008).

## C. WARRANTIES OF QUALITY

Both the UCC and the CISG contain warranties regarding the quality of the goods being sold. In the UCC, these are contained in sections 2-313 through 2-315; in the CISG they are contained in Article 35. The warranties are similar in that they include express warranties, warranties that the goods are fit for the ordinary purpose, and warranties that the goods are fit for the particular purpose of the buyer, under circumstances in which the seller had reason to know the buyer's purpose and that the buyer was relying on the seller's judgment in selecting the goods.

### 1. UNDER THE UCC

#### (a) Express Warranties

The UCC provision dealing with express warranties is section 2-313. Please read the section. An express warranty can be created by the seller saying something about the goods ("an affirmation of fact or promise" or "description of the goods") or by showing a sample or model to the buyer. Unless stated otherwise, the seller warrants that the goods will conform to the sample or model. In all of these cases, the statement by the seller or the sample model must be "part of the basis of the bargain" in order to be an actionable express warranty. Affirmations of value of the goods or statements purporting merely to be the seller's opinion or commendation of the goods are not warranties.

A couple of difficult questions are posed by section 2-313. What is meant by "part of the basis of the bargain"? How do we distinguish statements of value, opinion, or commendation from affirmations of fact or promise? With regard to the "basis of the bargain" language, the law used to require that the buyer show reliance on a statement by the seller for it to be considered actionable. Official Comment 3 indicates that "no particular reliance on [affirmations of fact] need be shown in order to weave them into the fabric of the agreement. Rather, any fact which is to take such affirmations, once made, out of the agreement requires clear affirmative proof." This language supports a rebuttable presumption test that once it is shown that an affirmation of fact or promise has been made regarding goods, the seller now must show that it wasn't part of the contract. The next case discusses how we distinguish between affirmations of fact or promise and statements that are merely of value of commendation, so-called puffery.

## Federal Signal Corporation v. Safety Factors, Inc.

Supreme Court of Washington

125 Wash. 2d 413, 886 P.2d 172, 25 UCC Rep. Serv. 2d 765 (1994)

MADSEN, Justice.

Appellant Safety Factors, Inc. (Safety Factors) bought seven Night Warrior light towers from Respondent Federal Signal Corporation (Federal Signal). Safety Factors experienced a number of problems with the equipment and never paid Federal Signal for the towers. Federal Signal sued Safety Factors to recover amounts due and Safety Factors counterclaimed for damages for breach of warranty. The trial court found in Federal Signal's favor. The case was then certified for appeal to this court. We reverse several of the trial court's conclusions and remand for additional findings.

### Facts

Safety Factors is in the business of renting, repairing, and selling equipment. The Night Warrior light towers were purchased for rental and sale. Steve Fors, president of Safety Factors, testified that before Safety Factors purchased the light towers, he and David Robbins of Federal Signal discussed the capabilities and features of the Night Warrior, and compared this newer product to the TPME, an older model with which Safety Factors had good experiences. These statements were made either orally or in an advertising brochure. Safety Factors purchased seven of these newer towers.

Before renting or selling the Night Warriors, Safety Factors tested the towers "through a full field of motion" for approximately five minutes without incident. However, problems arose as soon as the towers were used in the field, beginning in late February 1989 with the first rental customer, Tucci & Sons. The first night Tucci & Sons used the towers, they experienced what the parties referred to as the "restrike problem." The lamps would either fail to relight following an interruption of operation or shut down once the lamps reached full intensity. One of the towers would not run because the fuel lines were reversed. Safety Factors replaced these with other towers after it unsuccessfully attempted to repair the defective towers. On the second night, one of the replacement towers failed due to the restrike problem. Tucci & Sons experienced the problem with all of the rental towers over a four- or five-day period until it threw the towers off the job.

[The court discusses a number of other problems that the buyer had with the towers, including oil leakage from the generators that powered the towers, problems with the winches that were used in raising and lowering the towers, and rusting of the exhaust pipes.]

In his oral decision, the trial judge stated that "the only warranties that applied in this case were the implied warranties of merchantability and fitness for a particular purpose." He concluded that no express warranties were made.

### Analysis

Safety Factors argues that the trial court made erroneous findings of fact and conclusions of law with regard to issues of breach of warranty, mitigation, and damages.[1] We will address the issues in the order they arose in trial.

#### I. Express Warranties

The trial court concluded that Federal Signal made no express warranties to Safety Factors concerning the Night Warrior light towers. Safety Factors contends that the trial court's conclusion to this effect is contrary to the evidence presented. The trial judge made no findings of fact in support of his conclusion, stating that it was unnecessary.

In this case, significant evidence was presented regarding express warranties. Safety Factors's purchase of seven Night Warrior towers was made following personal contact between Steve Fors and David Robbins. Robbins said that they discussed "the feature changes" of the Night Warrior (the newer, not-yet-produced model) versus the TPME (an older model originally produced by another company). Fors testified that Robbins told him that the Night Warrior was comparable to and of higher quality than the TPME, a model with which Fors had good experiences and that Robbins knew Fors currently had in stock. Robbins testified that it was possible he told Fors that Night Warriors were sturdier than TPME's, but said he did not "remember exactly what went on in that discussion."

Fors also stated that Robbins left literature advertising and explaining the features of the Night Warrior. Fors testified that Robbins gave him the literature at the time Robbins was trying to sell the towers; Fors found the literature in his files of old quotes. Robbins testified that he was unsure whether he had given it to Fors. Among other things, the literature stated that the tower is "built tough for long-lasting, reliable performance" and "will stay ready and roadworthy in all kind[s] of weather and work environments." Fors testified that Robbins's oral representations for sale "basically spoke to what their brochure says." Based on this record, we believe that an adequate review requires a remand for entry of findings of fact that show an understanding of the conflicting contentions and evidence as well as a knowledge of the standards applicable to the determination.

To guide the court in its effort, we will briefly address the questions of law presented in this case which should be considered. This dispute involves a commercial goods transaction; thus, we turn to Article 2 of the Uniform Commercial Code (UCC) as enacted and codified in Title 62A.2 of the RCW. [The court quotes from UCC section 2-313.]

The comments elaborate: "'Express' warranties rest on 'dickered' aspects of the individual bargain, and go so clearly to the essence of that bargain that

---

1. Only the express warranty issue is considered here—Ed.

words of disclaimer in a form are repugnant to the basic dickered terms." UCC §2-313, Official Comment 1.

The trial court therefore must first identify whether any verbal representations were made equating the Night Warriors and the TPMEs, and, if so, whether these representations were of such character as to create an express warranty. The more specific a statement, the more likely it is an affirmation of fact or a promise. 1 James J. White and Robert S. Summers, *Uniform Commercial Code* §9-4, at 445-447 (3d ed. 1988). Further, affirmations of fact or promises will generally relate to the quality of a good. Debra L. Goetz et al., Special Project, *Article Two Warranties in Commercial Transactions: An Update,* 72 Cornell L. Rev. 1159, 1171 (1987). In contrast, more general statements, such as, "You meet the nicest people on a Honda," or a Honda bike is a good one for children, are a seller's opinion or commendation rather than affirmations of fact. *Baughn v. Honda Motor Co.*, 107 Wash. 2d 127, 152, 727 P.2d 655 (1986). Additional factors to consider are whether any hedging occurred, the experimental nature of the good, a buyer's actual or imputed knowledge of the true condition of the good, and the nature of the defect. Andrew M. Baker et al., Special Project, *Article Two Warranties in Commercial Transactions*, 64 Cornell L. Rev. 30, 61 (1978); *see also* White and Summers, at 446-447.

Second, the trial court must determine if and when Federal Signal gave Fors an advertising brochure and if it contained any affirmations of fact or promises. If the trial court here finds that the brochure was given to Fors during the sales negotiation, it must closely examine the language of that brochure. The analysis then is similar to the verbal instance. This court specifically dealt with the question of when advertisements create express warranties under the UCC in *Touchet Vly. Grain Growers, Inc. v. Opp & Seibold Gen. Constr., Inc.*, 119 Wash. 2d 334, 831 P.2d 724 (1992). In that case, a sales brochure contained statements that the advertising company could "design to your specifications," that fabrication "is carefully checked by our quality control department," that its designs would "meet the strictest building codes," and that "[y]our particular requirements will determine the most suitable style of construction." *Touchet Vly.,* at 348, 831 P.2d 724. This court found that such statements constituted express representations promising "a building of certain quality" rather than puffing in advertising; that is, an opinion or commendation about the goods. *Touchet Vly.,* at 348, 831 P.2d 724. Moreover, commentators agree that a written statement is less likely to be puffery. White and Summers, at 445-447.

Lastly, if the court finds that at least one affirmation of fact or promise was made either orally or through the brochure, the trial court must determine whether any of the affirmations of fact or promises were "part of the basis of the bargain" under section 2-313.

## QUESTIONS AND PROBLEMS

If you were the trial judge and were to apply the factors discussed by the court, would you find the statements in the brochures or statements made by the seller's agents to be actionable statements of express warranty? How do we determine if the statements were part of the "basis of the bargain" ? See UCC

§2-313, Official Comment 3. Does it matter if the statements were made *after* the buyer made the decision to purchase the good? See UCC §2-313, Official Comment 7 and UCC §2-209. What relevance, if any, would you give to the facts showing the considerable difficulties the buyer had with the goods in determining whether the statements made were express warranties?

***Problem 4-5.*** A manufacturer makes advertising claims to the general public regarding the quality of the goods that are being sold; the claims are sufficiently specific such that they would be considered express warranties if they were communicated directly to the buyer. Should these advertising statements be considered "warranties," even if they are not mentioned when the buyer contracts to buy the goods from a retailer (not the manufacturer)? See *Interco, Inc. v. Randustrial Corp.*, 533 S.W.2d 257 (Mo. App. 1976). Are they part of the "basis of the bargain" ? What if the buyer never saw the advertisement before purchasing the good? If you advise your client that prior knowledge of the advertisement is required and the client has a sudden recovery of recollection as to having seen the advertisement, how should you respond?

### (b) Implied Warranties

The UCC provides implied warranties in some cases. If goods are sold by merchants in the business of selling the goods of the kind involved, there is an implied warranty that the goods will be fit for the ordinary purpose—that they will work in a manner reasonably expected by the buyer. UCC §2-314. If the buyer relies on the seller to select the goods and informs the seller of the buyer's particular needs, there is an implied warranty that goods will be fit for that purpose. UCC §2-315. Both of these implied warranties can be disclaimed. UCC §2-316. The CISG has similar implied warranties in Article 35, subject to contrary agreement between the parties.

As the following case demonstrates, there is overlap between liability under contract law for breach of the implied warranty of merchantability and strict liability in tort. Later in the book, pages 209-218, *infra*, there is a discussion regarding when an action can be brought in tort as compared to contract. As will be discussed, if a defective product results in personal injury or damage to property other than the goods themselves, the injured party may sue in tort and also under contract as well (assuming the implied warranty of merchantability was not disclaimed). Under the *Restatement (Third) of Torts: Products Liability* section 2, defective products fall into three categories: (1) defectively manufactured products, where the product is manufactured contrary to its design; (2) defectively designed products, where a reasonable alternative design exists; and (3) products containing inadequate warnings, where foreseeable risks of harm could have been reduced with reasonable instructions or warnings.

When it comes to liability imposed under state tort law or the UCC, federal law must also be considered with respect to some products that are regulated by the federal government. The United States Supreme Court has ruled on the relationship between federal law and state law in several cases, sometimes finding that federal law preempts state tort and contract law imposing liability and sometimes finding that federal law does not preempt state law.

*Compare Wyeth v. Levine,* 555 U.S. 555 (2009)(holding that Food and Drug Administration labeling laws do not preempt state law failure-to-warn claims with respect to drugs) *with Riegel v. Medtronic, Inc.*, 552 U.S. 312 (2008)(Medical Device Amendments of 1976 preempt state law claims challenging the safety or effectiveness of a medical device marketed in a form that received premarket approval from the Food and Drug Administration) *and Cipollone v. Liggett Group*, 505 U.S. 504 (1992)(federal laws regulating the labeling and advertising of cigarettes preempt state law claims based on failure to warn but do not preempt state law claims based on express warranty, intentional fraud and misrepresentation, or conspiracy).

As noted previously, the CISG does not cover actions for death or personal injury—these actions are left to other domestic or international law. CISG Article 5. As an example of other non-U.S. law that might apply in such cases, the European Union has issued a products liability directive that imposes strict liability for defective products in a way similar to U.S. tort law.[2]

### Commonwealth v. Johnson Insulation

Supreme Judicial Court of Massachusetts

425 Mass. 650, 682 N.E.2d 1323 (1997)

Asbestos was widely used as an insulator and fire retardant until the 1970s, when it became evident that the material posed health hazards (including lung diseases and cancer) even at low levels of exposure. As a result, the Commonwealth undertook a program to identify and remove asbestos-containing materials that had been installed in its buildings over several decades. To recoup the costs of these remediation activities, the Commonwealth brought an action against numerous companies that had manufactured, supplied, and installed the asbestos-containing products, seeking damages for the costs of removing these materials on the theory that the companies had breached an implied warranty of merchantability. The trial judge ordered the action to be split into three phases, according to the type of asbestos product installed; the case before us involved thermal insulation products, such as those applied to pipes and boilers. All defendants in this phase settled before trial, with two exceptions: Owens-Corning Fiberglas Corporation and Johnson Insulation (Johnson). At trial, the jury found that the defendants had furnished products that were unfit for their intended use, and assessed damages for 21 of the 22 buildings at issue. After judgment was entered against both defendants for damages and interest, Johnson moved for judgment notwithstanding the verdict (judgment N.O.V.) or, in the alternative, for remittitur or a new trial on the damages awarded for two of the sites. Johnson also moved to amend the judgment to reduce the amount of prejudgment interest. The judge allowed the motion for judgment N.O.V., and dismissed entirely the complaint against Johnson. Owens also filed motions for judgment N.O.V. or a new

2. *See* Council Directive 85/374/EEC of July 25, 1985, amended by Directive 1999/34/EC, summarized at *http://eur-lex.europa.eu/LexUriServ/LexUriServ.do?uri=OJ:L:1999:141:0020:0021:EN:PDF* (accessed Oct. 2011).

trial, but subsequently settled with the Commonwealth. Therefore, Johnson is the only remaining defendant in this action. The Commonwealth appealed from the judge's grant of judgment N.O.V. to Johnson and his dismissal of the Commonwealth's G.L. c. 93A claim, and we granted the Commonwealth's application for direct appellate review. We now reverse the judgment N.O.V., and reinstate the jury's verdict.

1. *Johnson's liability under an implied warranty of merchantability.* The Commonwealth argued at trial that Johnson was liable for breach of the implied warranty of merchantability, as defined by provisions of the Uniform Commercial Code (UCC) governing sales, §§2-314 to 2-318. Under the UCC, a warranty that goods are merchantable is implied in a contract for their sale if the seller is a merchant with respect to goods of that kind.[5] To be merchantable, goods must be "fit for the ordinary purposes for which such goods are used." UCC §2-314(1),(2)(c). Although the notion of warranty is grounded in contract, we have recognized that breach of this implied warranty provides a cause of action in tort where the harm is a physical injury to person or property rather than an "economic" loss of value in the product itself (for which contractual remedies must still be pursued). Liability under this implied warranty is "congruent in nearly all respects with the principles expressed in *Restatement (Second) of Torts* §402A (1965)." *Back v. Wickes, supra* at 640, 378 N.E.2d 964. The *Restatement of Torts, supra,* takes the position that the seller of "any product in a defective condition unreasonably dangerous to the user or consumer or to his property is subject to liability for physical harm thereby caused to the ultimate user or consumer, or to his property," even though "the seller has exercised all possible care in the preparation and sale of his product." *Id.* at §402A(1),(2)(a). Thus, a claim for breach of the implied warranty of merchantability should be considered in light of the requirements for warranties contained in G.L. c. 106, §§2-314 to 2-318, as well as the principles expressed in section 402A of the *Restatement. Back v. Wickes Corp., supra.*

The UCC provides separately for an implied warranty of fitness for a particular purpose, which exists "[w]here the seller at the time of contracting has reason to know any particular purpose for which the goods are required and that the buyer is relying on the seller's skill or judgment to select or furnish suitable goods." UCC §2-315. The Commonwealth did not argue that such a warranty existed in this case. As discussed below, the existence of the two separate implied warranties, and of separate defenses to their existence, engenders some confusion and ambiguity in statutes, commentary, and case law.

By way of defense, Johnson contends that it cannot be held liable for having sold the asbestos-containing products, whether or not they were "unreasonably dangerous," because no implied warranty of merchantability existed as to those products. It argues that the warranty never arose because the

---

5. As the supplier of the asbestos-containing product and as its installer, Johnson provided both goods and services to the Commonwealth. We are satisfied that Johnson is a "merchant" with respect to the asbestos product. In its memorandum of law in support of its motion for judgment N.O.V., Johnson implied that it should be viewed as a service provider rather than as a merchant, but it has not pressed this argument on appeal.

products were supplied according to the Commonwealth's plans and specifications. Johnson argues that the Commonwealth specified the products that Johnson was to supply and install, and that it is fundamentally unfair to hold a seller liable for providing a product which it was bound by the buyer's specifications to provide. As indications that it had no discretion in supplying these products, Johnson points out that (1) the specifications were created by design engineers and reviewed by staff of the division of capital planning and operations before the projects were put out to bid, (2) Johnson had to obtain approval of the materials it proposed to use, and (3) a "clerk of the works" at each job site ensured that the approved materials were actually installed. Johnson does not cite any specific statutory language as the basis for its defense. We presume here that it relies on UCC section 2-316, which provides that an implied warranty can be excluded or modified "by course of dealing or course of performance or usage of trade," and on section 2-317(c), which states that an express warranty (here, Johnson's contractual promise to install the specified materials) displaces an inconsistent implied warranty of merchantability. As support for its position, Johnson cites 1A U.L.A. section 2-316, Official Comment 9, at 467 (Master ed. 1989):

> The situation in which the buyer gives *precise and complete specifications* to the seller is not explicitly covered in this section, but this is a frequent circumstance by which the implied warranties may be excluded. The warranty of fitness for a particular purpose would not normally arise since in such a situation there is usually no reliance on the seller by the buyer. The warranty of merchantability in such a transaction, however, must be considered in connection with [section 2-317] on the cumulation and conflict of warranties. Under [section 2-317(c),] in case of such an inconsistency the implied warranty of merchantability is displaced by the express warranty that the goods will comply with the specifications. Thus, where the buyer gives *detailed specifications* as to the goods, neither of the implied warranties as to quality will normally apply to the transaction unless consistent with the specifications. (Emphasis added.)

Logically, in the circumstances where a buyer specifies the desired goods, in detail, to a seller, the buyer has not relied on the seller's skill and judgment in selecting those goods, and hence, by the terms of section 2-315, a warranty of fitness for a particular purpose does not exist. By contrast, the effect of a buyer's specifications on the warranty of merchantability depends on a number of variables, including the nature and uniqueness of the product, the extent of the buyer's role in product design, the sophistication of the parties, and their prior course of dealing. We conclude that an implied warranty of merchantability did exist for the products supplied by Johnson, because the specifications supplied by the Commonwealth were not so detailed, precise, and complete as to exclude that warranty.

The specification by a buyer of a brand or trade name does not, by itself, negate an implied warranty of merchantability. That warranty would lose almost all significance if it ceased to apply any time that a consumer selected or requested a product by brand name. Even if Johnson was in fact bound to supply a product requested by the Commonwealth or lose the sale, all other sorts of manufacturers, distributors, and retailers, from automobile dealers to fast-food vendors, face a similar choice in supplying brand-name products requested or selected by customers.

Johnson cites several cases involving buyer specifications in which the implied warranty of merchantability was held not to apply, but we find these cases inapposite or unpersuasive. In *Cumberland Farms, Inc. v. Drehmann Paving & Flooring Co.,* 25 Mass. App. Ct. 530, 520 N.E.2d 1321 (1988), structural problems in a dairy plant's brick floor were attributed to the absence of expansion joints across the floor's surface. The plaintiff (a construction company affiliated with the plant's owner) had made the initial contact with the defendant installer, supplied blueprints to it, and informed it that the floor was to be similar to a floor, likewise lacking surface expansion joints, that the defendant had installed previously in another of the plaintiff's facilities. The plaintiff had also rejected the defendant's recommendation that expansion joints be added to the new floor's design. During installation, the plaintiff rejected a similar recommendation from its own construction supervisor. *Id.* at 531-533, 520 N.E.2d 1321. The appeals court held that the installer was not liable under either of the two possible warranty theories. The court concluded that (1) the implied warranty of fitness for a particular purpose never arose because the plans and specifications had been furnished by the plaintiff, the installer had no discretion, and the plaintiff had not relied on the installer's expertise; and (2) the implied warranty of merchantability had been displaced by an express warranty, namely, that the floor was to be similar to the one previously constructed. *Id.* at 535-536, 520 N.E.2d 1321. We do not accept the analogies that Johnson wishes us to draw between the *Cumberland Farms* case and the action before us. In the *Cumberland Farms* case, the failure of the floor was caused not by the quality of the materials (i.e., bricks) supplied by the installer, nor by a lack of craftsmanship on its part, but by innate flaws in engineering and design that were wholly attributable to the plaintiff. In the present case, the problem is not with the design of the Commonwealth's buildings or with its decision to insulate pipes, but with the materials provided by the installer, products that turned out to have undisclosed and nonobvious defects that rendered them unfit for their ordinary purposes. The asbestos-containing products supplied by Johnson were "off-the-shelf," commercially available goods that were not specially designed or manufactured for the Commonwealth.

Allowing Johnson's "specifications defense" to negate the implied warranty of merchantability here might create an anomaly in other cases involving brand-name products where both negligence and breach of the implied warranty of merchantability are potential theories for establishing product liability. Even if a buyer's selection of a product by brand name furnished a defense to a breach of warranty claim, the buyer's action would be unlikely to alter the seller's duty of care to the buyer with respect to the product. As a result, the buyer might find it more difficult to recover on a warranty theory than on a theory of negligence. This would undercut the social policy, advanced by the breach of warranty theory, of holding sellers liable for the quality and safety of their products.

Having concluded that an implied warranty of merchantability did exist, we proceed to consider whether a reasonable basis existed for the jury's affirmative findings that the asbestos-containing product furnished and installed by Johnson at 21 sites was unfit for its intended use.

As discussed above, we have equated a breach of the implied warranty of merchantability, that goods be "fit for the ordinary purposes for which such goods are used," with the sale of an "unreasonably dangerous" product. An article is not unreasonably dangerous merely because some risk of harm is associated with its use, but only where it is dangerous "to an extent beyond that which would be contemplated by the ordinary consumer who purchases it, with the ordinary knowledge common to the community as to its characteristics." *Restatement (Second) of Torts, supra* at §402A, comment i, at 352. A product may be unreasonably dangerous because of a defect in design. *See Back v. Wickes Corp., supra* at 640-642, 378 N.E.2d 964 (manufacturer must anticipate environment in which product will be used; where design defect is alleged, "fitness" is to be judged by social acceptability, considering such factors as consumer expectations, degree of danger, feasibility and cost of alternative designs, and adverse consequences of alternatives). Alternatively, a product may be considered to be unreasonably dangerous because of the absence of an adequate warning, sufficient to alert those who may be sensitive to the product and to allow users to balance the risk of harm against the product's social utility. *See Borel v. Fibreboard Paper Prods. Corp.,* 493 F.2d 1076, 1088-1089 (5th Cir. 1973); *Restatement* §402A, comments j,k. In this action, both the Commonwealth and Johnson focused on the "failure to warn" basis for finding a product unreasonably dangerous, and we therefore address only that issue.

The jury could reasonably have found that Johnson's products were unfit for their ordinary purposes, based on the evidence presented at trial concerning the absence of adequate warnings as to the dangers of exposure to asbestos. The Commonwealth introduced, as exhibits, product brochures and other descriptive materials that contained no warnings as to the dangers posed by even low levels of exposure to installed asbestos. It also introduced an interrogatory in which Johnson acknowledged that "[n]o specific warnings, advice or requirements [were] given regarding preparing, installing, [or] applying ... asbestos-containing materials to the plaintiff." This appears to address only the potential immediate hazards to workers handling the material during installation, and not the long-term dangers of exposure to in-place asbestos that in fact necessitated the Commonwealth's asbestos-removal programs. However, the jury could have reasonably inferred from this response that Johnson had offered no warnings of long-term hazards, either.[13]

In summary, an implied warranty of merchantability existed for the products supplied by Johnson to the Commonwealth, notwithstanding Johnson's defense that it was bound by the Commonwealth's specifications. The absence

---

13. We note that it is a matter of some dispute as to when the dangers of asbestos became either known or scientifically discoverable. *See Borel v. Fibreboard Paper Prods. Corp.*, 493 F.2d 1076, 1083-1086 (5th Cir. 1973), *cert. denied*, 419 U.S. 869, 95 S.Ct. 127, 42 L. Ed.2d 107 (1974) (reviewing history of knowledge as to risks of exposure to asbestos) [According to the court, asbestosis was a known disease as early as the 1920s—Ed.].

of adequate warnings as to the hazards of asbestos rendered those products unreasonably dangerous, in breach of that warranty. The judge's decision to grant judgment N.O.V. must therefore be reversed, and the jury's verdict reinstated. There was no inconsistency between the jury's findings that products were furnished according to the Commonwealth's specifications and their findings that those products were unfit for their ordinary purpose.

## PROBLEMS

***Problem 4-6.*** In the preceding case, the court holds that a good is not fit for the ordinary purpose under UCC section 2-314 if it would be considered a defective product under tort strict liability principles. How should cigarettes, alcohol, and other known dangerous products be considered? Products that are dangerous but where the dangers are not previously known? *See, e.g., American Tobacco Co. v. Grinnell*, 951 S.W.2d 420 (Tex. 1997); Owen, *Inherent Product Hazards*, 93 Ky. L.J. 377 (2004-2005).

***Problem 4-7.*** A nonmerchant buyer purchases ballasts for light fixtures. Five percent of the ballasts are defective. Is it relevant for the seller to argue that the accepted failure rate in the industry is 10 percent? See UCC §2-314(2) (a),(b),(d); *Episcopal Church Home of Western New York v. The Bulb Man*, 274 A.D.2d 961, 710 N.Y.S. 2d 503 (2000). Should a buyer be held to an industry failure rate of which it is unaware?

***Problem 4-8.*** A customer picks up a bottle of soda in a store and decides to purchase it. While carrying it to the checkout stand, the bottle explodes, cutting the customer's hand severely. Does the customer have a cause of action against the store for breach of the implied warranty of merchantability? Has there been a "sale" ? See UCC §2-106. Would it make a difference if the customer was examining the bottle when it exploded but had not yet decided whether to purchase it? *Compare McQuiston v. K-Mart Corp.*, 796 F.2d 1346 (1986), *with Sheeskin v. Giant Foods, Inc.*, 20 Md. App. 611, 318 A.2d 874, 14 UCC Rep. Serv. 892 (1974). If intent to purchase matters, how should you counsel a prospective client who comes into your office looking for representation?

***Problem 4-9.*** A diner purchases a chicken tostada in a restaurant and chokes on a chicken bone. Is the restaurant liable for breach of implied warranty of merchantability or fitness? Would it make a difference if the diner broke a tooth on a rock that was in the beans? *See Mexicali Rose v. Superior Court*, 1 Cal. 4th 617, 822 P.2d 1292, 4 Cal. Rptr. 2d 145 (1992).

***Problem 4-10.*** A large clothing manufacturer has a number of different computers that it uses in its business. Some of the computers are more high-powered than others. The business decides that it is going to purchase some new computers and offers some of the existing computers for sale through an advertisement in the newspaper. It has never sold computers before. A small-business owner responds to the advertisement and describes specifically her needs for a computer to perform bookkeeping and inventory-control functions to the clothing manufacturer's office manager. The office manager shows the business owner one of the machines and tells her that it should be adequate for the business owner's purposes. The business owner buys the computer, but it turns out to have insufficient memory and speed to perform the bookkeeping and inventory functions, although it could be used for word processing. What, if any, warranties were given by the clothing manufacturer to the small- business owner that might have been breached? See UCC §§2-313 to 2-315. If more than one warranty is given, does one warranty take priority over another? See UCC §2-317.

## 2. UNDER THE CISG

The CISG provisions requiring that the goods be of a certain quality are contained in CISG Article 35. Article 35(1) requires that the goods be "of the quantity, quality and description required by the contract and which are contained or packaged in the manner required by the contract." This rule requires courts or arbitral tribunals to interpret the contract to see what is requires. CISG Article 8 should be useful in this regard, focusing on the reasonable understandings of the parties and their knowledge of the other party's intent.

CISG Article 35(2) contains a number of implied promises from the seller about the quality of the goods, unless the parties have agreed otherwise. Please read Article 35(2). You will see that the implied promises here are similar to the UCC implied warranty of merchantability and fitness. There is also a requirement that the goods be consistent with any sample or model, which is in UCC section 2-313. Under Article 35(3), the buyer may not hold the seller responsible for any nonconformity under Article 35(2) if at the time the contract was formed ("concluded" under the parlance of the CISG) "the buyer knew or could not have been unaware of such lack of conformity."

The following case raises the problem of whether the seller is responsible for standards in the buyer's country that make the goods unsuitable. It also shows how arbitral awards are handled by courts.

### Medical Marketing International v. Internazionale Medico Scientifica

United States District Court, Eastern District of Louisiana

1999 W.L. 311945 (1999)

DUVAL, District Judge.

Before the court is an Application for Order Conforming Arbitral Award and Entry of Judgment, filed by plaintiff, Medical Marketing International, Inc. ("MMI"). Having considered the memoranda of plaintiff, and the memorandum in opposition filed by defendant, Internazionale Medico Scientifica, S.r.l. ("IMS"), the court grants the motion.

#### Factual Background

Plaintiff MMI is a Louisiana marketing corporation with its principal place of business in Baton Rouge, Louisiana. Defendant IMS is an Italian corporation that manufactures radiology materials with its principal place of business in Bologna, Italy. On January 25, 1993, MMI and IMS entered into a business licensing agreement in which IMS granted exclusive sales rights for Giotto Mammography H.F. Units to MMI.

In 1996, the Food and Drug Administration ("FDA") seized the equipment for noncompliance with administrative procedures, and a dispute arose over who bore the obligation of ensuring that the Giotto equipment complied with the United States Governmental Safety Regulations, specifically the Good Manufacturing Practices (GMP) for Medical Device Regulations. MMI formally demanded mediation on October 28, 1996, pursuant to Article 13 of the agreement. Mediation was unsuccessful, and the parties entered into arbitration, also pursuant to Article 13, whereby each party chose one arbitrator and a third was agreed upon by both.

An arbitration hearing was held on July 13-15, July 28, and November 17, 1998. The hearing was formally closed on November 30, 1998. The arbitrators rendered their decision on December 21, 1998, awarding MMI damages in the amount of $357,009 and legal interest on that amount from October 28, 1996. The arbitration apportioned 75 percent of the $83,640.45 cost of arbitration to MMI, and the other 25 percent to IMS. IMS moved for reconsideration on December 30, 1998, and this request was denied by the arbitrators on January 7, 1999. Plaintiff now moves for an order from this court confirming the arbitral award and entering judgment in favor of the plaintiff under 9 U.S.C. §9.

### Jurisdiction

The Federal Arbitration Act ("FAA") allows parties to an arbitration suit to apply to the "United States court in and for the district within which such award was made" for enforcement of the award. 9 U.S.C. §9. Because the arbitration in this case was held in New Orleans, Louisiana, this court has jurisdiction over petitioner's Application under 9 U.S.C. §9. This court also has diversity jurisdiction over the case, because the amount in controversy exceeds $75,000 and the parties are a Louisiana corporation and an Italian corporation.

### Analysis

The scope of this court's review of an arbitration award is "among the narrowest known to law." *Denver & Rio Grande Western Railroad Co. v. Union Pacific Railroad Co.,* 119 F.3d 847, 849 (10th Cir. 1997). The FAA outlines specific situations in which an arbitration decision may be overruled: (1) if the award was procured by corruption, fraud, or undue means; (2) if there is evidence of partiality or corruption among the arbitrators; (3) if the arbitrators were guilty of misconduct that prejudiced the rights of one of the parties; or (4) if the arbitrators exceeded their powers. Instances in which the arbitrators "exceed their powers" may include violations of public policy or awards based on a "manifest disregard of the law." *See W.R. Grace & Co. v. Local Union 759,* 461 U.S. 757, 766, 103 S. Ct. 2177, 2183 (1983), *Walcha v. Swan,* 346 U.S. 427, 436-437, 74 S. Ct. 182, 187-188 (1953), *overruled on other grounds*, 490 U.S. 477, 109 S. Ct. 1917 (1989).

IMS has alleged that the arbitrators' decision violates public policy of the international global market and that the arbitrators exhibited "manifest disregard of international sales law." Specifically, IMS argues that the arbitrators misapplied the United Nations Convention on Contracts for the International

Sales of Goods, commonly referred to as the CISG, and that they refused to follow a German Supreme Court case interpreting the CISG.

MMI does not dispute that the CISG applies to the case at hand. Under the CISG, the finder of fact has a duty to regard the "international character" of the convention and to promote uniformity in its application. CISG Article 7. The Convention also provides that in an international contract for goods, goods conform to the contract if they are fit for the purpose for which goods of the same description would ordinarily be used, or are fit for any particular purpose expressly or impliedly made known to the seller and relied upon by the buyer. CISG Article 35(2). To avoid a contract based on the nonconformity of goods, the buyer must allege and prove that the seller's breach was "fundamental" in nature. CISG Article 49. A breach is fundamental when it results in such detriment to the party that he or she is substantially deprived of what he or she is entitled to expect under the contract, unless the party in breach did not foresee such a result. CISG Article 25.

At the arbitration, IMS argued that MMI was not entitled to avoid its contract with IMS based on nonconformity under Article 49, because IMS's breach was not "fundamental." IMS argued that the CISG did not require that it furnish MMI with equipment that complied with the U.S. GMP regulations. To support this proposition, IMS cited a German Supreme Court case, which held that under CISG Article 35, a seller is generally not obligated to supply goods that conform to public laws and regulations enforced at the buyer's place of business. *Entscheidunger des Bundersgerichtshofs in Zivilsachen* (BGHZ) 129, 75 (1995). In that case, the court held that this general rule carries with it exceptions in three limited circumstances: (1) if the public laws and regulations of the buyer's state are identical to those enforced in the seller's state; (2) if the buyer informed the seller about those regulations; or (3) if due to "special circumstances," such as the existence of a seller's branch office in the buyer's state, the seller knew or should have known about the regulations at issue.

The arbitration panel decided that under the third exception, the general rule did not apply to this case. The arbitrators held that IMS was, or should have been, aware of the GMP regulations prior to entering into the 1993 agreement, and explained their reasoning at length. IMS now argues that the arbitration panel refused to apply CISG and the law as articulated by the German Supreme Court. It is clear from the arbitrators' written findings, however, that they carefully considered that decision and found that this case fit the exception and not the rule as articulated in that decision. The arbitrators' decision was neither contrary to public policy nor in manifest disregard of international sales law. This court therefore finds that the arbitration panel did not "exceed its powers" in violation of the FAA. Accordingly,

IT IS ORDERED that the Application for Order Conforming Arbitral Award is hereby GRANTED.

## NOTES AND QUESTIONS

1. This case is an instructional one for a couple of reasons. One is that it shows how an arbitration award is enforced and the deference that courts pay to

such awards. Does the limited scrutiny that courts give to arbitral awards make it advantageous or disadvantageous to have an arbitration provision included in the contract of sale? Do you think, however, that the case would have been decided the same way, even if the court had applied a more strict standard of review? Another reason why the case is instructional is that it shows the persuasive authority of cases decided from all over the world. This case involved U.S. and Italian parties, and yet the seller was asserting a German court decision. Use of authority from around the world seems to be encouraged by CISG Article 7(1), which states that in interpreting the Convention, "regard is to be had to its international character and the need to promote uniformity in international trade."

2. As to the substance of the rule itself, do you agree that the seller should generally not be responsible for its goods conforming to the regulatory rules of the buyer's place of business? If the seller knows that goods will be delivered and used in another nation, shouldn't the seller make certain that its goods are in conformity with standards for such goods in the country in question?

***Problem 4-11.*** In a contract for the sale of potatoes covered by the CISG, Buyer had approached Seller asking for potatoes that would be suitable for making into potato chips. Buyer was a potato chip manufacturer.[3] Seller brought Buyer a box of potatoes, and Buyer told Seller that the potatoes that were shown were suitable for Buyer's purposes because the color and size of the potatoes were appropriate for Seller's product. Buyer wanted its chips to have a uniform, white color. Buyer also liked the price that was quoted by Seller, as it was less than the price it paid to its other suppliers for potatoes guaranteed to be of the quality desired by Buyer. Buyer issued a purchase order for 40,000 pounds of potatoes "as per sample provided." Seller issued a "confirmation" that was in agreement as to price and quantity, but only indicated that it would be shipping "40,000 pounds of potatoes" without any statement as to whether the potatoes would be consistent with the sample. Buyer was aware that in a typical contract for the sale of potatoes, unless stipulated otherwise, the potatoes would not necessarily be of uniform color or size, as it cost extra money for Seller to segregate out potatoes of specific size and color. Nevertheless, Buyer did not pay much attention to Seller's confirmation and the potatoes were delivered and paid for. Buyer was confident that Seller understood Buyer's needs for a consistent product. Buyer was very disappointed to learn that a significant proportion of the potatoes delivered were not consistent with the sample. At what point in time was a contract formed and do the terms of the purchase order or the confirmation control? See CISG Articles 18 and 19. Were there any express or implied promises made by Seller that were breached? See CISG Articles 8 and 35.

***Problem 4-12.*** A German buyer contracts to purchase New Zealand mussels from a Swiss seller. The CISG applies to the transaction. The mussels have a higher cadmium content than suggested by German health regulations, but they are edible and can legally be resold and consumed there. They have a

3. For a case similar to this under the UCC, see *Hubbard v. UTZ Quality Foods, Inc.*, page 155 *infra*.

higher cadmium content than most New Zealand mussels. Has there been a violation of CISG Articles 35(2)(a) or (2)(b)? Compare UCC §2-314(2)(b) & (2)(d). This problem is based on, but is not identical to, a case decided by the German Federal Supreme Court, Bundesgerichthof March 8, 1995, CLOUT no. 123, *www.cisg.law.pace.edu/cisg/wais/db/cases2/950308g3.html* (accessed Oct. 2011).

## 3. DISCLAIMERS OF WARRANTIES

Under both the UCC and the CISG, sellers of goods are free to disclaim the implied warranties of merchantability and fitness in their contracts with buyers. Under the UCC, disclaimers must comply with the technical requirements of section 2-316.

Section 2-316(1) provides that express warranties may not be disclaimed. Language of disclaimer should be read in a manner consistent with the express warranty if possible, but the express warranty will control over any inconsistent disclaimer. The parol evidence rule may be an issue if an express warranty is given before the buyer signs a written contract containing a disclaimer that is inconsistent with the express warranty; that is, the buyer may have difficulty getting the court to permit admission of evidence of the express warranty. Parol evidence issues are considered in the next chapter.

Section 2-316(2) provides that to disclaim the implied warranty of merchantability, the disclaimer must mention the word "merchantability." If the disclaimer is in writing, it must be conspicuous. Any disclaimer of the implied warranty of fitness must be in writing and be conspicuous.

Section 2-316(3) provides an alternative way to disclaim implied warranties. The seller may use language that "in common understanding" indicates that warranties are being disclaimed. The section indicates that language such as "as is" or "with all faults" are that type of language. In addition, the seller may demand that the buyer inspect the goods. Failure to inspect will bar the buyer from suing on a defect that the inspection would have reasonably disclosed. Implied warranties may also be disclaimed through course of dealing, course of performance, or usage of trade.

The CISG has no specific technical requirements for disclaimers of warranties. Article 6 of the CISG is a broad provision permitting parties to the contract to derogate from provisions of the CISG (or the entire CISG, for that matter) and Article 35's implied warranties apply "except where the parties have agreed otherwise." The following case demonstrates application of UCC section 2-316.

### Borden, Inc. v. Advent Ink Company

Superior Court of Pennsylvania

701 A.2d 255, 33 UCC Rep. Serv. 2d 975 (1997)

Plaintiff/appellee Borden, Inc. ("Borden") sued defendant/appellant Advent Ink Company ("Advent") in the Court of Common Pleas of Lancaster County to recover moneys owed for goods delivered but not paid for. Advent counterclaimed for damages allegedly sustained as a result of a previous shipment of defective goods. The trial court granted Borden's motion for summary judgment on the counterclaim.

Advent, a Pennsylvania corporation, manufactured water-based inks for printers. Among those inks was a black ink that was sold to R.R. Donnelley & Sons Company ("Donnelley") for the printing of its telephone directories. In producing this ink, Advent used a water-based black dispersion, "Aquablak," which it purchased from Borden.

In 1992, Borden sued Advent to recover the sum of $16,227.50 on a book account for merchandise sold and delivered to Advent. In response, Advent asserted that it had rejected the shipments in question because prior shipments had failed to comply with implied warranties of merchantability and fitness for a particular purpose. Specifically, Advent alleged that Borden's failure to age the Aquablak resulted in material defects which, when the Aquablak was incorporated into the black ink, caused the ink to separate and to clog Donnelley's presses. As a result, Donnelley ceased buying water-based black ink from Advent. In its counterclaim Advent argued that it was "entitled to recover from Borden the profits which [it] lost and which [it had] reasonably expected to continue from the Donnelley contract that was cancelled solely as a result of Borden's failure to provide a merchantable black dispersion for use in the black ink."

Late in 1992, Advent filed for bankruptcy under Chapter 11. A stipulation was entered lifting the automatic stay so that Advent could proceed on its counterclaim.

Following discovery, Borden filed a motion for summary judgment on the counterclaim. In its motion Borden argued that it was entitled to summary judgment on either of two bases: First, it had validly and conspicuously disclaimed the implied warranties of merchantability and of fitness for a particular purpose, as it was allowed to do under Uniform Commercial Code ("UCC") section 2-316, by means of language included in its sales invoices and on labels affixed to each drum of Aquablak that was shipped to Advent; second, by the same means it had validly excluded any liability for consequential damages such as lost profits, as it was allowed to do under section 2-719 of the UCC.[4]

By order entered January 2, 1997, the trial court granted Borden's motion for summary judgment and dismissed the counterclaim. The trial court reasoned that Borden had conspicuously disclaimed the implied warranties of merchantability and fitness for a particular purpose. The court did not address Borden's alternative argument on the limitation of damages.

In this appeal, Advent contends that summary judgment was not warranted on either of the two grounds advanced by Borden. As to the disclaimer of warranties on the invoices and drum labels, Advent argues that the disclaimer was inoperative because it was inconspicuous. Advent asserts that the limitation of remedies clause was also inoperative because it failed its essential purpose and was unconscionable. Therefore, Advent argues, we should vacate the award of summary judgment and allow the case to proceed to trial.

---

4. Only the part of the opinion dealing with the disclaimer or warranties is reproduced here—Ed.

I. Disclaimer of Warranties

In order to resolve Advent's first issue (namely, its challenge to the disclaimer of warranties), we turn first to the pertinent provisions of the UCC as adopted in this Commonwealth. The implied warranty of merchantability, as set forth in the UCC, is "a warranty that the goods will pass without objection in the trade and are fit for the ordinary purposes for which such goods are used." *Moscatiello v. Pittsburgh Contractors Equipment Company*, 407 Pa. Super. 363, 368, 595 A.2d 1190, 1193 (1991), citing UCC §2-314, *appeal denied,* 529 Pa. 650, 602 A.2d 860 (1992). Such a warranty "serves to protect buyers from loss where the goods purchased are below commercial standards." *Hornberger v. General Motors Corporation,* 929 F. Supp. 884 (E.D. Pa. 1996). The superior court has observed that "this warranty is so commonly taken for granted that its exclusion from a contract is recognized as a matter threatening surprise and therefore requiring special precaution." *Moscatiello,* 407 Pa. Super. 369, 595 A.2d 1193, citing Comment 11 to UCC §2-314. The implied warranty that goods shall be fit for a particular purpose exists, under the UCC, where the seller at the time of contracting has reason to know of such purpose and of the buyer's reliance upon the seller's skill or judgment to select or furnish goods that are suitable for such purpose. See UCC §2-315.

The UCC sets forth the following requirements for excluding or modifying these implied warranties:

> Subject to subsection (c) [not relevant here], to exclude or modify the implied warranty of merchantability or any part of it the language must mention merchantability and in case of a writing must be conspicuous, and to exclude or modify any implied warranty of fitness the exclusion must be by a writing and conspicuous. Language to exclude all implied warranties of fitness is sufficient if it states, for example, that "There are no warranties which extend beyond the description on the face here of."

UCC §2-316(b). In the present case, the attempted exclusions of both warranties appear in writings, and, as will be shown *infra,* the writings mention merchantability. The question to be decided, therefore, is whether those attempted exclusions are conspicuous. This is a question of law for the court. UCC §1-201.

The UCC provides the following definition of the critical term "conspicuous":

> A term or clause is conspicuous when it is so written that a reasonable person against whom it is to operate ought to have noticed it. A printed heading in capitals ... is conspicuous. Language in the body of a form is conspicuous if it is in larger or other contrasting type or color. But in a telegram any stated term is conspicuous.

UCC §1-201. As explained in Comment 10 to section 1-201, the definition of "conspicuous" is "intended to indicate some of the methods of making a term attention calling. But the test is whether attention can reasonably be expected to be called to it."

Under Pennsylvania law, factors to be considered in determining whether a reasonable person should have noticed a warranty disclaimer include: (1) the disclaimer's placement in the document, (2) the size of the disclaimer's print, and (3) whether the disclaimer was highlighted by being printed in all capital letters or in a type style or color different from the remainder of the document. The reasonableness test accords with the primary purpose of the conspicuousness requirement, which is "to avoid fine print waiver of rights by the buyer[.]" *Moscatiello,* 407 Pa. Super. at 369, 595 A.2d at 1193.

In the present case, the trial court concluded on the basis of the invoices and drum labels that Borden had met these waiver requirements. On the front of Borden's standard invoice, in red capital letters, is the phrase "SEE REVERSE SIDE." On the reverse side is the heading "CONDITIONS OF SALE," followed by 19 conditions, the first of which is the following:

> **1. WARRANTIES AND DISCLAIMERS. SELLER MAKE [sic] NO WARRANTY, EXPRESS OR IMPLIED, CONCERNING THE PRODUCT OR THE MERCHANTABILITY OR FITNESS THEREOF FOR ANY PURPOSE, except: (a) that the product shall conform to the Seller's specifications, if any, and (b) that the product does not infringe any valid United States patent. Seller does not warrant, however, that the use of the product or articles made therefrom, either alone or in conjunction with other materials, will not infringe any United States patent.**

At the top of the label affixed to each drum of dispersion is the Borden logo. Beneath the logo are two centered lines:

**BORDEN PRINTING INKS**
**ZERO DEFECTS: THAT'S OUR GOAL**

These are followed by three centered lines, spaced as shown:

**FOR INDUSTRIAL USE ONLY**
**EMERGENCY TELEPHONE [NUMBER]**
**FOLLOW USE DIRECTIONS FROM BORDEN INC.**

Below these lines is the centered heading "DISCLAIMER" and the following text:

> **SELLER MAKES NO WARRANTY, EXPRESS OR IMPLIED, CONCERNING THE PRODUCT OR THE MERCHANTABILITY OR FITNESS THEREOF FOR ANY PURPOSE OR CONCERNING THE ACCURACY OF ANY INFORMATION PROVIDED BY BORDEN, except that the product shall conform to contracted specifications. . . . Buyer's exclusive remedy shall be for damages and no claim of any kind, whether as to product delivered or for non-delivery of product, and whether based on contract, breach of warranty, negligence or otherwise shall be greater in amount than the purchase price of the quantity of product in respect of which damages are claimed. In no event shall Seller be liable for incidental or consequential damages . . . .**

All of the type on the drum label appears to be in boldface.

The trial court, reasoning as follows, found that both disclaimers were conspicuous as a matter of law:

> The disclaimer on the drums was on the front and center of the drum labels in boldface. The disclaimer is the only paragraph on the drum label. The heading and disclaimer are typed in all capitals, all the rest of the paragraph is not.
>
> Similarly conspicuous, the disclaimer on Borden's invoice appears in the very first paragraph of the "CONDITIONS OF SALE" which is set apart from all other paragraphs and is in all capitals. Although the disclaimer is on the reverse side

> of the invoice, the front of the invoice states in red typeface, "SEE REVERSE SIDE." The red color is in contract [sic] with all surrounding typeface.

Relying principally upon this court's decision in *Moscatiello, supra,* Advent contends that the trial court erred in concluding that the disclaimers were conspicuous. The issue in *Moscatiello* was whether the seller's exclusion of warranties clause, located on the reverse side of a standard sales contract, was conspicuous. The superior court analyzed the issue as follows:

> The front of the form contains blank lines in which are typed a customer's name, shipping instructions, detailed description of the machine, price breakdown, and payment terms. All of the information is individually typed on separate lines at least one quarter of an inch wide. Toward the bottom of the form, inside the margins for the price breakdown, is the phrase in capital letters: "TERMS AND CONDITIONS ON REVERSE SIDE ARE AN INTEGRAL PART OF THIS ORDER." Immediately below is a sentence containing the clause, in smaller type, "subject to the provisions hereof and conditions contained on reverse side hereof."
>
> By contrast, the reverse side of the form contains eighteen numbered paragraphs which fill the page, top to bottom and side to side, in extremely small type, approximately one-sixteenth inch in height and one-fourth the size used on the front. The capital letters are slightly larger, but of the same color and in the same type style as the rest of the printing. The type used on the front of the contract is much larger and bolder than that used on the reverse side. The warranty disclaimer is buried in paragraph number sixteen at the bottom of the page. Though the operative language of the disclaimer is set forth in capital letters, the size of the type of even the capital letters is so minute that it simply does nothing to attract attention to the clause. As Moscatiello aptly observes, "to say that the print is 'fine' is an understatement." Appellee's brief at 12.

*Id.,* 407 Pa. Super. at 369-370, 595 A.2d at 1193-1194.

On the basis of these facts, the superior court affirmed the trial court's finding that the disclaimer was not adequate to put the buyer, Moscatiello, on notice that substantial rights were being relinquished. The disclaimer itself, according to the superior court, "was set forth in some of the 'finest' print this court ever has read." *Id.,* 407 Pa. Super. at 370, 595 A.2d at 1194. Moreover, the court noted, the language on the front of the invoice, referring to terms and conditions on the reverse side, suffered from two defects: (1) it was inconspicuous, being buried in the middle of the invoice, and (2) it was misleading, as it referred only to "terms" and "conditions" on the reverse side and not to a limitation of warranties. The court concluded that "[t]his language clearly does not meet the letter or the spirit of the UCC requirements." *Id.* In addition, the court noted that the seller had failed to notify Moscatiello of the exclusion of warranties despite having had numerous opportunities to do so.

We agree with Advent that the sales invoice in the present case is equally ineffective as a disclaimer of warranties. Advent asserts, and this court confirms, that the print on the reverse side of the invoice is no larger than one-sixteenth inch in height. All of the type appears to be boldface. Although the disclaimer of warranties is the first of 19 numbered paragraphs, as was not the case in *Moscatiello,* nevertheless there is nothing to indicate that the first paragraph is any more significant than, for example, the seventh ("WEIGHTS") or the tenth ("CARRIER AND ROUTING").

Even more important, the reference on the front of the invoice to the terms on the reverse side is even less informative, albeit more noticeable, than that in *Moscatiello*. The reference in *Moscatiello* at least served to indicate that the terms and conditions on the reverse side of the invoice were an integral part of the order. The reference in the present case simply states "SEE REVERSE SIDE"; there is absolutely no indication that among the terms on the reverse side is an exclusion of warranties, including a warranty (namely, the implied warranty of merchantability) "so commonly taken for granted that its exclusion from a contract is recognized as a matter threatening surprise. . . ." *Id.,* 407 Pa. Super. at 368-369, 595 A.2d at 1193.

In *Moscatiello*, the superior court observed that "[w]hile . . . the location of a disclaimer on the reverse side of a contract alone does not render the disclaimer inconspicuous, the disclaimer itself must be conspicuous *and* the front of the document must contain noticeable reference to the terms on the reverse side." *Id.,* 407 Pa. Super. at 370 n.2, 595 A.2d at 1194 n.2 (emphasis in original). If the language in *Moscatiello* lacked "noticeable reference to the terms on the reverse side," so much more pronounced was the lack of such reference in the present case.

According to the trial court, the superior court's decision in *Moscatiello* rested, inter alia, upon two factors that are not present in this case: 1) The seller was a merchant and a dealer of equipment, while the buyer was neither; and 2) the buyer and the seller had had no previous dealings with each other. As Advent points out, however, the superior court did not consider these factors in connection with the exclusion of warranties issue, but rather took them into account in its analysis of the seller's limitation of damages clause. These factors, therefore, do not serve to distinguish *Moscatiello* from the present case. Accordingly, we conclude that the disclaimer stated on Borden's invoice was inconspicuous and, consequently, ineffective.

Borden's argument that it disclaimed the warranties at issue therefore rests upon the language appearing on the drum labels. The trial court found this disclaimer to be conspicuous because it appeared "front and center" on the labels, it was in boldface type, it was the only paragraph on the label, and the heading "DISCLAIMER" and the disclaimer itself were printed in capitals, unlike the rest of the paragraph. As Advent points out, however, the disclaimer is printed in very small type. In fact, it appears to this court that the typeface, like that of the disclaimer on the back of the invoice, is one-sixteenth of an inch high. Moreover, all of the print on the label appears to be boldfaced; thus, the fact that the disclaimer and accompanying paragraph are boldfaced does not make them stand out. Finally, while the heading "DISCLAIMER" and the disclaimer itself are printed in capitals, so too are the preceding lines of text, and they are printed in larger type. Taking into account all of these factors, we conclude that this disclaimer, like that on the invoice, is inconspicuous and therefore ineffective.

## PROBLEMS

***Problem 4-13.*** Assume that a label on a product conspicuously disclaims all warranties. The first time the buyer sees the disclaimer, however, is when the product is delivered. Is the disclaimer effective? *See Bowdoin v. Showell Growers,*

*Inc.*, 817 F.2d 1543, 3 UCC Rep. Serv. 2d 1366 (11th Cir. 1987). *Cf. Hill v. Gateway 2000, Inc.*, pp. 43-46, *supra*.

***Problem 4-14.*** Should a seller be allowed to disclaim implied warranties through an inconspicuously worded provision indicating that goods are sold "as is" ? *See Lumber Mutual Insurance Co. v. Clarklift of Detroit*, 224 Mich. App. 737, 569 N.W.2d 681 (1997). Should an inconspicuous disclaimer be effective if the seller proves that the buyer knew of its existence? See White and Summers, *Uniform Commercial Code* §12.5b (5th ed.).

***Problem 4-15.*** Assume that you purchase a used car from a dealer. The dealer asks you if you would like to have a mechanic inspect the car but you refuse. Is there still an implied warranty of merchantability going along with the sale of the car? See UCC §§2-314, Official Comment 3, 2-316(3)(b) and its Official Comment 8.

***Problem 4-16.*** Suppose that you go to a swap meet and see someone selling various types of name-brand watches. One appears to be a gold Rolex watch, which the seller is selling for $50. You know that genuine Rolex watches sell for much more than that. If the watch stops running within a few months after you buy it, is there an implied warranty of merchantability that could be asserted against the seller? See UCC §2-314, Official Comment 7, and UCC §2-316(3)(c) and its Official Comment 6.

***Problem 4-17.*** A nonmerchant seller advertises a laptop in the newspaper and sells it to someone at a fair price for a used, working laptop. The seller knows that the laptop has a tendency to crash, causing loss of data, but does not tell the buyer about it. Instead, the seller tells the buyer that the computer is being sold "as is" and makes no express warranties regarding the quality of the machine. Does the seller have any liability when the laptop continues its practice of frequent crashing? Can you counsel the seller that the less the seller claims to know about the computer, the better? See UCC §2-314, Official Comment 3. See UCC §1-304.

***Problem 4-18.*** If the contract is covered by the CISG, may the seller make inconspicuous disclaimers? Should the enforceability of disclaimers be a question of "validity" that is excluded from the Convention under Article 4? Or should it instead be considered a question of contract interpretation governed by Article 8? If it is a question of "validity," should the disclaimers be analyzed under UCC section 2-316 if the UCC would apply but for the application of the CISG? See CISG Article 7(2). See also Longobardi, *Disclaimers of Implied Warranties: The 1980 United Nations Convention on Contracts for the International Sale of Goods*, 53 Fordham L. Rev. 863 (1985).

## 4. PRIVITY REQUIREMENTS

### (a) Under the UCC

Traditionally, in order to sue for breach of contract, the plaintiff would have had to be the party who contracted with the defendant or be a third-party beneficiary or assignee of a contract between the defendant and somebody else. In sale-of-goods contracts, one question that arises is whether a buyer of goods from a retailer can sue the manufacturer of goods. This is sometimes referred to as a "vertical" privity question because it involves the chain of distribution of goods from the manufacturer to the ultimate buyer. Another question that arises is whether someone who didn't buy the goods but used them can sue the seller if the goods adversely affect the user. For example, someone might purchase a toy and give the toy to her son. If the son is injured while using the unreasonably dangerous toy, could he sue the seller on a breach of warranty theory? This is sometimes referred to as a "horizontal" privity question. Vertical privity focuses on the proper defendant (e.g., the retailer or manufacturer?) while horizontal privity focuses on the proper plaintiff (e.g., the buyer or the buyer's son?). Vertical and horizontal privity questions might both exist in some cases—for example, could the son in the earlier example sue the manufacturer of the toy that was bought from a retailer?

UCC section 2-318 provides three alternatives to state legislatures for adoption dealing with privity issues. Of the three, Alternative A has been adopted by the majority of states.

Courts have gone beyond the UCC sections in imposing liability on remote sellers. In personal injury cases, courts generally do not require privity of contract because of the strict tort liability rules. Where lack of privity may still be a good defense is in the area of implied warranties and economic loss.

The following three cases show how courts handle privity issues. The first case involves personal injury and demonstrates the application of UCC section 2-318, Alternative A. As you will see, the court did not believe that Alternative A limited the situations in which an injured party could sue a seller that was not in privity with the injured party. The next two cases deal with economic loss and an attempt by the injured buyer to sue the manufacturer despite a lack of privity. The two courts take different views, the first one denying the ability of the injured party to sue based on lack of privity, and the second one permitting the action on a third-party beneficiary theory. Are the cases distinguishable? Do you prefer one approach over the other?

## REED V. CITY OF CHICAGO

United States District Court, Northern District of Illinois

263 F. Supp. 2d 1123 (2003)

Plaintiff Ruby Reed brought this action against defendants City of Chicago (City), police officers Timothy Gould, Bruce Young, Brian Pemberton, and Susan Madison (Officers), and Edwards Medical Supply, Inc. (Edwards), Cypress Medical Products, Ltd., and Cypress Medical Products, Inc. (together, Cypress), and Medline Industries (Medline), arising from her son's death in a Chicago jail cell. Defendant Cypress filed a motion to dismiss Count VI of the complaint—breach of warranty—pursuant to Federal Rule of Civil Procedure 12(b)(6). For the following reasons, Cypress's motion is denied.

### Background

Plaintiff Ruby Reed filed this suit as the special administrator of her son J.C. Reed's estate. On November 12, 2000, J.C. Reed (Reed) was allegedly arrested and brought to the City's Fifth District police station, where he was placed in a detention cell controlled and managed by the officers. The officers allegedly knew that Reed was mentally unstable, had witnessed him attempting suicide by slitting his wrists, and failed to adequately monitor the cell. The officers removed his clothing and provided him with a paper isolation gown. Plaintiff claims that Reed used this gown to hang himself and that officers found him in the cell and failed to give him proper medical care, resulting in his death.

Plaintiff further alleges that the gown was manufactured and designed by defendants Edwards, Cypress, and Medline and that these defendants breached implied and express warranties when the gown failed to tear away when used by Reed in an attempt to hang himself.

**Discussion**

The single issue we must decide is whether plaintiff, as a nonpurchaser, can recover from the manufacturer and designer of the gown for breach of warranty. Historically, Illinois law has required plaintiffs suing for breach of warranty to establish both horizontal and vertical privity. Section 2-318 of the Uniform Commercial Code ("UCC"), as adopted by the Illinois legislature, contains mandatory exceptions to the general requirement of privity:

> A seller's warranty whether express or implied extends to any natural person who is in the family or household of his buyer or who is a guest in his home if it is reasonable to expect that such person may use, consume, or be affected by the goods and who is injured in person by breach of the warranty. A seller may not exclude or limit the operation of this section.

The Illinois Supreme Court has determined that the privity is no longer an absolute requirement for breach of warranty actions. *Berry v. G.D. Searle & Co.*, 56 Ill. 2d 548, 309 N.E.2d 550 (Ill. 1974) (stating "privity is of no consequence when a buyer who purportedly has sustained personal injuries predicates recovery against a remote manufacturer for breach of an implied warranty under the code"). While section 2-318 lists specific exceptions to the privity requirement, Illinois courts have noted that this list is not necessarily exhaustive. *See Wheeler v. Sunbelt Tool Co., Inc.*, 181 Ill. App. 3d 1088, 1099, 537 N.E.2d 1332, 1340, 130 Ill. Dec. 863, 871 (1989); *see also* UCC §2-318, Comment 3 (stating that "the section in this form is neutral and is not intended to enlarge or restrict the developing case law on whether the seller's warranties, given to his buyer who resells, extend to other persons in the distributive chain").

The vast majority of cases examining the limits of section 2-318 in Illinois have dealt with the employment context, expanding the class of potential breach of warranty plaintiffs to employees of the ultimate purchaser. In these cases courts have allowed employees to sue for breach of warranty despite a lack of horizontal privity.[2]

In cases examining the limits of section 2-318 in other contexts, courts have been reluctant to find additional exceptions to the privity requirement.

---

2. We note that the cases expanding the potential plaintiff class deal with personal injury. The Illinois Supreme Court has declined to extend *Berry* and abolish the privity requirement in cases involving solely economic losses. *Szajna v. General Motors Corp.*, 115 Ill. 2d 294, 311, 503 N.E.2d 760, 767, 104 Ill. Dec. 898, 905 (Ill. 1986). The Illinois Supreme Court later made clear that the privity requirement was not abolished in *all* cases where plaintiff alleges physical harm as a result of breach of warranty. *Board of Educ. of City of Chicago v. A, C and S, Inc.*, 131 Ill. 2d 428, 461-62, 546 N.E.2d 580, 595-96, 137 Ill. Dec. 635, 650-51 (Ill. 1989).

*See Frank v. Edward Hines Lumber Co.*, 327 Ill. App. 3d, 113, 761 N.E.2d 1257, 260 Ill. Dec. 701 (2001); *Lukwinski v. Stone Container Corp.*, 312 Ill. App. 3d 385, 726 N.E.2d 665, 244 Ill. Dec. 690 (2000); *Hemphill v. Sayers*, 552 F. Supp. 685 (S.D. Ill. 1982). In *Hemphill*, the court refused to allow a breach of warranty claim by a university football player against the manufacturer of his helmet. 552 F. Supp. at 690-693. The court determined that while courts may expand the class of vertical non-privity plaintiffs, the class of horizontal non-privity plaintiffs is expressly limited by the language of section 2-318 to a "natural person who is in the family or household of his buyer or who is a guest in his home." *Id.* at 690-691. *Hemphill* was, however, decided prior to decisions expanding the plaintiff class to include employees of the ultimate purchaser. Subsequent decisions have recognized that the exceptions to horizontal privity are not absolutely limited by the language of the UCC.

While no Illinois courts have expanded the plaintiff class for breach of warranty actions beyond employees, we believe that the law requires us to do so here. The beneficiary of any warranty made by the manufacturer and designer of the gown is necessarily a potentially suicidal detainee like Reed. If protection is not provided to plaintiffs like Reed, any warranty as to the safety of the gown would have little, if any, effect. In designing and manufacturing the gown, defendants contemplated that the users of the gown would be detainees. Moreover, the safety of these detainees was necessarily a part of the bargain, whether explicitly or implicitly, between the seller and buyer. For these reasons, a detainee of the City like Reed must be able to enforce the protections of any warranties made by the manufacturer and designer of the gown.

**Conclusion**

For the foregoing reasons, defendants' motion to dismiss Count VI of the complaint is denied.

## QUESTIONS

1. Do you agree with the court that it is necessary to permit the plaintiff to sue to give effect to any warranty regarding the safety of the gown? What would happen if the motion to dismiss were granted?
2. On the merits, did the gown cause the prisoner's death? See UCC §2-314, Official Comment 13; *Daniell v. Ford Motor Co.*, 581 F. Supp. 728, 38 UCC Rep. Serv. 464 (D.N.M. 1984) (woman attempted to commit suicide by locking herself in trunk and had a change of heart; she then sued because she couldn't unlock herself from the inside).

## PROFESSIONAL LENS PLAN V. POLARIS LEASING CORP.

Supreme Court of Kansas

234 Kan. 742, 675 P.2d 887 (1984)

Professional Lens Plan, Inc., reached an agreement with Impact Systems for acquisition of an Ohio Scientific computer on or about August 15, 1979. The computer was delivered in September, 1979.

Problems in the operation of the computer commenced shortly after its delivery that were ultimately traced, at least in part, to an allegedly defective hard disc, a computer component part, that had been purchased by Ohio Scientific from the disc's manufacturer, Okidata Corporation.

The first such issue concerns whether the district court erred in finding Professional Lens had a cause of action against Okidata. Stated more specifically, the question is whether Kansas permits a corporate ultimate purchaser, who has incurred only economic loss, as opposed to personal injury or property damage, to recover on theories of breach of implied warranty of fitness and merchantability from a manufacturer with whom the ultimate purchaser was not in contractual privity.

Privity of contract is defined by *Black's Law Dictionary* 1362 (4th ed. rev. 1968) as follows:

> *Privity of contract* is that connection or relationship which exists between two or more contracting parties. It is essential to the maintenance of an action on any contract that there should subsist a privity between the plaintiff and defendant in respect of the matter sued on.

In *Booth v. Scheer,* 105 Kan. 643, 185 Pac. 898 (1919), 8 A.L.R. 663, the general common law rule requiring privity in sales contracts was stated as follows:

> Ordinarily there is no privity of contract between the original vendor of personal property and third persons who may purchase or acquire the property from the original vendee; and the original vendor's warranty is a personal obligation between him and his own vendee, and it does not run with the property like covenants concerning real estate.

Problems arose with the strict application of the requirement of privity where manufacturers sold inherently dangerous products to dealers who, in turn, sold them to consumers. An exception to the rule requiring privity was frequently held to exist in situations where a manufactured human foodstuff caused personal injury by virtue of a defect.

K.S.A. 84-2-318 sets limits on persons who may assert breach of implied warranty actions under 84-2-314 (merchantability) and 84-2-315 (fitness for a particular purpose). K.S.A. 84-2-318 is Alternative B of UCC section 2-318.

Professional Lens is the buyer of the computer; hence any question of extending the buyer's warranty to others (the whole purpose of 84-2-318) does not arise in regard to Professional Lens. Additionally, if same did apply in principle, Professional Lens is not a "natural person" who was personally injured. Determination of the issue before us is not a matter of statutory construction.

K.S.A. 84-2-318 has been characterized as relating wholly to "horizontal privity," that is, extending the class of plaintiff beyond that of the actual purchaser. The question of whether a plaintiff can extend the class of defendants beyond that of the seller is sometimes characterized as a matter of "vertical privity." These terms are technically misnomers as imposition of implied warranties between persons who are in the buyer-seller relationship is an exception to the requirement of privity.

The propriety of allowing a non-privity ultimate purchaser who has suffered only direct or consequential economic loss to recover from a remote manufacturer of an allegedly defective product under an implied warranty theory has been a matter of considerable debate within the legal profession.

White and Summers, *Uniform Commercial Code* (2d ed. 1980), have squarely addressed the issue of direct and consequential economic loss damages of a non-privity ultimate purchaser in implied warranty actions. Speaking of direct economic loss, Messrs. White and Summers have said:

> [T]he law permits a non-privity buyer to recover for direct economic loss if the remote seller has breached an *express* warranty. Where the buyer cannot show reliance on express representations by the remote seller, however, the case law is in conflict. *The majority of courts still appear to hold that absent such reliance, a non-privity buyer, whether commercial or consumer, cannot recover for direct economic loss on either an express or an implied warranty theory.* We have found only two commercial cases to the contrary.
>
> A minority of courts, however, permit "warranty" recovery for direct economic loss by non-privity buyers who are ordinary *consumers.* §11-5, pp. 407-08. (Emphasis supplied.)

Of consequential economic loss White and Summers have stated:

> *Consequential* economic loss includes loss of profits, loss of good will or business reputation and other loss proximately resulting from a defective product beyond direct economic loss as defined in the preceding section (loss of bargain, cost of repair, replacement cost, and the like). Recall that the Code neither authorizes nor bars recovery by a non-privity purchaser for economic loss—whether consequential or direct. *The vast majority of courts do not allow non-privity consumer purchasers to recover for consequential economic loss.* Even courts that allow non-privity consumer purchasers to recover for direct economic loss do not permit such purchasers to recover for consequential economic loss. Note that *consumer* buyers ordinarily do not suffer any consequential economic loss and only seek recovery for direct economic losses such as loss of bargain or costs of repair.
>
> We concur in this majority view. §11-6, p. 409. (Emphasis supplied.)

In *State ex rel. Western Seed v. Campbell,* 250 Or. 262, 442 P.2d 215 (1968), the Oregon Supreme Court commented:

> A buyer whose seller proves to be irresponsible will understandably seek relief further afield. But to allow a non-privity warranty action to vindicate every disappointed consumer would unduly complicate the code's scheme, which recognizes the consensual elements of commerce. Disclaimers and limitations of certain warranties and remedies are matters for bargaining. Strict-liability actions between buyers and remote sellers could lend themselves to the proliferation of unprovable claims by disappointed bargain hunters, with little discernible social benefit. Because the buyer and his seller will normally have engaged in at least one direct transaction, litigation between these parties should ordinarily be simpler and less costly than litigation between buyer and remote seller. Where the purchaser of an unmerchantable product suffers only loss of profits, his remedy for the breach of warranty is against his immediate seller unless he can predicate liability upon some fault on the part of a remote seller.

White and Summers have observed:

> Even if relevant policies justify allowing non-privity consumers to recover for direct economic loss, there can be no justification in the usual case for allowing non-privity consumer buyers to recover for consequential economic losses they sustain. Remote buyers may use a seller's goods for unknown purposes from which enormous losses might ensue. Since the remote seller cannot predict the purposes for which the goods will be used he faces unknown liability and may not be able to insure himself. Insurers are hesitant to insure against risks they cannot measure. Moreover, here more than in personal injury and property damage cases, it is appropriate to recognize the traditional rights of parties to make their own contract. If a remote seller wishes to sell at a lower price and exclude liability for consequential economic loss to sub-purchasers, why should we deny him that right? Why should we design a system that forces him to bear the unforeseeable consequential economic losses of remote purchasers? Indeed, by forcing the buyer to bear such losses we may save costly law suits and even some economic losses against which buyers, knowing they have the responsibility, may protect themselves. In short, we believe that *a buyer should pick his seller with care and recover any economic loss from that seller and not from parties remote from the transaction.* §11-6, pp. 409-10. (Emphasis supplied.)

The economic loss claimed by Professional Lens appears to be consequential rather than direct under the following White and Summers, *Uniform Commercial Code* (2d ed. 1980) definition:

> Direct economic loss . . . includes ordinary loss of bargain damages: the difference between the actual value of the goods accepted and the value they would have had if they had been as warranted. Courts will also frequently measure direct economic loss by the purchaser's cost of replacement or cost of repair. "Consequential economic loss," on the other hand, encompasses all economic harm a purchaser suffers beyond direct economic loss as defined above. Thus, consequential economic loss includes loss of profits resulting from failure of the goods to function as warranted, loss of goodwill and loss of business reputation. § 11-5, p. 406.

However, for purposes of this issue, we need only utilize the general term, economic loss, as we see no valid reason for distinguishing between direct and consequential economic loss in the circumstances herein.

Public policy reasons are the basis on which implied warranties have been extended to non-privity manufacturers whose inherently dangerous products cause physical injuries to buyers. However, imposing implied warranties on non-privity manufacturers for a buyer's economic loss is a major step, not to be taken lightly. If contractual privity is not necessary to maintain an action for breach of an implied warranty of fitness (UCC §2-315), how is it possible for a remote seller to have reason to know any particular purpose for which its goods are required by an unknown ultimate buyer? What is the time of contracting between a remote manufacturer and an ultimate purchaser? How does a buyer rely upon the skill or judgment of a seller it has never met or had any dealing with and maybe doesn't even know the existence of?

The problems do not end with section 2-315, they only begin. For example, how is a remote manufacturer to afford itself of the ability to exclude or modify warranties under UCC §2-316, when the remote manufacturer does not know to whom it must exclude or modify its warranties? In turn, how is an ultimate purchaser, pursuant to UCC §2-607(3)(a), to give notice of defect to a remote manufacturer whom it does not know? Further, how is UCC §2-719 authorizing contractual modification or limitation of remedy to operate between parties who have not dealt directly with each other? Specifically, how is a remote manufacturer to avail itself of UCC §2-719(3), which permits limitation or exclusion of consequential damage liability? An across-the-board extension of implied warranties to non-privity manufacturers or sellers, without regard to the nature of either the involved product or the type of damage sought, would spawn numerous problems in the operation of Article 2 of the Uniform Commercial Code.

The computer and its component part, the hard disc, are clearly not products that are inherently dangerous. Here damages are sought only for economic loss, no personal injuries or property damage being involved. We find no public policy dictates extending implied warranties of fitness and merchantability to the non-privity manufacturers herein.

We conclude implied warranties of fitness and merchantability are not extended to a remote seller or manufacturer of an allegedly defective product that is not inherently dangerous for only economic loss suffered by a buyer who is not in contractual privity with the remote seller or manufacturer. Accordingly, the district court erred in holding that Professional Lens had a cause of action against Okidata Corporation for economic loss based on breach of implied warranty.

## Touchet Valley Grain Growers v. Opp & Seibold General Construction, Inc.

Supreme Court of Washington

119 Wash. 2d 334, 831 P.2d 724 (1992)

Touchet Valley Grain Growers sued Opp & Seibold, National Surety Corp., and Truss-T Structures over the collapse of Touchet Valley's "flathouse"[1] grain storage building in October 1985. Opp & Seibold constructed the steel-frame building under a contract negotiated in 1984 with Touchet Valley. Opp & Seibold, in turn, contracted with Truss-T Structures to design the building and supply its components. National Surety carried Opp & Seibold's performance bond for the $1.2 million contract price.

Evidence of faulty construction or design appeared in the spring of 1985, when the flathouse building's frame buckled at the roof. Opp & Seibold and Truss-T Structures attempted repairs, but on October 24, 1985, an exterior wall failed, spilling grain from the storage building and damaging roof beams beyond repair.

Touchet Valley claimed breach of implied warranties of fitness for a particular purpose and merchantability and breach of express warranties. The trial

1. A "flathouse" is a noncylindrical grain-storage facility. It is basically a rectangular building with a heavy steel frame, sheet metal liner, and sheet metal walls and roof. The flathouse in this case is 1.5 times the length of a football field.

court granted Truss-T Structures's motion for summary judgment dismissing the warranty claims.

The court of appeals certified to this court the question of whether a third-party beneficiary analysis can be used to pursue claims for breach of implied warranties in a product liability claim.

Dismissing the warranty claims against Truss-T Structures, the trial court determined that privity did not exist under UCC section 2-318 between Truss-T, the manufacturer, and Touchet Valley, the end user. We reverse and reinstate Touchet Valley's breach of warranty claims. We hold that Touchet Valley is a third-party beneficiary of implied and express warranties made by Truss-T Structures to Opp & Seibold, and as such is entitled to raise these warranty claims.

Because designing and selling building components constitutes a transaction in goods, Touchet Valley's warranty claims are controlled by UCC Article 2. UCC section 2-318 limits warranty claims against a *seller* to those brought by natural persons in a household or such others as might reasonably be expected to use the product.

Touchet Valley correctly argues that UCC section 2-318 limits only horizontal privity; that is, privity between the seller and the immediate purchaser. The type of privity at issue here is *vertical* privity—privity between a manufacturer and end users down the distribution chain. Unlike horizontal privity, which is governed by statute, development of vertical privity is found in case law. UCC section 2-318, Official Comment 3. We note the Washington commentator's added emphasis:

> Official Comment 3 is most emphatic that this section is otherwise intended to be neutral on the question of whether a seller's warranties extend to other than the original buyer.

Washington Comment, RCWA 62A.2-318.

Truss-T argues that the Legislature's enactment of RCW 62A.2-318 deliberately rejected broader alternatives for section 2-318 presented by drafters of the Uniform Commercial Code. True, the National Conference of Commissioners on Uniform State Laws offered states more expansive vertical privity alternatives, but not until after Washington adopted section 2-318 in 1965. See Laws of 1965, 1st Ex. Sess., ch. 157, §2-318, p. 2365; 2 W. Hawkland, *Uniform Commercial Code Series* §2-318 (1992). When Washington adopted UCC Article 2, only one choice existed for section 2-318. And, as Hawkland explains, the UCC drafters' strict definition of horizontal privity was not meant to restrict the concept of vertical privity. 2 W. Hawkland, *supra*.

We believe the commentary to RCW 62A.2-318 is unmistakable: Vertical privity is a different concept from horizontal privity. We also believe the Legislature spoke clearly when it defined section 2-318 as neutral on vertical privity and left its development to the courts. We hold that vertical privity controls warranty issues here between a remote manufacturer and ultimate purchaser.

### A. Implied Warranties

Touchet Valley relies on *Kadiak Fisheries Co. v. Murphy Diesel Co.*, 70 Wash. 2d 153, 422 P.2d 496 (1967), arguing that privity is satisfied because Touchet

Valley is a third-party beneficiary of the implied warranties Truss-T gave Opp & Seibold under RCW 62A.2-314 and RCW 62A.2-315. In *Kadiak,* this court held that a purchaser of a specially built marine diesel motor could sue the manufacturer for breach of implied warranties even though the purchaser bought the diesel motor from a retail dealer. The court found that the manufacturer's implied warranties of merchantability and fitness for a particular purpose given to its purchaser, the dealer, extended to the end user. The decision relied on the sum of interaction and expectations between the purchaser and the manufacturer: The manufacturer knew the identity, purpose, and requirements of the purchaser's specifications and shipped the motor directly to the purchaser. *Kadiak,* at 164-165, 422 P.2d 496. In addition, the manufacturer sent a company official, the regional sales representative, and a service technician to help with installation of the motor in the purchaser's fishing boat. Then, after repeated mechanical problems, the manufacturer attempted to fix the engine. *Kadiak,* at 165, 422 P.2d 496.

Truss-T Structures argues that Touchet Valley's reliance on *Kadiak* is misplaced because *Kadiak* was decided before the UCC became effective in Washington. If anything, Truss-T argues, case law has tightened the privity requirement. It cites several post-UCC cases, all of which are distinguishable.

In *Baughn v. Honda Motor Co.,* 107 Wash. 2d 127, 727 P.2d 655 (1986), this court disallowed an action against a manufacturer for breach of implied warranties brought by parents of children injured while riding a motorscooter. The court held that the parents did not show privity between the manufacturer and ultimate purchaser. It relied on two decisions interpreting the horizontal privity provision of RCW 62A.2-318. *Baughn,* at 151 n.54, 727 P.2d 655 [citing *Daughtry v. Jet Aeration Co.,* 91 Wash. 2d 704, 592 P.2d 631 (1979); *Berg v. General Motors Corp.,* 87 Wash. 2d 584, 555 P.2d 818 (1976)]. However, *Baughn* is distinguishable from this case (and *Kadiak*) on the issue of implied warranties because the manufacturer was not actually involved with the ultimate purchaser and the analysis was not based on a third-party beneficiary argument. *Cf. Lidstrand v. Silvercrest Indus.,* 28 Wash. App. 359, 623 P.2d 710 (1981); *Schroeder v. Fageol Motors, Inc.,* 12 Wash. App. 161, 528 P.2d 992 (1974), *rev'd in part on other grounds in* 86 Wash. 2d 256, 544 P.2d 20 (1975).

The *Kadiak* analysis remains sound. Regardless of whether *Kadiak* predated the UCC in Washington, it supplements the code unless displaced by a code provision. UCC §1-103. Applying the *Kadiak* analysis to the facts before us, we note that Truss-T knew Touchet Valley's identity, its purpose, and its requirements for the grain storage building. Truss-T designed the building knowing the specifications were the purchaser's. As was its business practice, Truss-T delivered the components to Touchet Valley's construction site. And, when the first beams buckled in March 1985, Truss-T joined Opp & Seibold to attempt repairs.

We find the sum of this interaction indistinguishable from *Kadiak.* We reverse the trial court and hold that Touchet Valley Grain Growers was the intended beneficiary of Truss-T's implied warranties to Opp & Seibold. Those warranties assured the merchantability of Truss-T's fabricated building components and their fitness for Touchet Valley's known particular purpose.

## B. Express Warranties

Touchet Valley contends that Truss-T made express warranties in its advertising brochure, its price book, and its purchase order. Touchet Valley further argues that Opp & Seibold acted as agent for Truss-T, thus Opp & Seibold's representatives of quality and performance were also Truss-T's.

Truss-T Structures reiterates that privity must be shown in an express warranty action between a remote manufacturer and an end user, and claims no privity exists here. But we believe *Baughn* expands privity to include the express representations at issue here. "The privity requirement is relaxed, however, when a manufacturer makes express representations, in advertising or otherwise, to a plaintiff." *Baughn,* 107 Wash. 2d at 151-152, 727 P.2d 655. Recovery for breach of an express warranty is contingent on a plaintiff's knowledge of the representation. *Baughn,* at 152, 727 P.2d 655.

*Advertising Brochure.* The language we cite from *Baughn* incorporates the substance of UCC section 2-313. *Baughn* rejected an express warranty claim because the claim was based on puffing in advertising, not on an express representation. This court held the representations "appear to be Honda's opinion or commendation regarding minibikes rather than affirmations of fact about the goods." *Baughn,* at 152, 727 P.2d 655.

Touchet Valley argues that a sales brochure produced by Truss-T promises, directly or by description, a building of certain quality, which Truss-T failed to deliver. In this brochure, Truss-T Structures states that it "can design to your specifications" and that fabrication "is carefully checked by our quality control department." It also states Truss-T's designs will "meet the strictest building codes" and "[y]our particular requirements will determine the most suitable style of construction."

Truss-T counters that its brochure only generally describes its standards, products, and methods. It argues that Touchet Valley never suggested "that there is any deficiency in Truss-T's general qualifications or general product quality." Their argument misses the point: Truss-T tells the ultimate customers, not its dealers, that its designs will be tailor-made and of highest quality. Here, Touchet Valley claims that its grain storage building was improperly designed or constructed, and was not of highest quality, since it collapsed.

*Price Book and Purchase Order.* Touchet Valley claims provisions in Truss-T's price book, labeled "standard warranty," and in its purchase order guaranteeing quality assurance, benefits Touchet Valley. In particular, it points out that the price book warranty guarantees materials for a year.

Truss-T argues that a set duration in a warranty provision does not benefit the end user here, because neither *Lidstrand* nor *Schroeder* supports "the proposition that a manufacturer's warranty that extends to future performance always benefits the end user. . . ." Future performance does not *always* benefit the end user, but Touchet Valley's argument is not as simple as Truss-T suggests. The court in *Schroeder* held that a time-bound warranty against defects in a diesel truck motor protected the current operator, whether or not the operator was the original purchaser. Truss-T points out that a manufacturer's witness in *Schroeder* established that the diesel motor manufacturer intended its warranty to benefit the end user and that the warranty substantially followed one given by the dealer. Truss-T argues that none of the factors in *Schroeder* is present here.

However, Truss-T overlooks *Schroeder*'s reasoning, which supports Touchet Valley's claim. The court in *Schroeder* stated:

> The engine was warranted to be free of defects "for two years or 100,000 miles or 3,600 hours of *operation*." . . . Obviously, the warranty is for the benefit of the *operator*.

*Schroeder,* 12 Wash. App. at 165, 528 P.2d 992.

The court in *Schroeder* determined that the purchaser was a third-party beneficiary of the manufacturer's warranty because warranty benefits flowed directly to the third party and were not indirect, inconsequential, or incidental. The court noted the manufacturer attempted repairs without success. *Schroeder.*

In *Lidstrand,* Truss-T contends, the court specifically emphasized that a manufacturer did not limit a 12-month mobile home warranty to the original purchaser. But the court, by pointing out that omission, merely reinforced its conclusion.

> On its face, a warranty that the home will be defect-free for 12 months is a promise that there will be no defects during that time, regardless of who happens to own the product. We conclude that any owner of the mobile home during the one-year warranty period was intended to benefit from Silvercrest's warranty.

*Lidstrand,* 28 Wash. App. at 363-364, 623 P.2d 710. As in *Schroeder,* the court in *Lidstrand* found the end user to be the intended third-party beneficiary of a manufacturer's warranty that existed for a set time. The court cited *Schroeder* as a basis for its reasoning. *Lidstrand,* at 363, 623 P.2d 710.

Touchet Valley argues convincingly that the one-year duration for Truss-T's warranty must be read to benefit the owner, necessarily and directly. For all practical purposes, Truss-T's one-year warranty on its fabricated components would mean little to the contractor-dealer who builds the structure and moves on to the next job. We believe the court of appeals in *Schroeder* and *Lidstrand* correctly determined that warranties against product defects extend for a definite time, benefit the end user, and not just the first purchaser. We hold the price book warranty, as well as the quality assurance in Truss-T's purchase order form, benefited Touchet Valley.

*Agency.* Having ruled that Truss-T's express warranties extended to Touchet Valley as a third-party beneficiary, we need not reach the question whether Opp & Seibold extended express warranties as an agent for Truss-T. We hold the trial court erred in dismissing Touchet Valley's warranty claims.

## NOTES AND QUESTIONS

1. Is the lack of privity defense simply a technical defense that prevents a buyer from suing a manufacturer of defective products? Does it provide an inappropriate shield for such manufacturers? Or is there a good reason, at least

sometimes, to require privity? Note the policy discussion in *Professional Lens Plan* as to why lack of privity should be a defense in cases involving economic loss. Are these policy considerations being ignored in *Touchet Valley* or are the cases distinguishable factually? In considering these questions, it can be noted that the manufacturer loses control of the goods once they leave the manufacturer's possession. The manufacturer does not know what the retailer does with the goods and does not know what the retailer tells the ultimate buyer about the goods. The manufacturer does not know what the ultimate buyer intends to do with the goods. The manufacturer may have a difficult time disclaiming any warranties because it is not communicating directly with the ultimate buyer. The manufacturer may be in a different jurisdiction, raising choice-of-law problems. A question may also arise as to whether any statute of limitations begins to run when the goods leave the manufacturer or when the ultimate buyer purchases the goods. For a discussion of some of the pros and cons of the privity requirement, see Holdych, *A Seller's Responsibilities To Remote Purchasers For Breach of Warranty in Sales of Goods Under Washington Law*, 28 Seattle U. L. Rev. 239 (2005).

***Problem 4-19.*** BB & B, owners of a rock-crushing business bought a used tractor from Dravo Equipment Co. The tractor came with a warranty as follows: "This price includes new, rebuilt engine and to carry 1500 hours of 100 percent engine warranty." The warranty was specifically bargained for as part of the sale. BB & B then sold the tractor along with the rock-crushing business to German & Hunter. At the time of this sale, German & Hunter read the warranty and checked to make sure that 1500 hours had not yet run. Subsequently, when the engine proved to be defective, still within the 1500 hour period, German & Hunter sought to hold Dravo Equipment Co. responsible under the terms of the express warranty. Are German & Hunter barred from asserting breach of warranty because of lack of privity? Should express warranties be distinguished from implied warranties? Should it make a difference if German & Hunter never read the warranty before deciding to buy the tractor? Should it matter if the damages are direct or consequential (note the discussion of this distinction in *Professional Lens Plan* above)? See *Dravo Equipment Co. v. German*, 73 Or. App. 165, 698 P.2d 63 (1985).

### (b) Under the CISG

The CISG does not have any section comparable to UCC section 2-318 and says nothing about privity. Remember that the CISG does not apply to consumer goods transactions and also does not apply to any personal injury claims (CISG Articles 2 and 5), so it may not be as objectionable to require a buyer to proceed only against the immediate seller. With an international chain of distribution, it may also be less complicated to require privity of contract. In some situations, however, perhaps it is appropriate to permit a direct action by the buyer against the manufacturer. Please consider the following problem:

***Problem 4-20.*** Buyer Manufacturing Company, located in Country *A*, purchased a machine for use in its business from XYZ Dealership, also located in Country *A*. It purchased the machine after reading an advertisement from the machine's manufacturer, Remote Machine Co., which was located in Country *B*. Both countries have adopted the CISG. The advertisement touted the many fine qualities of the machine and directed interested purchasers to contact licensed dealerships from a list contained in the advertisement. XYZ was one of the dealerships mentioned. When Buyer took delivery of the machine, XYZ also gave Buyer a document from Remote entitled "Warranty" that indicated that the machine would perform the functions listed or that the purchaser could take the machine back to the dealer from which it was purchased for repairs. The machine never performed as indicated, and Buyer took the machine back to XYZ several times. Before the machine was repaired, XYZ went out of business. Buyer would like to sue Remote. Can it? What are some of the practical problems in answering this question either yes or no? See CISG Article 4. See also, J. Honnold, *Uniform Law for International Sales* §63 (3d ed. 1999).

## 5. RELATIONSHIP OF UCC WARRANTY ACTIONS TO CONSUMER PROTECTION LAW

Congress and the states have passed laws that give additional protections to consumers in sale of goods cases. The Magnuson-Moss Warranty Act, 15 USC section 2301, et seq., has sometimes been referred to as a "Truth in Warranting" act in that it requires sellers of goods to "conspicuously disclose in simple and readily ascertainable language the terms and conditions" of warranties. 15 USC §2302.

### (a) Scope of Magnuson-Moss

Under Magnuson-Moss, a "written warranty" is defined as "any written affirmation of fact or written promise made in connection with the sale of a consumer product by a supplier to a buyer" that "relates to the nature of the material or workmanship," promises a level of performance, or promises that goods will remain defect-free. Also included are promises to repair or provide refunds. As is the case with UCC section 2-313, the warranty must be part of the basis of the bargain. 15 USC §2301(6). When you buy a product, you may notice that it is conspicuously labeled a "limited warranty" or more infrequently a "full warranty." This disclosure is mandated by Magnuson-Moss, and if the warranty is labeled a "full warranty," it must comply with the Federal Minimum Standard for Warranties spelled out in section 104 of the Act. 15 USC §2304. If you take a look at the requirements listed, you will understand why most warranties are therefore "limited warranties" ! The Federal Trade Commission fleshes out the requirements of Magnuson-Moss in regulations to be found at 16 C.F.R. Parts 700-703.

Magnuson-Moss applies to goods which are "normally" used for personal, family, or household purposes. 15 USC §2301(1). "Consumer" is defined to include a "buyer (other than for purposes of resale) of any consumer product." 15 USC §2301(3). So would a passenger car purchased by a business be included within Magnuson-Moss's coverage? Why would it make sense to include it?

## Szubski v. Mercedes-Benz, U.S.A.

Court of Common Pleas of Ohio, Cuyahoga County

124 Ohio Misc. 2d 82, 796 N.E.2d 81(2003)

This is an action for consumer relief arising from the lease of an automobile. Plaintiffs Ralph Szubski and Computer Jungle, Inc. seek damages under the Magnuson-Moss Warranty Act, Section 2301 et seq., Title 15, U.S. Code (Counts I and II).

This matter is before the court on the motion of defendant Mercedes-Benz, U.S.A., L.L.C., ("MBUSA") to dismiss Counts I and II of the first amended complaint for failure to state a claim upon which relief can be granted.

In Count I of the first amended complaint, plaintiffs allege a claim for breach of written warranty pursuant to the Magnuson-Moss Warranty Act, Section 2301 et seq., Title 15, U.S. Code. In support of this claim, plaintiffs allege the following: that they are a lessee of a consumer product; that they received the vehicle during the duration of the written warranty period applicable to the vehicle; that MBUSA is a "person" engaged in the business of making a consumer product directly available to plaintiffs; that the Magnuson-Moss Warranty Act applies because the vehicle was manufactured and leased after July 4, 1975, and cost in excess of $10; that the lease was accompanied by written factory warranties covering any nonconformities or defects in material or workmanship; and that plaintiffs have suffered damages as a direct and proximate result of MBUSA's failure to comply with its written warranty.

In Count II, plaintiffs allege a claim for breach of implied warranty of merchantability pursuant to the Magnuson-Moss Warranty Act. In support of this claim, plaintiffs allege the following: that the leased vehicle was subject to an implied warranty of merchantability as defined in section 2301(7), running from MBUSA to plaintiffs; that MBUSA is a supplier of consumer goods as a "person" engaged in the business of making a consumer product directly available to plaintiffs; that the vehicle was impliedly warranted to be substantially free of defects and nonconformities in both material and workmanship, and thereby fit for the ordinary purpose for which it was intended; that the alleged defects render the vehicle unmerchantable, unreliable, and/or unsafe and not fit for the ordinary purpose for which the vehicle was intended; and that as a result of the breaches of implied warranty, plaintiffs are without the reasonable value of the vehicle and have suffered damages.

### II. Issues

The main issue before the court is whether the Magnuson-Moss Warranty Act, Section 2301 et seq., is applicable to breach-of-warranty actions involving leases. MBUSA argues that the unambiguous language of the statute excludes lease transactions. MBUSA urges the court to follow the holdings of other state and federal courts that have allegedly determined that Congress knowingly opted not to include leases within the scope of the statute. In addition, MBUSA argues that the legislative history of the statute supports a finding that lease transactions are excluded.

### III. Opinion

The Magnuson-Moss Warranty Act, Section 2301 et seq., Title 15, U.S. Code (the "Act"), was enacted by Congress in response to misuse by merchants of express warranties and disclaimers. The Act mandates certain guidelines in connection with written warranties. Where written warranties are given, they invalidate attempts to disclaim implied warranties. The law is aimed at written warranties and service contracts made in connection with the sale of "consumer products" (tangible personal property normally used for personal, family, or household purposes). Section 2301(1). Under the statute, no seller is required to give an express written warranty, but if one is offered, it must comply with the standards set forth in the law.

Under the Act, a consumer who is damaged by the failure of a supplier, warrantor, or service contractor to comply with any obligation under the Act, or under a written warranty, implied warranty, or service contract, may bring a suit for damages and other legal and equitable relief, and, if successful, may recover attorney's fees. Section 2310(d).

In this case, in order to state a viable cause of action, plaintiffs must establish that the automobile in question is a "consumer product." A "consumer product" is defined in section 2301(1) as:

> [A]ny tangible personal property which is distributed in commerce and which is normally used for personal, family, or household purposes (including any such property intended to be attached to or installed in any real property without regard to whether it is so attached or installed).

{¶14} The regulations promulgated under the Act further amplify this definition:

> This means that a product is a "consumer product" if the use of that product is not uncommon. The percentage of sales or the use to which a product is put by any individual buyer is not determinative. For example, products such as automobiles and typewriters, which are used for both personal and commercial purposes come within the definition of consumer product. Where it is unclear whether a particular product is covered under the definition of consumer product, any ambiguity will be resolved in favor of coverage.

*Business Modeling Techniques, Inc. v. Gen. Motors Corp.*(1984), 123 Misc. 2d 605, 607, 474 N.Y.S.2d 258, 260, quoting Section 700.1(a), Title 16, C.F.R. (1983).

It is generally recognized that an automobile is a "consumer product" under the Act. Here, plaintiffs have alleged that the automobile was leased for the personal use of Szubski. Clearly, the complaint states that the E320S is a "consumer product."

In addition, for purposes of the Act, a "supplier" is "any person engaged in the business of making a consumer product directly or indirectly available to consumers." Section 2301(4). In addition, a "warrantor" is defined to mean "any supplier or other person who gives or offers to give a written warranty or who is or may be obligated under an implied warranty." Here, plaintiffs have alleged that MBUSA is in the business of manufacturing, selling, and distributing motor vehicles and related equipment and services, as well as marketing, supplying, and selling written warranties. Therefore, plaintiffs have alleged that MBUSA is both a "supplier" and a "warrantor" under the Act.

Plaintiffs must also establish that they are "consumers" under the meaning of the Act. The term "consumer" is defined in section 2301(3) as:

> [A] buyer (other than for purposes of resale) of any consumer product, any person to whom such product is transferred during the duration of an implied or written warranty (or service contract) applicable to the product, and any other person who is entitled by the terms of such warranty (or service contract) or under applicable State law to enforce against the warrantor (or service contractor) the obligations of the warranty (or service contract).

Accordingly, there are three classes of individuals that may qualify as a "consumer" : (1) buyers, (2) transferees, and (3) persons entitled to enforce the warranty. Here, plaintiffs have alleged that they leased the automobile during the time period in which a written four-year or 50,000-mile "bumper to bumper" warranty issued by the manufacturer was in effect. Plaintiffs have also alleged that the automobile was subject to an implied warranty of merchantability. This is sufficient to establish that the automobile was transferred to plaintiffs during the effective period of the warranties. Thus, plaintiffs have alleged sufficient facts to show that they are "consumers" within the meaning of the Act.

MBUSA argues that the Act does not cover breach-of-warranty actions for leased vehicles. Specifically, MBUSA argues that the Act is ambiguous as to the meaning of the terms "buyer" and "sale" as those terms are used in the definitions of "written warranty" and "implied warranty."

Written warranty" is defined in Section 2301(6) as:

> (A) any written affirmation of fact or written promise made in connection with the sale of a consumer product by a supplier to a buyer which relates to the nature of the material or workmanship and affirms promises that such material or workmanship is defect free or will meet a specified level of performance over a specified period of time, or
>
> (B) any undertaking in writing in connection with the sale by a supplier of a consumer product to refund, repair, replace, or take other remedial action with respect to such product in the event that such product fails to meet the specifications set forth in the undertaking,
>
> which written affirmation, promise, or undertaking becomes part of the basis of the bargain between a supplier and a buyer for purposes other than resale of such product.

In addition, "implied warranty" is defined in section 2301(7) as "an implied warranty arising under State law * * * in connection with the sale by a supplier of a consumer product."

According to MBUSA, under the Act, a sale to a consumer with a passage of title is required in order for there to be a written or implied warranty. MBUSA suggests that since the Act does not define "buyer" or "sale" the court should rely on the Uniform Commercial Code ("UCC") to define those terms. Under the UCC, "sale" is defined to require "passing of title." UCC §2-106(1). "Buyer" is defined as "a person who buys or contracts to buy goods." UCC §2-103(1)(a). In addition, MBUSA argues that the common meaning of "sale" is "the transfer of ownership from one person to another for a price." Merriam-Webster Collegiate Dictionary (19th ed. 2000). According to MBUSA, plaintiffs are neither "buyers" nor parties to a "sale" because there is no transfer of title in a lease transaction. Therefore, MBUSA contends that plaintiffs cannot sue under the Act.

In support of its argument, MBUSA cites *DiCintio v. DaimlerChrysler Corp.* (2002), 97 N.Y.2d 463, 742 N.Y.S.2d 182, 768 N.E.2d 1121. In *DiCintio,* the New York Court of Appeals held that the Act did not apply to a 36-month lease with an option to buy. The court held that a lessee was not a "consumer" because he was neither a buyer, a transferee, nor a person entitled to enforce the warranty. In so holding, the court determined that no "written warranty" or "implied warranty" was in effect during the lease period because no "sale" had occurred as that term is defined under the UCC. *Id.* at 470-471, 742 N.Y.S.2d 182, 768 N.E.2d 1121. The court reasoned that the lessee enjoyed a different bundle of rights than a buyer, could always have chosen not to buy, and paid less than a buyer who opts for a monthly payment plan. *Id.* The *DiCintio* court also noted that Congress' inclusion of leases in other consumer protection statutes, such as the Truth in Lending Act, Section 1601 et seq., Title 15, U.S. Code, is evidence that Congress knew how to draft legislation to protect leases and opted not to include such protection in the Magnuson-Moss Warranty Act. *Id.* at 472, 742 N.Y.S.2d 182, 768 N.E.2d 1121. Finally, the *DiCintio* court rejected the plaintiff's argument that the Act covered his lease even though it was not a "sale," because the lease provided that after its execution, the vehicle would be assigned to a finance company as "holder." *Id.* at 474, 742 N.Y.S.2d 182, 768 N.E.2d 1121.

However, still other courts have held that the Act is applicable to leases. For instance, in *Cohen v. AM Gen. Corp.* (N.D. Ill.2003), 264 F. Supp.2d 616, the United States District Court for the Northern District of Illinois held that the Act applied to the lease of a 1999 American General Hummer where the lease terms included an option to buy at the end of the lease period. That court held that the warranty delivered from the manufacturer to the lessor was a written warranty as defined by the Act. The *Cohen* court reasoned that the terms of the warranty were part of the bargain between the manufacturer and the lessor; therefore, the warranty was issued "in connection with" the sale of the vehicle from the manufacturer to the lessor. Accordingly, the *Cohen* court held that the term "sale," as defined by the Act, "is not limited to transactions between the warrantor and the ultimate consumer."

The court in *Cohen, supra,* disagreed with the *DiCintio* court with respect to the significance of a lessee's rights as compared to a buyer's rights:

> The Act does not require us to look at the bundle of rights acquired by the purchaser and the lessee. Instead, a plain reading of the Act forces us to simply look for a warranty exchange in connection with a sale. Defendant clearly sold the vehicle to Mister Leasing and, when doing so, made a series of promises in connection with this sale. This is enough for the warranty to meet the first part of the definition of 'written warranty' in 15 U.S.C. §2301(6).

This court agrees with those courts that have found that the Act is applicable to breach-of-warranty actions involving leases. The interpretations in *DiCintio* and cases that concur with it are not required by the language of the Act, as *Cohen* and other opinions show. Moreover, the *DiCintio* interpretation is inconsistent with the purposes of the Act—to protect the ultimate user of the product. Contrary to the view in *DiCintio,* the statutorily defined terms "written warranty" and "implied warranty" do not require the sale to be made to an ultimate consumer with a passage of title to that party. The warranty section contains no such limitation as to the buyer. Its only limitation is that the transaction be made "in connection with" the sale of a consumer product by a supplier to a buyer. Here, the vehicle came with a manufacturer's written warranty at the time it was sold to the lessor. The vehicle is alleged to be a consumer product; therefore, the warranty was made "in connection with" the sale of a consumer product, pursuant to section 2301(6)(A). Although the lessor would not qualify as a consumer under section 2301(3) who could enforce the warranty, the lessor is, nonetheless, a buyer under section 2301(6)(A) to whom a warranty was made and the plaintiffs—transferees of the product—are consumers who may enforce the Act in connection with the consumer product.

## QUESTION AND PROBLEM

1. Couldn't Congress have been more clear if it had intended Magnuson-Moss to apply to lease transactions? The UCC considers leases separately from sales of goods in Article 2A. See Chapter 10, *infra*. From a policy perspective, do you agree with this court that Magnuson-Moss should apply to consumer lease transactions?

***Problem 4-21.*** Buyer wishes to sue a merchant seller for breach of the implied warranty of merchantability on a defective boat. No written warranties were given. May Buyer sue under the Magnuson-Moss Consumer Warranty Act? See 15 U.S.C. §2310(d)(1); *McCurdy v. Texar, Inc.*, 575 So.2d 299 (Fla. App. 1991). Why would Buyer wish to do so? See 15 U.S.C. §2310(d)(2) and the discussion in the next section of this book.

### (b) Substantive Protections Afforded by Magnuson-Moss and State Consumer Protection Law

One provision in Magnuson-Moss that is helpful to consumers is section 108 of the Act [15 U.S.C. §2308], which provides that if a written warranty is given, a supplier may not disclaim or modify any implied warranties, except that for limited warranties the supplier may limit the duration of the implied warranty to the duration of the written warranty if that duration is reasonable. The meaning of this provision is not clear, because implied warranties are either breached or not at the time the goods are delivered to the buyer. That is, the good is either merchantable or not merchantable when it is delivered, even though discovery of the defect may occur sometime after delivery. We will explore what is meant by limiting duration of an implied warranty in an upcoming problem.

The Magnuson-Moss Act creates a cause of action for consumers who are injured by failure to comply with the Act *or* under any express *or* implied warranty. The cause of action extends to "a supplier, warrantor, or service contractor," meaning that lack of privity is not a defense. 15 U.S.C. §2310(d). The consumer can sue the manufacturer who provides the warranty. As a prerequisite to a lawsuit under Magnuson-Moss, a warrantor may require a consumer to first go through an informal dispute resolution procedure established under rules promulgated by the Federal Trade Commission. 15 U.S.C. §2310(a)(2)(3). In the event that a lawsuit is ultimately filed and the consumer is successful, the court has discretion to award reasonable attorney's fees. The possible usefulness of Magnuson-Moss in some situations is demonstrated by the following case.

### Mekertichian v. Mercedes-Benz U.S.A.

Appellate Court of Illinois

347 Ill. App. 3d 828, 807 N.E.2d 1165 (2004)

Plaintiff Edmond Mekertichian brought the instant cause of action against defendant Mercedes-Benz U.S.A. for breach of express and implied warranties under the Magnuson-Moss Warranty-Federal Trade Commission Improvement Act (the Act or Magnuson-Moss) (15 U.S.C. §2301 *et seq.* (1994)). Defendant moved for partial summary judgment regarding plaintiff's claim for breach of implied warranty of merchantability, alleging there was no privity between plaintiff and defendant. The circuit court denied the motion and defendant now appeals. We affirm the denial of the motion for summary judgment.

#### Background

On November 27, 1999, plaintiff purchased a new 2000 Mercedes-Benz S500V from Autohaus on Edens, Inc., in Northbrook, Illinois. Defendant, the manufacturer, provided a 48-month or 50,000-mile limited written warranty with the new automobile. The warranty provided that any authorized dealership would make repairs or replacements necessary to correct defects in material or workmanship during the warranty period.

Following the purchase, plaintiff began experiencing problems with the vehicle and, on several occasions, took it to Autohaus for repairs. However, plaintiff claimed that Autohaus was unable to repair the vehicle, and he attempted to revoke his acceptance of the vehicle. Defendant refused plaintiff's revocation. Plaintiff subsequently filed a complaint against defendant for breach of written and implied warranties under Magnuson-Moss. Claiming a lack of vertical privity between the parties, defendant filed a motion for partial summary judgment regarding plaintiff's claim for breach of implied warranty of merchantability. Defendant argued that because plaintiff did not purchase the vehicle directly from defendant, no vertical privity existed and the breach of implied warranty claim could not be maintained. The trial court denied the motion, but certified the question as to whether such privity is required pursuant to Supreme Court Rule 308 (155 Ill. 2d R. 308).

Defendant thereupon filed in this court an application for leave to appeal under Rule 308, which we denied. Following a supervisory order from our supreme court, we vacated our order denying leave to appeal and now consider defendant's interlocutory appeal. For the following reasons, we affirm the denial of defendant's motion for partial summary judgment.

#### Analysis

The instant appeal was brought following the denial of defendant's motion for partial summary judgment. In its motion, defendant alleged, as it does before this court in its appeal, that an action for breach of an implied warranty of merchantability could not be maintained against it as the manufacturer. It argues that because it did not sell the vehicle in question to plaintiff, there was no vertical privity between it and plaintiff, a required element under Illinois law when seeking recovery for the breach of an implied warranty. Plaintiff responds that the action is proper because our supreme court has determined on two occasions, in *Szajna v. General Motors Corp.,* 115 Ill. 2d 294, 104 Ill. Dec. 898, 503 N.E.2d 760 (1986), and *Rothe v. Maloney Cadillac, Inc.,* 119 Ill. 2d 288, 116 Ill. Dec. 207, 518 N.E.2d 1028 (1988), that Magnuson-Moss expands our state law to provide for vertical privity where a manufacturer provides a written warranty to a consumer. As shall be discussed below, we find that we are bound by the doctrine of *stare decisis* to follow our supreme court's determination in *Szajna* and *Rothe.*

Under the Magnuson-Moss Warranty Act, "a consumer who is damaged by the failure of a supplier, warrantor, or service contractor to comply with any obligation under this chapter, or under a written warranty, implied warranty, or service contract" may sue for damages or other equitable relief, and, where a plaintiff prevails, for attorney fees and costs. 15 U.S.C. §§2310(d)(1), (d)(2) (1994). With respect to actions predicated on the breach of an implied warranty of merchantability, which is at issue here, the Act provides that such actions may arise only under state law. 15 U.S.C. §2301(7) (1994). The Act does not provide an independent avenue through which implied warranty actions may be filed. Accordingly, under the terms of the Act itself, any action for breach of implied warranty is governed and limited by state law (except to the extent that state law might be modified by section 2308, dealing with disclaimers of implied warranties, and section 2304(a), dealing with attempts to restrict the duration of an implied warranty, neither of which is at issue here).

In Illinois, actions for breach of implied warranty of merchantability are governed by the UCC. In order for a plaintiff to file a claim for economic damages under the UCC for the breach of an implied warranty, he or she must be in vertical privity of contract with the seller. This means that "the UCC Article II implied warranties give a buyer of goods a potential cause of action only against his immediate seller." *Rothe,* 119 Ill. 2d at 292, 116 Ill. Dec. 207, 518 N.E.2d at 1029. Although this vertical privity requirement has been challenged on a number of occasions, our supreme court has consistently declined to abolish the doctrine in cases where purely economic damages are sought.

Despite this preservation of the privity requirement, the Illinois Supreme Court in *Szajna* and *Rothe* found that Magnuson-Moss serves to modify the state law privity requirement in cases filed under the federal Act. In *Szajna,* our supreme court held that, because the purpose of Magnuson-Moss is to "furnish[] broad protection to the consumer" and the Act modifies state law in "several" other of its provisions, under the Act where a manufacturer has expressly warranted a product to a consumer, vertical privity will be deemed to exist with respect to that consumer, enabling him to file an action for breach of implied warranty as well. *Szajna,* 115 Ill. 2d at 315, 104 Ill. Dec. 898, 503 N.E.2d at 769. The *Szajna* court stated, "under [the Act] a warrantor, by extending a written warranty to the consumer, establishes privity between the warrantor and the consumer which, though limited in nature, is sufficient to support an implied warranty under * * * the UCC." *Szajna,* 115 Ill. 2d at 315-316, 104 Ill. Dec. 898, 503 N.E.2d at 769.

Although there has been no determination on the vertical privity requirement under Magnuson-Moss by the United States Supreme Court, the holding in *Szajna* and *Rothe* that under Magnuson-Moss the vertical privity requirement is eliminated has been rejected by a consensus of the federal circuit courts of appeal that have dealt with this question, as well as by the overwhelming majority of federal district court cases.

Given these premises, this case turns on the doctrine of *stare decisis*. The doctrine of *stare decisis* is a basic tenet of our legal system, which requires the courts to stand by legal precedent and not disturb settled points of law.

Federal circuit court decisions are considered persuasive, but not binding on us or our supreme court in the absence of a decision by the United States Supreme Court. As we have previously noted, the United States Supreme Court has not issued any opinions concerning state privity requirements under Magnuson-Moss. Accordingly, while the Illinois Supreme Court may opt to give weight to the decisions of lower federal courts interpreting a federal statute, it is under no compulsion to do so.

We, however, are bound by the decisions of the Illinois Supreme Court. After our supreme court has declared the law with respect to an issue, this court must follow that law, as only the supreme court has authority to overrule or modify its own decisions. As an inferior court of review, our serving as a reviewing court on our supreme court's interpretation of federal law would inject chaos into the judicial process. As a result, whether there is going to be any change or modification of the precedent set by *Rothe* and *Szajna* should first be determined by our supreme court and not by us.

Accordingly, the judgment of the circuit court is affirmed.

## NOTES, QUESTIONS, AND PROBLEMS

1. Do you agree with the Illinois precedent that a cause of action for breach of implied warranty should lie under Magnuson-Moss even when such a cause of action would not exist under state law? Why does Magnuson-Moss prohibit disclaimers of implied warranties when express warranties are given? Why should the court have the power to grant attorney's fees in these cases but generally not in a case brought under UCC Article 2 (unless the parties have an enforceable agreement to the contrary)?
2. As previously noted, a seller of goods can opt out of the more onerous provisions of Magnuson-Moss by clearly labeling a warranty as a "Limited Warranty." Feeling that the protection given to consumers by Magnuson-Moss was thus inadequate, a number of states adopted their own consumer protection laws to supplement both the UCC and Magnuson-Moss. Magnuson-Moss states that it does not preempt such laws. 15 U.S.C. §2311(b)(1). California, for example, has adopted the Song-Beverly Consumer Warranty Act, Cal. Civil Code section 1790, et seq., which provides additional protection to consumers. Under Song-Beverly, "consumer goods" are defined as "any new product or part thereof that is used, bought, or

leased for use primarily for personal, family, or household purposes, except for clothing and consumables." "Buyer" is defined as "any individual who buys consumer goods from a person engaged in the business of manufacturing, distributing, or selling consumer goods at retail." "Lessee" is defined as "an individual who leases consumer goods under a lease." Cal. Civil Code §1791. Distributors or retail sellers of used consumer goods in sales in which express warranties are given are also covered by Song-Beverly, with some limitations on their exposure. Cal. Civil Code §1795.5.

Under Song-Beverly, a seller is not allowed to disclaim, limit, or modify the implied warranty of merchantability or fitness if an express warranty is given. Cal. Civ. Code §1793. If no express warranty is given, the warranties can be disclaimed, but the disclaimer must be more precise and explanatory than the disclaimer allowed under UCC §2-316. Cal. Civ. Code §1792.4. The Song-Beverly Act is perhaps best known for its "lemon law," that requires a manufacturer of goods to replace the goods or refund the purchase price (less an amount attributable to the buyer's use of the goods) if the manufacturer or its representative is unable to repair the goods to conform to applicable express warranties after a reasonable number of attempts. Cal. Civ. Code §1793.2. Note that this provision applies to goods in addition to cars, although the lemon law is most frequently thought of (and probably applied) in cases involving cars. For cars, there is a presumption that a reasonable number of attempts have been made if, among other things, the same nonconformity has been subject to repair four or more times within 18 months from delivery to the buyer or 18,000 miles, whichever occurs first. Cal. Civ. Code §1792.22(b). For cars, buyers are also given the option of obtaining restitution rather than replacement. In determining restitution, the buyer's use of the car is taken into account in setting off the amount awarded. Cal. Civ. Code §1793.2(d)(2). In some cases, Song-Beverly also will permit limited civil penalties for willful failure to comply and attorney's fees. Cal. Civ. Code §1794. Other states also have "lemon laws" with varying degrees of consumer protection.[5] Is the approach of Song-Beverly (as described) superior to that of Magnuson-Moss? Is it an unwarranted infringement on "freedom of contract"?

***Problem 4-22.*** Buyer purchases a television set from a retailer. The manufacturer's "limited warranty" states that the television is warranted to be free from defects for one year, and that any implied warranty is limited to the duration of the written warranty. If the television set completely fails to operate 13 months after purchase, does Buyer have any remedy? If no written warranty was given at all and the implied warranty of merchantability was not disclaimed, would Buyer have any remedy? See UCC §2-314 and Magnuson-Moss Act §108 [15 U.S.C. §2308]. See *Carlson v. General Motors*, 883 F.2d 287 (4th Cir. 1989); C. Reitz, *Consumer Product Warranties Under Federal and State Law* 82, 86, 95(2d ed. 1987).

---

5. For a discussion of the lemon laws and a comparison of their terms, see Nowicki, *State Lemon Law Coverage Terms*, 11 Loy. Consumer L. Rev. 39 (1999).

***Problem 4-23.*** Buyer purchases a car from a dealership. The contract contains a limited warranty that is covered by the Magnuson-Moss Act. The contract does not provide for an informal dispute mechanism, but does provide that any disputes arising out of the contract are subject to binding arbitration. Is such an arbitration provision enforceable? See Magnuson-Moss Act §110 [15 U.S.C. §2310]. *Compare Davis v. Southern Energy Homes*, 305 F.3d 1268 (11th Cir. 2002), *with Browne v. Kline Tysons Imports, Inc.*, 190 F. Supp. 2d 827 (E.D. Va. 2002).

## CHAPTER 4 REVIEW PROBLEM

Frank's Family Farm, a small farming operation, was interested in buying equipment that would assist with its tomato harvest. It noticed that some used equipment was being offered for sale by Tomato Coop, the largest tomato farming operation in the area. Tomato Coop occasionally sold its used equipment to smaller farming operations. The manager at Tomato Coop told Frank that the equipment was "sound" and "would do the job for you." Frank purchased the equipment after inspecting it and noticing no apparent defects. It was just two years old. It was manufactured by Ag Equipment Manufacturers, Inc. Frank was mostly influenced, however, by the price, which was substantially less than what the equipment would cost new.

Tomato Coop created a bill of sale, which both parties signed, which stated in conspicuous language that "no warranties of any kind accompany the goods being sold." Frank did not pay much attention to the bill of sale, thinking it was just an acknowledgment of receipt of the goods. Frank soon learned that the equipment did not work well for his purposes—it processed more slowly than comparable equipment. He was also surprised to get a phone call from Farmer's & Merchant's Bank, which claimed that it had a security interest (lien) in the equipment arising out of a loan it had made to Tomato Coop. The equipment had been used as collateral in the loan, and the loan was in default. What recourse, if any, does Frank's Family Farm have against Tomato Coop or Ag Equipment Manufacturers? Please analyze under both the UCC and the CISG. Please disregard any unconscionability or parol evidence issues, which will be considered in the next chapter. The relevant UCC sections are 2-313, 2-314, 2-315, and 2-316. The relevant CISG articles are 6, 35, and 41.

CHAPTER 5

# OTHER CONTRACT TERMS, INTERPRETATION, AND UNCONSCIONABILITY

## A. RISK OF LOSS

The parties to the contract may by contract determine who bears the risk of loss in the event that the goods are damaged or destroyed at some point during the transaction. The risk of loss starts with the seller and at some point shifts to the buyer. The parties are free to allocate risk by contract. In the event that the contract is silent, both the UCC and the CISG provide default rules that allocate the loss. As noted in the first chapter, risk of loss used to be allocated on the basis of which party had title. The UCC changed that approach under U.S. law, and the CISG also allocates loss irrespective of title.

The UCC differentiates between situations in which the parties are properly performing under the contract and situations in which one of the parties is in breach. The relevant sections are 2-503, 2-504, 2-509, and 2-510. Section 2-510 deals with the question of risk allocation when one of the parties is in breach, and will be considered later when we take up the topic of performance and breach under the contract of sale. The CISG articles that are relevant are Articles 66 through 70.

### 1. CASES WHERE NO SHIPMENT IS INVOLVED

The UCC rule dealing with risk of loss absent breach of contract is section 2-509. It has rules that provide for two specific cases: (1) where the contract calls for the seller to ship the goods by carrier; and (2) where the goods are in the possession of a bailee (e.g., a warehouse operator) and are to be delivered without being moved. We will consider the rules dealing with shipment in the next section of the book. With respect to goods in possession of a bailee, section 2-509(2) provides that the risk of loss passes when the bailee acknowledges the buyer's right to possession of the goods or when the buyer receives a document of title representing title to the goods. We will talk more about documents of title in Chapter 9.

In cases other than those calling shipment or transfer of goods in possession of a bailee, section 2-509(3) provides that the risk of loss passes when the buyer takes possession of the goods if the seller is a merchant. Risk of loss passes upon tender of delivery if the seller is a non-merchant. Tender of delivery is defined in section 2-503, and requires that the seller "put and hold conforming goods at the buyer's disposition and give the buyer any notification reasonably necessary to enable him to take delivery." Among other things, it also requires that tender be at a reasonable hour and that the buyer be given a reasonable amount of time to pick up the goods.

Under the CISG, in non-shipment cases, the risk of loss passes to the buyer when the buyer takes over the good or when the buyer is in breach in not taking delivery. CISG Article 69(1). If the goods are located at a place other than the seller's place of business, the risk passes when delivery is due and the buyer is aware that the goods are placed at his disposal at that place. CISG Article 69(2).

The following problems deal with situations where the contract does not call for the goods to be shipped by an independent carrier. In these cases, either the buyer is to pick up the goods in the store or the seller is to deliver the goods to the buyer via the seller's own delivery truck.

## PROBLEMS

***Problem 5-1.*** Buyer agrees to purchase a valuable painting from Seller Art Gallery, which is in the business of selling fine art and also displaying it in a museum-like setting. Buyer agrees to leave the painting at Seller Art Gallery for a month so that it can be displayed. During the month, the painting is stolen through no fault of Seller and cannot be found. Has the risk of loss passed to Buyer in this case under Article 2? See section 2-509 and read the comments to that section as they explain the policy behind the loss allocation rules. Would it make a difference if the seller was a private collector who was not a merchant and Buyer simply didn't show up to claim the painting for a few days before it was stolen? See section 2-503. How would these cases come out under the CISG? See Article 69.

***Problem 5-2.*** Castellano, a plumbing subcontractor, through his agent ordered plumbing supplies from National Plumbing Supply Corp. to be delivered to a job site. There was some question as to whether the supplies would be needed by him, because he was going into the hospital for heart surgery and would perhaps not be able to perform as the subcontractor on the project. The plumbing supplies were delivered by the seller to the job site on June 25, and were signed for by unidentified employees of the general contractor who simply signed the name of the owner of the project. The seller was aware that neither Castellano nor his agent were present at the job site when the supplies were delivered. Neither Castellano nor his agent otherwise took physical possession of the goods—they were left at the site. As it turned out, Castellano did not serve as the subcontractor on the project, and National

Plumbing Supply returned to the job site in September to take back the supplies. When some of the supplies proved to be missing, National Plumbing Supply sued, alleging that the risk of loss had passed to Castellano. How should the court rule on the risk of loss issue? Would it matter if National Plumbing Supply were not a merchant? See UCC §§2-503 and 2-509(3). *See National Plumbing Supply Corp. v. Castellano*, 118 Misc. 2d 150, 460 N.Y.S.2d 248 (N.Y. Just. Ct. 1983).

## 2. CASES WHERE SHIPMENT IS INVOLVED

Often the contract will require that the goods be shipped by carrier, especially in international commercial transactions. In these cases, we must distinguish between "shipment" contracts and "destination" contracts. Under a "shipment" contract the obligation of the seller is to place the goods into possession of a carrier, make a reasonable contract for shipment, obtain and forward to the buyer documents necessary for the buyer to take possession of the goods upon delivery (e.g., a negotiable bill of lading), and promptly notify the buyer of shipment. The risk of loss and expense of shipment then passes to the buyer. See UCC §§2-504 and 2-509. Compare CISG Articles 30-34 and 67. Under a "destination" contract, the seller is obligated at its own risk and expense to deliver the goods to the destination indicated in the contract, probably the buyer's place of business.

If the parties contract to ship goods but do not express whether it is a shipment or destination contract, the default is that it is a shipment contract. See Comment 5 to §2-503. Compare CISG Article 31. Often, parties will use shorthand terms to indicate the duties of the parties, such as FOB ("free on board") or CIF ("cost, insurance, and freight"). UCC sections 2-319 through 2-325 explain what these shorthand terms mean, although they are always subject to contrary agreement between the parties. Parties may decide to use the Incoterms, discussed below, which have different meanings for FOB and CIF and which use other shorthand terms as well. The following case demonstrates how parties might use delivery terms in ways that differ from the UCC's definition of those terms.

### National Heater Company v. Corrigan Company Mechanical Contractors

United States Court of Appeals, Eighth Circuit

482 F.2d 87 (1973)

STEPHENSON, Circuit Judge.

This diversity action springs from a contract dispute between two subcontractors. Appellant-seller (National Heater) brought the action in the United States District Court for the Eastern District of Missouri to recover the balance allegedly due on a purchase contract for certain heaters. Corrigan Company, the buyer, counterclaimed. The trial court judgment was in favor of Corrigan on its counterclaim. Judge Regan found that harm to appellee Corrigan totaled $63,291.04 as a result of damage in transit, late delivery, and work done by Corrigan to conform the goods to contract specifications. On appeal the master issue raised by appellant is that the risk of loss for goods in transit should not have been attributed to it.

On March 1, 1969, National Heater made a proposal "to the trade" concerning the price of certain heating units to be used in construction at the Chrysler automobile plant in Fenton, Missouri. The proposal priced the merchandise FOB St. Paul, Minnesota, "with freight allowed." Based in part upon National Heater's proposal, Corrigan made its bid on the construction job and was awarded the contract. Thereafter, appellant received appellee's purchase order listing "Price $275,640—Delivered." Appellant then mailed to appellee an "Acknowledgment of Purchase Order" bearing the printed words "Sale Price Total" followed by this typed language: "$275,640.00 Total Delivered to Rail Siding." Expressly made a part of this acknowledgment was the condition that "delivery of equipment hereunder shall be made FOB point of shipment unless otherwise stated." The trial court determined that the parties had by these writings contracted for appellant to deliver the goods to the construction site and that the attendant risk of loss in transit therefore was appellant's burden. The court states:

> [t]he statement on the face of the acknowledgment which obligated plaintiff to deliver the merchandise "to rail siding" comes clearly within the "otherwise stated" provision of the condition. The manifest intention of the parties, in view of their entire course of conduct, was that delivery was to be made not FOB point of shipment but to the rail siding on the job.

We agree. To hold otherwise would contradict the writing. We must give effect to the intention of the parties as expressed in the unequivocal language employed.

Several circumstances surrounding this contract further convince us that the trial court was correct. Both litigants agree that the Uniform Commercial Code ("UCC"), having been adopted in Minnesota and Missouri prior to the formation of this contract, should apply to this lawsuit. The Code provides that evidence relating to course of performance between the parties is relevant in determining the meaning of the agreement. UCC §2-208.

Appellant argues that the term "delivered" in appellee's purchase order and the term "delivered to rail siding" in the acknowledgment referred only to price.[1] As heretofore mentioned, the original proposal to the trade made by appellant had previously established that freight would be allowed. Yet both parties typed in the provisions concerning delivery on their forms. In addition, appellant made no protest about the "delivered" term in a letter he sent to appellee accompanying the acknowledgment. He did take exception to another provision of the purchase order concerning a ten percent retainage by the buyer pending acceptance. It seems to us as it did to the trial court that the parties were contemplating where delivery would take place rather than price.

When a contract is partly written or typewritten and partly printed, any conflict between the printed portion and the written or typewritten portion will be resolved in favor of the latter. Appellant's form acknowledgment accepted the purchase order "subject to the conditions of sale and trade customs set forth on the reverse side."

1. There is no dispute that the rail siding contemplated was at the Chrysler plant in Fenton, Missouri.

Condition 7 on the back of the acknowledgment provided that "all risk of loss or damage following delivery to point of shipment shall be borne by the purchaser." If any ambiguity in fact exists between this condition and the typed provision "delivered to rail siding," the conflict should be resolved in favor of the typewriting. It is also true that any ambiguity in the acknowledgment must be construed against appellant since it drafted the document. We conclude that the parties by their written documents agreed that appellant was to deliver the goods to the job site.

In reaching our result we are not unmindful that the FOB term usually indicates the point at which delivery is to be made and will normally determine risk of loss. We also note that the "destination" type contract, which we envision this to be, is the variant rather than the norm. UCC §2-503 Comment 5; W. Hawkland, *Sales and Bulk Sales* at 58, 94 (2d ed. 1958). The provisions of the UCC may nevertheless be varied by agreement. UCC §1-102 and Comment 3. The written documents persuade us that National Heater specifically agreed to deliver the goods to their destination.

Affirmed.

## PROBLEMS

***Problem 5-3.*** If the contract had simply stated "FOB St. Paul, Minnesota, with freight allowed," who would have the risk of loss if the goods were damaged between St. Paul and Missouri? What if the carrier had inadequate insurance to cover the loss to the goods that occurred during the shipment? See UCC §§2-319, 2-504(a); *Cook Specialty Co. v. Schrlock*, 772 F. Supp. 1532, 16 UCC Rep. Serv. 2d 160 (E.D. Pa. 1991).

***Problem 5-4.*** If the contract had stated "CIF Fenton, Missouri," and seller complied with the requirements of UCC section 2-320, who would have the risk of loss if the goods were damaged between St. Paul and Missouri? Is a CIF contract a "shipment" or "destination" contract in terms of risk of loss?

## NOTE AND PROBLEM

In an international contract of sale, the parties may use "Incoterms," which provide the buyer's and seller's obligations regarding shipment and delivery. The Incoterms are devised by the International Chamber of Commerce and are similar, but not identical, to the shorthand delivery terms contained in UCC sections 2-319 through 2-323. Brief descriptions of the Incoterms can be found at the International Chamber of Commerce Web site, *www.iccwbo.org/Incoterms/index.html?id=40772* (accessed Oct. 2011). A helpful table showing which party bears various duties under the Incoterms can be found at *www.i-b-t.net/incoterms.html* (accessed Oct. 2011). The Incoterms are copyrighted by the International Chamber of Commerce; full descriptions of the terms are contained in International Chamber of Commerce publications available for purchase through their Web site. The Incoterms were most recently revised in 2010. Contracts referring to earlier versions of the Incoterms are governed by the definitions of those terms contained in the earlier versions. It is important to understand that the Incoterms are not "law" in that they have not been enacted by any government (at least not to the knowledge of the author). They are only effective if the parties have agreed to use them, and the parties are free to vary their meaning.

Some Incoterms are not found in the UCC, such as CIP ("carriage and insurance paid to"), which means that the price paid by the buyer includes the cost of shipment to the place of destination and insurance. The seller is obligated to deliver the goods to the carrier, pay the freight, and purchase insurance before the risk passes to the buyer. Also, FOB is always a shipment contract under the Incoterms, while it may be either a shipment or destination contract under the UCC. Under the Incoterms, a CIF contract always involves carriage by waterborne vessel and requires the seller to deliver the goods over the ship's rail at the port of shipment. For further discussion of the differences between the Incoterms and the UCC Article 2 shipment terms, see Spanogle, *Incoterms and UCC Article 2—Conflicts and Confusions*, 31 Int'l Lawyer 111 (1997).

***Problem 5-5.*** In an international sale of goods covered by the CISG, the contract provides that the price is $500 per unit "FCA Seller's Warehouse Hamburg Incoterms 2010." What are the seller's delivery obligations under such a contract? See *www.i-b-t.net/PDFs/Incoterms_2010_chart.pdf* (accessed Oct. 2011).

## B. GAP FILLERS

Both the UCC and the CISG contain a number of provisions designed to fill in the gaps in sales contracts if the parties have not expressly agreed to certain terms but have otherwise indicated an intent to be bound to a contract. Arguably, almost all of the provisions in the UCC and CISG are "gap fillers" because parties are generally permitted to derogate from most of the UCC and CISG's provisions. See UCC §1-302 and CISG Article 6.

UCC section 2-204 contemplates the need for gap-filler sections when it states, "Even though one or more terms are left open a contract for sale does not fail for indefiniteness if the parties have intended to make a contract and there is a reasonably certain basis for giving an appropriate remedy." In the UCC, the gap-filler provisions are generally found in Part 3 of Article 2. For example, section 2-308 tells us that if the parties have not agreed on a place for delivery of goods that are known at the time of contracting to be at the seller's place of business, the place of delivery is the seller's place of business. If the parties have not agreed to a time of shipment, it is to be a reasonable time. UCC §2-309. For the definition of "reasonable time," see UCC §1-205. Comparable CISG gap-filler provisions are sprinkled among the Articles dealing with "obligations of the seller" (Articles 30-34) and "obligations of the buyer" (Articles 53-59).

When considering whether there is a "gap" in the parties' contract that needs filling, the role of course of performance, course of dealing, and usage of trade needs to be kept in mind. "Course of performance" is how parties have been performing under the contract in question when the contract calls for repeated performances. "Course of dealing" is how parties have performed under prior contracts. "Usage of trade" is industry practice. See UCC §1-303. It is assumed, unless the written contract says otherwise, that parties will perform as they have been performing under the contract in question, as they have performed under prior contracts, and according to industry practices. If a term can be established through looking at course of performance, course of dealing, or usage of trade, there is no need to use a gap filler to supply the term. For example, if the contract is silent on delivery but in prior dealings the seller has always delivered within two weeks of the purchase order, that tells us that delivery should be within two weeks on this contract as well.

The UCC and arguably the CISG also provide provisions that help fill gaps on such fundamental terms as price and quantity. In your contracts class, you probably studied the gap fillers regarding price and UCC section 2-306 regarding output and requirements contracts. The following case demonstrates the UCC approach to cases in which the terms are somewhat indefinite.

## H. C. Schmieding Produce Company v. Cagle

Supreme Court of Alabama

529 So. 2d 243 (1988)

According to Cagle, [a] contract arose in part from at least two telephone conversations with Schmieding's employees, one of which occurred at the end of February 1985, and one of which took place in May 1985. Cagle introduced evidence at trial to the effect that Schmieding had agreed in these conversations to pay Cagle $5.50 per bag for approximately 10,000 bags of white potatoes, and to pay him the market price at harvest time for all of his red potatoes grown on 30 acres of land.

Schmieding denied the existence of this alleged contract and refused to pay Cagle for his potato crop at harvest time.

Schmieding argues that, assuming a potato sales contract of some form was in fact entered into, that contract is nevertheless unenforceable because its terms are indefinite. We disagree.

Schmieding argues that the alleged contract fails for indefiniteness due to its numerous "open terms," such as time and place of delivery and various warranties that the potatoes would meet certain specifications. In addition, Schmieding also argues that the price term for the red potatoes — that is, "market price at time of harvest" — is also too indefinite to allow enforcement of the contract.[1]

Although Schmieding's argument might have had some merit under pre-UCC cases, this argument has no chance of success on these facts under the UCC. The controlling section in this regard is UCC section 2-204(3), which provides as follows:

> Even though one or more terms are left open a contract for sale does not fail for indefiniteness if the parties have intended to make a contract and there is a reasonably certain basis for giving an appropriate remedy.

---

1. The statute of frauds was not raised in this case as a defense. There was some written evidence of a contract —Ed.

We have previously noted that evidence was presented at trial indicating that at least the following terms were agreed upon: (1) the type of potatoes ordered (red potatoes and white potatoes), (2) the quantity ordered (in terms of "bags" or acreage), (3) the price to be paid for the quantity ordered ($5.50 per bag for the whites, market price at harvest for the reds), and (4) the approximate delivery date (at harvest).

This evidence, as well as that noted in our previous discussion, puts to rest any argument as to whether, under the first prong of the test in section 2-204(3), the parties "intended to make a contract"—sufficient evidence was introduced by Cagle to require that this question of fact be submitted to the jury.

Similarly, these terms, if in fact entered into, would also provide a "reasonably certain basis for giving an appropriate remedy." Thus, the legal question posed by the second prong of section 2-204(3) must also be answered in the affirmative. The alleged contract clearly delineates a promise to sell identifiable goods of a specified type and quantity at a specified or reasonably determinable price and time. Consequently, we think the value of this contract to either party is susceptible to reasonably certain measurement by a court and jury, and that an appropriate remedy for its breach could be provided.

Accordingly, even though the contract contains several open terms in addition to those expressly noted, the contract does not fail for indefiniteness, because such open terms may be supplemented by the UCC's "gap-filler" provisions. For instance, time, place, and manner of delivery are dealt with in UCC sections 2-307, 2-308, and 2-309, and, similarly, the quality of the potatoes would likely have been guaranteed under one or more of the Code's warranty provisions. See UCC §§2-313 to 2-315. Moreover, a market-based open price term (such as that chosen for the red potatoes in the instant contract) is expressly recognized by the Code as an acceptable contract term. See UCC §2-305(1)(c). Accordingly, Schmieding's argument that the terms of this contract are indefinite is without merit, and the trial court did not err in submitting this claim to the jury.

## NOTES, QUESTIONS, AND PROBLEM

1. It is important to note that UCC section 2-305 will supply a price only if the parties have intended to form a contract even though the price is not settled. If they only intend to have a binding agreement upon settlement of the price, then there is no binding contract between them until they agree on price.
2. Note that the court indicates that the buyer would have had a better argument that no contract had been formed under the law predating the adoption of the UCC. Why would the drafters of the Code seek to enforce more agreements in which important terms, such as exact price and delivery date, had not been expressly agreed upon?

***Problem 5-6.*** The CISG is somewhat schizophrenic in its consideration of open price term contracts. Consider the following hypothetical: Seller, a manufacturer of equipment, offers to sell to Buyer a truck and a forklift. Delivery is to be in one month after acceptance. The price of the truck is listed in the offer at $30,000, but no price is listed for the forklift. Buyer accepts Seller's offer. At the time of the acceptance, the market price of the forklift was $10,000. At the time of delivery the market price of the forklift is $9,000. Was there an offer; that is, does the CISG require that an offer provide a price or a mechanism to determine it? See CISG Article 14. Is there a contract? Can we have a contract without an "offer"? If there is a contract, how is the price to be determined? See CISG Articles 23 and 55. How would the price be determined under the UCC? See UCC §2-305(1). Should Article 55 have meaning only in countries that have opted out of Part II of the CISG pursuant to CISG Article 92?[2] See also the Secretariat Commentary to the predecessor to Article 55. See *Transcript of a Workshop on the Sales Convention*, 18 J. of Law & Commerce 191-258 (1999), *www.cisg.law.pace.edu/cisg/biblio/workshop-14,55,18.html* (accessed Oct. 2011). See also Gillette & Walt, *Sales Law: Domestic and International* 117-123 (rev. ed.).

## C. CONTRACT INTERPRETATION

CISG Article 8 states that in interpreting the terms of the agreement, the actual intent of a party governs as long as the other party knows or could not be unaware of that intent. Otherwise, each party's statements or actions "are to be interpreted according to the understanding that a reasonable person of the same kind as the other party would have had in the same circumstances." CISG Article 8(2). The CISG indicates that in determining the intent of the parties "or the understanding a reasonable person would have had, due consideration is to be given to all relevant circumstances of the case including the negotiations, any practices which the parties have established between themselves, usages and any subsequent conduct of the parties." CISG Article 8(3). See also CISG Article 9.

In interpreting international contracts, the UNIDROIT Principles on International Commercial Contracts may also be helpful. Chapter 4 of the Principles contains several rules pertaining to contract interpretation. For example, Article 4.7 states that if a contract is drawn up in two languages and if there is a discrepancy between the two versions, the original version of the contract should control. The Principles also have rules with regard to standard form contracts and state that terms in a standard form are not enforceable if they are not within the reasonable expectations of the party who did not prepare the form. Principles Article 2.1.20. The Principles have a parol evidence rule, but indicate that parol evidence may be admissible to explain the meaning of an agreement. Principles Article 2.1.17.

The UCC does not contain rules of contract interpretation similar to CISG Article 8. Remember that in cases not covered by the UCC, general principles of law and equity supplement the Code. UCC §1-103. Courts will interpret sale of goods contracts as they do other contracts. *Restatement (Second) of Contracts*

2. Denmark, Finland, Norway, and Sweden have made such a declaration.

section 20 has rules dealing with contract interpretation that are similar to CISG Article 8 in that the focus is on what each party knows regarding the other party's intent and also on what each party has reason to know regarding the other party's intent.

In cases involving either the UCC or the CISG, courts may use some basic maxims of contract interpretation and construction. For example, courts may use the principle of *contra proferentem* ("against the proferror") to construe a contract against the party who drafted it if a term is ambiguous.[3]

The UCC has a version of the parol evidence rule, which you probably spent some time considering in your contracts class. See UCC §2-202. As you remember, the parol evidence rule bars evidence of prior agreements or contemporaneous oral agreements to contradict a partially integrated written contract or to supplement a completely integrated written contract.

In determining whether the parol evidence rule may apply, you must first see some form of a written contract. It could be a document signed by both parties, or it could be a confirmatory memorandum sent by one of the parties. Then you must see someone trying to introduce evidence of an agreement allegedly made between the parties before or at the same time that the written contract was entered into or the confirmatory memorandum was sent. Normally, the prior agreement will be oral, but it doesn't have to be for the parol evidence rule to apply. Note that the parol evidence rule does *not* apply to modifications. The parol evidence rule assumes that when parties have entered into a final written agreement, they intend to supercede any inconsistent prior agreements, whether they are written or oral.

The parol evidence rule will exclude evidence only if the written agreement is partially or completely integrated. What is meant by a "partially integrated" or "completely integrated" contract? The term partial integration refers to whether the parties intend the written contract to be the final expression of their intentions with respect to the terms that are contained in the writing. For example, if a writing has a price, quantity, and delivery date and we say that it is "partially integrated," that means we are saying that it is final with respect to price, quantity, and delivery date. Evidence will not be admitted of prior agreements that contradict the price, quantity, and delivery date in the writing. If the agreement is only partially integrated, it means that the parties may have had prior agreements on other matters that are not in the writing—for example, on warranties—and evidence of such agreements will be admitted. On the other hand, if we say that the written agreement is "completely integrated," it means that the writing is the final expression of the parties on all terms of the transaction, and no evidence of any prior agreement (written or oral) or contemporaneous oral agreement will be admitted to contradict or add terms to the agreement, even if they are consistent with the writing.

How do we tell if an agreement is partially or completely integrated? One thing to look at is whether the parties have included a "merger clause" in the writing, stating that the agreement is the final and complete expression of the

3. For more discussion on basic contract rules of interpretation and construction, see Farnsworth, *Contracts* §§7.4, 7.11 (4th ed. 2004).

parties' agreement. Another thing to look at is whether the writing is detailed and was carefully negotiated. The test proposed by Official Comment 3 to section 2-202 is whether the alleged prior agreement "would certainly have been included in the document," in which case the evidence of the prior agreement should be excluded.

There are some exceptions to the parol evidence rule. Parol evidence will generally be admitted to show conditions precedent to the enforceability of the contract (for example, whether financing needed to be obtained as a condition to go through with a car purchase), fraud and mistake (including a so-called scrivener's error where the written contract does not accurately reflect the parties' agreement). Parol evidence will also be admitted to resolve ambiguities. If the contract is not completely integrated, parol evidence will be admitted to show terms that are consistent with the written contract. It is very difficult to find cases in which courts refuse admission of evidence of agreements that are consistent with the terms of the written contract (remember that to bar admission, the court must determine that the terms "would *certainly* have been included in the document" if the parties had agreed to them (emphasis added)).

As to the CISG's treatment of parol evidence, as previously noted, Article 8(3) provides that all relevant evidence should be considered in determining the parties' intent under the contract, including evidence of negotiations prior to contracting. Does this mean that there is no parol evidence rule under the CISG? That question is considered in the *MCC-Marble* case, which follows shortly.

### Dall v. Certified Sales, Inc.

United States District Court, District of Connecticut

2011 WL 572387, 73 UCC Rep. Serv. 2d 622 (2011)

Pending before the court is the third party defendant's Motion *in Limine*, which asks the court to preclude the plaintiff from offering any testimony regarding oral representations that the defendant allegedly made prior to plaintiff's purchase of the boat at issue.

[The court quotes from UCC §2-202]

[T]he parol evidence rule is not a rule of evidence, but a substantive rule of contract law. The rule prohibits the use of extrinsic evidence to vary or contradict the terms of an integrated written contract.

The rule is premised upon the idea that when the parties have deliberately put their engagements into writing, in such terms as import a legal obligation, without any uncertainty as to the object or extent of such engagement, it is conclusively presumed, that the whole engagement of the parties, and the extent and manner of their understanding, was reduced to writing. After this, to permit oral testimony, or prior or contemporaneous conversations, or circumstances, or usages [etc.], in order to learn what was intended, or to contradict what is written, would be dangerous and unjust in the extreme.

Parol evidence is admissible, however, if relevant (1) to explain an ambiguity appearing in the instrument; (2) to prove a collateral oral agreement which does not vary the terms of the writing; (3) to add a missing term in a writing which indicates on its face that it does not set forth the complete agreement; or (4) to show mistake or fraud.

At oral argument, the plaintiff contended that defendant's verbal representations were terms of an oral contract between the plaintiff and the defendant. That contract, the plaintiff argues, included a verbal warranty that the boat had "fresh engines," and the defendant breached the contract by delivering a boat with damaged engines. This argument fails. Despite plaintiff's insistence to the contrary, it is apparent that he injects defendant's oral statements into the case in an attempt to vary the terms of the parties' written contract.

The plaintiff bought the boat by bidding at an auction. Under the Uniform Commercial Code's provision on sale by auction, a bid is an offer, and a contract is formed when accepted by the auctioneer upon the fall of the hammer. UCC §2-328.

The plaintiff's written bid form set forth the terms of the contract. Among other provisions, it states that the vessel was sold "as is," that "[n]o verbal agreement can be applied," and that there is "no warranty or guarantee expressed or implied." Thus, the plaintiff entered into a contract for an as-is sale with disclaimer of both express and implied warranties. See UCC §2-316(3). Plaintiff's attempt to introduce evidence of prior oral statements to prove the existence of warranties which vary the terms of the parties' written contract is exactly what is barred by the parol evidence rule.

The plaintiff also argued, in his briefs, that the evidence is admissible to prove fraud. He says that the defendant's verbal representations were intended to, and did, fraudulently induce him to enter into the contract.

Plaintiff is correct in observing that prior oral representations are admissible to show fraud. The opportunity to present evidence of fraud long has been recognized as an exception to the parol evidence rule. Fraud vitiates all contracts, written or otherwise; no rule of law, including the parol evidence rule, deprives a trial court of the power to allow oral testimony to prove fraud. To show fraudulent inducement, the defrauded party must prove the following elements:

> (1) a false representation was made as a statement of fact; (2) it was untrue and known to be untrue by the party making it; (3) it was made to induce the other party to act upon it; and (4) the other party did so act upon that false representation to his injury.

The plaintiff has lost sight of his complaint. The court previously dismissed his tort claims, including a fraudulent inducement claim, on statute of limitations grounds. Only Count 3 of the complaint remains, and it is a breach of contract claim. The plaintiff's argument is an attempt to resurrect his claims of fraudulent inducement.

For all the foregoing reasons, the Motion *in Limine* is GRANTED.

## NOTES AND PROBLEMS

1. Should the court have spent some time analyzing whether the plaintiff's written bid form was "a writing intended by the parties as a final expression

of their agreement" with respect to the terms that were included in the bid form, in other words a "partial integration?" Do you think it was a partial integration?

2. The court recognizes that fraud is an exception to the parol evidence rule, but the party seeking to assert it must be trying to rescind the contract on the basis of fraud. Fraud is a basis for rescission, as is a negligent material misrepresentation. *Restatement (Second) of Contracts* §164. There is a split of authority, however, on the question of whether evidence of negligent misrepresentation should be admitted to rescind a contract if it is inconsistent with the written contract. *See Keller v. A.O. Smith Harvestore Products, Inc.*, 819 P.2d 69 (Colo. 1991). If negligent misrepresentation is a valid basis for rescission of a contract, why distinguish between negligent misrepresentation and fraud in determining whether evidence should be admitted under the parol evidence rule?

***Problem 5-7.*** A contract for the sale of fertilizer requires the buyer to take a specified quantity at a specified price. The contract contains a standard "merger" clause, indicating that the written contract reflects the entire understanding of the parties regarding this transaction. When the market price for fertilizer falls, buyer refuses to take delivery of the specified minimum quantity. Buyer seeks to introduce evidence that, in the industry, it is common for buyers not to be required to take minimum quantities when market conditions change. Buyer also seeks to introduce evidence that in prior dealings between these parties, that the buyer had not taken the minimum quantity and that the seller had not held buyer responsible. Is the evidence of the industry practice and the prior dealings between the parties admissible? See UCC §2-202(a); *Columbia Nitrogen Corp. v. Royster Co.*, 451 F.2d 3 (4th Cir. 1971). Could the parties have drafted a clause that would prevent admission of such evidence? Would such a clause be wise? See UCC §2-202, Official Comment 2.

***Problem 5-8.*** A negotiated sales contract contains a merger clause and is very detailed. Buyer sues for breach of an express warranty that the buyer claims was made orally prior to the execution of the contract. The seller admits to you that the statement was made but was not included in the written contract. Would it be ethical to raise the parol evidence rule as a defense? What counsel would you give the client? See discussion in Problem 3-9, *supra*.

## MCC-Marble Ceramic Center v. Ceramica Nuova D'Agostino

United States Court of Appeals, 11th Circuit

144 F.3d 1384 (1998)

This case requires us to determine whether a court must consider parol evidence in a contract dispute governed by the United Nations Convention on Contracts for the International Sale of Goods ("CISG"). The district court granted summary judgment on behalf of the defendant-appellee, relying on certain terms and provisions that appeared on the reverse of a preprinted form contract for the sale of ceramic tiles. The plaintiff-appellant sought to rely on a number of affidavits that tended to show both that the parties had arrived at an oral contract before memorializing their agreement in writing and that they subjectively intended not to apply the terms on the reverse of the contract to their agreements. The magistrate judge held that the affidavits did not raise an issue of material fact and recommended that the district court grant summary judgment based on the terms of the contract. The district court agreed with the magistrate judge's reasoning and entered summary judgment in the defendant-appellee's favor. We REVERSE.

**Background**

The plaintiff-appellant, MCC-Marble Ceramic, Inc. ("MCC"), is a Florida corporation engaged in the retail sale of tiles, and the defendant-appellee, Ceramica Nuova d'Agostino S.p.A. ("D'Agostino"), is an Italian corporation engaged in the manufacture of ceramic tiles. In October 1990, MCC's president, Juan Carlos Monzon, met representatives of D'Agostino at a trade fair in Bologna, Italy, and negotiated an agreement to purchase ceramic tiles from D'Agostino based on samples he examined at the trade fair. Monzon, who spoke no Italian, communicated with Gianni Silingardi, then D'Agostino's commercial director, through a translator, Gianfranco Copelli, who was himself an agent of D'Agostino. The parties apparently arrived at an oral agreement on the crucial terms of price, quality, quantity, delivery, and payment. The parties then recorded these terms on one of D'Agostino's standard, preprinted order forms and Monzon signed the contract on MCC's behalf. According to MCC, the parties also entered into a requirements contract in February 1991, subject to which D'Agostino agreed to supply MCC with high-grade ceramic tile at specific discounts as long as MCC purchased sufficient quantities of tile. MCC completed a number of additional order forms requesting tile deliveries pursuant to that agreement.

MCC brought suit against D'Agostino claiming a breach of the February 1991 requirements contract when D'Agostino failed to satisfy orders in April, May, and August of 1991. In addition to other defenses, D'Agostino responded that it was under no obligation to fill MCC's orders because MCC had defaulted on payment for previous shipments. In support of its position, D'Agostino relied on the preprinted terms of the contracts that MCC had executed. The executed forms were printed in Italian and contained terms and conditions on both the front and reverse. According to an English translation of the October 1990 contract, the front of the order form contained the following language directly beneath Monzon's signature:

> [T]he buyer hereby states that he is aware of the sales conditions stated on the reverse and that he expressly approves of them with special reference to those numbered 1-2-3-4-5-6-7-8.

R2-126, Exh. 3 ¶5 ("Maselli Aff.").

Clause 6(b), printed on the back of the form states:

> [D]efault or delay in payment within the time agreed upon gives D'Agostino the right to . . . suspend or cancel the contract itself and to cancel possible other pending contracts and the buyer does not have the right to indemnification or damages.

*Id.*¶6.

D'Agostino also brought a number of counterclaims against MCC, seeking damages for MCC's alleged nonpayment for deliveries of tile that D'Agostino had made between February 28, 1991, and July 4, 1991. MCC responded that the tile it had received was of a lower quality than contracted for, and that, pursuant to the CISG, MCC was entitled to reduce payment in proportion to the defects. D'Agostino, however, noted that Clause 4 on the reverse of the contract states, in pertinent part:

> Possible complaints for defects of the merchandise must be made in writing by means of a certified letter within and not later than 10 days after receipt of the merchandise . . . .

Maselli Aff. ¶6.

Although there is evidence to support MCC's claims that it complained about the quality of the deliveries it received, MCC never submitted any written complaints.

MCC did not dispute these underlying facts before the district court, but argued that the parties never intended the terms and conditions printed on the reverse of the order form to apply to their agreements. As evidence for this assertion, MCC submitted Monzon's affidavit, which claims that MCC had no subjective intent to be bound by those terms and that D'Agostino was aware of this intent. MCC also filed affidavits from Silingardi and Copelli, D'Agostino's representatives at the trade fair, which support Monzon's claim that the parties subjectively intended not to be bound by the terms on the reverse of the order form. The magistrate judge held that the affidavits, even if true, did not raise an issue of material fact regarding the interpretation or applicability of the terms of the written contracts and the district court accepted his recommendation to award summary judgment in D'Agostino's favor. MCC then filed this timely appeal.

**Discussion**

The parties to this case agree that the CISG governs their dispute because the United States, where MCC has its place of business, and Italy, where D'Agostino has its place of business, are both States Party to the Convention. See CISG, Article 1. Article 8 of the CISG governs the interpretation of international contracts for the sale of goods, and forms the basis of MCC's appeal from the district court's grant of summary judgment in D'Agostino's favor. MCC argues that the magistrate judge and the district court improperly ignored evidence that MCC submitted regarding the parties' subjective intent when they memorialized the terms of their agreement on D'Agostino's preprinted form contract, and that the magistrate judge erred by applying the parol evidence rule in derogation of the CISG.

I. Subjective Intent under the CISG

Contrary to what is familiar practice in U.S. courts, the CISG appears to permit a substantial inquiry into the parties' subjective intent, even if the parties did not engage in any objectively ascertainable means of registering this intent. Article 8(1) of the CISG instructs courts to interpret the "statements . . . and other conduct of a party . . . according to his intent" as long as the other party "knew or could not have been unaware" of that intent. The plain language of the Convention, therefore, requires an inquiry into a party's subjective intent as long as the other party to the contract was aware of that intent.

In this case, MCC has submitted three affidavits that discuss the purported subjective intent of the parties to the initial agreement concluded between MCC and D'Agostino in October 1990. All three affidavits discuss the preliminary negotiations and report that the parties arrived at an oral agreement for D'Agostino to supply quantities of a specific grade of ceramic tile to MCC at an agreed-upon price. The affidavits state that the "oral agreement established the essential terms of quality, quantity, description of goods, delivery, price and payment." See R3-133 ¶9 ("Silingardi Aff."); R1-51 ¶7 ("Copelli Aff."); R1-47 ¶7 ("Monzon Aff."). The affidavits also note that the parties memorialized the terms of their oral agreement on a standard D'Agostino order form, but all three affiants contend that the parties *subjectively* intended not to be bound by the terms on the reverse of that form despite a provision directly below the signature line that expressly and specifically incorporated those terms.

The terms on the reverse of the contract give D'Agostino the right to suspend or cancel all contracts in the event of a buyer's nonpayment and require a buyer to make a written report of all defects within ten days. As the magistrate judge's report and recommendation makes clear, if these terms applied to the agreements between MCC and D'Agostino, summary judgment would be appropriate because MCC failed to make any written complaints about the quality of tile it received and D'Agostino has established MCC's nonpayment of a number of invoices amounting to $108,389.40 and 102,053,846.00 Italian lira.

Article 8(1) of the CISG requires a court to consider this evidence of the parties' subjective intent. Contrary to the magistrate judge's report, which the district court endorsed and adopted, Article 8(1) does not focus on interpreting the parties' statements alone. Although we agree with the magistrate judge's conclusion that no "interpretation" of the contract's *terms* could support MCC's position, Article 8(1) also requires a court to consider subjective intent while interpreting the *conduct* of the parties. The CISG's language, therefore, requires courts to consider evidence of a party's subjective intent when signing a contract if the other party to the contract was aware of that intent at the time. This is precisely the type of evidence that MCC has provided through the Silingardi, Copelli, and Monzon affidavits, which discuss not only Monzon's intent as MCC's representative but also discuss the intent of D'Agostino's representatives and their knowledge that Monzon did not intend to agree to the terms on the reverse of the form contract. This acknowledgment that D'Agostino's representatives were aware of Monzon's subjective intent puts this case squarely within Article 8(1) of the CISG, and therefore requires the court to consider MCC's evidence as it interprets the parties' conduct.

II. Parol Evidence and the CISG

Given our determination that the magistrate judge and the district court should have considered MCC's affidavits regarding the parties' subjective intentions, we must address a question of first impression in this circuit: whether the parol evidence rule, which bars evidence of an earlier oral contract that contradicts or varies the terms of a subsequent or contemporaneous written contract, plays any role in cases involving the CISG. We begin by observing that the parol evidence rule, contrary to its title, is a substantive rule of law, not a rule of evidence. See II E. Allen Farnsworth, *Farnsworth on Contracts,* §7.2 at 194 (1990). The rule does not purport to exclude a particular type of evidence as an "untrustworthy or undesirable" way of proving a fact, but prevents a litigant from attempting to show "the fact itself—the fact that the terms of the agreement are other than those in the writing." *Id.* As such, a federal district court cannot simply apply the parol evidence rule as a procedural matter—as it might if excluding a particular type of evidence under the Federal Rules of Evidence, which apply in federal court regardless of the source of the substantive rule of decision. *Cf. id.* §7.2 at 196.

The CISG itself contains no express statement on the role of parol evidence. *See* Honnold, *Uniform Law* §110 at 170. It is clear, however, that the drafters of the CISG were comfortable with the concept of permitting parties to rely on oral contracts because they eschewed any statutes of fraud provision and expressly provided for the enforcement of oral contracts. *Compare* CISG, Article 11 (a contract of sale need not be concluded or evidenced in writing) *with* UCC §2-201 (precluding the enforcement of oral contracts for the sale of goods involving more than $500). Moreover, Article 8(3) of the CISG expressly directs courts to give "due consideration . . . to all relevant circumstances of the case including the negotiations . . . " to determine the intent of the parties. Given Article 8(1)'s directive to use the intent of the parties to interpret their statements and conduct, Article 8(3) is a clear instruction to admit and consider parol evidence regarding the negotiations to the extent they reveal the parties' subjective intent.

Our reading of Article 8(3) as a rejection of the parol evidence rule is in accordance with the great weight of academic commentary on the issue. As one scholar has explained:

> [T]he language of Article 8(3) that "due consideration is to be given to *all relevant* circumstances of the case" seems adequate to override any domestic rule that would bar a tribunal from considering the relevance of other agreements. . . . Article 8(3) relieves tribunals from domestic rules that might bar them from "considering" any evidence between the parties that is relevant. This added flexibility for interpretation is consistent with a growing body of opinion that the "parol evidence rule" has been an embarrassment for the administration of modern transactions.

*Honnold,* Uniform Law §110 at 170-171. Indeed, only one commentator has made any serious attempt to reconcile the parol evidence rule with the CISG. See David H. Moore, Note, *The Parol Evidence Rule and the United Nations Convention on Contracts for the International Sale of Goods: Justifying Beijing Metals & Minerals Import/Export Corp. v. American Business Center, Inc.*, 1995 BYU L. Rev. 1347. Moore argues that the parol evidence rule often permits the admission of evidence discussed in Article 8(3), and that the rule could be an appropriate way to discern what consideration is "due" under Article 8(3) to evidence of a parol nature. *Id.* at 1361-1363. He also argues that the parol evidence rule, by limiting the incentive for perjury and pleading prior understandings in bad faith, promotes good faith and uniformity in the interpretation of contracts and therefore is in harmony with the principles of the CISG, as expressed in Article 7. *Id.* at 1366-1370. The answer to both these arguments, however, is the same: Although jurisdictions in the United States have found the parol evidence rule helpful to promote good faith and uniformity in contracts, as well as an appropriate answer to the question of how much consideration to give parol evidence, a wide number of other states party to the CISG have rejected the rule in their domestic jurisdictions. One of the primary factors motivating the negotiation and adoption of the CISG was to provide parties to international contracts for the sale of goods with some degree of certainty as to the principles of law that would govern potential disputes and remove the previous doubt regarding which party's legal system might otherwise apply. See Letter of Transmittal from Ronald Reagan, President of the United States, to the United States Senate, *reprinted at* 15 U.S.C. app. 70, 71 (1997). Courts applying the CISG cannot, therefore, upset the parties' reliance on the Convention by substituting familiar principles of domestic law when the Convention requires a different result. We may only achieve the directives of good faith and uniformity in contracts under the CISG by interpreting and applying the plain language of Article 8(3) as written and obeying its directive to consider this type of parol evidence.

This is not to say that parties to an international contract for the sale of goods cannot depend on written contracts or that parol evidence regarding subjective contractual intent need always prevent a party relying on a written agreement from securing summary judgment. To the contrary, most cases will not present a situation (as exists in this case) in which both parties to the contract acknowledge a subjective intent not to be bound by the terms of a preprinted writing. In most cases, therefore, Article 8(2) of the CISG will apply, and objective evidence will provide the basis for the court's decision. See Honnold, *Uniform Law* §107 at 164-165. Consequently, a party to a contract governed by the CISG will not be able to avoid the terms of a contract and force a jury trial simply by submitting an affidavit which states that he or she did not have the subjective intent to be bound by the contract's terms. Moreover, to the extent parties wish to avoid parol evidence problems they can do so by including a merger clause in their agreement that extinguishes any and all prior agreements and understandings not expressed in the writing.

Considering MCC's affidavits in this case, however, we conclude that the magistrate judge and the district court improperly granted summary judgment in favor of D'Agostino. Although the affidavits are, as D'Agostino observes, relatively conclusory and unsupported by facts that would *objectively* establish MCC's intent not to be bound by the conditions on the reverse of the form, Article 8(1) requires a court to consider evidence of a party's subjective intent when the other party was aware of it, and the Silingardi and Copelli affidavits provide that evidence. This is not to say that the affidavits are conclusive proof of what the parties intended. A reasonable finder of fact, for example, could disregard testimony that purportedly sophisticated international merchants signed a contract without intending to be bound as simply too incredible to believe and hold MCC to the conditions printed on the reverse of the contract. Nevertheless, the affidavits raise an issue of material fact regarding the parties' intent to incorporate the provisions on the reverse of the form contract. If the finder of fact determines that the parties did not intend to rely on those provisions, then the more general provisions of the CISG will govern the outcome of the dispute.

Accordingly, we REVERSE and REMAND this case for further proceedings consistent with this opinion.

### PROBLEM

***Problem 5-9.*** How would you draft a clause to prevent the evidence of the prior agreement from being admitted in the foregoing case? Would the clause have any meaning if it was also contained on the back of the form and if it was in Italian?

## D. UNCONSCIONABILITY

Under the UCC, terms in a contract will not be enforced if the court considers them to be "unconscionable." You probably spent some time discussing unconscionability in your contracts course. When is a provision "unconscionable"? Perhaps the test that Justice Potter Stewart used for obscenity is appropriate: You know it when you see it![4] The drafters of the UCC attempt to give some guidance in the official comments to section 2-302: "The basic test is whether, in light of the general commercial background and the commercial needs of the particular trade or case, the clauses involved are so one-sided as to be unconscionable under the circumstances existing at the time of the making of the contract . . . The principle is one of the prevention of oppression and unfair surprise . . . and not of disturbance of allocation of risks because of superior bargaining power." The drafters provide some examples of clauses that might be considered unconscionable in Official Comment 1 to section 2-302.

Most courts will require the existence of both a procedural and substantive element before invalidating a contract or a clause of a contract on the basis of unconscionability. The procedural element goes to flaws in the bargaining process, unequal bargaining power and the use of "take it or leave it" form contracts (called contracts of adhesion). The substantive element goes to the fairness of the term. Section 2-302 makes it clear that the question of unconscionability is one for the court to decide, based on the evidence presented. The court is allowed to invalidate the entire contract, a clause of the contract, or limit the application of a clause.

The CISG does not have any provisions dealing with unconscionability. Unconscionability would be a question of a contract's validity, and is thus not considered under Article 4. If choice-of-law rules would indicate that the UCC fills gaps left by the CISG in a transaction otherwise covered by the CISG, a court might use UCC section 2-302 to invalidate any provisions that it

---

4. *See Jacobellis v. Ohio*, 378 U.S. 184 (Stewart, J., concurring).

thought were unconscionable. Keep in mind, however, that transactions covered by the CISG are commercial transactions involving merchants who are expected to be able to look out for themselves. In the following case, however, the court used unconscionability to protect a buyer in a domestic commercial transaction.

## A&M Produce Co. v. FMC Corp.

California Court of Appeal

135 Cal. App. 3d 473, 186 Cal. Rptr. 114 (1982)

Defendant FMC Corporation (FMC) appeals from the judgment entered in favor of plaintiff A&M Produce Co. (A&M) in the net sum of $255,000 plus $45,000 attorney's fees.

A&M, a farming company in the Imperial Valley, is solely owned by C. Alex Abatti who has been farming all of his life. In late 1973, after talking with two of his employees, he decided to grow tomatoes. Although they had grown produce before, they had never grown tomatoes or any other crop requiring a weight-sizer and were not familiar with weight-sizing equipment. They first spoke with a salesman from Decco Equipment Company regarding the purchase of the necessary equipment. The salesman explained A&M would need a hydrocooler in addition to a weight-sizer and submitted a bid of $68,000 for the equipment. Abatti thought the Decco bid was high, and contacted FMC for a competitive bid.

According to Abatti, Isch [of FMC] recommended FMC equipment because it operated so fast that a hydrocooler was unnecessary, thereby saving A&M about $25,000.

Isch obtained Abatti's signature to a "field order" for the equipment. The order was on a standard form, printed on both sides, the terms of which were identical to the written contract that Abatti later received. Along with the order, Abatti delivered his $5,000 check as a deposit. The total price was $32,041.80.

The provisions of the agreement which are important are: paragraph 3, "Seller's Remedies," outlining the buyer's obligation to pay seller's reasonable attorney's fees in connection with any defaults by the buyer; paragraph 4, "Warranty," containing a disclaimer of warranties, in bold print; and paragraph 5, "Disclaimer of Consequential Damages," stating in somewhat smaller print that "Seller in no event shall be liable for consequential damages arising out of or in connection with this agreement . . . . "

Abatti signed the agreement and returned it to FMC with his check for an additional $5,680.60 as a down payment. In April 1974, FMC delivered and installed the machinery. A&M's problems with the FMC equipment began during the third week of May, when it started to pick the tomatoes. Tomatoes piled up in front of the singulator belt, which separated the tomatoes for weight-sizing. Overflow tomatoes had to be sent through the machinery again, causing damage to the crop. The damage was aggravated because the tomatoes were not cooled by a hydrocooler, allowing a fungus to spread more quickly within the damaged fruit.

A&M offered to return the weight-sizer to FMC provided FMC would refund A&M's down payment and pay the freight charges. FMC rejected this offer and demanded full payment of the balance due.

A&M then filed this action for damages against FMC for breach of express warranties and breach of an implied warranty for a particular use.

After hearing evidence presented to the jury, and additional evidence in the absence of the jury on the nature of the contract's formation and the bargaining position of the respective parties, the court ruled:

> [I]t would be unconscionable to enforce [the waivers of warranties and waiver of consequential damage] provisions of the agreement, and further that they are not set out in a conspicuous fashion.

The court's ruling is based on all of the circumstances in this case in connection with how the negotiations were conducted, the fact that initially a substantial down payment of $5,000 was made, and later on the contract was signed.

Accordingly, the jury viewed only the front of the contract, not the reverse side with its lengthy provisions.

The jury returned a general verdict for $281,326 [for plaintiff].

FMC's initial attack on the judgment alleges prejudicial error by the trial court in not allowing the jury to see the reverse side of the written agreement, which contained both a disclaimer of all warranties as well as a provision stating that in the event a warranty was made, the buyer was precluded from recovering consequential damages resulting from a breach of the warranty. The trial court's decision to exclude evidence of the contents of the agreement's reverse side was based on its determination that the warranty disclaimer and the consequential damage exclusions were unconscionable and therefore unenforceable. If this determination was correct the reverse side of the contract was appropriately withheld from the jury.

FMC argues that unconscionability is inapplicable to disclaimers of warranty, being supplanted by the more specific policing provisions of UCC section 2-316. We conclude otherwise, however.

Unconscionability is a flexible doctrine designed to allow courts to directly consider numerous factors that may adulterate the contractual process. Uniform Commercial Code section 2-302 specifies that "any clause of the contract" may be unconscionable. The policing provisions of section 2-316 are limited to problems involving the visibility of disclaimers and conflicts with express warranties. But oppression and unfair surprise, the principal targets of the unconscionability doctrine, may result from other types of questionable commercial practices.

Unconscionability has both a "procedural" and a "substantive" element. Procedural unconscionability appears to be present on the facts of this case. Although the printing used on the warranty disclaimer was conspicuous, the terms of the consequential damage exclusion are not particularly apparent, being only slightly larger than most of the other contract text. Both provisions appear in the middle of the back page of a long preprinted form contract that was only casually shown to Abatti. It was never suggested to him, either verbally or in writing, that he read the back of the form. Abatti testified he never read the reverse side terms. There was thus sufficient evidence before the trial court to conclude that Abatti was in fact surprised by the warranty disclaimer and the consequential damage exclusion. How "unfair" his surprise was is subject to some dispute. He certainly had the opportunity to read the back of the contract or to seek the advice of a lawyer. Yet as a factual matter, given the complexity of the terms and FMC's failure to direct his attention to them, Abatti's omission may not be totally unreasonable.

In fact, one suspects that the length, complexity, and obtuseness of most form contracts may be due at least in part to the seller's preference that the buyer will be dissuaded from reading that to which he is supposedly agreeing.

Even if we ignore any suggestion of unfair surprise, there is ample evidence of unequal bargaining power here and a lack of any real negotiation over the terms of the contract. Although it was conceded that A&M was a large-scale farming enterprise by Imperial Valley standards, employing five persons on a regular basis and up to 50 seasonal employees at harvest time, and that Abatti was farming some 8,000 acres in 1974, FMC Corporation is in an entirely different category. The 1974 gross sales of the Agriculture Machinery Division alone amounted to $40 million. More important, the terms on the FMC form contract were standard. FMC salesmen were not authorized to negotiate any of the terms appearing on the reverse side of the preprinted contract. Although FMC contends that in some special instances, individual contracts are negotiated, A&M was never made aware of that option. The sum total of these circumstances leads to the conclusion that this contract was a "bargain" only in the most general sense of the word.

Although the procedural aspects of unconscionability are present in this case, we suspect the substantive unconscionability of the disclaimer and exclusion provisions contributed equally to the trial court's ultimate conclusion. As to the disclaimer of warranties, the facts of this case support the trial court's conclusion that such disclaimer was commercially unreasonable. The warranty allegedly breached by FMC went to the basic performance characteristics of the product. In attempting to disclaim this and all other warranties, FMC was in essence guaranteeing nothing about what the product would do. Since a product's performance forms the fundamental basis for a sales contract, it is patently unreasonable to assume that a buyer would purchase a standardized mass-produced product from an industry seller without any enforceable performance standards. From a social perspective, risk of loss is most appropriately borne by the party best able to prevent its occurrence. Rarely would the buyer be in a better position than the manufacturer-seller to evaluate the performance characteristics of a machine.

A&M had no previous experience with weight-sizing machines and was forced to rely on the expertise of FMC in recommending the necessary equipment. FMC was abundantly aware of this fact. The jury here necessarily found that FMC either expressly or impliedly guaranteed a performance level which the machine was unable to meet. Especially where an inexperienced buyer is concerned, the seller's performance representations are absolutely necessary to allow the buyer to make an intelligent choice among the competitive options available. A seller's attempt, through the use of a disclaimer, to prevent the buyer from reasonably relying on such representations calls into question the commercial reasonableness of the agreement and may well be substantively unconscionable. The trial court's conclusion to that effect is amply supported by the record before us.

## QUESTION AND PROBLEMS

**1.** If a disclaimer meets the requirements of section 2-316, is it appropriate to invalidate it on the basis of unconscionability, especially if the buyer is a commercial entity? What are the policy problems raised by this case? Would it make more sense to analyze this case under UCC section 2-316(1)?

***Problem 5-10.*** Buyer purchased a computer and service contract from Dell Computers over the internet. After receiving the order, Dell sent Buyer an order acknowledgment form, the back of which contained Dell's "Terms and Conditions Agreement." A copy of the agreement was also included in the box in which the computer was shipped, and was available for Buyer to view on Dell's Web site before placing orders. The pertinent part of the agreement read as follows:

PLEASE READ THIS DOCUMENT CAREFULLY!
IT CONTAINS VERY IMPORTANT INFORMATION ABOUT YOUR RIGHTS
AND
OBLIGATIONS, AS
WELL AS LIMITATIONS AND EXCLUSIONS THAT MAY APPLY TO YOU.
THIS
DOCUMENT
CONTAINS A DISPUTE RESOLUTION CLAUSE

13. Binding Arbitration. ANY CLAIM . . . AGAINST DELL, its agents, employees, successors, assigns or affiliates (collectively for purposes of this paragraph, "Dell") arising from or relating to this Agreement, its interpretation, or the breach, termination or validity thereof, the relationships which result from this Agreement (including, to the full extent permitted by applicable law, relationships with third parties who are not signatories to this Agreement), Dell's advertising, or any related purchase SHALL BE RESOLVED EXCLUSIVELY AND FINALLY BY BINDING ARBITRATION ADMINISTERED BY THE NATIONAL ARBITRATION FORUM (NAF). . . . The arbitration will be limited solely to the dispute or controversy between Customer and Dell.

Buyer claimed that Dell improperly calculated the $10.65 sales tax that it charged on the transaction, and wants to file a class action lawsuit. Dell seeks to have the lawsuit dismissed, and to have Buyer's individual claim arbitrated pursuant to the sales contract. Under the rules of the NAF in place at the time of the dispute for this type of dispute, Buyer would incur a $25 filing fee to initiate arbitration, which could be completed without a hearing through written submissions, and an additional $75 fee if a participatory hearing was scheduled. Buyer would also incur an additional $100 fee if written findings from the arbitrator were requested. These fees included the fees of the arbitrator. Rule 37(c) of the NAF Code of Procedure provides that an arbitration "[a]ward may include fees and costs awarded by an Arbitrator in favor of any Party."

Based on these facts, should the arbitration provision be declared unconscionable? *See Stenzel v. Dell, Inc.*, 2005 ME 37, 870 A.2d 133 (2005). *Cf. Armendariz v. Foundation Health Psychare Services, Inc.*, 24 Cal. 4th 83, 6 P.3d 669, 99 Cal. Rptr. 745 (2000) (holding that for an arbitration provision to be enforceable in a dispute between an employer and an employee, the provision must be mutual, must permit some limited discovery, must provide for written findings for at least some judicial review, must provide for a neutral arbitrator, and must require the employer to cover the costs unique to arbitration). As to the provision indicating "[t]he arbitration will be limited solely to the dispute or controversy between Customer and Dell" (referred to as a "class action waiver"), see *AT&T Mobility v. Concepcion*, __U.S.___, 131 S.Ct. 1740 (2011)(holding that class action waivers are enforceable in arbitration agreements under the Federal Arbitration Act, even if such waivers are unconscionable under applicable state law).

## PROBLEM

***Problem 5-11.*** In a home solicitation sale, buyers, who are welfare recipients, agreed to purchase a freezer for $900. With the addition of time credit charges, credit life insurance, credit property insurance, and sales tax, the purchase price totaled $1,234.80. To date, buyers have paid $619.88. Evidence indicates that the fair market retail cash price for this freezer is $300. May buyers stop paying and defend on the grounds that the price is unconscionable? Would it matter if the buyers were not welfare recipients but instead were middle-class consumers? *Jones v. Star Credit*, 59 Misc. 2d 189, 298 N.Y.S.2d 264 (1969). *Cf. Remco Enterprises, Inc. v. Houston*, 9 Kan. App. 2d 296, 677 P.2d 567 (1984) ("where the contract price is more than 2 times the fair retail value of the goods, there is a greatly increased possibility that the contract will be declared to be unconscionable").

## CHAPTER 5 REVIEW PROBLEM

Buyer, a car collector, was interested in purchasing a special model Chevrolet Corvette, the same model of which had served as the pace car for the Indianapolis 500 auto race. Buyer went to a Chevrolet auto dealer and contracted to buy one before they arrived at the dealership—it was anticipated that there would be a large demand and a limited supply. Buyer put down $500 as a deposit on the purchase price, and signed a contract that had the price left blank. The contract also had a merger clause. It also provided that the risk of any loss to the car would pass to Buyer on the date that the car was tendered by the dealer to the buyer.

When the Corvettes arrived at the dealership, Dealer designated one for Buyer, called Buyer, and told Buyer that the car was available and that it would cost Buyer $70,000. The sticker price (manufacturer's suggested retail price) of the car was $50,000, but because of the demand for the car, dealers were able to get around $70,000 for them. Buyer objected, claiming that before the parties had signed the contract, they had agreed that the price charged would be the sticker price, and that it had been left blank because the parties were waiting to see what it would be. Dealer denied any such agreement, and stated that the reason the price was left blank was because Dealer wanted to see what the market would bear for the car.

One day later, the car was stolen from Dealer's lot through no fault of Dealer, and Dealer now wants to hold Buyer under the risk of loss provision of the contract for loss of a $70,000 car. Is there a contract between the parties? If so, what was the price of the car? Was the risk of loss provision enforceable? Please analyze under both the UCC and the CISG. Some of the issues in this problem are based on *Landrum v. Devenport*, 616 S.W.2d 359 (Tex. App. 1981). Under the UCC, please see §§2-202, 2-302, 2-305, 2-503, and 2-509. Under the CISG, please see Articles 4, 6, 14, 55, and 69.

CHAPTER 6

# PERFORMANCE, BREACH, AND EXCUSE

## A. PROSPECTIVE NONPERFORMANCE—INSECURITY AND REPUDIATION

Both the CISG and the UCC recognize that there is an obligation on each party to the sales contract not to impair the other party's expectation of receiving performance. In some circumstances, a party is entitled to demand adequate assurance of performance and to suspend performance until adequate assurance is forthcoming. Two important questions are raised: (1) When does a party have grounds to demand adequate assurance, and (2) what constitutes adequate assurance? The Official Commentary to UCC section 2-609 provides some guidance as to the answers to these questions and should be read. For example, if a buyer falls behind in paying accounts owed to the seller, Comment 3 indicates that a seller's expectation of future performance is impaired. Trustworthy reports that a seller has been shipping defective goods would normally give the buyer reasonable grounds for insecurity.

In other situations, one party will either directly state that it will not perform in the future or will take steps that make it apparently unable to perform. This is referred to as repudiation or anticipatory breach. Failure to provide adequate assurance when the other party is justified in demanding it will also constitute repudiation. In such a situation, the other party is justified in terminating the contract if the repudiation would result in a substantial impairment in value in a UCC case or a fundamental breach in a CISG case. We will discuss the concept of "substantial impairment" and "fundamental breach" later in this chapter. A question may exist in some cases as to whether a repudiation has occurred. In such a situation, the other party is at risk if it terminates the contract as that termination may itself constitute a repudiation.

## Hornell Brewing Co. v. Spry

Supreme Court, New York County, New York

174 Misc. 2d 451, 664 N.Y.S.2d 698 (1997)

Plaintiff Hornell Brewing Co., Inc. ("Hornell"), a supplier and marketer of alcoholic and nonalcoholic beverages, including the popular iced-tea drink "Arizona," commenced this action for a declaratory judgment that any rights of defendants Stephen A. Spry and Arizona Tea Products Ltd. to distribute Hornell's beverages in Canada have been duly terminated, that defendants have no further rights with respect to these products, including no right to market and distribute them, and that any such rights previously transferred to defendants have reverted to Hornell.

In late 1992, Spry approached Don Vultaggio, Hornell's chairman of the board, about becoming a distributor of Hornell's Arizona beverages. Vultaggio had heard about Spry as an extremely wealthy and successful beer distributor who had recently sold his business. In January 1993, Spry presented Vultaggio with an ambitious plan for distributing Arizona beverages in Canada. Based on the plan and on Spry's reputation, but without further investigation, Hornell in early 1993 granted Spry the exclusive right to purchase Arizona products for distribution in Canada, and Spry formed a Canadian corporation, Arizona Iced Tea Ltd., for that express purpose.

Initially, the arrangement was purely oral. In response to Spry's request for a letter he needed to secure financing, Hornell provided a letter in July 1993 confirming their exclusive distributorship arrangement, but without spelling out the details of the arrangement. Although Hornell usually had detailed written distributorship agreements and the parties discussed and exchanged drafts of such an agreement, none was ever executed. In the meantime, Spry, with Hornell's approval, proceeded to set himself up as Hornell's distributor in Canada. During 1993 and until May 1994, the Hornell line of beverages, including the Arizona beverages, was sold to defendants on ten-day credit terms. In May 1994, after an increasingly problematic course of business dealings, Hornell de facto terminated its relationship with defendants and permanently ceased selling its products to them.

The problem dominating the parties' relationship between July 1993 and early May 1994 was defendants' failure to remit timely payment for shipments of beverages received from plaintiff. Between November and December 1993 and February 1994, defendants' unpaid invoices grew from $20,000 to over $100,000, and their $31,000 check to Hornell was returned for insufficient funds. Moreover, defendants' 1993 sales in Canada were far below Spry's initial projections.

In March and April 1994, a series of meetings, telephone calls, and letter communications took place between plaintiff and defendants regarding Spry's constant arrearages and the need for him to obtain a line and/or letter of credit that would place their business relationship on a more secure footing. These contacts included a March 27, 1994, letter to Spry from Vanguard Financial Group, Inc., confirming "the approval of a $1,500,000 revolving credit facility" to Arizona Tea Products Ltd., which never materialized into an actual line of credit; Spry sent Hornell a copy of this letter in late March or early April 1994.

All of these exchanges demonstrate that during this period plaintiff had two distinct goals: to collect the monies owed by Spry, and to stabilize their future business relationship based on proven, reliable credit assurances. These exchanges also establish that during March and April 1994, Spry repeatedly broke his promises to pay by a specified deadline, causing Hornell to question whether Vanguard's $1.5 million revolving line of credit was genuine.

On April 15, 1994, during a meeting with Vultaggio, Spry arranged for Vultaggio to speak on the telephone with Richard Worthy of Metro Factors, Inc. The testimony as to the content of that brief telephone conversation is conflicting. Although Worthy testified that he identified himself and the name of his company, Metro Factors, Inc., Vultaggio testified that he believed Worthy was from an "unusual lending institution" or bank that was going to provide Spry with a line of credit, and that nothing was expressly said to make him aware that Worthy represented a factoring company.[1] Worthy also testified that Vultaggio told him that once Spry cleared up the arrears, Hornell would provide Spry with a "$300,000 line of credit, so long as payments were made on a net 14-day basis." According to Vultaggio, he told Worthy that once he was paid in full, he was willing to resume shipments to Spry "so long as Steve fulfills his requirements with us."

Hornell's April 18, 1994, letter to Spry confirmed certain details of the April 15 conversations, including that payment of the arrears would be made by April 19, 1994. However, Hornell received no payment on that date. Instead, on April 25, Hornell received from Spry a proposed letter for Hornell to address to a company named "Metro" at a post office box in Dallas, Texas. Worthy originally sent Spry a draft of this letter with "Metro Factors, Inc." named as the addressee, but in the copy Vultaggio received the words "Factors, Inc." were apparently obliterated. Hornell copied the draft letter on its own letterhead and sent it to Metro over Vultaggio's signature. In relevant part, the letter stated as follows:

> **Gentlemen:**
> Please be advised that Arizona Tea Products, Ltd. (ATP), of which Steve Spry is president, is presently indebted to us in the total amount of $79,316.24 as of the beginning of business Monday, April 25, 1994. We sell to them on "Net 14 days" terms. Such total amount is due according to the following schedule:
>
> * * *
>
> Upon receipt of $79,316.24. (which shall be applied to the oldest balances first) by 5:00 P.M. (EST) Tuesday, May 2, 1994, by wire transfer(s) to the account described below, we shall recommence selling product to ATP on the following terms:
>
> (1) All invoices from us are due and payable by the 14th day following the release of the related product.

1. A "factoring company" is in the business of purchasing accounts receivable. One way for a business to obtain credit is to sell its accounts receivable to a factor, at a discount. That way, the business receives money immediately rather than waiting for its customers to pay. —Ed.

> (2) We shall allow the outstanding balance owed to us by ATP to go up to $300,000 so long as ATP remains "current" in its payment obligations to us. Wiring instructions are as follows:
>
> * * *

Hornell received no payment on May 2, 1994. It did receive a wire transfer from Metro of the full amount on May 9, 1994. Upon immediate confirmation of that payment, Spry ordered 30 trailer loads of "product" from Hornell, at a total purchase price of $390,000 to $450,000. In the interim, between April 25, 1994, and May 9, 1994, Hornell learned from several sources, including its regional sales manager Baumkel, that Spry's warehouse was empty, that he had no managerial, sales, or office staff, that he had no trucks, and that in effect his operation was a sham.

On May 10, 1994, Hornell wrote to Spry, acknowledging receipt of payment and confirming that they would extend up to $300,000 of credit to him, net 14 days cash "based on your prior representation that you have secured a $1,500,000 U.S. line of credit." The letter also stated,

> Your current balance with us reflects a $0 balance due. As you know, however, we experienced considerable difficulty and time wasted over a five-week time period as we tried to collect some $130,000 which was 90-120 days past due.
>
> Accordingly, before we release any more product, we are asking you to provide us with a letter confirming the existence of your line of credit as well as a personal guarantee that is backed up with a personal financial statement that can be verified. Another option would be for you to provide us with an irrevocable letter of credit in the amount of $300,000.

Spry did not respond to this letter. Spry never even sent Hornell a copy of his agreement with Metro Factors, Inc., which Spry had signed on March 24, 1994, and which was fully executed on March 30, 1994. On May 26, 1994, Vultaggio met with Spry to discuss termination of their business relationship. Vultaggio presented Spry with a letter of agreement as to the termination, which Spry took with him but did not sign. After some months of futile negotiations by counsel this action by Hornell ensued.

Plaintiff has demonstrated a basis for lawfully terminating its contract with defendants in accordance with section 2-609 of the Uniform Commercial Code. Section 2-609(1) authorizes one party upon "reasonable grounds for insecurity" to "demand adequate assurance of due performance and until he receives such assurance . . . if commercially reasonable suspend any performance for which he has not already received the agreed return." The Official Comment to section 2-609 explains that this

> section rests on the recognition of the fact that the essential purpose of a contract between commercial men is actual performance and they do not bargain merely for a promise, or for a promise plus the right to win a lawsuit and that a continuing sense of reliance and security that the promised performance will be forthcoming when due, is an important feature of the bargain. If either the willingness or the ability of a party to perform declines materially between the time of contracting and the time for performance, the other party is threatened with the loss of a substantial part of what he has bargained for. A seller needs protection not merely against having to deliver on credit to a shaky buyer, but also against having to procure and manufacture the goods, perhaps turning down other customers. Once he has been given reason to believe that the buyer's performance has become uncertain, it is an undue hardship to force him to continue his own performance.

UCC §2-609 Official Comment 1.

Whether a seller, as the plaintiff in this case, has reasonable grounds for insecurity is an issue of fact that depends upon various factors, including the buyer's exact words or actions, the course of dealing or performance between the parties, and the nature of the sales contract and the industry. Subdivision (2) defines both "reasonableness" and "adequacy" by commercial rather than legal standards, and the Official Comment notes the application of the good faith standard.

Once the seller correctly determines that it has reasonable grounds for insecurity, it must properly request assurances from the buyer. Although the Code requires that the request be made in writing (UCC §2-609(1)), courts have not strictly adhered to this formality as long as an unequivocal demand is made. After demanding assurance, the seller must determine the proper "adequate assurance." What constitutes "adequate" assurance of due performance is subject to the same test of commercial reasonableness and factual conditions. UCC §2-609 Official Comment 4.

Applying these principles to the case at bar, the overwhelming weight of the evidence establishes that, at the latest by the beginning of 1994, plaintiff had reasonable grounds to be insecure about defendants' ability to perform in the future. Defendants were substantially in arrears almost from the outset of their relationship with plaintiff, had no financing in place, bounced checks, and had failed to sell even a small fraction of the product defendant Spry originally projected.

Reasonable grounds for insecurity can arise from the sole fact that a buyer has fallen behind in his account with the seller, even where the items involved have to do with separate and legally distinct contracts, because this "impairs the seller's expectation of due performance." UCC §2-609 Official Comment 2.

Here, defendants do not dispute their poor payment history, plaintiff's right to demand adequate assurances from them, and that plaintiff made such demands. Rather, defendants claim that they satisfied those demands by the April 15, 1994, telephone conversation between Vultaggio and Richard Worthy of Metro Factors, Inc., followed by Vultaggio's April 18, 1994, letter to Metro, and Metro's payment of $79,316.24 to Hornell, and that thereafter plaintiff had no right to demand further assurance.

The court disagrees with both plaintiff and defendants in their insistence that only one demand for adequate assurance was made in this case to which there was and could be only a single response. Even accepting defendants' argument that payment by Metro was the sole condition Vultaggio required when he spoke and wrote to Metro, and that such condition was met by Metro's actual payment, the court is persuaded that on May 9, 1994, Hornell had further reasonable grounds for insecurity and a new basis for seeking further adequate assurances.

By placing a single order worth $390,000 to $450,000 immediately after receipt of Metro's payment, Spry not only demanded a shipment of product that exceeded the proposed limit, but placed Hornell in a position where it would have *no* opportunity to learn whether Spry would meet the 14-day payment terms, before Spry again became indebted to Hornell for a very large sum of money.

At this point, neither Spry nor Worthy had fully informed Hornell what assurance of payment Metro would be able to provide. Leaving aside the question whether the factoring arrangement with Metro constituted adequate assurance, Hornell never received any documentation to substantiate Spry's purported agreement with Metro.

These circumstances, coupled with information received in early May (on which it reasonably relied) that Spry had misled Hornell about the scope of his operation, created new and more acute grounds for Hornell's insecurity and entitled Hornell to seek further adequate assurance from defendants in the form of a documented line of credit or other guarantee. Defendants' failure to respond constituted a repudiation of the distributorship agreement, which entitled plaintiff to suspend performance and terminate the agreement. UCC §2-609(4).

Even if Hornell had seen Spry's agreement with Metro, in the circumstances of this case the agreement did not provide the adequate assurance to which plaintiff was entitled in relation to defendants' $390,000 to $450,000 order. Spry admitted that much of the order was to be retained as inventory for the summer, for which there would be no receivables to factor within 14 days. Although the question of whether every aspect of Hornell's May 10 demand for credit documentation was reasonable is a close one, given the entire history of the relationship between the parties, the court determines that the demand was commercially reasonable.

The court notes in conclusion that its evaluation of the evidence in this case was significantly influenced by Mr. Spry's regrettable lack of credibility. The court agrees with plaintiff that to an extent far greater than was known to Hornell in May 1994, Mr. Spry was not truthful, failed to pay countless other creditors almost as a matter of course, and otherwise engaged in improper and deceptive business practices.

For the foregoing reasons, it is hereby

ORDERED and ADJUDGED that plaintiff Hornell Brewing Co., Inc., have a declaratory judgment that defendants Stephen A. Spry and Arizona Tea Products, Ltd., were duly terminated and have no continuing rights with respect to plaintiff Hornell Brewing Co.'s beverage products in Canada or elsewhere.

## QUESTIONS AND PROBLEMS

1. It appears that Spry had arranged with Metro for Metro to purchase accounts receivable that were due to Spry from its sale of Hornell products. This would provide funds to Spry in order to pay Hornell the amount owed for the products. Why was this arrangement not as satisfactory as a bank loan? Even if Spry had fully disclosed to Hornell its arrangement with Metro, would that have constituted adequate assurance?

***Problem 6-1.*** If this case were covered by the CISG, could Hornell have suspended performance? See CISG Article 71. Could it have avoided the contract? You may assume that failure to pay for the goods in the future would constitute a "fundamental breach." See CISG Articles 25, 26, 72, and 73.

***Problem 6-2.*** A contract for the sale of a car calls for the buyer to provide a "trade-in" at the time of delivery. The parties set an initial price for the trade-in at $6,500, but since the new car would not be delivered for about two months, the contract provided that there would be a reappraisal done at that time. Shortly before the delivery of the new car, the seller reappraised the trade-in for $500 less ($6,000). The buyer protested and suggested that the parties split the difference. The seller refused. The buyer asked that the seller notify the buyer when the new car arrived, then left the dealership. The seller then canceled the contract and sold the new car to somebody else when it arrived. Assume that there was an enforceable contract pursuant to which the buyer was required to accept the appraisal done by the seller and go through with the deal. Which party repudiated the contract? If it was the buyer, could the buyer call back the seller and retract the repudiation? See UCC §2-610, Comment 2 and §2-611. *See also McDonald v. Bedford Datsun,* 59 Ohio App. 3d 38, 570 N.E.2d 299 (1989). Are these types of cases analyzed the same way under CISG Article 72?

# B. PERFORMANCE AND BREACH UNDER THE UCC

## 1. NONINSTALLMENT SALES

In analyzing performance and breach under the UCC, we must first ask whether the contract calls for delivery of the goods all at once or over time in installments? If the goods are to be delivered all at once, then section 2-601 applies. If the goods are to be delivered in installments, then section 2-612 applies. We will first consider noninstallment sales.

UCC section 2-301 provides that "(t)he obligation of the seller is to transfer and deliver and that of the buyer is to accept and pay in accordance with the contract." Section 2-507 indicates that "(t)ender of delivery is a condition to the buyer's duty to accept the goods and, unless otherwise agreed, to his duty to pay for them." In a noninstallment sales contract under the UCC, the so-called "perfect tender rule" applies. Under that rule, section 2-601, unless otherwise agreed, the buyer may reject any tender of goods that fails in any respect to conform to the terms of the contract. This right is subject to contrary contractual agreement, and we will see that usually sellers limit the buyer's rights to have the seller repair any defects. See §2-719. This right is also subject to the seller's statutory right to cure defects in some circumstances, which we will also explore. See §2-508.

Unless otherwise agreed, a buyer has a reasonable opportunity to inspect the goods before accepting them or paying for them. UCC §§2-513 and 2-606. If the buyer decides to reject the goods, the buyer must give notice to the seller of the rejection. UCC §2-602(1). The buyer is also required to hold the goods with reasonable care at the seller's disposition. UCC §2-602(2). In some situations, if the buyer is a merchant, the buyer may be required to follow reasonable instructions of the seller with respect to the goods, and in the absence of instructions to resell the goods if they are perishable or threaten to decline speedily in value. UCC §2-603.

If the buyer decides to accept the goods, the buyer becomes liable to pay the contract price for the goods. UCC §2-607(1). The buyer may, however, be able to recover any damages that are caused by any nonconformity of the tender. UCC §2-714(1). In some situations, the buyer will accept the goods with the understanding that the seller will attempt to cure defects but the seller fails to do so. In other situations, a defect will be discovered subsequent to acceptance. If the failure to cure or the subsequently discovered defect result in a "substantial impairment in the value of the goods to the buyer," the buyer may revoke acceptance of the goods and recover the purchase price.[2] The buyer may in addition recover damages caused by the breach, as will be discussed in the next chapter.

If the buyer fails to make a payment to the seller when due on or before the goods are delivered to the buyer, the seller is permitted to cancel the contract. UCC §2-702. In some situations in which the goods have been delivered but are not paid for or where the buyer is insolvent, the seller has limited rights to reclaim the goods. See UCC §§2-507, 2-511, and 2-702. Seller's remedies will be considered more fully in the next chapter.

The following famous case demonstrates some of these principles.

## Zabriskie Chevrolet v. Smith

Superior Court of New Jersey

99 N.J. Super. 441, 240 A.2d 195 (1968)

This action arises out of the sale by plaintiff to defendant of a new 1966 Chevrolet automobile. Within a short distance after leaving the showroom the vehicle became almost completely inoperable by reason of mechanical failure. Defendant the same day notified plaintiff that he cancelled the sale and simultaneously stopped payment on the check he had tendered in payment of the balance of the purchase price. Plaintiff sues on the check and the purchase order for the balance of the purchase price plus incidental damages and defendant counterclaims for the return of his deposit and incidental damages.

The facts are not complex nor do they present any serious dispute.

On February 2, 1967, defendant signed a form purchase order for a new 1966 Chevrolet Biscayne Sedan, which was represented to him to be a brand-new car that would operate perfectly. On that occasion he paid plaintiff $124 by way of deposit. On February 9, 1967, defendant tendered plaintiff his check for $2,069.50 representing the balance of the purchase price ($2,064) and $5.50 for license and transfer fees. Delivery was made to defendant's wife during the early evening hours of Friday, February 10, 1967, at which time she was handed the keys and the factory package of printed material, including the manual and the manufacturer-dealer's warranty, none of which she or her husband ever read before or after the sale was made, nor were the details thereof specifically explained to or agreed to by defendant. While en route

2. For a discussion of the workings of the UCC rules governing tender, acceptance, rejection, and revocation, see Whaley, *Tender, Acceptance, Rejection and Revocation—The UCC's "TARR-Baby,"* 24 Drake L. Rev. 52 (1974).

to her home, about 2.5 miles away, and after having gone about 7/10 of a mile from the showroom, the car stalled at a traffic light, stalled again within another 15 feet, and again thereafter each time the vehicle was required to stop. When about halfway home the car could not be driven in "drive" gear at all, and defendant's wife was obliged to then propel the vehicle in "low-low" gear at a rate of about five to ten miles per hour, its then maximum speed. In great distress, defendant's wife was fearful of completing the journey to her home and called her husband, who thereupon drove the car in "low-low" gear about seven blocks to his home. Defendant, considerably upset by this turn of events, thereupon immediately called his bank (which was open this Friday evening), stopped payment on the check, and then called plaintiff to notify them that they had sold him a "lemon," that he had stopped payment on the check, and that the sale was cancelled. The next day plaintiff sent a wrecker to defendant's home, brought the vehicle to its repair shop and after inspection determined that the transmission was defective.

Plaintiff's expert testified that the car would not move, that there was no power in the transmission, and in that condition the car could not move. Plaintiff replaced the transmission with another one removed from a vehicle then on plaintiff's showroom floor, notifying defendant thereafter of what had been done. Defendant refused to take delivery of the vehicle as repaired and reasserted his cancellation of the sale. Plaintiff has since kept the vehicle in storage at his place of business. Within a short period following these occurrences plaintiff and defendant began negotiations for a new 1967 Chevrolet, but these fell through when plaintiff insisted that a new deal could only be made by giving defendant credit for the previously ordered 1966 Chevrolet. This defendant refused to do because he considered the prior transaction as cancelled.

Plaintiff urges that defendant accepted the vehicle and therefore under the Code (UCC §2-607(1)) is bound to complete payment for it. Defendant asserts that he never accepted the vehicle and therefore under the Code properly rejected it; further, that even if there had been acceptance he was justified under the Code in revoking the same. Defendant supports this claim by urging that what was delivered to him was not what he bargained for; that is, a new car with factory-new parts, which would operate perfectly as represented and, therefore, the Code remedies of rejection and revocation of acceptance were available to him. These remedies have their basis in breach of contract and failure of consideration although they are also viewed as arising out of breach of warranty. The essential ingredient which determines which of these two remedies is brought into play is a determination, *in limine,* whether there had been an "acceptance" of the goods by the buyer. Thus, the primary inquiry is whether the defendant had "accepted" the automobile prior to the return thereof to the plaintiff.

It is clear that a buyer does not accept goods until he has had a "reasonable opportunity to inspect." Defendant sought to purchase a new car. He assumed what every new car buyer has a right to assume and, indeed, has been led to assume by the high-powered advertising techniques of the auto industry—that his new car, with the exception of very minor adjustments, would be mechanically new and factory-furnished, operate perfectly, and be free of substantial defects. The vehicle delivered to defendant did not measure up to these representations. Plaintiff contends that defendant had "reasonable opportunity to inspect" by the privilege to take the car for a typical "spin around the block" before signing the purchase order. If by this contention plaintiff equates a spin around the block with "reasonable opportunity to inspect," the contention is illusory and unrealistic. To the layperson, the complicated mechanisms of today's automobiles are a complete mystery. To have the automobile inspected by someone with sufficient expertise to disassemble the vehicle in order to discover latent defects before the contract is signed, is assuredly impossible and highly impractical. Consequently, the first few miles of driving become even more significant to the excited new car buyer. This is the buyer's first reasonable opportunity to enjoy his new vehicle to see if it conforms to what it was represented to be and whether he is getting what he bargained for. How long the buyer may drive the new car under the guise of inspection of new goods is not an issue in the present case. It is clear that defendant discovered the nonconformity within 7/10 of a mile and minutes after leaving plaintiff's showroom. Certainly this was well within the ambit of "reasonable opportunity to inspect." That the vehicle was grievously defective when it left plaintiff's possession is a compelling conclusion, as is the conclusion that in a legal sense defendant never accepted the vehicle.

Even if defendant had accepted the automobile tendered, he had a right to revoke under UCC section 2-608. [The court quotes from section 2-608.]

The New Jersey Study Comment to 12A:2-608 reads:

> 3. Subsection 2-608(1) permits revocation of acceptance only where there has been a nonconformity which substantially impairs the value of the lot or commercial unit which was accepted. No similar restriction is placed on the buyer's rights to rescind under section 69 of the U.S.A. (N.J.S. 46:30-75). Under the U.S.A., however, the courts have not allowed rescission for a trivial breach of warranty. Therefore, the UCC requirement of substantial impairment does not differ radically from the decisions under the U.S.A. *See*, in this connection, *Miller & Sons Bakery Co. v. Selikowitz*, 4 N.J. Super. 97, 66 A.2d 441 (1949) ("The right to rescind, however, is an extreme one and does not arise from every breach. * * * The general rule is that rescission will not be permitted for a slight or casual breach of contract, but only for such breaches as are so substantial * * * as to defeat the objective of the parties * * *"). 12 C.J. Sec. 661, p. 613; 17 C.J.S. Contracts §435, p. 918.

Nor did plaintiff have reasonable grounds to believe that a new automobile that could not even be driven a bare few miles to the buyer's residence would be acceptable. The dealer is in an entirely different position from the layperson. The dealer, with his staff of expert mechanics and modern equipment, knows or should know of substantial defects in the new automobile that it sells. There was offered into evidence the dealer's inspection and adjustment schedule containing more than 70 alleged items that plaintiff caused to be inspected, including the transmission. According to that schedule, the automobile in question had been checked by the seller for the satisfaction of the buyer, and such inspection included a road test. The fact that the automobile underwent a tortured operation for about 2.5 miles from the showroom to defendant's residence demonstrates the inherent serious deficiencies in this vehicle that were present when the so-called inspection was made by plaintiff, and hence plaintiff was aware (or should have been) that the vehicle did not conform to the bargain the parties had made, and plaintiff had no reasonable right to expect that the vehicle in that condition would be accepted.

There having been no acceptance, the next issue presented is whether defendant properly rejected under the Code. That he canceled the sale and rejected the vehicle almost concomitantly with the discovery of the failure of his bargain is clear from the evidence.

Section 2-602 indicates that one can reject after taking possession. Possession, therefore, does not mean acceptance and the corresponding loss of the right of rejection; nor does the fact that buyer has a security interest along with possession eliminate the right to reject. [The court quotes from section 2-602 and from section 2-106, which defines "conforming goods."]

The Uniform Commercial Code Comment to section 2-106 states:

> 2. Subsection (2): It is in general intended to continue the policy of requiring exact performance by the seller of his obligations as a condition to his right to require acceptance. However, the seller is in part safeguarded against surprise as a result of sudden technicality on the buyer's part by the provisions of section 2-508 on seller's cure of improper tender or delivery. Moreover usage of trade frequently permits commercial leeways in performance and the language of the agreement itself must be read in the light of such custom or usage and also, prior course of dealing, and in a long-term contract, the course of performance.

There was no evidence at the trial concerning any "custom or usage," although plaintiff in its brief argued that it is the usage of the automobile trade that a buyer accept a new automobile, although containing defects of manufacture, if such defects can be and are seasonably cured by the seller. Perhaps this represents prevailing views in the automobile industry, which have, over the years, served to blanket injustices and inequities committed upon buyers who demurred in the light of the unequal positions of strength between the parties. In the present case we are not dealing with a situation such as was present in *Adams v. Tramontin Motor Sales*, 42 N.J. Super. 313, 126 A.2d 358 (App. Div. 1956). In that case, brought for breach of implied warranty of merchantability, the court held that minor defects, such as adjustment of the motor, tightening of loose elements, fixing of locks and dome light, and a correction of rumbling noise, were not remarkable defects, and therefore there was no breach. Here the breach was substantial. The new car was practically inoperable and endowed with a defective transmission. This was a "remarkable defect" and justified rejection by the buyer.

Lastly, plaintiff urges that under the Code, section 2-508, it had a right to cure the nonconforming delivery. [The court quotes from section 2-508.]

It is clear that in the instant case there was no "forced breach" on the part of the buyer, for he almost immediately began to negotiate for another automobile. The inquiry is as to what is intended by "cure," as used in the Code. This statute makes no attempt to define or specify what a "cure" shall consist of. It would appear, then, that each case must be controlled by its own facts. The "cure" intended under the cited section of the Code does not, in the court's opinion, contemplate the tender of a new vehicle with a substituted transmission, not from the factory and of unknown lineage from another vehicle in plaintiff's possession. It was not the intention of the Legislature that the right to "cure" is a limitless one to be controlled only by the will of the seller. A "cure" that endeavors by substitution to tender a chattel not within the agreement or contemplation of the parties is invalid.

For a majority of people the purchase of a new car is a major investment, rationalized by the peace of mind that flows from its dependability and safety. Once their faith is shaken, the vehicle not only loses its real value in their eyes, but also becomes an instrument whose integrity is substantially impaired and whose operation is fraught with apprehension. The attempted cure in the present case was ineffective.

Accordingly, and pursuant to UCC section 2-711, judgment is rendered on the main case in favor of defendant. On the counterclaim judgment is rendered in favor of defendant and against plaintiff in the sum of $124, being the amount of the deposit, there being no further proof of damages.

Defendant shall, as part of this judgment, execute for plaintiff, on demand, such documents as are necessary to again vest title to the vehicle in plaintiff.

## PROBLEMS

***Problem 6-3.*** Note that the court in *Zabriskie Chevrolet* holds that receipt of the goods does not necessarily constitute "acceptance" as that term is defined in UCC section 2-606. Before "acceptance" occurs, the buyer must have a reasonable opportunity to inspect. Driving the car home from the dealership was within the reasonable opportunity provided. Assume that you purchase a crystal vase from a store. You don't notice a crack in the vase until you arrive home with the vase. Have you "accepted" the vase, thus precluding rejection? Is there a difference between the sale of the vase and the sale of the car in terms of the time permitted to inspect the goods?

***Problem 6-4.*** Assume a contract for the sale of two industrial machines used in a manufacturing plant. Each machine performs its functions separately. When the machines arrive, Buyer notices a minor scratch on the side of one of the machines. The machines were warranted to be merchantable. Do the goods "conform" to the contract? See UCC §2-106(2), Official Comment 2. If the goods do not conform, may the buyer reject both machines? UCC §§2-601, 2-105(6). When the buyer rejects the goods, what is the buyer required to tell the seller? See UCC §2-605.

***Problem 6-5.*** Assume that a buyer purchases a television set and the contract has an enforceable disclaimer stating that the television is sold "as is." When the buyer first plugs the television set into the wall, it works for a minute and then dies. May the buyer reject or revoke acceptance of the television? Does the television "conform" to the contract?

***Problem 6-6.*** Assume that goods are sold "FOB Seller's Plant." See UCC §2-319. If the goods are damaged in transit between the seller's plant and the buyer's place of business, may the buyer reject the goods? What if the seller fails to make a reasonable contract for shipment under section 2-504 and the damage to the goods is minor? See UCC §2-504.

***Problem 6-7.*** Assume a contract for the sale of watermelons in bulk to a wholesale food distributor. By mistake, the seller ships cantaloupes instead. What must the buyer do in this case to preserve its rights? See UCC §§2-602-2-606.

***Problem 6-8.*** In *Zabriskie Chevrolet,* if the seller had offered the buyer a new car rather than simply taking a transmission out of another car and putting it into the one that was sold to the buyer, would the buyer be legally required to accept that tender? To what extent does section 2-508 permit a seller to repair a defect rather than substitute a new, conforming product? Would Zabriskie Chevrolet have had a better argument for cure if it had delivered the defective Chevy to the buyer before the date indicated in the contract? Compare §§2-508(1) to 2-508(2). Would Zabriskie Chevrolet have had a right to cure if the court found that the buyer had revoked acceptance rather than having rejected the car? See UCC §2-608(3).

***Problem 6-9.*** Assume that the buyer was willing to accept the repaired transmission in *Zabriskie Chevrolet.* Over the next year, however, numerous other problems arose with the car. The dealer was able to repair each one, but the buyer grew tired of having to bring the car back to the dealer again and again. When the next problem arose, even though it was a minor one, the buyer wanted to get his money back. Remember the "lemon law" under the Song-Beverly Consumer Warranty Act? See p. 115, *supra.* Can an argument for revocation be made under the UCC? To what extent is the buyer's subjective need for a working car relevant? Does the car's depreciation during use which is unrelated to the defects prevent the buyer from legally revoking acceptance? See UCC §2-608 and *Rester v. Morrow*, 491 So. 2d 204 (Miss. 1986).

***Problem 6-10.*** Assume that your car is a "lemon," and that you have a right to demand your money back. The dealer refuses. You need some way to get to work and don't have enough money to buy or lease another car (and the bus is out of the question!). If you continue to drive your car to work, defects and all, do you sacrifice your ability to get your money back? See the next case.

## McCullough v. Bill Swad Chrysler-Plymouth, Inc.

Ohio Supreme Court

5 Ohio St. 3d 181, 449 N.E.2d 1289 (1983)

On May 23, 1978, appellee Deborah A. McCullough purchased a 1978 Chrysler LeBaron from appellant Bill Swad Chrysler-Plymouth, Inc. (now Bill Swad Datsun, Inc.). Following delivery of the vehicle, appellee and her (then) fiance informed appellant's sales agent of problems they had noted with the car's brakes, lack of rustproofing, paint job, and seat panels. The next day, the brakes failed, and appellee returned the car to appellant for the necessary repairs.

When again in possession of the car, appellee discovered that the brakes had not been fixed properly and that none of the cosmetic work had been done.

On June 26, 1978, appellee returned the car to appellant for correction both of the still-unremedied defects and of other flaws that had surfaced since the last failed repair effort. Appellant retained possession of the vehicle for more than three weeks in order to service it, but even then many of the former problems persisted. Moreover, appellant's workmanship had apparently caused new defects to arise, affecting the car's stereo system, landau top, and exterior. Appellee also experienced difficulties with vibrations, the horn, and the brakes.

The following month, while appellee was on a short trip away from her home, the automobile's engine abruptly shut off. The car eventually had to be towed to appellant's service shop for repair. A few days later, when appellee and her husband were embarked on an extensive honeymoon vacation, the brakes again failed. Upon returning from their excursion, the newlyweds, who had prepared a list of 32 of the automobile's defects, submitted the list to appellant and again requested their correction. By the end of October 1978, few of the enumerated problems had been remedied.

In early November 1978, appellee contacted appellant's successor, Chrysler-Plymouth East ("East"), regarding further servicing of the vehicle. East was not able to undertake the requested repairs until January 1979. Despite the additional work that East performed, the vehicle continued to malfunction. After May 1979, East refused to perform any additional work on the automobile, claiming that the vehicle was in satisfactory condition, appellee's assertions to the contrary notwithstanding.

On January 8, 1979, appellee, by letter addressed to appellant, called for the rescission of the purchase agreement, demanded a refund of the entire purchase price and expenses incurred, and offered to return the automobile to appellant upon receipt of shipping instructions. Appellant did not respond to appellee's letter, and appellee continued to operate the car.

On January 12, 1979, appellee filed suit against appellant, seeking rescission of the sales agreement. By the time of trial, June 25, 1980, the subject vehicle had been driven nearly 35,000 miles, approximately 23,000 of which were logged after appellee mailed her notice of revocation. The trial court entered judgment for appellee against appellant in the amount of $9,376.82, and ordered the return of the automobile to appellant.

Appellant asserts that appellee's continued operation of the vehicle after advising appellant of her revocation was inconsistent with her having relinquished ownership of the car, that the value of the automobile to appellee was not substantially impaired by its alleged nonconformities, and that the warranties furnished by appellant provided the sole legal remedy for alleviating the automobile's defects. Each of appellant's contentions must be rejected.

Whether continued use of goods after notification of revocation of their acceptance vitiates such revocation is solely dependent upon whether such use was reasonable.

The genesis of the "reasonable use" test lies in the recognition that frequently a buyer, after revoking his earlier acceptance of a good, is constrained by exogenous circumstances—many of which the seller controls—to continue using the good until a suitable replacement may realistically be secured. Clearly, to penalize the buyer for a predicament not of his own creation would be patently unjust.

In ascertaining whether a buyer's continued use of an item after revocation of its acceptance was reasonable, the trier of fact should pose the following queries: (1) Upon being apprised of the buyer's revocation of his acceptance, what instructions, if any, did the seller tender the buyer concerning return of the now rejected goods? (2) Did the buyer's business needs or personal circumstances compel the continued use? (3) During the period of such use, did the seller persist in assuring the buyer that all nonconformities would be cured? (4) Did the seller act in good faith? (5) Was the seller unduly prejudiced by the buyer's continued use?

It is manifest that, upon consideration of the aforementioned criteria, appellee acted reasonably in continuing to operate her motor vehicle even after the revocation of acceptance. First, the failure of the seller to advise the buyer, after the latter has revoked his acceptance of the goods, how the goods were to be returned entitles the buyer to retain possession of them.

Secondly, appellee, a young clerical secretary of limited financial resources, was scarcely in position to return the defective automobile and obtain a second in order to meet her business and personal needs. A most unreasonable obligation would be imposed upon appellee were she to be required, in effect, to secure a loan to purchase a second car while remaining liable for repayment of the first car loan.

Additionally, appellant's successor (East), by attempting to repair the appellee's vehicle even after she tendered her notice of revocation, provided both express and tacit assurances that the automobile's defects were remediable, thereby, inducing her to retain possession. Moreover, whether appellant acted in good faith throughout this episode is highly problematic, especially given the fact that whenever repair of the car was undertaken, new defects often miraculously arose while previous ones frequently went uncorrected. Both appellant's and East's refusal to honor the warranties before their expiration also evidences less than fair dealing.

Finally, it is apparent that appellant was not prejudiced by appellee's continued operation of the automobile. Had appellant retaken possession of the vehicle pursuant to appellee's notice of revocation, the automobile, which at the time had been driven only 12,000 miles, could easily have been resold. Indeed, the car was still marketable at the time of trial, as even then the odometer registered less than 35,000 miles. In any event, having failed to reassume ownership of the automobile when requested to do so, appellant alone must bear the loss for any diminution of the vehicle's resale value occurring between the two dates.

[UCC section 2-711] provides an additional basis for appellee's retention after revocation of the automobile. [The court quotes section 2-711(3).] A buyer who possesses, as appellee does in the instant action, a security interest in the rejected goods may continue to use them even after revoking his acceptance. Consequently, appellee's continued use of the defective vehicle was a permissible means of protecting her security interest therein.[4]

4. Appellant would be entitled to an offset for the reasonable value of appellee's continued use of the automobile after revocation but for the former's failure to adduce evidence of such value at trial.

## NOTES AND QUESTIONS

1. Is this result consistent with sections 2-602(2)(a) and 2-606(1)(c)? Not all courts would agree with this court's analysis. *See Bowen v. Young*, 507 S.W.2d 600 (Tex. App. 1974). Does the "reasonable use" test make sense from a policy perspective?
2. Do you agree with the court that section 2-711(3) gives the buyer the right to use the car?
3. At the end of the case, the court states that the dealer is entitled to restitution for the benefit that the buyer derived from driving the car, except that the seller did not introduce evidence of such value. How should such a benefit be calculated when the car has defects? Under the Song-Beverly Consumer Warranty Act, the amount of restitution to which the seller is entitled is determined by multiplying the price paid by the buyer for the car by a fraction, the numerator of which is the number of miles driven by the buyer before the car was first given back to the dealer for repair and the denominator of which is 120,000. See Cal. Civ. Code §1793.2(d)(2)(C). That would not provide the dealer with any restitution for benefits derived after revocation of acceptance. Is that fair?

## 2. INSTALLMENT SALES

If the contract for sale either requires or authorizes the delivery of goods in separate lots, then it is considered an installment contract and is governed by section 2-612. Two questions are raised when the seller delivers nonconforming goods under an installment contract: (1) Can the installment itself be rejected, and (2) can the entire contract be canceled? No longer does the "perfect tender rule" of section 2-601 apply.

The test for rejection of the installment is whether the nonconformity substantially impairs the value of the installment and cannot be cured. The test for cancellation of the entire contract is whether the nonconformity substantially impairs the value of the whole contract.

What is meant by "substantial impairment"? Is it to be determined with reference to the particular buyer, or objectively? Compare UCC §2-608's definition of "substantial impairment." Professors White and Summers suggest that the concept of "substantial impairment" is related to the concept of material breach, which you probably studied in your contracts class.[3] *Restatement (Second) of Contracts* section 241 indicates that the following factors are relevant in determining whether a breach is material, and whether a contract can be terminated[4] as a result:

1. To what extent is the injured party deprived of a reasonably expected benefit of the bargain?
2. To what extent can the injured party be compensated in damages?

---

3. White & Summers, *Uniform Commercial Code* §8.3 (5th ed.).

4. In UCC parlance the contract would be "canceled" if the contract was ended due to breach. A contract is "terminated" under Article 2 if the contract is ended for reasons other than breach. See UCC §2-106(3), (4).

3. To what extent will the party failing to perform suffer forfeiture if the contract is canceled?
4. What is the likelihood of cure?
5. To what extent is the breaching party acting in bad faith?

## HUBBARD v. UTZ QUALITY FOODS, INC.

United States District Court, W.D. New York

903 F. Supp. 444 (1995)

This is a breach of contract action brought by Daniel Hubbard ("Hubbard") against UTZ Quality Foods, Inc. ("UTZ"). Hubbard is a Bath, New York, potato farmer and UTZ is a Pennsylvania corporation that purchases potatoes for processing into potato chips.

On April 20, 1992, Hubbard executed a written contract to supply UTZ with a quantity of potatoes. The contract, a two-page, form contract prepared by UTZ, required that the potatoes comply with certain quality standards. Hubbard claims that he was ready and able to deliver the required shipments of potatoes but that UTZ wrongfully and without basis rejected his potatoes. Hubbard contends that the sample potatoes provided to UTZ complied with all the quality requirements and, therefore, he complied with all terms of the contract. Hubbard claims that UTZ breached the contract and claims damages for the full contract price, $68,750.

UTZ denies Hubbard's allegations. UTZ contends that the potatoes supplied by Hubbard did not meet the quality requirements of the contract and, therefore, they were properly rejected. UTZ filed a counterclaim against Hubbard contending that he breached the contract by failing to provide the potatoes required by contract.

The case was tried to the court for five days. The court took testimony from 13 witnesses and received numerous documents and deposition testimony in evidence. This decision constitutes my findings of fact and conclusions of law.

### Facts

#### April 20, 1992, Potato Contract

On April 20, 1992, Hubbard signed the two-page contract prepared by UTZ for farmers who produced potatoes for UTZ. The contract required Hubbard, beginning "approximately September 5, 1992," to ship 11,000 hundred-weight of Norwis (657) new chipping potatoes. Hubbard was to ship 2,000 to 4,000 hundred-weight per week with schedules to be arranged with UTZ. The price was $6.25 per hundred-weight, FOB New York.

The contract provided that the potatoes must meet certain quality standards. The buyer, UTZ, was entitled to reject the potatoes if they failed to do so. The potatoes had to meet United States Department of Agriculture ("USDA") standards for No. 1 white chipping potatoes. They had to have a minimum size and be free from bruising, rotting, and odors that made them inappropriate for use in the processing of potato chips.

The principal standard at issue in this lawsuit is the color standard. UTZ did not want dark potato chips but white or light ones and, therefore, the potatoes had to be the whitest or lightest possible color. The specific paragraph in the contract relating to color reads as follows:

> "Color" shall be at least #1 or #2 on the 1978 Snack Food Association "Fry Color Chart."

The Fry Color Chart is a color chart prepared by the Potato Chip/Snack Food Association that has five color designations. Color designation No. 1 is the best or lightest, and the chart contains a visual depiction of potato chips with that color. The last color designation, No. 5, is the darkest reading. The contract required that the chips produced from Hubbard's potatoes must at least meet the No. 2 color designation.

Claims of the Parties

In a nutshell, this lawsuit revolves around the color of the potato chips processed from potatoes submitted by Hubbard to UTZ. UTZ rejected all of the submitted potatoes, claiming that they did not meet the required "color" standard. UTZ claims that the samples were too dark and did not meet UTZ's standards for producing white or light chips. Hubbard, on the other hand, contends that UTZ was arbitrary in its refusal to accept his potatoes and that his potatoes substantially complied with the color requirement. Hubbard contends in his pleadings that UTZ's rejection was motivated by concerns about price, not by quality. Hubbard alleges that after rejecting his potatoes, UTZ obtained similar potatoes from other sources at prices below his contract price.

The ultimate factual issue in this case is whether the potato chips made from Hubbard's potatoes failed to meet the color specifications of the contract. In other words, was UTZ's rejection of the installments proper.

Rejection of Hubbard's Potatoes

Hubbard contends that he sent several sample loads of potatoes to UTZ for inspection. On or about September 22, 1992, he sent 1,000 pounds of potatoes from one of his fields to UTZ for testing. These were rejected. Hubbard thought that they looked good when he harvested them, but UTZ reported that when they were processed the color was poor. Hubbard discussed this rejection with Richard P. Smith, UTZ's Potato Manager, who told Hubbard to keep sending samples.

Thereafter, on October 1, 1992, Hubbard sent an entire truckload of potatoes to UTZ for processing under the contract. This installment consisted of 425-450 100-pound bags. Hubbard did not accompany this shipment to Pennsylvania, but he was advised by telephone that none of the potatoes would be accepted due to their poor color.

Hubbard requested that UTZ put the reasons for this rejection in writing, and Smith did so in a letter dated October 1, 1992 (Ex. 404).

About a week later, on October 7, Hubbard and his brother prepared a 1,000-pound load of potatoes and drove it to UTZ's facility in Pennsylvania to see if the potatoes would pass muster.

After Hubbard returned from Pennsylvania, on October 8, 1992, he had a telephone conversation with Smith, during which Smith told him that based on the samples, it did not appear that Hubbard's potatoes "would work" because they did not meet the contract specifications. Smith, however, told

Hubbard that he could send additional samples and shipments to Pennsylvania for inspection.

After October 7, Hubbard never delivered, or caused to be delivered, any other shipments of potatoes for UTZ pursuant to the contract.

After allegedly conversing with certain government officials, Hubbard advised UTZ by telegram that he intended to sell his potatoes on the open market and charge UTZ for the difference in price.

### Motivation of UTZ

Hubbard has also failed to convince me, by a preponderance of the evidence, that UTZ benefited by its rejection of Hubbard's potatoes. Smith and Corriere testified that they had suffered significant losses in the past when their potatoes had turned bad in storage. In 1992, UTZ took steps to see that such a disaster did not reoccur and so they were careful in their decisions to accept or reject potatoes.

Furthermore, there is no compelling evidence that UTZ purchased potatoes at lower market prices after it rejected Hubbard's crop. On the contrary, the evidence (Ex. 39) suggests that the market price during late 1992 and early 1993 was equal to or higher than Hubbard's contract price. Hubbard has failed to convince me that UTZ's motivation for rejecting his potatoes was to obtain similar potatoes but at a reduced cost. Therefore, I find as a fact, that UTZ's reason and motivation for rejection was its belief that the potatoes failed to meet the quality standards in the contract.

## Discussion

### UTZ's Rejection of Hubbard's Potatoes

It is also clear that the contract between the parties is an "installment contract" as that term is defined in UCC section 2-612(1): It contemplates "delivery of goods in separate lots to be separately accepted." That the contract is an installment contract does not appear to have been disputed by the parties.

As an installment contract, the question of whether UTZ's rejection was wrongful or proper is governed by UCC section 2-612(2) and (3). UCC section 2-612(2) states that a "buyer may reject any installment that is nonconforming if the nonconformity substantially impairs the value of that installment and cannot be cured. . . . " UCC section 2-612(3) states that "whenever nonconformity or default with respect to one or more installments substantially impairs the value of the whole contract there is a breach of the whole."

The purpose of this "substantial impairment" requirement is "to preclude a party from canceling a contract for trivial defects." *Emanuel Law Outlines, Inc. v. Multi-State Legal Studies,* 1995 WL 519999, No. 93 Civ. 7212 (S.D.N.Y. 1995). In this case, UTZ rejected Hubbard's potatoes based upon their failure to satisfy the color standard set forth in paragraph 3(c) of the contract. Thus, the issue for me to decide is whether the failure of Hubbard's potatoes to meet the required #1 or #2 color minimum constitutes a "substantial impairment" of the installments.

Whether goods conform to contract terms is a question of fact. Moreover, in determining whether goods conform to contract terms, a buyer is bound by the "good faith" requirements set forth in UCC section 1-304: "Every . . .

duty within this Act imposes an obligation of good faith in its enforcement or performance." Thus, UTZ's determination that Hubbard's potatoes failed to satisfy the contract terms must have been fairly reached.

The UTZ-Hubbard contract contains many specific requirements regarding the quality of the potatoes. In paragraph 1, the contract states that "only specified varieties as stated in contract will be accepted . . . . " Paragraph 3(a) states that

> All shipments shall meet the United States Standards for Grades of Potatoes for Chipping, USDA, January 1978 . . . , in addition to other provisions enumerated in this 'Section 3.' Loads that do not meet these standards may be subject to rejection. . . . (Emphasis added.)

Paragraph 3(b) sets forth specific size requirements (85 percent or better . . . graded to a 1-inch minimum size); paragraph 3(c) sets forth specific gravity requirements (at least 1.070 in a standard eight-pound test); paragraph 3(d) contains the color requirements at issue in this case; and paragraph 3(f) sets forth a number of other defects or incidents of improper treatment or handling of the potatoes that provide UTZ with the right to reject the potatoes.

Clearly, the quality standards are of great importance to UTZ. They are the most detailed aspect of the contract — far more so than timing or even quantity specifications.

In a contract of this type, where the quality standards are set forth with great specificity, the failure to satisfy one of the specifically enumerated standards is a "substantial impairment." UTZ obviously cares the most about the specific quality specifications, as is evident from the numerous references throughout the contract.

Additionally, I find that UTZ's determination that the potatoes did not meet the required #2 color standard was made in good faith, as required by UCC section 1-304. As noted above, the manner of visual testing utilized by UTZ was reasonable and customary. Further, Smith and DeGroft, the UTZ testers who rejected Hubbard's potatoes, provided credible testimony about their respective experience (Smith — 30 years, DeGroft — five to six years) and method of making such determinations. Accordingly, I find that UTZ fairly and in good faith determined that Hubbard's potatoes were nonconforming.

Thus, I find that Hubbard's failure to meet the proper color standard amounted to a "substantial impairment" of the installments (§2-612(2)), substantially impairing the whole contract (§2-612(3)). Accordingly, I find that UTZ's rejection of Hubbard's potatoes was proper.[3]

---

3. This is not a case where UTZ has rejected the potatoes because they were a week (or a month) late or where the quantities were lower than anticipated. Such nonconformity would not constitute "substantial impairment" of this contract because timing and quantity are not its critical components. *See, e.g., Emanuel, supra* (delay in installment shipment of bar review study aids not significant where shipment was still timely for the purposes of the contract); *Hudson Feather & Down Products, Inc. v. Lancer Clothing Corp.*, 128 A.D.2d 674, 513 N.Y.S.2d 173 (2d Dep't 1987) (delay in installment payment did not substantially impair value of whole contract).

## QUESTIONS AND PROBLEM

1. If only 84.9 percent (as compared to 85 percent) of a shipment of potatoes had graded to 1-inch minimum size, would the buyer have been permitted to reject the installment? Of what significance is the contractual provision stating "only specified varieties as stated in contract will be accepted"? See UCC §1-302. See also UCC §2-612, Official Comment 4.
2. In this case, the seller decided not to ship any more potatoes. What would result if on October 8, 1992, the buyer had told the seller that the contract was canceled and that no further shipments would be accepted? See UCC §2-612, Official Comment 6.

***Problem 6-11.*** Buyer contracted to buy a set of commemorative plates depicting all of the Presidents of the United States. The plates were limited edition, signed by the artist, who was very famous, and were made of very fine materials. The price of the complete set was $10,000. As the plates were to be manufactured over time, delivery would be in installments. Buyer would pay $200 upon delivery of each plate with the balance due after all of the plates had been delivered. Buyer was a collector of various objects, and believed that a complete set of these plates would appreciate significantly in value. The plates were indeed popular, and the limited edition was quickly sold out.

Although there were some slight delays in shipment, the first few plates were everything that Buyer expected in terms of quality. Unfortunately, the Thomas Jefferson plate had a slight scratch on it that was apparently attributable to mishandling by seller's shipment department. In Buyer's expert opinion as a collector, the defect would substantially diminish the value of the collection as a whole, although each nondefective plate still would be worth at least as much as Buyer was paying for them.

No precise estimate could be given for the amount of diminishment of value in the future, but Buyer thought it could be in the thousands of dollars. When Buyer complained to Seller and demanded a replacement plate, Seller refused. It would cost too much money for Seller to obtain the necessary materials to produce one more plate—it had only obtained enough to make the limited edition and it had also destroyed the molds for the plates to ensure that its promise to the buyers that no additional plates would be made would be honored. Seller did offer to give Buyer a money allowance—Buyer would be given an allowance of $2000 on the rest of the plates.

Use section 2-612 and its Official Comments to answer these questions: (1) Should Buyer be allowed to reject the Jefferson plate? (2) Should Buyer be allowed to cancel the entire contract? (3) Should Buyer be permitted to revoke acceptance of the plates already delivered? See UCC §2-608. Why do you think it is that the drafters of the UCC make it more difficult for a buyer to cancel an installment sales contract than a noninstallment sales contract?

### CHERWELL-RALLI, INC. v. RYTMAN GRAIN CO., INC.

Connecticut Supreme Court

180 Conn. 714, 433 A.2d 984 (1980)

PETERS, Justice.

This case involves a dispute about which of the parties to an oral installment contract was the first to be in breach. The plaintiff, Cherwell-Ralli, Inc., sued the defendant, Rytman Grain Co., Inc., for the nonpayment of moneys due and owing for accepted deliveries of products known as Cherco Meal and C-R-T Meal. The defendant, conceding its indebtedness, counterclaimed for damages arising out of the plaintiff's refusal to deliver remaining installments under the contract. The trial court, having found all issues for the plaintiff, rendered judgment accordingly, and the defendant appealed.

The parties, on July 26, 1974, entered into an installment contract for the sale of Cherco Meal and C-R-T Meal. The contract called for shipments according to weekly instructions from the buyer, with payments to be made within ten days after delivery. Almost immediately the buyer was behind in its payments, and these arrearages were often quite substantial. The seller repeatedly called these arrearages to the buyer's attention but continued to make all shipments as requested by the buyer from July 29, 1974, to April 23, 1975.

By April 15, 1975, the buyer had become concerned that the seller might not complete performance of the contract, because the seller's plant might close and because the market price of the goods had come to significantly exceed the contract price. In a telephone conversation between the buyer's president and the seller's president on that day, the buyer was assured by the seller that deliveries would continue if the buyer would make the payments for which it was obligated. Thereupon, the buyer sent the seller a check in the amount of $9,825.60 to cover shipments through March 31, 1975.

Several days later, on April 23, 1975, the buyer stopped payment on this check because he was told by a truck driver, not employed by the seller, that this shipment would be his last load. Two letters, both dated April 28, 1975, describe the impasse between the parties: The seller again demanded payment, and the buyer, for the first time in writing, demanded adequate assurance of further deliveries. The buyer made no further payments, either to replace the stopped check or otherwise to pay for the 19 accepted shipments for which balances were outstanding. The seller made no further deliveries after April 23, 1975, when it heard about the stopped check. Inability to deliver the goods forced the seller to close its plant on May 2, 1975, because of stockpiling of excess material.

The trial court concluded that the party in breach was the buyer and not the seller.

The buyer on this appeal challenges first the conclusion that the buyer's failure to pay "substantially impaired the value of the whole contract," so as to constitute "a breach of the whole contract," as is required by the applicable law governing installment contracts. [UCC] §2-612(3). What constitutes impairment of the value of the whole contract is a question of fact. The record below amply sustains the trial court's conclusion in this regard, particularly in light of the undenied and uncured stoppage of a check given to comply with the buyer's promise to reduce significantly the amount of its outstanding arrearages.

The buyer argues that the seller in an installment contract may never terminate a contract, despite repeated default in payment by the buyer, without first invoking the insecurity methodology of [UCC] §2-609. That is not the law.

If there is reasonable doubt about whether the buyer's default is substantial, the seller may be well advised to temporize by suspending further performance until it can ascertain whether the buyer is able to offer adequate assurance of future payments. But if the buyer's conduct is sufficiently egregious, such conduct will, in and of itself, constitute substantial impairment of the value of the whole contract and a present breach of the contract as a whole. An aggrieved seller is expressly permitted, by [UCC] §2-703(f), upon breach of a contract as a whole, to cancel the remainder of the contract "with respect to the whole undelivered balance."

The buyer's attack on the court's conclusions with respect to its counterclaim is equally unavailing. The buyer's principal argument is that the seller was obligated, on pain of default, to provide assurance of its further performance. The right to such assurance is premised on reasonable grounds for insecurity. Whether a buyer has reasonable grounds to be insecure is a question of fact. The trial court concluded that in this case the buyer's insecurity was not reasonable and we agree. A party to a sales contract may not suspend performance of its own for which it has "already received the agreed return." At all times, the buyer had received all of the goods that it had ordered. The presidents of the parties had exchanged adequate verbal assurances only eight days before the buyer itself delayed its own performance on the basis of information that was facially unreliable.

There is no error.

## NOTE AND QUESTION

The author of the opinion in the foregoing case is Justice Ellen Peters. Before becoming a Justice, she was a professor at Yale Law School. She was, and is, considered an expert on the UCC. One of her articles deals with issues such as the one presented in this case, *Remedies for Breach of Contracts Relating to the Sale of Goods Under the Uniform Commercial Code: A Roadmap for Article 2*, 73 Yale L.J. 199 (1963). Nevertheless, do you think this opinion is consistent with the following language from Official Comment 6 to section 2-612: "If only the seller's security in regard to future installments is impaired, he has the right to demand adequate assurances of proper future performance but has not an immediate right to cancel the entire contract"?

### 3. SELLER'S ABILITY TO LIMIT BUYER'S RIGHT TO REJECT OR REVOKE AND TO RECOVER CONSEQUENTIAL DAMAGES

#### (a) Limits on Rights to Reject or Revoke

The buyer's ability to reject goods or revoke acceptance can be limited by contract, according to UCC section 2-719. You will thus see in many contracts a provision limiting the right of a buyer in the event of a defective product to "repair or replacement of defective parts." This means that the seller has the opportunity to fix the goods and the buyer cannot demand money back or claim additional damages. How long does the seller have to repair the goods?

Section 2-719 further adds that "where circumstances cause an exclusive or limited remedy to fail of its essential purpose, remedy may be had as provided by this act." So, at some point, the buyer may ignore the limitation of remedy and demand rights that are available under the UCC, such as the right to revoke acceptance of the goods and obtain a refund. When the limited remedy fails is a question of fact. The following case discusses factors that are relevant in determining when a limited remedy fails of its essential purpose. One should keep in mind the purpose of the limited remedy—to give the buyer what the buyer bargained for.

### Riegel Power Corp. v. Voith Hydro

United States Court of Appeals, Third Circuit

888 F.2d 1043 (4th Cir. 1989)

This is an action by a buyer-plaintiff to recover of a seller-defendant damages for breach of a warranty of merchantability and freedom of defects in connection with the sale of an electric turbine. The buyer-plaintiff originally was Riegel Textile Company, but Riegel Power Corporation and Mount Vernon Mills, Inc., are the successors in "interest or assignees of Riegel Textile rights under the contract" and sue as such. The plaintiffs are collectively referred to by the parties and the district court as "Riegel" ; we do likewise. Defendant Voith Hydro is the successor in interest of the initial defendant, Allis-Chalmers Hydro, Inc. We refer herein to the defendant as "Voith Hydro." The defendant pled by way of defense (1) the provision in the contract of sale of an exclusive limitation of liability for a breach of warranty to an obligation to repair or replace, and (2) the provision proscribing recovery of consequential damages. Admitting the exclusive limitation of the liability provision, the plaintiff responded that under Delaware law, which was controlling, an exclusive limitation of warranty liability is ineffective "where circumstances cause an exclusive or limited remedy to fail of its essential purpose," (UCC §2-719(2)) and that in this case there is such failure of "essential purpose."

On motion for summary judgment, based on affidavits filed by the parties, the district court sustained, under Delaware law, the validity of the exclusive limitation of the liability clause in the contract of sale herein and found that such provision had not failed of its "essential purpose." It therefore granted judgment in favor of the defendant on that ground and did not address the provision in the contract proscribing recovery of consequential damages. We affirm.

On February 12, 1982, the plaintiff accepted a written offer of the defendant to supply a hydroelectric turbine for use in the plaintiff's Ware Shoals (South Carolina) installation. The installation of the turbine was contracted by Riegel to a third party. The defendant shipped, as agreed, certain parts to be imbedded into the concrete foundation below the turbine, and in January 1983 was ready to deliver and tendered, as if actually shipped, the turbine. The plaintiff, however, was not ready to accept delivery and requested the defendant not to ship the turbine. Due to this delay by the plaintiff and its installation contractor, the turbine was not actually installed and put in operation until June 11, 1984.

The repair or replace warranty obligation of the plaintiff under the contract of sale had a time limit of 18 months for delivery or tender of delivery. Such warranty would expire in July 1984, two or three weeks after the turbine was put in operation. The defendant called this fact to the plaintiff's attention by letter of February 17, 1984, and offered, for a fee, to extend the warranty. The plaintiff did not avail itself of the offer. Even though the warranty had expired, caused, as defendant says, largely by the fact that "the construction and installation schedules (which were the responsibility of third parties engaged by the plaintiff) were in excess of one year late," the defendant declared in a letter to the plaintiff that nonetheless it committed itself to "the successful start-up and commissioning of the Ware Shoals unit," and it carried out this commitment by promptly responding to every complaint of the plaintiff and of correcting every problem until full operation.

After joinder of issues, the parties engaged in certain discovery. In answer to an interrogatory, the plaintiff listed four times during which the turbine was down for repairs on account of which it premised its claim of failure of its essential purpose defense. The first of these occurred in July 1984. The other problems occurred at various times from July 1984 until 1987, all after the warranty had expired. The turbine operated without any significant problems from October 1985 to October 1986. Any problems were corrected and the turbine was fully operational on July 26, 1984, thereby satisfying the commitment made by the defendant.

In the affidavit of the defendant's project manager for the Ware Shoals project, he stated that "most or all of these problems (between 1984 and 1987) were caused by Riegel Textile's (or its contractor's) negligent installation of the turbine; Riegel Textile's and the plaintiffs' negligent maintenance and operation of the turbine; and the negligence of Riegel Textile, the plaintiffs, and their agents in overriding, bypassing, or disabling certain protective devices on the turbine." It seems undisputed that, whatever differences may have existed as to the cause of the problems encountered in the shakedown of the turbine, between 1984 and early 1987 "Voith Hydro or A-C Hydro promptly sent, at no cost to Riegel or the plaintiffs, repair personnel to Ware Shoals to perform the diagnostic and repair services necessary to render and keep the turbine operational." The plaintiffs made no attempt to refute this affidavit.

The real issue in the case, as posed by the plaintiffs, was whether the lost time in the operation of the turbine while the defendant was repairing the turbine was such that in a commercial sale such as this one it could be said that the exclusionary remedy for breach of warranty under the contract of sale had failed its "essential purpose." The district judge found that the plaintiffs had failed to offer any credible proof to support the claim that the exclusive limitation had failed its "essential purpose" and, therefore, granted defendant's motion for summary judgment. We agree.

As we have observed, there is no question of the applicability and validity of the exclusive repair or replace remedy in this case under controlling Delaware law. Nor is there any dispute that, under Delaware law, the exclusive repair or replace may be invalidated if the seller's performance is such that it can be said that the limitation or remedy had failed its "essential purpose." UCC §2-719(2). The Code, however, has not identified the circumstances that will justify a finding of failure of "essential purpose" in this context. This indefiniteness in the statutory language was found by the court in *J. A. Jones Const. Co. v. Dover,* 372 A.2d 540, 549 (Del. Super. Ct.), *appeal dismissed,* 377 A.2d 1 (Del.1977), to have been intended in order "to provide flexibility in molding contractual liability according to the actual nature of the transaction." Accordingly, "[i]n determining whether the contract limitation fails of its essential purpose, the facts and circumstances surrounding the contract, the nature of the basic obligations of the party, the nature of the goods involved, the uniqueness or experimental nature of the items, the general availability of the items, and the good faith and reasonableness of the provision are factors which should be considered." *Ibid.* Applying these factors, there are, as a leading text has put it, "relatively few situations where a remedy [such as the repair or replace provision] can fail of its essential purpose." 1 White & Summers, *Uniform Commercial Code,* 602 (West, 3d ed. 1988). This is not one of such "few situations" where the limitation of liability is rendered invalid by failure of its "essential purpose."

One of the most relevant factors to be considered under the *Dover* statement is the type of goods or product involved; that is, whether the sale is classified as a commercial or consumer sale. The importance of this difference in type of products sold is well stated by Professor Hawkland in 3 *Uniform Commercial Code Series,* 447 (Callaghan 1984):

> A more difficult case arises where the seller makes good faith but unsuccessful efforts to repair the defective goods. Where the buyer is a consumer this state of affairs should usually be sufficient to invalidate the prescribed remedy term on the basis of failure of essential purpose, and the same result ought to obtain as between merchants where standard goods are sold because the assumption in each case is that the seller can cure the defects that may crop up with regard to such goods. The situation and result may be different where the goods are experimental items, of complicated design, or built especially for the buyer. In those cases, the repair or replacement clause may simply mean that the seller promises to use his best efforts to keep the goods in repair and in working condition and that the buyer must put up with the inconvenience and loss of down time.

It has been often said that a sale of an electric turbine qualifies as a commercial and not as a consumer sale; in fact, we have been cited no decisions to the contrary. The rule that the agreed-upon allocation of commercial risk should not be disturbed is particularly appropriate where, as here, the warranted item is a highly complex, sophisticated, and in some ways experimental piece of equipment. Moreover, compliance with a warranty to repair or replace must depend on the type of machinery in issue. In the case of a multimillion-dollar turbine-generator, we are not dealing with a piece of equipment that either works or does not, or is fully repaired or not at all. On the contrary, the normal operation of a turbine-generator spans too large a spectrum for such simple characterizations.

Generally, in the commercial cases, the "essential purpose" exclusion arises only where the seller has refused to make repairs as he was required or where he cannot repair the product. In *American Electric,* which involved a turbine sale as does this case, the claim of the buyer, supported by evidence in the record, was that the seller in that case had "acted in bad faith in repairing the Unit," had "been wilfully dilatory in rendering repairs," but had "not merely failed to repair or replace but [had] repudiated its obligation to repair and replace." 418 F. Supp. at 453. In such a case, it was for the jury to determine whether the limited warranty had failed of its "essential purpose."

This, however, is not a case such as *American Electric*. The buyer and seller were enterprises managed by sophisticated businessmen who were thoroughly acquainted with and experienced in the electric-generating business. The parties acted in good faith both in agreeing on the contract and in performance under the contract. Unlike the seller in *American Electric*, the seller in this case is not charged with bad faith or with being "wilfully dilatory" in rendering repairs nor did it repudiate its obligation to repair. Even though its warranty had expired, the defendant in this case responded promptly to every complaint of the buyer, sent its personnel to the Ware Shoals unit, and made the necessary repairs. It continued to follow this course for three years after the warranty expired until the turbine could be pronounced fully operational in every way. Taking into account the type of product involved, it is understandable that there were five times when some difficulty arose in the break-in of the turbine. Moreover, the seller-defendant acted promptly to correct the difficulty. The defendant, even though its obligation under the sale agreement had expired, carried out its "commitment to the successful start-up and commissioning of the Ware Shoals unit." It went beyond its obligation under its limited warranty and the district court correctly granted summary judgment in its favor. Even were this a consumer case, it is doubtful that the plaintiff would have been able to sustain failure of an "essential purpose" claim.

The judgment of the district court is accordingly

AFFIRMED.

## PROBLEM

***Problem 6-12.*** Milgard Tempering contracted to purchase a glass tempering furnace from Selas Corporation. Milgard cuts and installs glass for residential construction. The furnace is for the purpose of manufacturing tempered glass. The contract contained a provision limiting Milgard's remedy to "repair or replacement" of defective parts. Selas agreed to design and manufacture the furnace for $1.45 million. The furnace was complex and, in the eyes of Selas, experimental. It was marketed, however, as a working piece of equipment. Three years after the date that the furnace was to be operational, Selas had failed to make it substantially conform to the contract's performance specifications. While it worked hard to make the furnace conform, evidence suggests that Selas did not take some steps that might have been more successful, stubbornly sticking with some aspects of the original design. Finally, Milgard had enough and decided to sue for damages. Is the "repair or replace" limitation enforceable? Is there a distinction between this case and the case preceding this problem? UCC §2-719(2). *See Milgard Tempering v. Selas Corp.*, 902 F.2d 703 (9th Cir. 1990).

### (b) Limits on Buyer's Rights to Recover Consequential Damages

As will be discussed in the next chapter, breaches of contract by the seller entitle the buyer in appropriate cases to recover consequential damages under UCC section 2-715. Such damages would include lost profits on resale of goods if the seller doesn't deliver or losses in the event that goods do not work as promised. For example, if a computer system does not perform according to specification, the buyer may be required to hire additional employees to perform work that the computer was supposed to perform. The wages of those additional employees would be consequential damages. If goods fail to perform and personal injury or property damage result, those damages would also be potentially recoverable as consequential damages. As you can imagine, consequential damages might greatly exceed direct damages in some cases and might be many times higher than the contract price for the goods.

Because of the potential exposure posed by consequential damages, sellers will often attempt to limit liability for those damages. Along with a contractual provision limiting the buyer to repair or replacement of defective parts might be a provision indicating that the seller will in no way be responsible for any consequential damages resulting from a breach of the sales contract. UCC section 2-713(3) permits such a provision, as long as it is not unconscionable. One question that has come up in litigation is whether the consequential damage limitation should fail automatically when a limited remedy of repair or replace fails of its essential purpose. It could be argued that since section 2-719(2) gives the buyer any "remedy . . . provided in this Act" in such cases, that consequential damages should be available since they are provided by the Act (the UCC). On the other hand, perhaps the drafters intended consequential damage limitations to be considered separately, since section 2-719(3) specifically deals with such provisions. The following case analyzes the issue.

#### CHATLOS SYSTEMS v. NATIONAL CASH REGISTER CORP.

United States Court of Appeals, Third Circuit

635 F.2d 1081 (1980)

In this diversity case governed by the Uniform Commercial Code, the district court assessed damages for breach of warranty after finding that the seller's failure to timely program a computer system caused a contractual remedy to fail of its essential purpose. Despite an express provision in the agreement prohibiting recovery of consequential damages, the court also made an award for such losses. Although we accept the determination on the failure of the contractual remedy, we do not agree that the disclaimer of consequential damages is ineffective as a result. We conclude that that clause must be evaluated on its own merits and, in this case, enforced. In addition, we are unable to accept certain trial court determinations on the factors used to compute the other items of damage, and we remand for recalculation.

I

Chatlos Systems, Inc. (Chatlos), filed suit in the New Jersey Superior Court against National Cash Register Corp. (NCR), alleging, inter alia, breach of warranty in connection with the sale of a computer system. The case was removed to the United States District Court for the District of New Jersey, and after a bench trial, judgment was entered in favor of the plaintiff for $120,710.92.

Chatlos designs and manufactures cable pressurization equipment for the telecommunications industry. In the spring of 1974, the company decided to purchase a computer system and contacted several manufacturers, among them NCR. That firm suggested a magnetic ledger card system, but, after further inquiry by Chatlos, agreed to provide the 399/656 disc system, a computer utilizing more advanced technology, as the appropriate model for the customer's need.

This system was designed to provide six functions for Chatlos: (1) accounts receivable, (2) payroll, (3) order entry, (4) inventory deletion, (5) state income tax, (6) cash receipts. NCR represented to Chatlos that the system would solve inventory problems, result in direct savings of labor costs, and be programmed by capable NCR personnel to be "up and running" (in full operation) within six months.

On July 24, 1974, Chatlos signed a system service agreement with NCR as part of the transaction, and the computer hardware was delivered the following December. Because NCR would not extend credit, Chatlos made a leasing arrangement with Midlantic National Bank, agreeing to pay $70,162.09 on a monthly installment basis. This is a common practice in the trade; the computer company sells the system to a bank, which in turn leases it to the customer.

Chatlos understood that the system would be operational about three months after delivery and therefore expected it to be "up and running" by March 1975. An NCR employee began programming in January 1975, but by March, only one of the functions, payroll, was in operation. Efforts to install the inventory deletion and order entry programs were unsuccessful. These functions used multiple records per sector technology—the storing of several items of information in one section of a disc. But the NCR programmer was unable to delete any information within the same section without erasing it all. Since Chatlos had purchased the computer to record its extensive parts inventory, the inability to solve the multiple records sector problem posed a major difficulty if the withdrawal of one part in a unit erroneously deleted the entire unit.

One year later the problem persisted. NCR analysts attempted a demonstration of the order entry and accounts receivable functions in March 1976, but significant problems surfaced with both. In June 1976 Chatlos asked that the lease be canceled and the computer removed, but, at NCR's request, agreed to allow additional time to make the system operational. On August 31, 1976, Chatlos experienced problems with the payroll function, the only operation the computer had been performing properly.

On September 1, 1976, the state income tax program was installed. The next day an NCR representative arrived at the Chatlos plant to install the order entry program. Chatlos refused to allow the work to proceed and again asked NCR to terminate the lease and remove the computer. NCR refused, stating that it had no ownership rights in the system, having been paid by the bank.

The district judge, applying New Jersey law, reasoned that despite the service aspects and lease arrangement, the transaction was for the sale of goods within the meaning of Article 2 of the Uniform Commercial Code. He determined that certain express warranties had been made in various writings executed by the parties.

The court found that NCR had warranted its product for "12 months after delivery against defects in material, workmanship, and operational failure from ordinary use," and further that "services (would be) performed in a skillful and workmanlike manner." In addition, there was an oral, express warranty, memorialized in a purchase order prepared by the Midlantic Bank, providing that "since the goods . . . are purchased by us expressly for the use of (Chatlos), (NCR) further warrants that the goods are in good working order, fit for the use (Chatlos) intends them, and fulfill all representations made by (NCR) to (Chatlos)." 479 F. Supp. at 743. The purchase order also provided that Chatlos was "to obtain all the benefits of all warranties." Finally, the court held that since Chatlos's reliance upon the skill and judgment of NCR was known to it, an implied warranty of fitness for Chatlos's particular purposes was created as well. *Id.*; see N.J. Stat. Ann. §12A:2-315 (West 1962).

Finding that these warranties had been breached, the court looked to UCC. §2-714(2). That section measures damages for breach of warranty as the difference between the value of what was accepted and what was warranted, N.J. Stat. Ann. §12A:2-714(2), which in this case was determined to be $57,152.76. The court awarded additional damages of $63,558.16 for items such as employee salaries and lost profits, since it concluded that NCR's disclaimer of consequential damages was ineffective.

No evidence of wrongful intent on the part of NCR was found, nor did the plaintiff prove fraudulent misrepresentation. Consequently, a claim for punitive damages was denied.

## II

Both parties have appealed, and while they concede the applicability of the UCC, each contests liability and damage determinations. We have examined the contentions of the parties with respect to the court's conclusions on warranties, their breach, lack of fraud, and punitive damages. The district court's findings and reasoning on these aspects of the case are not erroneous and will be affirmed.

## III

We are unable to concur, however, with the trial court's computation of damages. Accepting the finding that NCR breached its warranties, our next step is to examine the contract and determine whether the parties limited otherwise applicable remedies. UCC section 2-719(1) provides that the parties may so agree.

The contract states that services would be performed in a skillful and professional manner, and further provides that NCR's obligation was limited to correcting any "error in any program or routine as appears within 60 days after such has been furnished." Another part of the contract reads: "In no event shall NCR be liable for special or consequential damages from any cause whatsoever." We will discuss these two restrictions separately.

Before a limitation on a party's remedies may be enforced, it must be established that the contract contains "an exclusive or limited remedy." UCC §2-719(1)(b). The agreement here does say that NCR's obligation is "limited." Although an argument might be made that this is not clearly expressed, we will assume arguendo that the contract satisfies this Code requirement.

An exclusive or limited remedy, however, must be viewed against the background of UCC section 2-719(2), which provides, "Where circumstances cause an exclusive or limited remedy to fail of its essential purpose, remedy may be had as provided in this Act."

NCR repeatedly attempted to correct the deficiencies in the system, but nevertheless still had not provided the product warranted a year and a half after Chatlos had reasonably expected a fully operational computer. In these circumstances, the delay made the correction remedy ineffective, and it therefore failed of its essential purpose. Consequently, the contractual limitation was unenforceable and did not preclude recovery of damages for the breach of warranty.

This conclusion, however, does not dispose of the contractual clause excluding consequential damages. UCC section 2-719(2) states that when an exclusive or limited remedy fails of its purpose, remedy may be had as provided in the Act. Recognizing that consequential damages may be a subject of agreement between the parties, section 2-719(3) provides:

[The court quotes from section 2-719(3).]

Several cases have held that when a limited remedy fails of its purpose, an exclusion of consequential damages also fails, but approximately the same number of decisions have treated that preclusion as a separate matter. New Jersey has not taken a position on this question, so in this diversity case we must predict which view the New Jersey Supreme Court would adopt if the question were presented to it.

It appears to us that the better-reasoned approach is to treat the consequential damage disclaimer as an independent provision, valid unless unconscionable. This poses no logical difficulties. A contract may well contain no limitation on breach of warranty damages but specifically exclude consequential damages. Conversely, it is quite conceivable that some limitation might be placed on a breach of warranty award, but consequential damages would expressly be permitted.

The limited remedy of repair and a consequential damages exclusion are two discrete ways of attempting to limit recovery for breach of warranty. The Code, moreover, tests each by a different standard. The former survives unless it fails of its essential purpose, while the latter is valid unless it is unconscionable. We therefore see no reason to hold, as a general proposition, that the failure of the limited remedy provided in the contract, without more, invalidates a wholly distinct term in the agreement excluding consequential damages. The two are not mutually exclusive.

Whether the preclusion of consequential damages should be effective in this case depends upon the circumstances involved. The repair remedy's failure of essential purpose, while a discrete question, is not completely irrelevant to the issue of the conscionability of enforcing the consequential damages exclusion. The latter term is "merely an allocation of unknown or undeterminable risks."

UCC §2-719, Official Comment 3. Recognizing this, the question here narrows to the unconscionability of the buyer retaining the risk of consequential damages upon the failure of the essential purpose of the exclusive repair remedy.

One fact in this case that becomes significant under the Code is that the claim is not for personal injury but for property damage. Limitations on damages for personal injuries are not favored, but no such prejudice applies to property losses. It is also important that the claim is for commercial loss and the adversaries are substantial business concerns. We find no great disparity in the parties' bargaining power or sophistication. Apparently, Chatlos, a manufacturer of complex electronic equipment, had some appreciation of the problems that might be encountered with a computer system. Nor is there a "surprise" element present here. The limitation was clearly expressed in a short, easily understandable sales contract. This is not an instance of an ordinary consumer being misled by a disclaimer hidden in a "linguistic maze."

Thus, at the time the contract was signed there was no reason to conclude that the parties could not competently agree upon the allocation of risk involved in the installation of the computer system.

From the perspective of the later events, it appears that the type of damage claimed here came within the realm of expectable losses. Some disruption of normal business routines, expenditure of employee time, and impairment of efficiency cannot be considered highly unusual or unforeseeable in a faulty computer installation. Moreover, although not determinative, it is worth mentioning that even though unsuccessful in correcting the problems within an appropriate time, NCR continued in its efforts. Indeed, on the date of termination NCR was still actively working on the system at the Chatlos plant. In fact, the trial court thought that Chatlos should have cooperated further by accepting the installation of the programs. This is not a case where the seller acted unreasonably or in bad faith.

In short, there is nothing in the formation of the contract or the circumstances resulting in failure of performance that makes it unconscionable to enforce the parties' allocation of risk. We conclude, therefore, that the provision of the agreement excluding consequential damages should be enforced, and the district court erred in making an award for such losses.

## NOTES, QUESTIONS, AND PROBLEM

1. This case involved a lease of goods, but the court applied UCC Article 2. This case was decided before the adoption of UCC Article 2A, which deals with leases of goods. Many of the Article 2A provisions are similar to Article 2. In particular, section 2A-503 is similar to section 2-719, and section 2A-519 (4) is similar to UCC section 2-715. The court's analysis would probably be the same even if it were to apply the Article 2A provisions. For more on Article 2A and leases, see Chapter 10, *infra*.
2. Not all courts would agree that the consequential damages limitation can be enforced even when the limited remedy of repair or replace fails of its essential purpose. *See RRX Industries v. Lab-Con, Inc.*, 772 F.2d 543 (9th Cir. 1985) (consequential damages available despite limitation when breach was "total and fundamental"); *Milgard Tempering v. Selas Corp.*, 902 F.2d 703

(9th Cir. 1990) (whether the limitation on consequential damages survives the failure of the limited remedy depends on a factual analysis of whether the damages sustained by the buyer were fairly part of the risk assumed by the buyer in the contract). Why should consequential damage limitations be considered differently from other remedy limitations?

***Problem 6-13.*** Buyer contracted to purchase a car from an auto dealer in a consumer transaction. The contract had a provision limiting the buyer's remedy to repair or replacement of defective parts and limited the buyer's ability to recover consequential or incidental damages resulting from breach. Shortly after purchase, the car began to develop a number of problems, including periodic stalling, a leaky transmission, and a defective speedometer. Over a nine-month period, buyer took the car back to the seller eight times. The car was never fully repaired, and finally buyer decided to revoke acceptance. Since the seller was unwilling to agree, buyer stored the car at home, rented a substitute car to provide transportation, and continued to pay insurance on the defective car. Buyer would like to recover the costs of insurance and the rental car under UCC section 2-715. Should the limited remedy and limit on consequential damages be allowed to stand and prevent recovery? UCC §2-719. *See King v. Taylor Chrysler-Plymouth, Inc.*, 184 Mich. App. 204, 457 N.W.2d 42 (1990).

## 4. RISK OF LOSS—BREACH

Under the UCC, the risk of loss rules change when one of the parties is in breach. Section 2-510 covers three cases: (1) where a nonconformity gives the buyer a right of rejection; (2) where the buyer rightfully revokes acceptance; and (3) where conforming goods are identified to the contract and the buyer repudiates or is otherwise in breach before the risk of loss passes to the buyer. The following case deals with one of these situations.

### JAKOWSKI v. CAROLE CHEVROLET

New Jersey Superior Court

180 N.J. Super. 122, 433 A.2d 841 (1981)

Plaintiff seeks summary judgment on Count I of the complaint alleging breach of a new car sales contract by defendant Carole Chevrolet, Inc.

The essential facts are not in dispute. On March 8, 1980, plaintiff Jakowski (hereinafter "buyer") entered into a contract of sale with defendant Carole Chevrolet, Inc. (hereinafter "seller"), calling for the purchase of one new 1980 Chevrolet Camaro. The parties also agreed that the car would be undercoated and that its finish would have a polymer coating. While there is some disagreement as to exactly when the buyer ordered the coatings, it is undisputed that prior to delivery the seller agreed to deliver the car with the coatings applied. Likewise, it is undisputed that the car in question was delivered to the buyer without the required coatings on May 19, 1980.

The next day, May 20, 1980, the seller contacted the buyer and informed him that the car delivered to him lacked the coatings in question and seller instructed buyer to return the car so that the coatings could be applied. On May 22, 1980, the buyer returned the auto to the seller for application of the coatings. Sometime during the evening of May 22 or the morning of May 23 the car was stolen from the seller's premises and it was never recovered. Seller has refused to either provide a replacement auto to buyer or to refund the purchase price. Buyer remains accountable on the loan, provided through GMAC, for the purchase of the car.

The narrow question thus presented is upon whom, as between buyer and seller, this loss should fall. In UCC terminology, on May 22, 1980, which party bore the risk of the car's loss?

Seller argues that the risk of loss passed to the buyer upon his receipt of the auto. This is consistent with UCC section 2-509(3) pursuant to which the risk of loss passes to the buyer upon his receipt of the goods. Section 2-509(4), however, expressly provides that the general rules of section 2-509 are subject to the more specific provisions of section 2-510, which deals with the effect of breach upon risk of loss.

Buyer relies upon section 2-510(1), which provides:

Where a tender or delivery of goods so fails to conform to the contract as to give a right of rejection the risk of their loss remains on the seller until cure or acceptance.

Application of this section to the instant facts requires that three questions be answered. First, did the car "so fail to conform" as to give this buyer a right to reject it? If so, did the buyer "accept" the car despite the nonconformity? Finally, did the seller cure the defect prior to the theft of the auto?

The first question must be answered in the affirmative. The contract provided that the car would be delivered with undercoating and a polymer finish, and it is undisputed that it was delivered without these coatings. The goods were thus clearly nonconforming and, despite seller's assertion to the contrary, the degree of their nonconformity is irrelevant in assessing the buyer's concomitant right to reject them. UCC section 2-106 is clear in its intent to preserve the rule of strict compliance, that is, the "perfect tender" rule:

> Goods . . . are "conforming" or conform to the contract when they are in accordance with the obligations under the contract.

The language of section 2-510(1), "so fails to conform," is misleading in this respect: No particular quantum of nonconformity is required where a single delivery is contemplated. The allusion is to section 2-612 which substitutes a rule of substantial compliance where, and only where, an installment deal is contemplated. White & Summers, *Uniform Commercial Code* (2d ed. 1980), §5.5 at 187-188.

Secondly, did buyer "accept" the auto by taking possession of it? This question was presented in *Zabriskie Chevrolet, Inc. v. Smith*, 99 N.J. Super. 441, 240 A.2d 195 (Law Div. 1968). In *Zabriskie* it was held that the mere taking of possession by the purchaser is not equivalent to acceptance. Before he can be held to have accepted, a buyer must be afforded a "reasonable opportunity to inspect" the goods. UCC §2-606.

Seller's actions in this matter preclude analysis in conventional "acceptance" terms. Buyer had no opportunity, indeed no reason, to reject, given seller's own communication to buyer shortly after delivery, to the effect that the goods did not conform and that the seller was exercising its right to cure said nonconformity. See UCC §2-508 (seller's right to cure). This communication, in effect an acknowledgement of nonconformity, obviated the need for a formal rejection on buyer's part, if, indeed, section 2-510(1) imposes such an obligation. Put another way, it precluded the buyer from rejecting the car. Consistent with this analysis, I find as a matter of law that there was no acceptance by buyer of this nonconforming auto.

As to the final question of whether the seller effected a cure, there is no evidence, in fact defendant does not even contend, that cure was ever effected.

Given the undisputed facts, the operation of section 2-510(1) is inescapable. The goods failed to conform, the buyer never accepted them, and the defect was never cured. Accordingly, the risk of loss remained on the seller and judgment is granted for plaintiff.

For present purposes it is adequate to hold simply that where a seller obtains possession of the goods in an effort to cure defects in them so as to comply with his end of the bargain, he is under a contractual duty to redeliver them to the buyer. In failing to do so, he has breached the contract.

Pursuant to UCC section 2-711, buyer is entitled to a refund of so much of the purchase price as has been paid to seller. Included in the cost of the automobile are the finance charges incurred by the buyer, who secured financing from GMAC pursuant to a retail installment sales contract entered into with the seller. There is no dispute about including these charges in the purchase cost, and the buyer, as of March 30, 1981, indicated the total amount due on any judgment to be $9,398.75. However, since this case was first heard some additional time has passed and a current pay-off figure should be obtained for inclusion in this judgment.

## PROBLEMS

***Problem 6-14.*** A contract for the sale of a pool heater requires the seller to both deliver and install the product. The pool heater was delivered to buyer's premises. It sat there for four days. The heater was too large to move, and the buyer warned the seller that the delivery was being made to a high-crime area. Before it was installed, it was stolen. Who had the risk of loss? See UCC §2-510(1); *In re Thomas*, 182 B.R. 347, 26 UCC Rep. Serv. 2d 774 (S.D. Fla. 1995).

***Problem 6-15.*** While goods identified to the contract were in the seller's warehouse, the buyer wrongfully repudiated the contract. The goods were destroyed in a fire. Seller has insurance that covers the loss. When an insurance company pays a claim made by its insured customer, it is given an equitable right of subrogation to step into the shoes of the insured and to assert the insured's rights. For example, if you are involved in a car accident that is the fault of the other driver, you may nevertheless seek recovery from your insurance company under the provisions of the policy calling for the company to pay to repair any damage to your car no matter who was at fault (the "collision" part of the policy as compared to the "liability" part). If the insurance company pays, it is subrogated to your right to recover from the driver who was at fault. In this problem, if Seller's insurance company pays Seller, is the insurance company subrogated to any right that the Seller might have to sue Buyer? See the last sentence of Official Comment 3 to §2-510.

## C. PERFORMANCE AND BREACH UNDER THE CISG

The obligations of the seller under the CISG are spelled out in Articles 30-44, and the obligations of the buyer are contained in Articles 53-60. Basically, the seller is required to deliver goods that are in conformity with the requirements of the contract and the buyer is required to take delivery and pay for them as required under the contract.

Perhaps the biggest difference between the CISG and the UCC on the question of performance is that neither party is permitted to cancel, or in the parlance of the CISG, "avoid," the contract for an insignificant breach. There is no "perfect tender rule" under the CISG. Rather, the buyer may avoid the contract only if the seller has committed a "fundamental breach" or, in the case of nondelivery, the seller does not deliver goods within the additional period of time set by the buyer under CISG Article 47. CISG Art. 49. Likewise, the seller may avoid the contract only if the buyer has committed a "fundamental breach" or if the buyer has not performed its obligations within the additional period of time set by the seller under CISG Article 63. CISG Article 64. If the injured party is not entitled to avoid because the breach is not fundamental, the injured party may still be able to obtain specific performance or damages, as discussed in the next two chapters.

What is meant by "fundamental breach"? It is defined in Article 25, and requires substantial deprivation of what the injured party was entitled to expect under the contract. In addition, the substantial deprivation resulting from the breach must have been reasonably foreseeable to the breaching party. The U.N. Secretariat Commentary to the predecessor section to Article 25 elaborates somewhat by stating that the monetary value of the contract, the monetary value of the harm caused by the breach, and the interference with the activities of the injured party are all relevant factors. As to whether the results of the breach must be foreseeable at the time of contracting or at the time of breach, the Commentary suggests that it is up to the tribunal deciding the case to decide based on the facts of the given case.

Cases and commentators focus on a number of factors in determining whether there has been a fundamental breach. One question would be whether the parties in the contract have defined what is fundamental. For example, have they agreed that the designated time of delivery is an essential condition to the buyer's obligation to accept and pay for the goods (often called "time is of the essence")? Have they agreed that the goods must be suitable for a particular purpose in order to be acceptable? Other factors include willingness of the breaching party to perform, ability of the breaching party to cure, and adequacy of damages.[5] As you can see, these factors are similar to those considered in determining material breach or substantial impairment in value.

---

5. For a very good discussion of the factors taken into account in determining if a breach is fundamental, see Robert Koch, *The Concept of Fundamental Breach of Contract Under the United Nations Convention on Contracts for the International Sale of Goods,* in Pace, ed., *Review of the Convention on Contracts for the International Sale of Goods* 177-354 (1998). This discussion can be found on the Internet at *www.cisg.law.pace.edu/cisg/biblio/koch.html* (accessed Oct. 2011). See also CISG Advisory Council Opinion No. 5, *www.cisg.law.pace.edu/cisg/CISG-AC-op5.html* (accessed Oct. 2011).

On the foreseeability question, it can be argued that foreseeability should be determined at the time of contracting since it is at that time that the party decides to undertake the risks of performing. If the party is aware that a late delivery by one day will have catastrophic results for which that party will be liable, the party may decide not to enter into the contract. On the other hand, if the party subsequently becomes aware of the other party's special needs and it is not difficult for the party to perform exactly according to the contract, perhaps notions of good faith require exact performance on pain of finding fundamental breach in the event that such performance is not forthcoming. So this may explain why a "one size fits all" rule does not exist.[6]

Another concept in the CISG that is different from the UCC is the concept of the *nachfrist*, or extension, notice. As previously noted, either the seller or the buyer may give the other party a reasonable period of additional time to perform. If performance is still not forthcoming after that time, then the contract may be avoided. Of course, there is a question as to what constitutes a reasonable period of time, and the question of what is reasonable probably is related to the concept of fundamental breach.

The CISG requires the buyer to inspect the goods for nonconformities as soon as is practicable. CISG Article 38. The CISG requires that the buyer give notice to the seller of any nonconformity with respect to the goods within a reasonable time after the buyer knew or should have known of the nonconformity if the buyer wishes to assert that lack of nonconformity against the seller. CISG Article 39. The seller is not permitted to assert the buyer's failure to examine the goods or give notice if the seller knew or could not have been unaware of the nonconformities. CISG Article 40. If either the buyer or seller wishes to avoid the contract, notification of avoidance must be given within the time indicated in Articles 49 and 64.

## Delchi Carrier SpA v. Rotorex Corp.

United States Court of Appeals, Second Circuit

71 F.3d 1024 (1995)

Rotorex Corporation, a New York corporation, appeals from a judgment of $1,785,772.44 in damages for lost profits and other consequential damages awarded to Delchi Carrier SpA following a bench trial before Judge Munson. The basis for the award was Rotorex's delivery of nonconforming compressors to Delchi, an Italian manufacturer of air conditioners. Delchi cross-appeals from the denial of certain incidental and consequential damages. We affirm the award of damages; we reverse in part on Delchi's cross-appeal and remand for further proceedings.

### Background

In January 1988, Rotorex agreed to sell 10,800 compressors to Delchi for use in Delchi's "Ariele" line of portable room air conditioners. The air conditioners were scheduled to go on sale in the spring and summer of 1988. Prior to

6. These factors are discussed in the Koch paper cited above.

executing the contract, Rotorex sent Delchi a sample compressor and accompanying written performance specifications. The compressors were scheduled to be delivered in three shipments before May 15, 1988.

Rotorex sent the first shipment by sea on March 26. Delchi paid for this shipment, which arrived at its Italian factory on April 20, by letter of credit. Rotorex sent a second shipment of compressors on or about May 9. Delchi also remitted payment for this shipment by letter of credit. While the second shipment was en route, Delchi discovered that the first lot of compressors did not conform to the sample model and accompanying specifications. On May 13, after a Rotorex representative visited the Delchi factory in Italy, Delchi informed Rotorex that 93 percent of the compressors were rejected in quality control checks because they had lower cooling capacity and consumed more power than the sample model and specifications. After several unsuccessful attempts to cure the defects in the compressors, Delchi asked Rotorex to supply new compressors conforming to the original sample and specifications. Rotorex refused, claiming that the performance specifications were "inadvertently communicated" to Delchi.

In a faxed letter dated May 23, 1988, Delchi canceled the contract. Although it was able to expedite a previously planned order of suitable compressors from Sanyo, another supplier, Delchi was unable to obtain in a timely fashion substitute compressors from other sources and thus suffered a loss in its sales volume of Arieles during the 1988 selling season. Delchi filed the instant action under the United Nations Convention on Contracts for the International Sale of Goods ("CISG" or "the Convention") for breach of contract and failure to deliver conforming goods. On January 10, 1991, Judge Cholakis granted Delchi's motion for partial summary judgment, holding Rotorex liable for breach of contract.

**Discussion**

The district court held, and the parties agree, that the instant matter is governed by the CISG, reprinted at 15 U.S.C.A. Appendix (West Supp. 1995), a self-executing agreement between the United States and other signatories, including Italy. Because there is virtually no case law under the Convention, we look to its language and to "the general principles" upon which it is based. See CISG Article 7(2). The Convention directs that its interpretation be informed by its "international character and . . . the need to promote uniformity in its application and the observance of good faith in international trade." See CISG Article 7(1); see generally John Honnold, *Uniform Law for International Sales Under the 1980 United Nations Convention* 60-62 (2d ed. 1991) (addressing principles for interpretation of CISG). Case law interpreting analogous provisions of Article 2 of the Uniform Commercial Code ("UCC") may also inform a court where the language of the relevant CISG provisions tracks that of the UCC. However, UCC caselaw "is not per se applicable." *Orbisphere Corp. v. United States,* 726 F. Supp. 1344, 1355 (Ct. Int'l Trade 1989).

Under the CISG, "[t]he seller must deliver goods which are of the quantity, quality and description required by the contract," and "the goods do not conform with the contract unless they . . . [p]ossess the qualities of goods which the seller has held out to the buyer as a sample or model." CISG Article 35. The CISG further states that "[t]he seller is liable in accordance with the contract and this Convention for any lack of conformity." CISG Article 36.

Judge Cholakis held that "there is no question that [Rotorex's] compressors did not conform to the terms of the contract between the parties" and noted that "[t]here are ample admissions [by Rotorex] to that effect." We agree. The agreement between Delchi and Rotorex was based upon a sample compressor supplied by Rotorex and upon written specifications regarding cooling capacity and power consumption. After the problems were discovered, Rotorex's engineering representative, Ernest Gamache, admitted in a May 13, 1988, letter that the specification sheet was "in error" and that the compressors would actually generate less cooling power and consume more energy than the specifications indicated. Gamache also testified in a deposition that at least some of the compressors were nonconforming. The president of Rotorex, John McFee, conceded in a May 17, 1988, letter to Delchi that the compressors supplied were less efficient than the sample and did not meet the specifications provided by Rotorex. Finally, in its answer to Delchi's complaint, Rotorex admitted "that some of the compressors . . . did not conform to the nominal performance information." There was thus no genuine issue of material fact regarding liability, and summary judgment was proper.

Under the CISG, if the breach is "fundamental" the buyer may either require delivery of substitute goods, CISG Article 46, or declare the contract void, CISG Article 49, and seek damages. With regard to what kind of breach is fundamental, Article 25 provides:

> A breach of contract committed by one of the parties is fundamental if it results in such detriment to the other party as substantially to deprive him of what he is entitled to expect under the contract, unless the party in breach did not foresee and a reasonable person of the same kind in the same circumstances would not have foreseen such a result.

CISG Article 25. In granting summary judgment, the district court held that "[t]here appears to be no question that [Delchi] did not substantially receive that which [it] was entitled to expect" and that "any reasonable person could foresee that shipping nonconforming goods to a buyer would result in the buyer not receiving that which he expected and was entitled to receive." Because the cooling power and energy consumption of an air conditioner compressor are important determinants of the product's value, the district court's conclusion that Rotorex was liable for a fundamental breach of contract under the Convention was proper.

[The part of the opinion dealing with damages will be reproduced in the next chapter.]

## NOTES, QUESTIONS, AND PROBLEMS

1. What factors do you think are important in determining that the seller's failure to perform in this case constituted a fundamental breach? Is it enough that 93 percent of the first shipment failed the test? Why have a fundamental breach rule in international sales as compared to a perfect tender rule?
2. Could the seller have cured in this case if it had wanted to? See CISG Article 48.

***Problem 6-16.*** Assume a contract for the sale of shoes for resale purposes. The contract does not indicate that time is of the essence, and the shoes are not seasonal items. Half the shoes were to be delivered in November and half the following January. None of the shoes are delivered by the first delivery date. In December, the buyer contacts the seller by telephone and complains about the late delivery, reminding the seller of the January deadline. In January, about half of the shoes are delivered and buyer accepts the goods but does not pay for them. In February and March the buyer contacts the seller and complains about the failure of the seller to deliver the remaining shoes. The buyer continues to refuse to pay. Finally, the buyer declares the contract avoided. Does it appear that there has been a fundamental breach, warranting avoidance? Should it matter if, in January, the buyer told the seller that the shoes were immediately needed for a big sale the buyer was planning? Has the buyer given a valid extension notice under Article 47? See U.N. Secretariat Commentary on the predecessor section to Article 47, paragraph 7, which can be found on the Internet at *www.cisg.law.pace.edu/cisg/text/secomm/secomm-47.html* (accessed Oct. 2011). What factors should be relevant in determining whether the extension notice provides a reasonable time? See Kimbel, *Nachfrist Notice and Avoidance Under the CISG*, 18 J. of Law & Comm. 301, 310-312 (1999), *www.cisg.law.pace.edu/cisg/biblio/kimbel.html#kli* (accessed Oct. 2011). The foregoing hypothetical is roughly based on a German case, Oberlandesgericht Dusseldorf April 24, 1997, CLOUT abstract no. 275, *http://cisgw3.law.pace.edu/cases/970424g1.html* (accessed Oct. 2011).

***Problem 6-17.*** A retailer contracts with a manufacturer for the delivery of men's dress shoes. The contract is covered by the CISG. Instead of shipping dress shoes, the seller mixes up the order and ships work boots (the dress shoes went elsewhere). Buyer receives the boots, and rather than complain about it decides to try to sell them. Eight months later, Buyer is dissatisfied with the number of boots that have been sold and wants to either (a) avoid the contract, or (b) sue for damages for sales that have been lost since boots were shipped rather than dress shoes. Does the Buyer have a remedy against the Seller? See CISG Articles 26, 38, 39, 40, 44, and 49(2). As to whether Seller is precluded from asserting lack of timely notice of nonconformity under Article 40, see Schlechtriem, *Uniform Sales Law—The UN-Convention on Contracts For the International Sale of Goods* 69-72 (1986), reproduced at *www.cisg.law.pace.edu/cisg/biblio/schlechtriem-40.html* (accessed Oct. 2011). For a discussion of when Article 44 might apply, see Lookofsky, *Editorial Analysis of Article 44, www.cisg.law.pace.edu/cisg/text/cross/cross-44.html* (accessed Oct. 2011).

***Problem 6-18.*** Buyer contracts to purchase a computer system. The contract is covered by the CISG. Assume that after months of trying, the Seller is unable to make the system run according to contract specifications. The contract contains a provision indicating "Buyer's sole remedy under this contract is to permit Seller to repair or replace defective parts in the goods, and to correct programming errors." Finally, Buyer is fed up and wishes to avoid the contract. You may assume that proper notices are given and that the breach is fundamental. Does the contractual provision prevent Buyer from avoiding? See CISG Articles 6 and 8.

***Problem 6-19.*** In a sale covered by the CISG, Buyer's agent is supposed to pick up the goods at a warehouse that is operated by a warehouse operator (not Seller). The date of delivery is to be June 1. The warehouse operator is told by Seller that Buyer is to pick up the goods. Seller tells Buyer that the goods are ready to be picked up. The goods are clearly identifiable to the contract. Due to inadvertence, Buyer's agent fails to pick up the goods. On June 2, the warehouse and the goods are destroyed by fire through no fault of any party. As between Buyer and Seller, who had the risk of loss? What if Buyer was to pick up the goods from Seller's place of business, which was destroyed by fire along with the goods? See CISG Article 69. Assume instead that Buyer took possession of the goods and discovered that they had serious defects that would amount to fundamental breach. The next day and before Buyer had an opportunity to give notice of avoidance, the goods were destroyed by fire. Who had the risk of loss? See CISG Article 66.

## D. EXCUSE FROM PERFORMANCE— IMPRACTICABILITY AND FRUSTRATION OF PURPOSE

In your contracts class, you probably spent some time focusing on the doctrines of impossibility of performance and frustration of purpose. If you recall, sometimes performance of a contractual duty may be discharged where, due to some unforeseen event, the performance becomes either physically impossible or becomes unduly onerous. You might have studied the English case of *Taylor v. Caldwell*, 122 Eng. Rep. 309 (K.B. 1863), in which the owner of a music hall was excused from performance under a contract for use of the hall when it burned down. In addition, performance may be discharged where the parties understood at the time of contracting that there was a specific purpose for the contract, and due to some unforeseen event the purpose has become substantially frustrated. You might have studied the English case of *Krell v. Henry*, [1903] 2 K.B. 740, in which a person who contracted to rent a room to view the coronation of King Edward VII was excused from performance when the King was stricken with perityphlitis. It is also quite possible that you have suffered frustration while studying impossibility and frustration because the rules are murky and court decisions are somewhat unpredictable.

The UCC has several rules dealing with excuse on the basis of impracticability and frustration, sections 2-613 through 2-616. At first read, it does not appear that the doctrine of frustration of purpose is dealt with by these sections, but Official Comment 9 to section 2-615 suggests that frustration may be a proper excuse under the UCC in some cases. Courts might also apply frustration under general principles of law and equity. See UCC §1-103.

The CISG provides that a party to a contract is not liable for failure to perform if such "failure was due to an impediment beyond his control and that he could not reasonably be expected to have taken the impediment into account at the time of the conclusion of the contract or to have avoided or overcome it or its consequences." This provision has been described as one of the more difficult of the CISG Articles to apply. What constitutes an "impediment"? It is unclear whether it encompasses economic impracticability, meaning that performance is possible but perhaps economically ruinous, or frustration of purpose.[7] As is often the case with the CISG, the provision was drafted in a vague manner to accommodate the fact that different legal systems have different approaches. By comparison, the UNIDROIT Principles of International Commercial Contracts grant relief on the basis of hardship, which is defined as including situations in which the cost of performing has increased or the value of the contract has decreased due to unforeseen circumstances. UNIDROIT Principles of International Commercial Contracts Article 6.2.2.

## Maple Farms, Inc. v. City School District

Supreme Court, Chemung County, New York, Special Term

76 Misc. 2d 1080, 352 N.Y.S.2d 784 (1974)

This is a motion for summary judgment in an action for declaratory judgment whereby the plaintiff seeks a determination that the contract wherein the plaintiff agreed to supply milk to the defendant school district at an agreed price be terminated without further liability on the grounds of legal "impossibility" or "impracticality" because of the occurrence of events not contemplated by the parties which makes performance impracticable.

The background of this dispute is that the price of raw milk at the farm site is and has been controlled for many years in this area by the United States Department of Agriculture through the New York-New Jersey Market Administrator. The president of the plaintiff milk dealer has for at least ten years bid on contracts to supply milk for the defendant school district and is thoroughly conversant with prices and costs. Though the plaintiff avers that the defendant was aware of the prices of raw milk and the profit picture, the fiscal officer of the defendant denies that either the price of raw milk or the profit structure of suppliers was known or of any concern to him or the defendant. The defendant's only concern was the assurance of a steady supply of milk for the school lunch program at an agreed price on which the school's budget had to be based.

The mandated price of raw milk has in the past fluctuated from a cost of \$6.73 cwt. in 1969 to a high of \$7.58 cwt. in 1972, or 12 percent, with fluctuation within a calendar year ranging from 1 percent to 4.5 percent. The plaintiff agreed to supply milk to the defendant for the school year 1973-1974 by agreement of June 15, 1973, at a price of \$.0759 per half pint, at which time the mandated price of raw milk was \$8.03 cwt. By November 1973 the price of raw milk had risen to \$9.31 cwt., and by December 1973 to \$9.89 cwt., an increase of 23 percent over the June 1973 price. However, it should be noted that there was an increase from the low price in 1972 to the June 1973 price (date of the contract) of 9.5 percent. Because of considerable increase in the

7. Ziegel, *Report to the Uniform Law Conference of Canada on Convention on Contracts for the International Sale of Goods, Article 79*, found on the Internet at *www.cisg.law.pace.edu/cisg/text/ziegel79.html* (accessed Oct. 2011).

price of raw milk, the plaintiff, beginning in October 1973, has requested the defendant to relieve the plaintiff of its contract and to put the contract out for rebidding. The defendant has refused.

The plaintiff spells out in detail its costs based on the June and December prices of raw milk, and shows that it will sustain a loss of $7,350.55 if it is required to continue its performance on the same volume with raw milk at the December price. Its contracts with other school districts, where it is faced with the same problem, will triple its total contemplated loss.

The plaintiff goes to great lengths to spell out the cause of the substantial increase in the price of raw milk, which the plaintiff argues could not have been foreseen by the parties, because it came about in large measure from the agreement of the United States to sell huge amounts of grain to Russia and, to a lesser extent, to unanticipated crop failures.

The legal basis of the plaintiff's request for being relieved of the obligation under the contract award is the doctrine known variously as "impossibility of performance" and "frustration of performance" at common law and as "Excuse by Failure of Presupposed Conditions" under the Uniform Commercial Code §2-615.

Performance has been excused at common law where performance has become illegal, where disaster wipes out the means of production, and where governmental action prevents performance.

In *Mineral Park Land Co. v. Howard*, 172 Cal. 289, 156 P. 458 (1916), the defendants agreed to take all the gravel from the plaintiff's land up to a certain quantity. The defendants took only half the agreed amount because the balance of the gravel was under the water level. The court relieved the defendants from the obligation to pay for the balance under water, because it was not within the contemplation of the parties that the gravel under the water level would be taken, and secondly because the cost of doing so would be 10 to 12 times as expensive. The court stated the common law rule, 172 Cal. 293, 156 P. at p.460:

> (4) "A thing is impossible in legal contemplation when it is not practicable; and a thing is impracticable when it can only be done at an excessive and unreasonable cost." (1 Beach on Contr. §216.) We do not mean to intimate that the defendants could excuse themselves by showing the existence of conditions which would make the performance of their obligation more expensive than they had anticipated, or which would entail a loss upon them. But, where the difference in cost is so great as here, and has the effect, as found, of making performance impracticable, the situation is not different from that of a total absence of earth and gravel.

[The court quotes from UCC section 2-615]
Official Comment 3 to that section points out that the test of impracticability is to be judged by commercial standards. Official Comment 4 states:

> Increased cost alone does not excuse performance unless the rise in cost is due to some unforeseen contingency which alters the essential nature of the performance. Neither is a rise or a collapse in the market in itself a justification, for that is exactly the type of business risk which business contracts made at fixed prices are intended to cover. But a severe shortage of raw materials or

> of supplies due to a contingency such as war, embargo, local crop failure, unforeseen shutdown of major sources of supply or the like, which either causes a marked increase in cost or altogether prevents the seller from securing supplies necessary to his performance, is within the contemplation of this section. (See *Ford & Sons, Ltd., v. Henry Leetham & Sons, Ltd.*, 21 Com. Cas. 55 (1915, K.B.D.).)

Official Comment 10 states in part that " . . . governmental interference cannot excuse unless it truly 'supervenes' in such a manner as to be beyond the seller's assumption of risk."

We find little authority dealing with this section based on facts that are similar to those in this case. See, however, *Transatlantic Financing Corporation v. United States*, 124 U.S. App. D.C. 183, 363 F.2d 312.

The Transatlantic case is somewhat analogous to the question raised here. In that case the Suez Canal was closed causing the plaintiff's ship en route to Iran to have to go around Africa to deliver its cargo of wheat. The plaintiff sought to recover the increased expense from the defendant. The court found that shipping dangers in the Suez Canal area could have been anticipated; that the risk should be allocated to the plaintiff and that the increased cost was not of such magnitude to say that it was not within the accepted degree of risk. The doctrine enunciated by Uniform Commercial Code section 2-615 was explained by the court, 363 F.2d at page 315:

> The doctrine ultimately represents the evershifting line, drawn by courts hopefully responsive to commercial practices and mores, at which the community's interest in having contracts enforced according to their terms is outweighed by the commercial senselessness of requiring performance. When the issue is raised, the court is asked to construct a condition of performance based on the changed circumstances, a process which involves at least three reasonably definable steps. First, a contingency—something unexpected—must have occurred. Second, the risk of the unexpected occurrence must not have been allocated either by agreement or by custom. Finally, occurrence of the contingency must have rendered performance commercially impracticable.

Applying these rules to the facts here we find that the contingency causing the increase of the price of raw milk was not totally unexpected. The price from the low point in 1972 to the price on the date of the award of the contract in June 1973 had risen nearly 10 percent. Any businessman should have been aware of the general inflation in this country during the previous years and of the chance of crop failures.

However, should we grant that the first test had been met and thus the substantial increase in price was due to the sale of wheat to Russia, poor crops, and general market conditions that were unexpected contingencies, then the question of allocation of risk must be met. Here, the very purpose of the contract was to guard against fluctuation of price of half pints of milk as a basis for the school budget. Surely had the price of raw milk fallen substantially, the defendant could not be excused from performance. We can reasonably assume that the plaintiff had to be aware of escalating inflation. It is chargeable with knowledge of the substantial increase of the price of raw milk from the previous year's low. It had knowledge that for many years the Department of Agriculture had established the price of raw milk and that that price varied. It nevertheless entered into this agreement with that knowledge. It did not provide in the contract any exculpatory clause to excuse it from performance in the event of a substantial rise in the price of raw milk. On these facts the risk of a substantial or abnormal increase in the price of raw milk can be allocated to the plaintiff.

As pointed out in the Transatlantic case, 363 F.2d at p. 319, where the circumstances reveal a willingness on the part of the seller to accept abnormal rises in costs, the question of impracticability of performance should be judged by stricter terms than where the contingency is totally unforeseen. The increase in the price of raw milk from June to December 1973 was 23 percent, and the estimated loss to the plaintiff in completing the contract on the same assumed volume and estimated cost of raw milk would be $7,350.55.

Based on the plaintiff's December 1973 figures, including increased transportation cost, the cost of a delivered half pint of milk would be 10.4 percent greater than the bid price. The percentage would be 8.7 percent without the increased transportation cost.

There is no precise point, though such could conceivably be reached, at which an increase in price of raw goods above the norm would be so disproportionate to the risk assumed as to amount to "impracticality" in a commercial sense. However, we cannot say on these facts that the increase here has reached the point of "impracticality" in performance of this contract in light of the risks that we find were assumed by the plaintiff.

The plaintiff's motion is denied and the defendant is granted summary judgment dismissing the complaint.

## NOTES, QUESTIONS, AND PROBLEMS

The court in this case suggests that some increase in the seller's costs might justify excuse on the basis of impracticability. See also UCC §2-615, Comment 4. How much of an increase? Thirty percent? Forty percent? How much of a loss should the seller be expected to take? The court in *Iowa Electric Light and Power Corp. v. Atlas Corp.*, 467 F. Supp. 129 (N.D. Iowa, 1978), refused to grant relief where the increase in seller's costs was 52.2 percent and the loss incurred by the seller was more than $2.6 million. The court noted that cost increases of 50 to 58 percent are generally insufficient to grant relief. By comparison, relief was granted in *Aluminum Company of America (ALCOA) v. Essex Group*, 499 F. Supp. 53 (W.D. Pa. 1980), where the loss to the plaintiff would be $60,000,000 while the defendant would make a profit of the same amount.

Many commentators have tried to make sense out of the impracticability cases. Judge Richard Posner suggests that the cases should be viewed from an economic perspective, with the question being which party is the cheapest insurer? Factored into this analysis is the question of which party can best measure the magnitude and likelihood of the loss and can take steps to reduce or eliminate the risk.[8] Others suggest that many factors must be looked at to determine whether an adjustment should be made, perhaps including

8. See R. Posner, *Economic Analysis of the Law* 107, 117-119 (5th ed. 1998).

the forseeability of the risk, whether one party is profiteering over the other, and the loss that would be suffered by either party in the event that relief is either granted or not granted. Relational contracts theorists posit that parties in long-term contractual relationships should expect to make adjustments as time goes by and circumstances change; not being willing to make adjustments may be bad faith.[9]

Should the courts' analysis in cases such as these be "all or nothing"? See Comment 6 to §2-615. Why do you think that courts actually prefer the "all or nothing" approach?

***Problem 6-20.*** Buyer contracts to purchase Seller's used home computer. While the computer is still at Seller's home and before the risk of loss passes to Buyer, the desk on which the computer is located collapses, damaging the computer but not completely destroying it. The Seller was not at fault in the incident. What are the rights of the parties? See UCC §2-613.

***Problem 6-21.*** Buyer contracts to purchase a specified model computer from Seller Computer Retailers, Inc. The computer will be shipped to Buyer. Before Seller was able to get a computer out of its warehouse and prepare it for shipment to Buyer (i.e., identify the good to the contract, §2-501(1)(b)), Seller's warehouse was destroyed by fire, including all of its inventory. The fire was not the fault of Seller. Does section 2-613 cover this situation, or does section 2-615? See UCC §2-615, Comment 5. If only half of the inventory was destroyed, can Seller pick and choose which of the contracts it wishes to fill? See UCC §2-615(b) & (c) and §2-616.

***Problem 6-22.*** Assume a contract for the sale of a vine wax that is used to protect vines from drying out and becoming infected. The wax delivered by Seller to Buyer is defective. Seller argues that it obtained the wax from a supplier and that it was defective when so obtained. It was thus an impediment beyond Seller's control that prevented Seller from being able to perform the contract, and therefore Seller should be excused from liability under CISG Article 79. Should this argument succeed? See *Bundesgericht* March 24, 1999, CLOUT abstract no. 271, *www.cisg.law.pace.edu/cisg/wais/db/cases2/990324g1.html* (accessed Oct. 2011).

## Chase Precast Corporation v. John J. Paonessa Company, Inc.

Supreme Judicial Court of Massachusetts

409 Mass. 371, 566 N.E.2d 603 (1991)

This appeal raises the question whether the doctrine of frustration of purpose may be a defense in a breach of contract action in Massachusetts, and, if so, whether it excuses the defendant John J. Paonessa Company, Inc. (Paonessa), from performance.

The claim of the plaintiff, Chase Precast Corporation (Chase), arises from the cancellation of its contracts with Paonessa to supply median barriers in

9. See Macneil, *Contracts: Adjustment of Long-Term Economic Relations under Classical, Neoclassical and Relational Contract Law*, 72 Nw. U.L. Rev. 854 (1978); Speidel, *The New Spirit of Contract*, 2 J. Law & Comm. 193 (1982) (discussing *Aluminum Co. of America v. Essex Group*, 499 F. Supp. 53 (W.D. Pa. 1980)).

a highway reconstruction project of the Commonwealth. Chase brought an action to recover its anticipated profit on the amount of median barriers called for by its supply contracts with Paonessa but not produced. After a jury-waived trial, a superior court judge ruled for Paonessa on the basis of impossibility of performance. The appeals court affirmed, noting that the doctrine of frustration of purpose more accurately described the basis of the trial judge's decision than the doctrine of impossibility. We agree.

The pertinent facts are as follows. In 1982, the Commonwealth, through the Department of Public Works (department), entered into two contracts with Paonessa for resurfacing and improvements to two stretches of Route 128. Part of each contract called for replacing a grass median strip between the north and southbound lanes with concrete surfacing and precast concrete median barriers. Paonessa entered into two contracts with Chase under which Chase was to supply, in the aggregate, 25,800 linear feet of concrete median barriers according to the specifications of the department for highway construction. The quantity and type of barriers to be supplied were specified in two purchase orders prepared by Chase.

The highway reconstruction began in the spring of 1983. By late May, the department was receiving protests from angry residents who objected to use of the concrete median barriers and removal of the grass median strip. Paonessa and Chase became aware of the protest around June 1. On June 6, a group of about 100 citizens filed an action in superior court to stop installation of the concrete median barriers and other aspects of the work. On June 7, anticipating modification by the department, Paonessa notified Chase by letter to stop producing concrete barriers for the projects. Chase did so upon receipt of the letter the following day. On June 17, the department and the citizens' group entered into a settlement which provided, in part, that no additional concrete median barriers would be installed. On June 23, the department deleted the permanent concrete median barriers item from its contracts with Paonessa.

Before stopping production on June 8, Chase had produced approximately one-half of the concrete median barriers called for by its contracts with Paonessa, and had delivered most of them to the construction sites. Paonessa paid Chase for all that it had produced, at the contract price. Chase suffered no out-of-pocket expense as a result of cancellation of the remaining portion of barriers.

This court has long recognized and applied the doctrine of impossibility as a defense to an action for breach of contract. Under that doctrine, where from the nature of the contract it appears that the parties must from the beginning have contemplated the continued existence of some particular specified thing as the foundation of what was to be done, then, in the absence of any warranty that the thing shall exist the parties shall be excused when performance becomes impossible from the accidental perishing of the thing without the fault of either party.

On the other hand, although we have referred to the doctrine of frustration of purpose in a few decisions, we have never clearly defined it. Other jurisdictions have explained the doctrine as follows: When an event neither anticipated nor caused by either party, the risk of which was not allocated by the contract, destroys the object or purpose of the contract, thus destroying the value of performance, the parties are excused from further performance.

In *Mishara Constr. Co.*, we called frustration of purpose a "companion rule" to the doctrine of impossibility. Both doctrines concern the effect of supervening circumstances upon the rights and duties of the parties. The difference lies in the effect of the supervening event. Under frustration, "[p]erformance remains possible but the expected value of performance to the party seeking to be excused has been destroyed by [the] fortuitous event. . . ." The principal question in both kinds of cases remains "whether an unanticipated circumstance, the risk of which should not fairly be thrown on the promisor, has made performance vitally different from what was reasonably to be expected."

Paonessa bore no responsibility for the department's elimination of the median barriers from the projects. Therefore, whether it can rely on the defense of frustration turns on whether elimination of the barriers was a risk allocated by the contracts to Paonessa. *Mishara Const. Co.* articulates the relevant test:

> The question is, given the commercial circumstances in which the parties dealt: Was the contingency which developed one which the parties could reasonably be thought to have foreseen as a real possibility which could affect performance? Was it one of that variety of risks which the parties were tacitly assigning to the promisor by their failure to provide for it explicitly? If it was, performance will be required. If it could not be so considered, performance is excused.

This is a question for the trier of fact.

Paonessa's contracts with the department contained a standard provision allowing the department to eliminate items or portions of work found unnecessary. The purchase order agreements between Chase and Paonessa do not contain a similar provision. This difference in the contracts does not mandate the conclusion that Paonessa assumed the risk of reduction in the quantity of the barriers. It is implicit in the judge's findings that Chase knew the barriers were for department projects. The record supports the conclusion that Chase was aware of the department's power to decrease quantities of contract items. The judge found that Chase had been a supplier of median barriers to the department in the past. The provision giving the department the power to eliminate items or portions thereof was standard in its contracts. The judge found that Chase had furnished materials under and was familiar with the so-called "Unit Price Philosophy" in the construction industry, whereby contract items are paid for at the contract unit price for the quantity of work actually accepted.[6] Finally, the judge's finding that "[a]ll parties were well aware that lost profits were not an element of damage in either of the public works

---

6. The contracts contained the following provision:

"4.06 Increased or Decreased Contract Quantities.

"When the accepted quantities of work vary from the quantities in the bid schedule, the Contractor shall accept as payment in full, so far as contract items are concerned, payment at the original contract unit prices for the accepted quantities of work done.

"The Engineer may order omitted from the work any items or portions of work found unnecessary to the improvement and such omission shall not operate as a waiver of any condition of the Contract nor invalidate any of the provisions thereof, nor shall the Contractor have any claim for anticipated profit.

"No allowance will be made for any increased expenses, loss of expected reimbursement therefor or from any other cause."

projects in issue" further supports the conclusion that Chase was aware of the department's power to decrease quantities, since the term prohibiting claims for anticipated profit is part of the same sentence in the standard provision as that allowing the engineer to eliminate items or portions of work.

In *Mishara Constr. Co.* we held that, although labor disputes in general cannot be considered extraordinary, whether the parties in a particular case intended performance to be carried out, even in the face of a labor difficulty, depends on the facts known to the parties at the time of contracting with respect to the history of and prospects for labor difficulties. In this case, even if the parties were aware generally of the department's power to eliminate contract items, the judge could reasonably have concluded that they did not contemplate the cancellation for a major portion of the project of such a widely used item as concrete median barriers, and did not allocate the risk of such cancellation.

Judgment affirmed.

## NOTES, QUESTIONS, AND PROBLEM

1. If the seller had already spent money in reliance on the contract, do you think the court would have come to the same conclusion? What if Paonessa could have used the medians on a future project?

***Problem 6-23.*** What kind of argument could be made under CISG Article 79 for the same result? What is the "impediment"? Is Article 8 of any help, especially given the plaintiff's knowledge of state contracting? See CISG Advisory Council Opinion No. 7, *www.cisg.law.pace.edu/cisg/CISG-AC-op7.html* (accessed Oct. 2011).

## CHAPTER 6 REVIEW PROBLEM

Buyer contracted to purchase some valves that were to be used in transmission lines that were used in moving chemicals through its chemical plant. The valves were specially designed and manufactured by Seller to meet Buyer's specifications, which were unusual in the chemical industry. The contract price was $50,000. The contract provided that Buyer's only remedy was "repair or replacement of defective parts." The contract further provided that under no circumstances could Buyer recover consequential damages. The contract was fairly negotiated between Buyer and Seller, who were both sophisticated merchants.

Eight months after the valves were installed, they were only working at 75 percent of the promised capacity—the chemicals moved more slowly through the valves than promised and there was some leakage. Seller was frequently called to come out to Buyer's plant during this eight-month period and diligently tried to make the valves work properly. After the eight-month period, it was quite clear, however, that Seller was not going to be able to make the valves work any better.

Buyer estimates that if it retains the valves for their useful life (five years), the failure of the valves to perform to specification will cost Buyer $200,000 in terms of leakage and delays in production. Buyer would like to reject or revoke acceptance of the goods, or recover $200,000 in consequential damages to cover the loss from failure of the valves to work properly. You may assume that if the consequential damage limitation is ineffective, Buyer could recover the $200,000. Should Buyer be allowed to reject, revoke, or recover consequential damages? Please analyze under both the CISG and the UCC. Under the CISG the relevant Articles are 6, 8, 25, 26, and 49. Under the UCC the relevant sections are 2-508, 2-601, 2-602, 2-606, 2-608, and 2-719.

CHAPTER 7

# BUYER'S REMEDIES

## A. REMEDIES UNDER THE UCC

The policy of UCC remedies is reflected in section 1-305, and that is that the injured party should be placed in as good a position as if the breaching party had performed. Section 1-305 also states, "neither consequential nor penal damages may be had except as specifically provided in this Act or other rule of law." Article 2 does not provide punitive damages for breach of a contract of sale, although in some cases it does permit consequential damages. The Code thus codifies the expectation principle of contract remedies and in not otherwise punishing the breaching party also reflects the "efficient breach" principle—that breach of contract is not a tort and that a breach is fine as long as the injured party is placed in the position that the party would have been in if the contract had been performed.

Section 2-711 provides a "menu" of buyer's remedies in situations in which the seller fails to make delivery or the buyer rightfully rejects or justifiably revokes acceptance. In other words, these are situations in which the buyer does not obtain or retain possession of the goods. Section 2-714 provides the measure of damages for goods that are accepted.

### 1. GOODS NOT ACCEPTED

Section 2-711 provides that in the event that the goods are not delivered or are rightfully rejected or where acceptance is rightfully revoked, the buyer is entitled to "cover," meaning purchase substitute goods, or obtain the difference between the market price of the goods and the contract price. See UCC §§2-712 and 2-713. In the event that the buyer makes a proper cover, the buyer is entitled to recover the difference between what the buyer had to pay for the goods and the contract price. UCC §2-712(2). If the buyer does not cover under section 2-712, the buyer recovers the difference between the contract price and the market price at the time the buyer learns of the breach. The remedies are in the alternative: If the buyer covers under section 2-712, the buyer may not use the contract/market formula even if it is more advantageous. Under both sections 2-712 and 2-713, consequential damages may also be available. The buyer is not required to cover, although failure to purchase substitute goods may limit the amount of consequential damages the buyer is permitted to recover.

### (a) Cover

#### MUELLER v. MCGILL

Court of Appeals of Texas

870 S.W.2d 673 (1994)

Appellant Rick Mueller brought an action for damages against appellees Don McGill, Don McGill, Inc., Don McGill Imports, Inc., and Greg Radford (collectively "McGill, Inc."), arising out of the breach of an agreement for the purchase of a new automobile. The trial court directed a verdict in favor of McGill, Inc., and Mueller appeals. We reverse and remand.

In December 1985, Rick Mueller decided to buy his dream car, a black 1985 Porsche 911 Targa. He located such an automobile at McGill, Inc., and negotiated the terms of a sale for several hours with a salesman, Steve Richter. Richter and Mueller finally agreed upon a sales price and a trade-in allowance for Mueller's Mazda RX-7, and signed a written contract memorializing the agreement.

After the contract was signed, Richter suggested that Mueller talk to the finance manager about the possibility of financing the car through Chase Manhattan Bank. Although Mueller had already obtained financing for the vehicle, he agreed to talk to the finance manager because of the low interest rate offered by Chase Manhattan.

When Richter directed Mueller to the finance department, he informed him that the car would be ready to be picked up the next morning. After filling out the loan application in the finance department, Mueller was informed for the first time that there was another contract on the car. Mueller had not been previously informed that he was negotiating a "backup" contract. Mueller was told not to worry because the individual with the earlier contract was having trouble obtaining financing, and probably would not be approved.

The next morning Mueller called the dealership to ask when he could pick up his car. After several attempts, he finally reached Richter and was told that the car had been sold to another customer. Mueller then spoke with Mike Reed, the sales manager, who told him that if McGill, Inc., could not deliver the car covered by the contract, they would find him another car. Reed signed and delivered to Mueller a document indicating that McGill, Inc., would find a replacement automobile and would allow Mueller the same $8,370 trade-in allowance that had been provided for in the original contract.

Several weeks later, Seth Brown, a McGill, Inc. employee, called Mueller and informed him that the dealership had not yet found a replacement. In February 1986, Mueller received a call from Greg Radford, the new sales manager for the dealership. Mueller was informed that the dealership would no longer honor the $8,370 trade-in allowance that had been previously negotiated. Radford indicated that they could sell Mueller a 1986 Porsche, but they would have to renegotiate the terms.

Mueller never received the car specified in the contract. The dealership apparently never found a 1985 vehicle like the car Mueller had contracted for. There is some testimony that it was difficult to find 1985 Porsche Targas so late in the year. Mueller himself called several dealerships in the Gulf Coast area in an effort to locate a 1985 Porsche. However, he was never able to find a satisfactory 1985 replacement.

In April 1986, Mueller went to one of McGill, Inc.'s competitors, and sometime thereafter purchased a 1986 Porsche 911 Targa. He paid more for the 1986 model and received less for his trade-in allowance. There is testimony that the 1985 and 1986 models were virtually identical vehicles, but the cost of the 1986 was somewhat higher.

At the conclusion of Mueller's case, the trial court, on its own motion, directed a verdict for McGill, Inc. In his sole point of error, Mueller contends that the trial court erred by doing so.

In this case, the trial judge decided that Mueller had established a breach of contract as a matter of law, but concluded that Mueller had failed to prove that he suffered any damages. More specifically, the trial judge concluded that the correct measure of damages was the difference between the contract price and the market value at the time of the breach, and that because Mueller had failed to introduce any evidence as to the market price of the automobile, he was not entitled to recover. He further concluded that there was no evidence that the 1986 automobile was a reasonable replacement for the 1985 automobile, or that the cost of the next closest available replacement was a proper measure of damages.

Mueller claims on appeal that he is entitled to recover damages representing the difference between the contract price on the 1985 Porsche and the price he was required to spend on the 1986 Porsche. A buyer's remedies upon a breach of a contract of sale by the seller are set forth in chapter two of the Texas Business and Commerce Code. Upon a seller's failure to deliver the goods, a buyer may either (1) "cover" by purchasing goods in substitution of those due from the seller, and recovering damages for the difference in the price of the contract and the "cover"; or (2) recover the difference between the contract price and market price at the time he learned of the breach. UCC §§2-712, 2-713. If a buyer elects to "cover" he need not show the market price at the time of the breach. Therefore, the fact that Mueller failed to introduce evidence about the market price of the Porsche at the time he discovered the breach is not fatal to his case, if he can show that he properly "covered" under section 2-712.

The issue this court must decide is whether there were any questions of fact relating to the issue of proper "cover" that should have been presented to a jury. If such questions of fact exist, the trial court erred by ordering a directed verdict.

A buyer may properly "cover" by "making in good faith and without unreasonable delay any reasonable purchase of or contract to purchase goods in substitution of those due from the seller." UCC §2-712. The issue of good faith in effecting "cover" is a question of fact to be resolved by the fact finder.

In his findings of fact and conclusions of law, the trial judge found that the purchase of a 1986 Porsche was not a reasonably similar replacement for the

1985 Porsche described by the contract. Comment 2 to section 2-712 provides that the goods purchased as "cover" need not be identical to those provided in the contract, but must be commercially usable as reasonable substitutes. The evidence presented in the case showed that it was very difficult to obtain a 1985 Porsche so late in the year. The dealership tried to obtain a 1985 substitute, and Mueller himself attempted to locate a 1985. However, no acceptable 1985 was ever located. Whether a cover purchase is reasonable poses a "classic jury issue." We hold that the issue of whether the 1986 Porsche was a reasonable substitute for the 1985 Porsche should have been presented to the jury.

Because the evidence presented by Mueller at trial was sufficient to raise fact questions regarding good faith and the reasonableness of his attempt to "cover," we hold that the trial court erred by granting a directed verdict in favor of McGill, Inc.

Accordingly, we reverse the judgment and remand the cause for further proceedings.

## QUESTION AND PROBLEM

1. If the 1986 model had some different features on it that made it a more desirable car, should an adjustment be made on the amount of damages received to reflect the difference? Otherwise, is the buyer improperly being put in a better position than if the contract had been performed?

***Problem 7-1.*** Buyer contracts to purchase a used 2002 model-year car for $30,000. The car has 20,000 miles on it. The contract price is roughly the same as the market price. When the seller breaches, Buyer is unable to find a similar 2002 model with comparable miles. Instead, Buyer purchases a 2001 model of the same car with 40,000 miles for $25,000. The 2001 model is roughly the same as the 2002 model. Has the buyer suffered any damages?

### (b) Contract-Market Differential—Buyer Does Not Cover

**JON-T FARMS, INC. v. GOODPASTURE, INC.**

Texas Court of Civil Appeals

554 S.W.2d 743 (1977)

Goodpasture, Inc., as plaintiff, instituted two consolidated breach of contract suits involving the purchase of grain from Jon-T Farms, Inc., the defendant. Judgment was rendered on a jury verdict favorable to the plaintiff.

The first contract was dated January 17, 1973, and obligated Jon-T to sell Goodpasture 10,000,000 pounds of Number 2 yellow grain sorghum at $2.70 per hundredweight. Grades were to be "official," and the grain was to be shipped during October and November 1973.

In accordance with the contract terms, Jon-T began shipping the grain in October 1973. By November 30 (the end of the stated delivery period), however, only 2,023,480 pounds of grain had been shipped.

The evidence is undisputed that the price of grain began to rise subsequent to the execution of the first contract on January 17, 1973, and continued to rise until November 1974, when it reached a price of $7.00 per hundredweight. On December 11 or 12, 1973, the market price was $4.48; in March 1974, between $5.35 and $5.50; and in October or November 1974, approximately $7.00 per hundredweight.

This suit for breach of contract was instituted by Goodpasture on December 17, 1973.

Goodpasture accepted and unloaded six carloads of grain between December 10 and December 21. As of this last date, Jon-T had delivered 4,167,550 pounds of the 10,000,000 it had contracted to deliver.

This case was tried to a jury in November 1975. The jury found that Jon-T had breached and/or repudiated the contract, causing Goodpasture to sustain $121,179.84 in damages.

Jon-T has appealed. We affirm.

Jon-T asserts that Goodpasture pleaded and proved an incorrect measure of damages because it had effected the remedy of "cover" under UCC section 2-712, and that its basic recovery should be the difference between the cost of cover and the contract price. Jon-T further argues that Goodpasture submitted no evidence as to the cost of cover and thus was not entitled to recover damages. Goodpasture contends that it was entitled under the provision of UCC section 2-713 to recover the difference between the contract price and the market price at the time it learned of the breach. It is undisputed that Goodpasture submitted evidence as to market value as of the time Goodpasture learned of the alleged breach.

Under section 2-712(3), upon seller's breach the buyer is not required to cover as a means of minimizing damages, and his failure to effect cover does not bar him from any other remedy. Thus, on seller's breach a buyer is free to choose between damages based upon the difference between the contract price and the cost of cover under section 2-712, and damages for nondelivery, consisting of the difference between the market price at the time when the buyer learns of the breach and the contract price, under section 2-713(1).

Goodpasture pleaded and proved the measure of damages set forth in section 2-713. Jon-T has argued that testimony established that Goodpasture "covered" for the grain due from, but undelivered by, Jon-T. The testimony of the plaintiff's witnesses was that Goodpasture normally bought sufficient grain in order to meet its contracts for sale. The grain purchased is commingled with other grain. Although in the overall operation Goodpasture may have bought some grain to compensate for the undelivered Jon-T grain to ensure an adequate supply to meet its commitments, there is no testimony that Goodpasture went out and bought specific grain to make up for the specific amount of grain undelivered by Jon-T.

In view of the foregoing, it is our opinion that the pleadings and evidence show that Goodpasture opted to pursue its remedy for damages, as it had the right to do, pursuant to section 2-713. Accordingly, we hold that the proper measure of damages was applied in this case.

## NOTES, QUESTIONS, AND PROBLEMS

1. Section 2-713 is sometimes referred to as the buyer's "hypothetical cover" remedy because it assumes that the buyer went into the marketplace and purchased substitute goods at the prevailing market price at the time that the buyer learned of the seller's breach. As the court holds in the foregoing case, it is available only if the buyer does not cover under section 2-712. Based on that, what questions would you ask Goodpasture regarding its business practices if it came to you for counsel? Would it be appropriate to label purchases at higher prices as being "cover" while purchases at lower prices are not? If the purchases are at prices higher than the market price, can they be asserted as "cover" while if they are at lower prices can they be asserted as ordinary purchases not intended as substitutes for the breached contract?

   If we assume that the buyer had sufficient inventory on hand to satisfy all of its resale contracts and did not have to purchase any grain in substitution for the grain it was to buy from the breaching seller, doesn't an award of damages place the buyer in a better position than if the contract had been performed? In other words, it does not appear that any money was lost on resale contracts and no additional money was paid to buy grain in substitution of the grain the seller was to sell. Doesn't an award of damages thus violate the policy of UCC section 1-305? *Compare Allied Canners & Packers, Inc. v. Victor Packing Co.*, 162 Cal. App. 3d 905, 209 Cal. Rptr. 60 (1984) *with Tongish v. Thomas*, 16 Kan. App. 2d 809, 829 P.2d 916 (1992).
2. If the seller repudiates its obligations before the time of delivery, how is the market price to be determined? UCC section 2-713 says that the market price is to be determined at the time the buyer "learns of the breach." UCC section 2-723 says that if the case comes to trial before the time for performance, the market price is to be determined "at the time the buyer learned of the repudiation." UCC section 2-610 says that upon repudiation, the injured party may await performance for a commercially reasonable time. The Code is clearer when it comes to seller's remedies, stating that market price is to be determined at "the time and place for tender." UCC §2-708. This rule is consistent with the approach of courts in non–sale of goods cases. *See, e.g., Bachewicz v. American Nat'l Bank & Trust Co.*, 126 Ill. App. 3d 298, 466 N.E.2d 1096 (1984) (damages for repudiation of contract to sell an apartment building measured at the time the sale was to close). How do sections 2-610 and 2-713 work together when a seller repudiates and the case comes to trial *after* the time for performance? This question is explored in Problem 7-4, *infra*.

***Problem 7-2.*** Buyer contracts to purchase wheat at a price of $10 per bushel. On the delivery date, the market price is $15 per bushel, and Seller breaches by not delivering. Because of shortages due to crop failure and the resulting rising market, buyer is unable to immediately purchase substitute wheat. Buyer waits for a few months in the hopes that the market will go down. The market doesn't fall, and Buyer finally decides to purchase substitute wheat at $20 per bushel several months after the contract was breached. May Buyer recover under UCC section 2-712, or is Buyer forced to recover under UCC section 2-713? *See Dangerfield v. Markel*, 26 UCC Rep. Serv. 419 (N.D. Sup. Ct. 1979).

***Problem 7-3.*** A contract for the sale of equipment has a price term of "$4,000 CIF Dallas, Texas." The equipment is to be shipped from Kansas City. The cost of insurance is $50 and the cost of shipment is $200. The equipment is to be delivered to Dallas, Texas. The Seller does not deliver the goods. Buyer chooses not to cover. At the time that Buyer learns of the breach, the equipment can be purchased in Dallas for $4,500 and in Kansas City for $4,300. The Kansas City price does not include insurance or shipping. How should Buyer's damages be determined under section 2-713? See UCC §§2-503, 2-504.

***Problem 7-4.*** Lightning Oil Company contracted to sell natural gas to Hess Energy. Delivery was to take place in one year. Three months after contracting, Lightning repudiated the contract because it was able to find a buyer who would pay more for the gas. Hess did not purchase substitute gas, as it had sufficient sources under contract to meet its needs. At all times, it would be possible for Hess Energy to purchase substitute gas at the prevailing market price without much difficulty. At the time of repudiation, assume that the difference between the market price and the contract price was $1 million. One month after repudiation, the difference between the market price and the contract price was $1.2 million. At the time of delivery, under the contract, the difference between the market price and the contract price was $2 million. The case is tried after the time for delivery. How should Hess Energy's damages be measured? See UCC §§2-610, 2-713, and 2-723. Compare UCC §2-708(1). *Compare Hess Energy v. Lightning Oil Co.,* 338 F.3d 357 (4th Cir. 2003), *with Oloffson v. Coomer*, 11 Ill. App. 3d 918, 296 N.E.2d 871 (1973). At what point would damages be measured under the CISG? See CISG Articles 72, 76, and 77.

3. The UCC permits the buyer to recover incidental and consequential damages under both UCC sections 2-712 and 2-713. As is the case under common law, the ability of the buyer to recover these types of damages is limited by the foreseeability of those damages at the time of contracting, the certainty of calculation of those damages, and the ability of the injured buyer to reasonably avoid them. Remember that the contract may attempt to limit the seller's liability for consequential damages. See UCC §2-719 and the discussion at pages 166-171, *supra*. The following case discusses the ability of the buyer to recover consequential damages in a case in which the seller failed to deliver the goods.

## MIGEROBE, INC. v. CERTINA USA, INC.

United States Court of Appeals, Fifth Circuit

924 F.2d 1330 (1991)

A watch manufacturer appeals a jury verdict that held it had breached an oral contract to deliver an order of watches to a retail operator. The jury held that the manufacturer was liable to the retailer for $157,133.00 in damages as a result of the breach. Finding that the retail operator presented sufficient evidence to support a finding of breach and sufficient evidence to justify the damage award, we AFFIRM.

### Facts and Procedural History

Appellant Certina USA is a watch manufacturer located in Lancaster, Pennsylvania. Appellee Migerobe, Inc., is a Mississippi corporation that owns and operates jewelry counters in McRae's department stores, which are located throughout the Southeast. This suit is based on the breach of an alleged oral contract that the two companies entered into in October 1987.

Certina sells its watches through the efforts of traveling salesmen, who are either salaried employees of Certina or independent representatives paid on a commission basis. Gerald Murff was one such representative, and his sales territory included Mississippi. Migerobe had purchased watches through Murff before, and, during the summer of 1987, Migerobe contacted Murff to notify him that Migerobe would be interested in buying Certina watches if the company decided to sell a large portion of its inventory at reduced prices. Migerobe suspected that Certina might make such an offer because another retailer recently had decided to stop carrying the Certina line of watches, and Migerobe believed that this would create a backlog of inventory for the manufacturer. In fact, Certina had decided to institute a special promotion to eliminate its inventory as a result of a corporate decision to withdraw its watches from the U.S. market.

Migerobe was hoping to acquire the Certina watches so that they could be used as "doorbusters" for an after-Thanksgiving sales promotion. Doorbusters, or "loss leaders," are items offered at a low price that are designed to increase the traffic flow through a store and, thereby, increase corollary sales (the sale of nonadvertised items). Murff later became aware that Migerobe was planning to use the watches in this special after-Thanksgiving promotion.

In a letter dated September 14, 1987, Murff responded to Migerobe's request, saying that he was "pursuing a special price on the Certina inventories on [Migerobe's] behalf" and that he would keep the company informed of his progress. At the time, Murff was attempting to negotiate a special discounted price with Certina's vice president of retail sales, William Wolfe. On October 21, 1987, Wolfe provided Murff with a list of watches from Certina's inventory that Murff could offer to Migerobe at a price of $45 each. Murff scheduled an October 29 meeting with Migerobe to present the offer. Prior to this meeting, Murff requested and received an additional list of watches from Wolfe, which were to be included in the offer to Migerobe.

Murff kept his October 29 appointment with Migerobe. During the course of the day, Murff made several phone calls to Certina's home office in Lancaster, Pennsylvania, to verify the number of watches in Certina's inventory and to secure specific payment terms. After a full day of negotiating for particular quantities and styles, as well as payment terms and a shipping date, Migerobe agreed to purchase more than 2,000 Certina watches at a price of $45 each. Murff phoned Certina's Lancaster office one final time to report the sale, and Wolfe's administrative assistant recorded it onto a Certina order form.

On November 4, 1987, Certina's national accounts manager, Don Olivett, called Migerobe to say that Certina would not ship the watches that had been ordered on October 29. The president of Certina, John Gelson, later explained that the order was being rejected because the offered price was lower than that offered to other customers, and he feared that the offer might constitute a violation of the Robinson-Patman Act.[1] Migerobe brought suit in district court for repudiation of the contract and, after a five-day trial, a jury awarded it $157,133.

**Discussion**

When Murff visited Migerobe on October 29, he was told that Migerobe planned to use the Certina watches as a "loss-leader" item, featuring them in a "doorbuster" Thanksgiving advertisement at a 50 percent discount. A loss-leader is an item normally offered for sale at or below cost, which functions to draw customers into the store, where they can make additional (nonadvertised or corollary) sales. Retailers justify reduced profits on the sale of loss-leaders by focusing on the increase in corollary sales that can be attributed to the loss-leader advertisement. Migerobe had seen its corollary sales increase in the past when similar "doorbuster" or loss-leader promotions were held. These past promotions also featured watches at a 50 percent discount. In 1982, the advertisement featured Seiko watches, and Migerobe saw its corollary sales increase by 87 percent when compared with the week preceding the sale. In 1983 the advertisement featured Seiko and Pulsar watches, and corollary sales rose by 69 percent. Based on their experience within the retail industry and their knowledge of the Certina brand, the decision makers at Migerobe expected that a first-time offer of Certina watches at a 50 percent discount would provide similar increases in corollary sales.

In order to recover for any losses it may have suffered in corollary sales as a result of Certina's breach, Migerobe must show that Certina, at the time of contracting, had reason to know that such losses were possible and that the damages were proximately caused by the breach. See UCC §2-715(2)(a). "Loss may be determined in any manner which is reasonable under the circumstances" and does not require "mathematical precision." UCC §2-715 Comment 4 (1968).

At trial, Migerobe presented evidence that it suffered $118,521 in lost profits that would have been realized on the direct resale of Certina watches, and an additional $77,224 in losses from corollary sales. The jury, however, did not award Migerobe the total amount of damages requested ($195,745), but instead awarded it a total of $157,133.

Certina does not dispute the jury's award for that portion of Migerobe's loss attributable to the direct resale of Certina watches. It does, however, find fault with the evidence supporting that portion of the award attributable to the loss in corollary sales. Certina argues that Migerobe failed to demonstrate that Certina's breach was the proximate cause of the loss in corollary sales, and it claims that the evidence was too speculative and uncertain to support such an award.

---

1. The Robinson-Patman Act, 15 U.S.C. §13, forbids a seller of goods from engaging in price discrimination (i.e., charging lower prices to some of its distributors than others) when the effect would be to create a monopoly. Whether the contract in this case would violate that law was not further discussed in the case—Ed.

We begin by noting that "the requirement of foreseeability is a more severe limitation of liability than is the requirement of substantial or 'proximate' cause in the case of an action in tort or for breach of warranty." *Restatement (Second) of Contracts* §351 Comment A (1979) (comparing *Restatement (Second) of Torts* §431 and UCC §2-715(2)(b)). The loss of corollary sales by Migerobe was a foreseeable consequence of Certina's breach; the very purpose of a loss-leader promotion is to increase the amount of corollary sales, and Migerobe has shown that Certina knew that the watches would be used for this purpose.

Through a combination of expert testimony and circumstantial evidence, Migerobe successfully provided the jury with a reasonable basis on which it could conclude that corollary sales would have been higher if Certina had performed its part of the bargain. Migerobe began by presenting historical data that showed that it could expect such promotions to increase its corollary sales by an average of 78 percent. Migerobe then solicited testimony from an expert economist that a first-time offer of Certina watches at a 50 percent discount would provide results similar to those experienced in 1982 and 1983. The expert relied on additional evidence suggesting that Certina was peaking in name recognition among Migerobe customers and that Certina's strongest market was in the southeastern United States, where Migerobe retail outlets were located. Under the circumstances, Migerobe presented the best possible evidence available to demonstrate proximate cause. "[I]t is the function of the jury as the traditional finder of the facts, and not the court, to weigh conflicting evidence and inferences, and determine the credibility of witnesses." *Boeing Co. v. Shipman,* 411 F.2d 365, 375 (5th Cir. 1969) (en banc). The evidence presented was such that a reasonable jury could conclude that Certina's breach was the proximate cause of Migerobe's loss in corollary sales.

Certina next argues that Migerobe's estimate of corollary damages must be rejected as being too speculative and uncertain. Migerobe's estimate of these losses was based on the success of similarly advertised "doorbuster" sales that it had held in 1982 and 1983. Certina begins by noting that Migerobe had never used Certina watches as a doorbuster item in the past, and, therefore, its potential for increasing corollary profits was unknown. It also claimed that the watches used in doorbuster sales during 1982 (Seiko) and 1983 (Seiko and Pulsar) were better known than Certina and could not provide an accurate comparison. As already noted, it is unnecessary for a plaintiff to prove his losses with mathematical precision, and we do not believe that a sales estimate based on historical data from similar advertising campaigns would have rendered this estimate speculative or uncertain. Certina is not entitled to complain about Migerobe's inability to provide a more precise estimate when such precision has been made all but impossible because of Certina's own breach. *See Story Parchment Co. v. Paterson Parchment Paper Co.,* 282 U.S. 555, 563, 51 S.Ct. 248, 250, 75 L. Ed. 544 (1931); *see also Terrell,* 494 F.2d at 24 ("Very often the nature of the wrong makes ascertainment of the damages difficult."); *Autowest,* 434 F.2d at 565 ("The wrongdoer should bear the risk of uncertainty that his own conduct has created.").

Certina next complains that the variables used to measure Migerobe's corollary sales did not remain constant throughout the years being compared. At the trial stage of this lawsuit, corollary sales were defined as all jewelry items that were sold except for those items that were advertised. In 1982 and 1983, watches were the only items that were advertised; therefore, any other item of jewelry sold during those years constituted the total amount of corollary sales. In 1987, however, three additional items besides watches were advertised. Therefore, the amount of sales generated by these three additional items, in addition to the sales generated by the advertised watches, were removed from the definition of corollary sales for 1987. Certina argues that the removal of these additional items from the pool constituting corollary sales produced a false perception that corollary sales had fallen as compared to prior years. Under different circumstances, this might be a persuasive argument, but a noticeable drop in corollary sales is apparent even when these three items are placed back into the pool constituting corollary sales. Certina's own calculations show that under such conditions, corollary sales would have risen by only 17 percent, still far short of the increases seen in 1982 and 1983.

We stress once again that Migerobe is not required to prove corollary sales to an established level of mathematical precision. The evidence only needs to provide an approximation of the damages as a matter of just and reasonable inference. *See Story Parchment,* 282 U.S. at 563, 51 S.Ct. at 250; *Terrell,* 494 F.2d at 24; *see also Nichols v. Stacks,* 485 So.2d 1034, 1038 (Miss. 1986) (recovery will not be denied to a plaintiff presenting the best available evidence as long as it is sufficient to afford a reasonable basis for estimating the loss); *Cain v. Mid-South Pump Co.,* 458 So. 2d 1048, 1050 (Miss. 1984) (same). The evidence presented by Migerobe provided the jury with a sufficient basis on which to estimate corollary damages, and we will not disturb that determination.

## NOTES, QUESTIONS, AND PROBLEM

1. If the seller's representative had not been told of the buyer's intent to use the watches as part of a post-Thanksgiving promotion, would lost profits from the corollary sales be sufficiently foreseeable?
2. Could the loss have been avoided through the purchase of other items for resale? Who should have the burden of proof on whether the buyer could have avoided the loss? *See Carnation Co. v. Olivet Egg Ranch,* 189 Cal. App. 3d 809, 229 Cal. Rptr. 261 (1986).

***Problem 7-5.*** If a buyer purchased a Certina watch and developed a severe skin rash due to the watch band, would the buyer be able to recover damages under Article 2? Does the same foreseeability test apply that was used by the court in the preceding case? See UCC §2-715(2)(b). Would there be a breach if the rash was due to an allergic reaction?

### (c) Specific Performance

In some situations, the buyer might prefer to get the court to order the seller to specifically perform the sales contract. As is the case under common law, specific performance is not the preferred remedy for breach of a sales contract. Generally speaking, the buyer is forced to sue for damages based on the difference between the cost of substitute goods and the contract price. The

UCC does provide a few circumstances in which the buyer is allowed to sue for what amounts to specific performance or replevin. These circumstances are set forth in UCC sections 2-502 and 2-716. As you read the next case and the problems that follow, you might ask yourself whether the UCC is more expansive than the common law in permitting specific performance, and if so, whether that is a good idea? Would it be an even better idea to permit specific performance in all cases?

### Copylease Corp. of America v. Memorex Corp.

United States District Court, Southern District of New York

408 F. Supp. 758 (1976)

[Memorex manufactures goods used in the operation of automatic copying machines, and Copylease distributes and sells such goods. On April 4, 1974, the parties entered into a contract whereby Memorex agreed to sell three types of products to Copylease: Memorex Premium Toner, Memorex Developer, and private-label toner. The contract was to run for an "initial term," defined to commence on the date of execution and "to continue for a period of 12 months from the date of the first shipment of [private label]," and granted Copylease the right to renew for successive 12-month periods provided that it maintained a certain level of purchases.]

By Memorandum Opinion, we determined the Memorex Corporation (Memorex) by repudiating certain of its obligations breached its contract with Copylease Corporation of America (Copylease) for the sale of toner and developer, and directed the parties to submit proposed judgments relating to the availability of specific performance. We have studied the submissions and conclude that further testimony is necessary to determine the propriety of such relief.

We agree with Memorex that the provision in the contract granting Copylease an exclusive territory to sell the designated Memorex products, on which Copylease places primary reliance in its request for specific performance, is not in itself an adequate basis under California law for an award of such relief. California law does not consider a remedy at law inadequate merely because difficulties may exist as to precise calculation of damages. California cases also demonstrate the more fundamental refusal of California courts to order specific performance of contracts that are not capable of immediate enforcement, but that require a "continuing series of acts" and "cooperation between the parties for the successful performance of those acts." Absent some exception to this general rule, therefore, Copylease will be limited to recovery of damages for the contract breach.

An exception that may prove applicable to this case is found in UCC section 2-716(1). That statute provides that in an action for breach of contract a buyer may be entitled to specific performance "where the goods are unique or in other proper circumstances." UCC §2-716(1). In connection with its claim for interim damages for lost profits from the time of the breach Copylease argues strongly that it could not reasonably have covered by obtaining an alternative source of toner because the other brands of toner are distinctly inferior to the Memorex product. If the evidence at the hearing supports this claim, it may well be that Copylease faces the same difficulty in finding a permanent alternative supplier. If so, the Official Comment to section 2-716 suggests that a grant of specific performance may be in order:

> Specific performance is no longer limited to goods which are already specific or ascertained at the time of contracting. The test of uniqueness under this section must be made in terms of the total situation which characterizes the contract. Output and requirements contracts involving a particular or peculiarly available source or market present today the typical commercial specific performance situation . . . However, uniqueness is not the sole basis of the remedy under this section for the relief may also be granted "in other proper circumstances" and *inability to cover is strong evidence of "other proper circumstances."* UCC §2-716, Comment 2. (Emphasis added.)

If Copylease has no adequate alternative source of toner the Memorex product might be considered "unique" for purposes of section 2-716, or the situation might present an example of "other proper circumstances" in which specific performance would be appropriate.

If such a showing is made it will be necessary to reconcile California's policy against ordering specific performance of contracts which provide for continuing acts or an ongoing relationship with section 2-716 of the Code. Although we recognize that the statute does not require specific performance, the quoted portion of the Official Comment seems clearly to suggest that where a contract calls for continuing sale of unique or "noncoverable" goods, this provision should be considered an exception to the general proscription. Output and requirements contracts, explicitly cited as examples of situations in which specific performance may be appropriate, by their nature call for a series of continuing acts and an ongoing relationship. Thus, the drafters seem to have contemplated that at least in some circumstances specific performance will issue contrary to the historical reluctance to grant such relief in these situations. If, at the hearing, Copylease makes a showing that it meets the requirements of section 2-716, the sensible approach would be to measure, with the particulars of this contract in mind, the uniqueness or degree of difficulty in covering against the difficulties of enforcement that have caused courts to refrain from granting specific performance. It would be premature to speculate on the outcome of such analysis in this case.

## QUESTION AND PROBLEMS

1. What further evidence is relevant in deciding if the trial court should award specific performance in this case?

***Problem 7-6.*** A buyer contracts to purchase a limited-edition Chevrolet Corvette that was the same model as a pace car used in the Indianapolis 500 automobile race. The car had some special options selected by the buyer. When the car designated for the buyer arrived at the dealership, the dealership refused to deliver the car unless the buyer agreed to pay a higher price. It would be difficult to purchase another one of these cars, as it is a limited edition, especially with the options selected by the buyer and at anything near the contract price. Would the buyer be able to sue for replevin? See UCC §2-716(3). If the car had never been identified to the particular contract, could the buyer sue for specific performance? See UCC §2-716(1) and *Sedmak v. Charlie's Chevrolet*, 622 S.W.2d 694 (Mo. App. 1981).

***Problem 7-7.*** Assume that Buyer contracts to purchase a painting from Seller to hang in Buyer's home for Buyer's personal enjoyment. Buyer pays Seller $500 as a deposit. Seller decides that it doesn't want to sell the painting. Can the painting be recovered by Buyer? See UCC §2-502.

## 2. ACCEPTED GOODS

### (a) Notice Requirement

Section 2-607(3)(a) requires the buyer to notify the seller of any breach within a reasonable time after the buyer discovers or should have discovered the breach. Failure to notify bars the buyer from any remedy. The following case demonstrates the application of this requirement.

### AQUALON COMPANY v. MAC EQUIPMENT, INC.

United States Court of Appeals, Fourth Circuit

149 F.3d 262 (1998)

Aqualon Company, a chemical manufacturer, asked MAC Equipment, Incorporated, to produce rotary valves, also called airlocks, for use in a pneumatic conveying system. The system was designed by C.W. Nofsinger Company to move a chemical, blended carboxymethyl cellulose. Before MAC was awarded a contract to produce the valves, it provided estimates of how much air its valves would leak. However, once the valves were actually constructed, they leaked much more than expected.

After almost a year of complaints and negotiations between Aqualon and MAC, it became apparent that the valves could not be made to leak any less. Aqualon modified its system design so that it would still be able to move the chemical despite the leakage. In the spring of 1993 Aqualon reissued a purchase order for the leaky valves; Aqualon accepted the valves in June; and Aqualon paid for them in full as of December 19, 1993. MAC did not conceal, and Aqualon knew, the valves' air-leakage rate.

Three years thereafter Aqualon served MAC with a complaint for breach of contract and warranty. The district court granted summary judgment to MAC, holding that Aqualon had not given MAC notice within a reasonable time of its claim for breach. Aqualon appeals.

[The court quotes from UCC section 2-607(3)(a).] The notice required by section 2-607(3) "need merely be sufficient to let the seller know that the transaction is still troublesome and must be watched." UCC §2-607, Comment 4.

Aqualon makes four related arguments: 1) Section 2-607(3) does not apply to the circumstance presented here; 2) Aqualon's preacceptance complaints that the valves leaked more than it had estimated constituted reasonable notice of the breach; 3) MAC's actual knowledge that the valves leaked more than MAC had estimated fulfilled the purposes of the UCC notice requirement; and 4) Aqualon's serving MAC with a complaint three years after acceptance constituted notice within a reasonable time. We address each contention in turn.

### A. UCC Section 2-607(3) Does Apply

By its terms, UCC section 2-607(3) applies to this case because this is a situation "[w]here a tender [of goods, i.e., the valves] has been accepted." Section 2-607(3) bars a breach of contract claim by a buyer, such as Aqualon, who has accepted the seller's, such as MAC's, tender of goods unless Aqualon gave MAC notice of the alleged breach within a reasonable time.

Aqualon has argued that the UCC provision does not apply to this case because MAC had actual knowledge that its valves were inadequate long before Aqualon's acceptance. Requiring further notice after acceptance would be pointless, Aqualon argues.

This confuses two quite different things. The notice "of the breach" required is not of the facts, which the seller presumably knows quite as well as, if not better than, the buyer, but of buyer's claim that they constitute a breach. The purpose of the notice is to advise the seller that he must meet a claim for damages, as to which, rightly or wrongly, the law requires that he shall have early warning.

### B. Aqualon's Preacceptance Complaints Did Not Satisfy the Requirements of UCC Section 2-607(3)

Aqualon next argues that its complaints to MAC before the March 1993 reissuance of the purchase order for the valves satisfied the requirements of section 2-607(3). Aqualon sent a letter to MAC on August 3, 1992, in which it asserted that the valve leakage rates were "outside the performance requirements of our purchase order" and that Aqualon "cannot accept valves that will not perform." That letter was followed by continuous correspondence "for the next six months regarding recommendations on how to correct and solutions to the deficiency of the valves."

However, Aqualon's acceptance of the valves without comment *after* the six months of letters dissipated the effect of its earlier complaints. Knowing the leakage rates, Aqualon nevertheless reissued its purchase order for the valves in March 1993 and amended it in April 1993. In June 1993 MAC's tender of the valves was accepted, and in December Aqualon paid for the valves in full. Finally, in the winter of 1993 Aqualon told MAC that its system was working well, and the only problem it mentioned was blower noise, which MAC fixed.

In short, MAC probably knew that Aqualon was not happy with the leakage rates, but it could reasonably have believed that Aqualon was satisfied with the valves. Because Aqualon did not inform MAC after accepting the tender that the transaction was "*still* troublesome," MAC had no way to know that there was any remaining problem to be cured, or any controversy to be negotiated about or settled, or any impending litigation with which to be concerned, after Aqualon reissued the purchase order for, accepted, and paid for the valves. Without any post-acceptance notice otherwise, MAC deserved to be able to rely on the certainty of its contractual arrangement and to believe that a way had been found to make the valves satisfactory.

### C. The Purposes of the Notice Requirement Were Not Met

Aqualon contends that three purposes of the notice requirement were met in this case. The three purposes that Aqualon identifies for the UCC's notice requirement are:

(1) to prevent surprise and allow the seller the opportunity to make recommendations on how to cure the nonconformance;
(2) to permit the seller the fair opportunity to investigate and prepare for litigation; and
(3) to open the way for normal settlement of claims through negotiation.

Aqualon, however, neglects to include a further purpose identified by the district court:

(4) to protect the seller from stale claims and provide certainty in contractual arrangements.

*Cf.* 1 James J. White & Robert S. Summers, *Uniform Commercial Code* §11-10, at 612-613 (4th ed. 1995) (listing these purposes, as well as the purpose of recognizing a general disbelief of tardy claims). Assuming, without deciding, that satisfaction of these four purposes would obviate the need to comply with the terms of the statute, Aqualon cannot demonstrate that the purposes were satisfied.

First, the notice requirement provides an opportunity for the seller to cure the defect. MAC knew in August 1992 that its valves would leak far more than stated in its original proposal. Both MAC and Aqualon worked together for the next six months to try to modify Aqualon's system design to use those valves, because both parties knew that nothing more could be done to improve the performance of the valves. Because MAC had in excess of six months to effect a cure and was unable to do so, Aqualon contends that the first purpose of the notice requirement was satisfied.

Second, the notice requirement is intended to give the seller a fair chance to prepare for litigation; for example, by gathering documents and taking depositions while the evidence is still available and memories are still fresh. Aqualon asserts that this purpose was fulfilled because MAC knew of the possibility of litigation by virtue of its knowledge that the system as originally designed did not work with the leaky valves. However, as explained above, the aforementioned knowledge demonstrates that MAC knew the *facts,* but not that MAC knew that Aqualon would consider these facts to constitute a breach of warranty. Aqualon's acceptance of and full payment for the valves without further complaint, knowing their leakage rates, communicated to MAC that the valves were acceptable.

Third, the notice requirement prompts negotiation and settlement of claims. If MAC had been notified more promptly after Aqualon's acceptance of the valves that Aqualon intended to sue MAC (specifically, before Aqualon filed its complaint), it might have settled the underlying claim. Because MAC would not have had to undertake the expenses of litigation that arose when it had to respond to Aqualon's complaint, MAC would likely have offered more money in settlement of the claim. And because Aqualon would not yet have invested in litigation by paying lawyers to prepare and file the complaint, Aqualon would presumably have agreed to receive less money in settlement of its claim. In this way, earlier notice would have led to a greater chance of settlement. Aqualon's bare assertion that "MAC has suffered no detriment with respect to the options of settlement," just because settlement efforts were unsuccessful, is mistaken.

Finally, the notice requirement is intended to protect the seller from stale claims and provide certainty in contractual arrangements. Aqualon argues that using a notice requirement to give peace of mind to a defendant and to protect against stale claims is inappropriate and unnecessary because that purpose is served by a statute of limitations. It is true that a state may decide to serve these policies through a strict statute of limitations. But a state may also choose to enact a notice requirement in addition to a longer statute of limitations. Such a two-part scheme preserves claims of which the defendant has *not* been notified for only a short period of time, but if the defendant *has* been notified, it preserves those claims for a longer period. Because Aqualon made no complaints to MAC for three years after accepting the valves, MAC was entitled to assume a position of repose.

### D. Aqualon's Delay of Three Years Was Not Notification within a Reasonable Time

Finally, Aqualon argues that even if its preacceptance complaints did not serve to notify MAC that it found the transaction "still troublesome," Aqualon's service of a civil complaint on MAC approximately three years after accepting the valves was notification within a "reasonable time," satisfying UCC section 2-607(3).[3]

Aqualon asserts that it had good reasons for delay. The reasons it provides boil down to simply that Aqualon was slow in figuring out that it wanted to blame MAC for the cost overrun in designing its system. Furthermore, Aqualon offers no explanation whatsoever for the delay of a year after filing its complaint against MAC before Aqualon served MAC with the complaint.

Aqualon also asserts that the delay was not unreasonable because MAC has not suffered any prejudice from the delay. MAC claims that there was prejudice to its case because of faded memories and lost documents, and gives an example of a lost document. Aqualon argues in rebuttal that the named document would have been irrelevant to MAC's case. We cannot tell whether the document would have been helpful because, it being lost, we cannot know exactly what information it contained. Furthermore, we cannot tell whether there may have been other pertinent documents available three years before

---

3. MAC urges that we should follow the "majority" of courts to address the issue and hold that notice-via-lawsuit is insufficient as a matter of law, citing cases such as *Chemtrol Adhesives, Inc. v. American Mfrs. Mut. Ins. Co.*, 42 Ohio St. 3d 40, 537 N.E.2d 624, 638 (1989), and *Lynx, Inc. v. Ordnance Prods., Inc.*, 273 Md. 1, 327 A.2d 502, 514 (1974). But MAC's assertion that this is the "majority" position recognizes that courts in other jurisdictions disagree. In fact, the *Chemtrol Adhesives, Inc.* court declined to adopt such a per se rule. *See* 537 N.E.2d at 638. We decline to resolve this issue of first impression under Delaware law.

MAC was served that were lost and have been forgotten during its period of repose. These considerations demonstrate why, although prejudice is relevant to whether a delay was reasonable, no showing of prejudice is required to make section 2-607(3) applicable.

## NOTES AND QUESTIONS

1. Would the seller have been interested in inspecting the goods under UCC section 2-515?
2. The court declines to address the issue of whether the filing of a lawsuit should constitute sufficient notice under section 2-607, assuming that the lawsuit is filed in a timely manner. In your opinion, should some preliminary notice be required before the lawsuit is filed?

### (b) Measurement of Damages

Section 2-714 provides the buyer's remedy for goods that are accepted. Subsection 1 provides the general rule, which as you can see is a very loose rule that should probably be interpreted in light of the policy of putting the injured party in the position that it would have been in if the contract had been performed. Subsection 2 provides a measure of damages for breach of warranty, but Official Comment 3 indicates that this is not the exclusive rule, leaving the court with discretion to fashion another rule in an appropriate case. As is the case with the buyer's cover and contract market remedies, UCC section 2-714 provides that in a proper case, the buyer may also recover incidental and consequential damages as provided in section 2-715.

## GEM JEWELERS V. DYKMAN

Supreme Court, Appellate Division, New York

160 A.D.2d 1069, 553 N.Y.S.2d 890 (1990)

In August 1984 plaintiff entered into an agreement with defendant Columbia-Art Store Equipment Company (hereinafter defendant) for the construction and installation of new, custom-designed jewelry cabinets, cases, and fixtures for plaintiff's retail jewelry store in the City of Gloversville, Fulton County, for a total price of $36,000. The items were to be built in accordance with plans and specifications drawn by a California-based designer specializing in jewelry stores who had been retained to design the renovation of plaintiff's store. Cabinets, cases, and fixtures were installed in the fall of 1984. After paying more than $32,000 on the contract, plaintiff wrote to defendant's president in May 1986 complaining of the workmanship and of the fact that solid cherry hardwood cases were "ordered and paid . . . for," but "we received [only] veneered particle board." Defendant's president responded by denying that there were any defects and suggested that the unpaid balance was sufficient to cover any unsatisfactory items. Plaintiff subsequently brought this action for breach of contract, breach of warranty, and fraud. Defendant counterclaimed for $3,000, representing the alleged unpaid balance on the contract. After dismissal of plaintiff's fraud cause of action, the case proceeded to trial, at the conclusion of which the jury found in plaintiff's favor, awarding $40,000 in damages and rejecting defendant's counterclaim. This appeal by defendant ensued.

Defendant argues that reversal was required because supreme court erred in its instructions on damages. The parties had agreed that, since the contract items had been accepted by plaintiff, the damage issue was controlled by UCC section 2-714. Under that section of the UCC, a buyer can recover damages "for any nonconformity of tender the loss resulting . . . from the seller's breach as determined in any manner which is reasonable." However, the measure of damages for breach of warranty "is the difference . . . between the value of the goods accepted and the value they would have had if they had been as warranted, unless special circumstances show proximate damages of a different amount." UCC §2-714(2). The reference to value in UCC section 2-714(2) is to the fair market value of the goods (see 4 Anderson, *Uniform Commercial Code* §2-714:5, at 471 (3d ed.)).

In its instructions to the jury on plaintiff's breach of contract cause of action, supreme court charged alternative measures of damages; that is, the "actual cost of making the goods meet the requirements of the contract," and "the difference in value between the goods as accepted and the value of the goods had they been in conformance with the contract." Supreme court then directed the jury to select a reasonable measure of damages. Defendant excepted to that portion of the charge which permitted the jury to award damages on the basis of cost to correct, and also excepted on the same ground to the court's supplemental charge on the general definition of damages, in response to the jury's request. Defendant claims that, in this case, the evidence only supported an award of damages based upon the difference between the value of the goods as accepted and their value had they been as warranted. It is asserted that supreme court's departure from this measure of damages in its charge was prejudicial, in that it invited the jury to compensate plaintiff on the basis of the replacement costs for solid wood cabinets and cases, an unacceptable standard under UCC section 2-714.

We find no error in the charge that was preserved for review that prejudiced defendant. First, plaintiff's evidence clearly showed that the cabinets and cases called for under the agreement were custom-designed specifically for plaintiff's store and further supported the inference that solid wood was specifically required for aesthetic reasons, as communicated to defendant; thus, special circumstances existed justifying a departure from the ordinary standard of damages based upon the difference between value of the goods as accepted and value as warranted. As this case can be found to involve unique goods not bought and sold on the open market, it can reasonably be concluded that the standard breach of warranty measure of damages under UCC section 2-714(2) was inadequate. While supreme court's instructions could have been more explicit regarding such special circumstances, any deficiency was not preserved by defendant's exception to the submission to the jury of any measure of damages other than one based upon the value of the goods as accepted and value as warranted. Under the foregoing special circumstances, cost of replacement was a proper measure of damages.

Moreover, particularly in the case of goods not regularly traded on the open market, replacement cost is a proper method of determining the value of goods as warranted under UCC section 2-714(2). 1 White and Summers, *Uniform Commercial Code* §10-2, at 504 (3d ed.). Thus, the jury could validly have used the replacement cost of solid cherry wood cabinets and cases in making its award, even if no alternative measure of damages had been submitted to it by supreme court.

Defendant also argues that the jury's award of $40,000 to plaintiff was excessive. We find that there is evidence substantially supporting this amount. Specifically, there was testimony that the cost in 1984 to replace the cabinets, cases, and fixtures with items conforming to the contract was approximately $44,000. The designer of the cabinets and cases, who saw them in plaintiff's store in May 1986, described their appearance as "horrible," and plaintiff's qualified expert appraiser described them as made of "a very thin veneer on a pressed board . . . of a sawdust composition," with the veneer "bubbling and peeling" on many cases, and colors that did not match. The jury, therefore, could reasonably have concluded that the value of the contract items as supplied by defendant was not more than their salvage value in 1984 as used fixtures, as testified to by plaintiff's expert. Thus, damages of $40,000 were not excessive, despite being more than the contract price.

We are likewise unpersuaded that the jury's rejection of defendant's counterclaim was unwarranted. Accordingly, the judgment should be affirmed in all respects.

Judgment affirmed, with costs.

## PROBLEM

***Problem 7-8.*** This problem is based on *Chatlos Systems v. National Cash Register*, which is reproduced on pages 166-171, *supra*. In that case, Chatlos contracted to purchase a computer system from National Cash Register (NCR) that would perform six bookkeeping functions. The contract price was $46,020. Ultimately, the system was only able to perform one of those functions. According to Chatlos's expert's testimony, there was no single computer system on the market that would perform the six functions that the NCR system had been warranted to perform. He testified that by combining the software and hardware of various vendors of computer products, he could put together a system that would perform according to Chatlos's specifications for $207,000. The value of the NCR system as it was currently functioning was estimated at being worth around $6,000. How should Chatlos's damages be calculated? Is comparing the hypothetical system put together by Chatlos's expert to the NCR system like comparing a Rolls-Royce to a Volkswagen? Is it like comparing the value of equipment that is warranted to lift 1,000 pounds to equipment that will lift only 200 pounds? Is it reasonable for a sophisticated buyer to expect to purchase equipment worth $207,000 for $46,020 from a sophisticated seller? *See Chatlos Systems v. National Cash Register*, 670 F.2d 1304 (3d Cir. 1982).

## 3. AVAILABILITY OF TORT REMEDIES

If there has been a breach of a sale of goods contract, the injured party may in some cases wish to proceed in tort. As was noted in *Commonwealth v. Johnson*, pages 73-78, *supra*, a breach of the implied warranty of merchantability may also give rise to strict liability in tort. An action for negligence may also lie in the event that there was a failure on the part of the seller to exercise reasonable care in the manufacture of the product. In addition, some of the conduct of the parties in performance of the contract (or in inducing the contract) may be tortious. An action in tort does not require privity of contract and also does not require the giving of notice as per UCC section 2-607. Statutes of limitation are different, thus sometimes barring the contract action as compared to the tort action (or vice versa). And tort actions may result in different damage calculations—sometimes punitive damages may be available.

When does the injured party have the option of suing in tort as compared to contract? In *East River Steamship Corp. v. Transamerica Delaval, Inc.*, 476 U.S. 858, 1 UCC Rep. Serv. 2d 609 (1986), the United States Supreme Court under its admiralty jurisdiction noted three different approaches to the question of whether an action in tort for negligence or strict liability exists when damages arise for breach of warranty in a sale of goods. The three approaches are: (1) A tort action is available only if there is damage to person or property other than the goods themselves (the "economic loss" rule); (2) a tort action is available in noneconomic-loss cases if the defect in the goods would be potentially dangerous to person or property other than the goods themselves (even if no such loss occurs); and (3) a tort action is available if a tort was committed even if the damage is economic in nature. The Supreme Court observed that the majority rule was the "economic loss" rule, and applied it to bar the tort action in *East River Steamship Corp.* There were no allegations of fraud in the case, simply negligence on the part of the defendant.

Courts will also allow a tort action if the tort is considered independent of the contract. For example, the seller might intentionally misrepresent the quality of the goods to the buyer in order to induce the buyer to enter into the contract in the first place. An action for fraud would be appropriate for the purpose of avoiding the sales contract. The fraudulent inducement is independent of performance under the contract itself. The next case raises the question of whether fraudulent statements made in connection with performance under the contract should be considered independently tortuous, thus allowing a tort cause of action, where the damages are purely economic in nature.

### Robinson Helicopter Company v. Dana Corporation

Supreme Court of California

34 Cal. 4th 979, 102 P.3d 268, 22 Cal. Rptr. 3d 352 (2004)

BROWN, J.

In this case, we decide whether the economic loss rule, which in some circumstances bars a tort action in the absence of personal injury or physical damage to other property, applies to claims for intentional misrepresentation or fraud in the performance of a contract. Because plaintiff Robinson Helicopter Company, Inc.'s (Robinson) fraud and intentional misrepresentation claim, with respect to Dana Corporation's (Dana) provision of false certificates of conformance, is an independent action based in tort, we conclude that the economic loss rule does not bar tort recovery.

### Facts

Robinson is a manufacturer of helicopters. Its R22 model is a two-seat helicopter used as a primary trainer for pilots. The R44 model is a heavier model used for a wide variety of purposes. Both of these models use sprag clutches manufactured by Dana's Formsprag division. The sprag clutch on a helicopter functions like the "freewheeling" clutch mechanism on a bicycle where the rider transmits power to the rear wheel by operating the pedals, but when the rider stops pedaling, the wheel continues to rotate. A sprag clutch is primarily a safety mechanism. If a helicopter loses power during flight, the sprag clutch allows the rotor blades to continue turning and permits the pilot to maintain control and land safely by the "autorotating" of the rotor blades. At all relevant times, Dana's Formsprag division was the only manufacturer of the sprag clutches that Robinson required for its R22 and R44 helicopters.

All aircraft manufacturers in the United States, including Robinson, must obtain a "type certificate" from the Federal Aviation Administration (FAA). The type certificate freezes the design as of the date the certificate is issued. Every aircraft made pursuant to the certificate must be produced exactly in accordance with that certificate. Any proposed changes must first be submitted to and approved by the FAA. The components of the sprag clutch must be ground to precise tolerances, measured in thousandths of an inch, to avoid distortions that lead to cracking and failure. Pursuant to the type certificate issued to Robinson by the FAA for the R22 and R44 models, the parts of the sprag clutches, including the sprag ears, were required to be ground at a particular level of hardness to assure their metallurgical integrity. The *required* level of hardness of the R22 and the R44 clutches, pursuant to the type certificates, was described as "50/55 Rockwell" (50/55).

Between 1984 and July 1996, Robinson purchased 3,707 sprag clutches from Dana. Each was ground to the required 50/55 level of hardness. There were only three incidents of cracking or failure of these sprag ears, a rate of 0.03 percent. In July 1996, Dana changed its grinding process to a higher "61/63 Rockwell" (61/63) level of hardness. Dana did not notify Robinson or the FAA of this change. After such change was made in the grinding process, Dana nonetheless continued to provide written certificates to Robinson with each delivery of clutches that the clutches had been manufactured in conformance with Robinson's written specifications (which specifications prohibited unapproved changes in Dana's manufacturing process).

In October 1997, again without notifying either Robinson or the FAA, Dana changed its grinding process back to the 50/55 level of hardness that was required by its contract with Robinson. Beginning in early 1998, the sprag clutch ears that had been ground at the 61/63 level of hardness and sold to Robinson experienced a failure rate of 9.86 percent. This compared with a failure rate for clutches manufactured before July 1996 of 0.03 percent and 00.0 percent for clutches manufactured after October 1997.

Between August 24, 1998, and November 30, 1998, Robinson sent several letters to Dana reporting that 11 clutch assemblies with cracked sprags had been returned to Robinson from its operator customers. Each of these assemblies was ultimately traced to serial numbers of Dana sprag clutches that had been sold to Robinson during the period that Dana was grinding the clutches to the higher 61/63 level of hardness. On November 30, 1998, during a conference call between Robinson and Dana officials, Dana disclosed, for the first time, that it had used the 61/63 hardness level in its manufacturing process during the period July 1996 to October 1997.

Although it was a disputed issue, the record reflects that substantial evidence was presented at trial demonstrating that the higher failure rate of Dana's sprag clutches manufactured during the July 1996 to October 1997 period was due to the higher hardness level to which they had been ground. Fortunately, these clutch failures did not result in any helicopter accident and there were no incidents of injury or property damage that were caused by any clutch defect or failure, nor did any of the defective clutches cause any damage to other parts of the helicopters in which they had been installed.

Nonetheless, Robinson was ultimately required by the FAA and its British equivalent, the Air Accidents Investigation Branch of the United Kingdom's Department of Transport, to recall and replace all of the faulty clutch assemblies (i.e., those manufactured with Dana's sprag clutches ground to the higher hardness level of 61/63 rather than the 50/55 level required by the Robinson specifications). This led to a total claimed expense to Robinson of $1,555,924, which represented the cost of (1) replacement parts; and (2) substantial employee time spent investigating the cause of the malfunctioning parts, and the identification and replacement of parts on helicopters that had already been sold to customers.

Robinson went forward, incurred the costs described above, purchased the new clutches, and effected the necessary replacements. It then filed this action alleging causes of action for breach of contract, breach of warranty, and negligent and intentional misrepresentations. After a nine-day trial, the jury returned a verdict in favor of Robinson for $1,533,924 in compensatory damages and $6 million in punitive damages. The jury found that Dana had not only breached its contract with Robinson and the warranties made thereunder, but also had made false misrepresentations of fact and had knowingly misrepresented or concealed material facts with the intent to defraud. The award of punitive damages was based on this latter finding.

Dana appealed. The court of appeal affirmed the judgment on the contract and warranty causes of actions. However, applying the economic loss rule, the court of appeal held that because Robinson suffered only economic losses, it could not recover in tort. Accordingly, the court of appeal reversed the judgment in part, based on the misrepresentation claims. As a result, the court of appeal held the punitive damages award could not be maintained.

Robinson seeks review of the court of appeal's application of the economic loss rule to its fraud and intentional misrepresentation claims.

### Discussion

Robinson contends the court of appeal erred in its decision because the economic loss rule does not bar its fraud and intentional misrepresentation claims. We conclude that, with respect to Dana's provision of false certificates of conformance, Robinson is correct.

We begin with a brief background on the economic loss rule. Economic loss consists of "damages for inadequate value, costs of repair and replacement of the defective product or consequent loss of profits—without any claim of personal injury or damages to other property. . . . " [Citation.] *Jimenez v. Superior Court* (2002) 29 Cal. 4th 473, 482, 127 Cal. Rptr. 2d 614, 58 P.3d 450. Simply stated, the economic loss rule provides: "[W]here a purchaser's expectations in a sale are frustrated because the product he bought is not working properly, his remedy is said to be in contract alone, for he has suffered only 'economic' losses. . . . This doctrine hinges on a distinction drawn between transactions involving the sale of goods for commercial purposes where economic expectations are protected by commercial and contract law, and those involving the sale of defective products to individual consumers who are injured in a manner which has traditionally been remedied by resort to the law of torts." *Neibarger v. Universal Cooperatives, Inc.* (Mich. 1992) 439 Mich. 512, 486 N.W.2d 612, 615, fns. omitted. The economic loss rule requires a purchaser to recover in contract for purely economic loss due to disappointed expectations, unless he can demonstrate harm above and beyond a broken contractual promise. Quite simply, the economic loss rule "prevent[s] the law of contract and the law of tort from dissolving one into the other." *Rich Products Corp. v. Kemutec, Inc.* (E.D. Wis. 1999) 66 F. Supp. 2d 937, 969.

In *Jimenez v. Superior Court, supra,* 29 Cal. 4th 473, 127 Cal. Rptr. 2d 614, 58 P.3d 450, we set forth the rationale for the economic loss rule: "The distinction that the law has drawn between tort recovery for physical injuries and warranty recovery for economic loss is not arbitrary and does not rest on the 'luck' of one plaintiff in having an accident causing physical injury. The distinction rests, rather, on an understanding of the nature of the responsibility a manufacturer must undertake in distributing his products. [Citation.] We concluded that the nature of this responsibility meant that a manufacturer could appropriately be held liable for physical injuries (including both personal injury and damage to property other than the product itself), regardless of the terms of any warranty. [Citation.] But the manufacturer could not be held liable for 'the level of performance of his products in the consumer's business unless he agrees that the product was designed to meet the consumer's demands. [Citation.]" *Id.* at p.482, 127 Cal. Rptr. 2d 614, 58 P.3d 450.

In support of its argument that the economic loss rule does not apply to its case, Robinson argues that its claims for fraud and deceit were based on an independent duty that Dana breached. In *Erlich v. Menezes* (1999) 21 Cal. 4th 543, 551, 87 Cal. Rptr. 2d 886, 981 P.2d 978, we held that a party's contractual obligation may create a legal duty and that a breach of that duty may support a tort action. We stated, "[C]onduct amounting to a breach of contract becomes tortious only when it also violates a duty independent of the contract arising from principles of tort law. [Citation.]" *Ibid.*

We went on to describe several instances where tort damages were permitted in contract cases. "Tort damages have been permitted in contract cases where a breach of duty directly causes physical injury [citation]; for breach of the covenant of good faith and fair dealing in insurance contracts [citation]; for wrongful discharge in violation of fundamental public policy [citation]; or where the contract was fraudulently induced. [Citation.]" (*Id.* at pp.551-552, 87 Cal. Rptr. 2d 886, 981 P.2d 978. "[I]n each of these cases, the duty that gives rise to tort liability is either completely independent of the contract or arises from conduct which is both intentional and intended to harm. [Citation.]" *Id.* at p.552, 87 Cal. Rptr. 2d 886, 981 P.2d 978; see also *Harris v. Atlantic Richfield Co.* (1993) 14 Cal. App. 4th 70, 78, 17 Cal. Rptr. 2d 649 ("when one party commits a fraud during the contract formation or performance, the injured party may recover in contract and tort").

With respect to situations outside of those set forth above, we stated: "Generally, outside the insurance context, 'a tortious breach of contract . . . may be found when (1) the breach is accompanied by a traditional common law tort, such as fraud or conversion; (2) the means used to breach the contract are tortious, involving deceit or undue coercion; or (3) one party intentionally breaches the contract intending or knowing that such a breach will cause severe, unmitigable harm in the form of mental anguish, personal hardship, or substantial consequential damages.'[Citation.] Focusing on intentional conduct gives substance to the proposition that a breach of contract is tortious only when some independent duty arising from tort law is violated. [Citation.] If every negligent breach of a contract gives rise to tort damages the limitation would be meaningless, as would the statutory distinction between tort and contract remedies." *Erlich v. Menezes, supra,* 21 Cal. 4th at pp.553-554, 87 Cal. Rptr. 2d 886, 981 P.2d 978.

Robinson's misrepresentation and fraud claims were based on: (1) Dana's provision of false certificates of conformance; (2) Dana's failure to provide the serial numbers of affected clutches until five months after the clutches failed; and (3) Robinson's claim that a Dana employee redacted reference to the hardness of the clutches on a list of products requested by Robinson. At trial, the jury found that Dana had (1) made false representations of material fact; (2) knowingly misrepresented or concealed material facts with intent to defraud; (3) and by clear and convincing evidence was guilty of oppression, fraud, or malice in its intentional misrepresentations and concealments.

For purposes of our decision, we focus solely on the fraud and misrepresentation claim based on Dana's provision of the false certificates of conformance. The elements of fraud are: (1) a misrepresentation (false representation, concealment, or nondisclosure); (2) knowledge of falsity (or scienter); (3) intent to defraud; that is, to induce reliance; (4) justifiable reliance; and (5) resulting damage. *Lazar v. Superior Court* (1996) 12 Cal. 4th 631, 638, 49 Cal. Rptr. 2d 377, 909 P.2d 981. Dana's issuance of the false certificates of conformance were unquestionably *affirmative* misrepresentations that Robinson justifiably relied on to its detriment. But for Dana's affirmative misrepresentations by supplying the false certificates of conformance, Robinson would not have accepted delivery and used the nonconforming clutches over the course of several years, nor would it have incurred the cost of investigating the cause of the faulty clutches. Accordingly, Dana's tortious conduct was separate from the breach itself, which involved Dana's provision of the nonconforming clutches. In addition, Dana's provision of faulty clutches exposed Robinson to liability for personal damages if a helicopter crashed and to disciplinary action by the FAA. Thus, Dana's fraud is a tort independent of the breach.

We hold the economic loss rule does not bar Robinson's fraud and intentional misrepresentation claims because they were independent of Dana's breach of contract. Because Dana's affirmative intentional misrepresentations of fact (i.e., the issuance of the false certificates of conformance) are dispositive fraudulent conduct related to the performance of the contract, we need not address the issue of whether Dana's intentional concealment constitutes an independent tort.

California's public policy also strongly favors this holding. "[C]ourts will generally enforce the breach of a contractual promise through contract law, except when the actions that constitute the breach violate a social policy that merits the imposition of tort remedies." *Freeman & Mills, Inc. v. Belcher Oil Co.* (1995) 11 Cal. 4th 85, 107, 44 Cal. Rptr. 2d 420, 900 P.2d 669 (conc. and dis. opn. of Mosk, J.). Similarly, "[c]ourts should be careful to apply tort remedies only when the conduct in question is so clear in its deviation from socially useful business practices that the effect of enforcing such tort duties will be . . . to aid rather than discourage commerce." *Erlich v. Menezes, supra,* 21 Cal. 4th at p.554, 87 Cal. Rptr. 2d 886, 981 P.2d 978. "In pursuing a valid fraud action, a plaintiff advances the public interest in punishing intentional misrepresentations and in deterring such misrepresentations in the future. [Citation.] Because of the extra measure of blameworthiness inhering in fraud, and because in fraud cases we are not concerned about the need for 'predictability about the cost of contractual relationships'[citation], fraud plaintiffs may recover 'out-of-pocket' damages in addition to benefit-of-the-bargain damages." *Lazar v. Superior Court, supra,* 12 Cal. 4th at p.646, 49 Cal. Rptr. 2d 377, 909 P.2d 981. In addition, California also has a legitimate and compelling interest in preserving a business climate free of fraud and deceptive practices. Needless to say, Dana's fraudulent conduct cannot be considered a socially useful business practice. Allowing Robinson's claim for Dana's affirmative misrepresentation discourages such practices in the future while encouraging a business climate free of fraud and deceptive practices.

We do not believe that our decision will open the floodgates to future litigation. Our holding today is narrow in scope and limited to a defendant's affirmative misrepresentations on which a plaintiff relies and which expose a plaintiff to liability for personal damages independent of the plaintiff's economic loss.

### Conclusion

Had Dana simply been truthful and declined to provide a certificate for the nonconforming orders, Robinson could have refused to accept them, thereby avoiding the damages it later suffered when it had to mitigate and replace the defective clutches. Dana's action denied Robinson this opportunity. Because the court of appeal erred by applying the economic loss rule to Robinson, we reverse and remand for proceedings consistent with this opinion.

WE CONCUR: GEORGE, C. J., KENNARD, BAXTER, CHIN, AND MORENO, J. J.

---

Dissenting Opinion by WERDEGAR, J.

Dana Corporation (Dana) entered into a commercial contract with Robinson Helicopter Company, Inc. (Robinson) to supply helicopter parts. It warranted that the parts would be manufactured in conformance with particular specifications. It later changed its manufacturing process and began delivering parts that no longer conformed to the contract specifications, accompanied by contractually required certificates of compliance that represented the parts were still being manufactured according to those specifications. Robinson discovered the manufacturing change and was forced to replace the nonconforming parts. Was this a contract breach? Absolutely. The contract called for a particular performance, and the breaching party, Dana, failed to deliver that performance.

Was this conduct also a basis for tort damages? As the majority notes, Robinson makes no claim that Dana had any fraudulent intent when it changed its manufacturing process. Thus, Robinson's misrepresentation claim rests in its entirety on a series of form certificates of compliance typically providing: "This is to certify that . . . pieces of part number . . . related to your purchase order . . . have been processed, fabricated and received final inspection in accordance with the applicable blueprint specifications and the purchase order requirements, with pertinent date relative thereto, maintained and on file." By providing these certificates, Dana represented that its parts satisfied the contract. In effect, it refused to admit that it was breaching the contract while in fact it was doing so. If Dana misrepresented its compliance intentionally, with knowledge that its parts did not satisfy the contract, then its conduct might be described variously as a bad faith breach of contract, a breach of contract by fraudulent means, or a bad faith denial of breach.

Until today, we have rejected the notion that such conduct could give rise to punitive damages. As a matter of both statute and common law, a breach of a commercial contract cannot be the basis for punitive damages. The law eschews inquiry into a breaching party's motives; whether acting in good faith or bad faith, a party that breaches a commercial contract must pay only contract damages.

This rule reflects a circumspect approach to attaching tort liability to conduct occurring in the course of contract performance. As we have frequently explained, the reason for this justifiable circumspection is the value commercial parties place on predictable potential costs and the chilling effect tort exposure in routine breach cases would have on commercial enterprise. As we have said in the context of rejecting tort liability for interference with one's own contract, if every breach creates a potentially triable tort claim, "the potential consequences of any breach of contract—efficient or inefficient, socially desirable or undesirable—become uncertain and unpredictable. Tort liability may or may not follow, depending on a myriad of imponderable factors. As a result, a business fearful of unfathomable tort exposure might lose the ability to respond flexibly to changing economic conditions or hesitate to enter into contracts at all in fast-moving aspects of commercial enterprise." *Applied Equipment,* at p.520, 28 Cal. Rptr. 2d 475, 869 P.2d 454.

The challenged conduct in this case is a breach of contract accompanied by false contractually required representations that the party was *not* in breach. This, the majority holds, is enough to allow a jury to inquire into whether the breaching party *knew* it was breaching the contract at the time and, if so, whether such a knowing misrepresentation might appropriately give rise to punitive damages. Of course, rare is the commercial contract that does not involve ongoing statements by the parties relating to their performance. In all such cases, under the majority's rule, it is now possible to plead a fraud claim. This raises the specter that every alleged breach will yield satellite litigation over whether contemporaneous remarks by one side or the other amounted to intentional misrepresentations about the existence of a breach, thus subjecting the breaching party to the possibility of punitive damages for such conduct. The implications of such a result for commercial predictability and certainty are considerable.

I do not disagree with the majority's desire to sanction deceit in commercial relationships. Commercial parties should be entitled to rely on the representations their contractual partners make. Indeed, the stability of commercial relationships depends on such trust, and the legal rules governing those relationships should foster it. The problem is not with the principle but the practice. Allowing a tort claim to be pleaded in every case where a breach is accompanied by representations about performance forces all parties, not just those engaged in malfeasance, to bargain in the shadow of potential tort liability. That cannot be a good thing.

## II

The application of the economic loss rule solves the problem of how to sanction deceit without chilling commercial relationships. It allows tort liability in those instances where a misrepresentation may have led to *actual* property damage or personal injury and, in doing so, both sanctions and deters opprobrious conduct. But by excluding tort recovery in those cases, like this one, where the only damages are economic, it preserves the valuable distinction between tort and contract remedies and avoids the problems that would arise if every routine breach were susceptible to both tort and contract claims.

## III

The majority purports to limit its holding to cases in which a misrepresentation exposes a plaintiff to a risk of liability for personal damage. The problem with this asserted limiting principle is that, unlike the requirement that there actually *be* noneconomic damage, this requirement is no limit at all. It is safe to say that in a large percentage of denial of breach cases, a plaintiff will be able to plead and perhaps prove that it was exposed to at least the risk of liability for personal damage by virtue of the defendant's failure to immediately confess its sins. Instead, we ought to continue to apply the economic loss rule in the absence of actual injury or property damage, adhering to the principle that "[w]hen no safety concerns are implicated because the damage is limited to the product itself, the [commercial party]'s recourse is in contract law to enforce the benefit of the bargain." *Jimenez v. Superior Court, supra,* 29 Cal. 4th at p.490, 127 Cal. Rptr. 2d 614, 58 P.3d 450 (conc. and dis. opn. of Brown, J.).

IV

The majority disavows any views on application of the economic loss rule to fraudulent concealment. Whenever the issue is settled, today's decision will leave no easy options. On the one hand, if fraudulent concealment is not tortious, the distinction between tortious misrepresentation and nontortious concealment may prove untenable and virtually impossible to administer. If a party makes statements that are true but incomplete and that may or may not have false implications, is this a tortious misrepresentation or a nontortious nondisclosure? Such line drawing will not be easy for parties seeking to order their affairs, judges obligated to instruct juries, or juries forced to split hairs by such a set of rules.

On the other hand, if the majority's decision is taken to its logical conclusion, then deceit by nondisclosure is a tort independent of any breach, just like deceit by misrepresentation. If so, every litigator can be expected to attach such a piggyback tort claim to each breach of contract claim, and every breach case can be expected to focus on when a party learned it was in breach and why it failed to disclose that fact to the other side. The threat of tort damages in every such instance can do no good for parties weighing the likely benefits and risks before entering any commercial contract.

V

Let us be clear: What Dana did was not admirable. A jury awarded Robinson $1.5 million in compensatory damages. Dana's conduct should be sanctioned, and it has been. But to allow tort recovery for bad faith denial of a breach that led only to economic damages is to prescribe a cure worse than the disease. Today's decision greatly enhances the ease with which every breach of contract claim can don tort clothes. I fear that in doing so, it opens a Pandora's box better left sealed. Because I would not do so, I respectfully dissent.

## NOTE, QUESTIONS, AND PROBLEM

The significance of the decision in *Robinson Helicopter* is that the plaintiff is allowed to recover punitive damages in tort. Note that the jury awarded $6 million in punitive damages and roughly $1.5 million in compensatory damages. In California, a plaintiff can recover punitive damages only in tort cases. Cal. Civ. Code §3294. This rule is consistent with *Restatement (Second) of Contracts* section 355. This rule is justified under the "efficient breach" theory of contract law that a breach of contract should not be punished other than through the award of compensatory damages. The rule is also justified on the grounds that the threat of punitive damages in the event of breach would have a chilling effect on the willingness of parties to contract (as noted in *Robinson Helicopter*).

Under the "efficient breach" theory, some breaches of contract may actually be beneficial to the economy because the breaching party moves goods or services to another party who values them more highly. For example, assume Company *A* needs a piece of equipment and contracts with Seller to purchase it for $50,000. Delivery is set for June 1. Company *B* needs the same piece of equipment but has a more urgent need for it than Company *A*. Company *B* agrees to pay $70,000 if Seller can deliver the equipment by May 1. The only way that Seller can perform for Company *B* is if it breaches its contract with Company *A* by not delivering on time. Seller decides to breach the contract, and does not tender delivery of the equipment to Company *A* until July 1. Company *A* is willing to accept the equipment, but claims that the delay resulted in $5,000 in damages due to the need to hire overtime workers to compensate for the delayed equipment. Under the "efficient breach" theory, if Company *A* is compensated in damages by Seller, the breach is efficient because Seller was able to make two sales rather than one and Company *B* got the equipment that it needed. Assuming Seller's profit on the sale to Company *B* is greater than $5,000, the breach is beneficial or neutral for all parties. Of course, the practical problem is determining exactly how much harm is actually done by the breach in many cases.[2]

Is the court in *Robinson Helicopter* rejecting the economic loss rule entirely? Did the buyer in *Robinson Helicopter* suffer any additional losses as a result of the intentional misrepresentation? In other words, if the seller had not been aware that the goods did not conform to the contract but had nevertheless certified that they did conform, would the buyer have suffered damages of any different amount? Was the breach by the seller in *Robinson Helicopter* an "efficient breach"? Do you agree with the dissent that this decision opens a "Pandora's box better left sealed"?

***Problem 7-9.*** A construction company contracts for the delivery of concrete to a construction site. The contract calls for 50,000 pounds. Each bag states that it contains 50 pounds. The seller of concrete intentionally fills each bag with only 45 pounds, hoping that the buyer will not actually weigh the bags. After the concrete has been delivered and paid for, the buyer weighs one of the bags and notices the shortfall. Assume that the time for delivery has passed. The buyer chooses not to cover—the buyer has sufficient concrete on hand to complete the construction project. Under the reasoning in *Robinson Helicopter*, could the buyer sue in tort and possibly recover punitive damages? If not, how would buyer's remedies be calculated under Article 2?

## B. BUYER'S REMEDIES UNDER THE CISG

Similar to the UCC, the CISG's remedial provisions seek to place the injured party in the position that the party would have been in but for breach. See Secretariat Commentary on Article 70 of the 1978 Draft (counterpart to CISG Article 74). A difference, as we will see, is that the CISG is more liberal in terms of granting specific performance than the UCC. Articles 45 through 52 provide the remedies available for buyers. Articles 74 through 78 provide the methods for calculating damages and interest for both injured buyers and sellers.

---

2. See Perillo, *Misreading Oliver Wendell Holmes on Efficient Breach and Tortious Interference*, 68 Fordham L. Rev. 1085 (2000).

Article 45 provides the options that are available to an injured buyer in the event of breach of contract by the seller. Article 45 rejects the doctrine of election of remedies in permitting the buyer to obtain damages even if the buyer pursues other remedies in addition. We previously discussed the concept of fundamental breach and when the buyer may avoid the contract. Some of the remedies available to the buyer are only available in the event of fundamental breach.

## Delchi Carrier SpA v. Rotorex Corp.

United States Court of Appeals, Second Circuit

71 F.3d 1024 (1995)

Rotorex Corporation, a New York corporation, appeals from a judgment of $1,785,772.44 in damages for lost profits and other consequential damages awarded to Delchi Carrier SpA following a bench trial before Judge Munson. The basis for the award was Rotorex's delivery of nonconforming compressors to Delchi, an Italian manufacturer of air conditioners. Delchi cross-appeals from the denial of certain incidental and consequential damages. We affirm the award of damages; we reverse in part on Delchi's cross-appeal and remand for further proceedings.

### Background

In January 1988, Rotorex agreed to sell 10,800 compressors to Delchi for use in Delchi's "Ariele" line of portable room air conditioners. The air conditioners were scheduled to go on sale in the spring and summer of 1988. Prior to executing the contract, Rotorex sent Delchi a sample compressor and accompanying written performance specifications. The compressors were scheduled to be delivered in three shipments before May 15, 1988.

Rotorex sent the first shipment by sea on March 26. Delchi paid for this shipment, which arrived at its Italian factory on April 20, by letter of credit. Rotorex sent a second shipment of compressors on or about May 9. Delchi also remitted payment for this shipment by letter of credit. While the second shipment was en route, Delchi discovered that the first lot of compressors did not conform to the sample model and accompanying specifications. On May 13, after a Rotorex representative visited the Delchi factory in Italy, Delchi informed Rotorex that 93 percent of the compressors were rejected in quality-control checks because they had lower cooling capacity and consumed more power than the sample model and specifications. After several unsuccessful attempts to cure the defects in the compressors, Delchi asked Rotorex to supply new compressors conforming to the original sample and specifications. Rotorex refused, claiming that the performance specifications were "inadvertently communicated" to Delchi.

In a faxed letter dated May 23, 1988, Delchi cancelled the contract. Although it was able to expedite a previously planned order of suitable compressors from Sanyo, another supplier, Delchi was unable to obtain in a timely fashion substitute compressors from other sources and thus suffered a loss in its sales volume of Arieles during the 1988 selling season. Delchi filed the instant action under the United Nations Convention on Contracts for the International Sale of Goods ("CISG" or "the Convention") for breach of contract and failure to deliver conforming goods. On January 10, 1991, Judge Cholakis granted Delchi's motion for partial summary judgment, holding Rotorex liable for breach of contract.

### Discussion

[The court determines that the seller had committed a fundamental breach of contract justifying avoidance of the contract by the buyer. That discussion is contained in the prior chapter. The court now turns to the question of damages.]

The CISG provides:

> Damages for breach of contract by one party consist of a sum equal to the loss, including loss of profit, suffered by the other party as a consequence of the breach. Such damages may not exceed the loss that the party in breach foresaw or ought to have foreseen at the time of the conclusion of the contract, in the light of the facts and matters of which he then knew or ought to have known, as a possible consequence of the breach of contract.

CISG Article 74. This provision is "designed to place the aggrieved party in as good a position as if the other party had properly performed the contract." Honnold, *supra,* at 503.

Rotorex argues that Delchi is not entitled to lost profits because it was able to maintain inventory levels of Ariele air conditioning units in excess of the maximum number of possible lost sales. In Rotorex's view, therefore, there was no actual shortfall of Ariele units available for sale because of Rotorex's delivery of nonconforming compressors. Rotorex's argument goes as follows: The end of the air conditioner selling season is August 1. If one totals the number of units available to Delchi from March to August 1, the sum is enough to fill all sales. We may assume that the evidence in the record supports the factual premise. Nevertheless, the argument is fallacious. Because of Rotorex's breach, Delchi had to shut down its manufacturing operation for a few days in May, and the date on which particular units were available for sale was substantially delayed. For example, units available in late July could not be used to meet orders in the spring. As a result, Delchi lost sales in the spring and early summer. We therefore conclude that the district court's findings regarding lost sales are not clearly erroneous. A detailed discussion of the precise number of lost sales is unnecessary because the district court's findings were, if anything, conservative.

Rotorex contends, in the alternative, that the district court improperly awarded lost profits for unfilled orders from Delchi affiliates in Europe and from sales agents within Italy. We disagree. The CISG requires that damages be limited by the familiar principle of foreseeability established in *Hadley v. Baxendale*, 156 Eng. Rep. 145 (1854). CISG Article 74. However, it was objectively foreseeable that Delchi would take orders for Ariele sales based on the number of compressors it had ordered and expected to have ready for the season. The district court was entitled to rely upon the documents and testimony regarding these lost sales and was well within its authority in deciding which orders were proven with sufficient certainty.

Rotorex also challenges the district court's exclusion of fixed costs and depreciation from the manufacturing cost used to calculate lost profits. The trial judge calculated lost profits by subtracting the 478,783 lire "manufacturing cost" —the total variable cost—of an Ariele unit from the 654,644 lire average sale price. The CISG does not explicitly state whether only variable expenses, or both fixed and variable expenses, should be subtracted from sales revenue in calculating lost profits. However, courts generally do not include fixed costs in the calculation of lost profits. *See Indu Craft, Inc. v. Bank of Baroda,* 47 F.3d 490, 495 (2d Cir. 1995) (only when the breach ends an ongoing business should fixed costs be subtracted along with variable costs); *Adams v. Lindblad Travel, Inc.,* 730 F.2d 89, 92-93 (2d Cir. 1984) (fixed costs should not be included in lost profits equation when the plaintiff is an ongoing business whose fixed costs are not affected by the breach). This is, of course, because the fixed costs would have been encountered whether or not the breach occurred. In the absence of a specific provision in the CISG for calculating lost profits, the district court was correct to use the standard formula employed by most American courts and to deduct only variable costs from sales revenue to arrive at a figure for lost profits.

In its cross-appeal, Delchi challenges the district court's denial of various consequential and incidental damages, including reimbursement for: (i) shipping, customs, and incidentals relating to the first and second shipments—rejected and returned—of Rotorex compressors; (ii) obsolete insulation materials and tubing purchased for use only with Rotorex compressors; (iii) obsolete tooling purchased exclusively for production of units with Rotorex compressors; and (iv) labor costs for the period of May 16-19, 1988, when the Delchi production line was idle due to a lack of compressors to install in Ariele air conditioning units. The district court denied damages for these items on the ground that they "are accounted for in Delchi's recovery on its lost profits claim," and, therefore, an award would constitute a double recovery for Delchi. We disagree.

The Convention provides that a contract plaintiff may collect damages to compensate for the full loss. This includes, but is not limited to, lost profits, subject only to the familiar limitation that the breaching party must have foreseen, or should have foreseen, the loss as a probable consequence. CISG Article 74; *see Hadley v. Baxendale, supra.*

An award for lost profits will not compensate Delchi for the expenses in question. Delchi's lost profits are determined by calculating the hypothetical revenues to be derived from unmade sales less the hypothetical variable costs that would have been, but were not, incurred. This figure, however, does not compensate for costs actually incurred that led to no sales. Thus, to award damages for costs actually incurred in no way creates a double recovery and instead furthers the purpose of giving the injured party damages "equal to the loss." CISG Article 74.

The only remaining inquiries, therefore, are whether the expenses were reasonably foreseeable and legitimate incidental or consequential damages. The expenses incurred by Delchi for shipping, customs, and related matters for the two returned shipments of Rotorex compressors, including storage expenses for the second shipment at Genoa, were clearly foreseeable and recoverable incidental expenses. These are up-front expenses that had to be paid to get the goods to the manufacturing plant for inspection and were thus incurred largely before the nonconformities were detected. To deny reimbursement to Delchi for these incidental damages would effectively cut into the lost profits award. The same is true of unreimbursed tooling expenses and the cost of the useless insulation and tubing materials. These are legitimate consequential damages that in no way duplicate lost profits damages.

The labor expense incurred as a result of the production line shutdown of May 16-19, 1988, is also a reasonably foreseeable result of delivering nonconforming compressors for installation in air conditioners. However, Rotorex argues that the labor costs in question were fixed costs that would have been incurred whether or not there was a breach. The district court labeled the labor costs "fixed costs," but did not explore whether Delchi would have paid these wages regardless of how much it produced. Variable costs are generally those costs that "fluctuate with a firm's output," and typically include labor (but not management) costs. *Northeastern Tel. Co. v. AT&T,* 651 F.2d 76, 86 (2d Cir. 1981). Whether Delchi's labor costs during this four-day period are variable or fixed costs is in large measure a fact question that we cannot answer because we lack factual findings by the district court. We therefore remand to the district court on this issue.

The district court also denied an award for the modification of electrical panels for use with substitute Sanyo compressors. It denied damages on the ground that Delchi failed to show that the modifications were not part of the regular cost of production of units with Sanyo compressors and were therefore attributable to Rotorex's breach. This appears to have been a credibility determination that was within the court's authority to make. We therefore affirm on the ground that this finding is not clearly erroneous.

Finally, Delchi cross-appeals from the denial of its claimed 4,000 additional lost sales in Italy. The district court held that Delchi did not prove these orders with sufficient certainty. The trial court was in the best position to evaluate the testimony of the Italian sales agents who stated that they would have ordered more Arieles if they had been available. It found the agents' claims to be too speculative, and this conclusion is not clearly erroneous.

## NOTES AND QUESTIONS

1. Note the court's language that, "In the absence of a specific provision in the CISG for calculating lost profits, the district court was correct to use the standard formula employed by most American courts and to deduct only variable costs from sales revenue to arrive at a figure for lost profits." The court also analogizes Article 74 to UCC section 2-715, and the *Hadley v. Baxendale* rule limiting consequential damages to those that can be shown that were foreseeable as a probable consequence of breach at the time the contract was formed. Is the court's use of U.S. law in interpreting the CISG proper? Does Article 74 provide the same rule as UCC section 2-715 or *Hadley v. Baxendale*? See CISG Article 7 and Kritzer, *Editorial Remarks—Delchi Carrier S.p.A. v. Rotorex Corp., www.cisg.law.pace.edu/cisg/wais/db/editorial/951206u1editorial.html* (accessed

Oct. 2011). See also Eiselen, *Remarks on the Manner in which the UNIDROIT Principles of International Commercial Contracts May Be Used to Interpret or Supplement Article 74 of the CISG, www.cisg.law.pace.edu/cisg/principles/uni74.html* (accessed Oct. 2011).

***Problem 7-10.*** If Delchi had wanted to, could it have compelled Rotorex to provide substitute goods that were in conformity with the contract, or to repair the goods that were delivered to make them conform? Please keep in mind that the case was litigated in the United States. See CISG Articles 28 and 46.

***Problem 7-11.*** If Delchi bought goods in substitution of the goods it had sought to purchase from Rotorex, could it have recovered the difference between what it paid for those goods and its contract price with Rotorex in addition to the lost profits it was awarded in the case? CISG Article 75. If Delchi did not buy substitute goods, what, if anything, could it recover in addition to its lost profits? CISG Article 76. Could it be argued that failure to purchase substitute goods should limit Delchi's lost profit recovery? See CISG Article 77.

***Problem 7-12.*** Buyer purchases packaging machines for $10,000. When the machines arrive, they do not package at anything near the speed that was promised—the breach is fundamental. Buyer noticed the problem shortly after the machines arrived, and notified Seller. While Seller was working with Buyer to try to get the machines to operate properly, Buyer continued to use them because it would have been more costly to shut down Buyer's production line. Buyer's use continued for several months and, during that time, the machines showed normal wear and tear from use. They had depreciated significantly in value. Finally, when it was clear that Seller could not make the machines conform to contract specifications, Buyer decided that it would like to avoid the contract. Is it possible for it to do so? CISG Articles 82 and 84. Can Buyer recover damages, and how would they be calculated? CISG Articles 74 and 83. Compare to UCC §2-608(2) and *McCullough v. Bill Swad Chrysler-Plymouth, Inc.*, 5 Ohio St. 3d 181, 449 N.E.2d 1289 (1983), *supra*.

***Problem 7-13.*** Assume that the contract price for goods is $100 per unit. When the goods are delivered to the buyer, it turns out that they do not conform to the contract. Assume that it would cost $10 per unit to make the goods conform to the contract. In the meantime, the market price for these goods (assuming they conformed to the contract) has dropped to $80 per unit, so that the value of the goods as defective at the time of delivery is $70 per unit. The CISG contains a provision, Article 50, that permits the buyer to reduce the price by a fraction, the numerator of which is the value of the goods at the time of the delivery and the denominator of which is the value the goods would have had at that time if they had been as warranted. Article 50 comes from civil law systems, and it may be used even if the buyer has already paid the complete price, in which case the buyer may sue for a partial refund. If the buyer decides to retain the goods, should the buyer opt to reduce the price under CISG Article 50 or proceed under CISG Article 74? Does it make sense to permit the buyer to reduce the price in situations such as this one? See Gillette & Walt, *Sales Law—Domestic and International* 361-365 (rev. ed.). If the buyer opts to proceed under Article 50, could the buyer also recover lost profits resulting from the defective goods' malfunction? See CISG Article 45(2).

## C. THE STATUTE OF LIMITATIONS

The statute of limitations for breaches of contracts covered by UCC Article 2 is four years after the cause of action has accrued. UCC §2-725.

For international sales, UNCITRAL has promulgated the Convention on the Limitation Period in the International Sale of Goods (CLPISG), which also provides a four-year period and which considers similar issues to the UCC regarding the time that the cause of action has accrued.[3] For example, generally the cause of action accrues at the time the breach occurs, which in cases nvolving nonconforming goods is when the goods are handed over to the buyer.[4] If, however, the seller warranties that the goods will perform for a specified period of time, the breach occurs at the earlier of (i) the buyer's notification to the seller of the nonconformity, or (ii) when the specified period of time for performance expires.[5]

Under choice-of-law principles, ordinarily the forum state will apply its own statute of limitations, although it may apply the shorter statute of limitations of a jurisdiction that had a closer relationship to the transaction and the parties. *Restatement (Second) of Conflict of Laws* §142. Thus, if an international sale of goods case is litigated in a U.S. state that has adopted the UCC, the UCC rule or the shorter statute of limitations of the jurisdiction more closely related to the transaction will apply unless the other nation involved has also acceded to the CLPISG. As is the case with the CISG, the United States has declared that its citizens will be bound to the CLPISG only if the nation of the other party involved in the transaction has also acceded to it.

In these materials, we will focus on the UCC statute of limitations. On the question of when the cause of action accrues, the UCC distinguishes between cases in which the warranty given does or does not explicitly extend to future performance, as discussed in the next case.

### WESTERN RECREATIONAL VEHICLES v. SWIFT ADHESIVES

United States Court of Appeals, Ninth Circuit

23 F.3d 1547 (1994)

3. The CLPISG was promulgated in 1974 and amended in 1980 to make it conform to the CISG. The CLPISG, as amended in 1980, has been acceded to by 21 nations, including the United States. Some of the nations that adopted the 1974 CLPISG have not adopted the 1980 amendments. For a complete listing, see *www.uncitral.org/uncitral/en/uncitral_texts/sale_goods/1974Convention_status .html* (accessed Oct. 2011).
4. CLPISG Article 10.
5. CLPISG Article 11.

I.

Western Recreational Vehicles, Inc., manufactures travel trailers, truck campers, and fifth-wheel trailers ("RVs"), the production of which requires bonding exterior sidewalls to interior RV components. In 1979, Western began to use a roll-coater lamination process, through which it could bond sidewalls with adhesive instead of staples. At that time, Western asked Swift Adhesives, Inc., to recommend a glue for the lamination process. After testing various products with the roll-coater machinery and aluminum sidewalls, Swift advised Western to use Adhesive #47344 ("Adhesive"). Western agreed and soon became a regular customer, using Adhesive on thousands of RVs over the next eight years. Ultimately, the product worked quite well, producing a minuscule .5 percent rate of exterior-skin delamination on aluminum-sided vehicles.

In 1984, Western decided to produce RVs with reinforced fiberglass ("Filon") instead of aluminum sidewalls. Western asked Swift to recommend a glue that would be compatible with the new material and, after conducting tests on Filon samples, Swift advised the RV manufacturer that Adhesive would work satisfactorily on the fiberglass. Relying on this advice, Western commenced production of Filon-sided RVs laminated with Adhesive.

Within a year and a half, Western began to receive customer complaints regarding delamination of Filon siding. Upon inspection of the damaged RVs, Western discovered that the glue line was discolored and had lost tack, particularly in panels exposed to natural elements. From this inspection, Western concluded that Adhesive had caused the delamination problems.[1] In total, Western has had, or will have, to repair more than 20 percent of the Filon-sided RVs that it laminated with Adhesive.

As a result, Western filed suit in state court against Swift for breach of express and implied warranties. Swift removed the action to federal court, defending primarily on the grounds that the statute of limitations had run and that the sales invoices and product data sheets disclaimed all warranties. After a bench trial, the district court found that, because fiberglass contracted and expanded more than aluminum, Adhesive did not bond properly with Filon and proximately caused the delamination problems. The court further determined that Swift had assured Western that, "You can go ahead and use [Adhesive] just like you have on the aluminum," and concluded that Western was protected by an express warranty that extended to future performance, thereby tolling the statute of limitations. Finally, the court held Swift's disclaimers invalid and awarded Western more than $3 million in damages.

Swift filed a timely appeal, arguing that the statute of limitations bars Western's claims, that the disclaimers are valid, that the district court erred by admitting certain evidence at trial, and that the alleged breach of warranty did not proximately cause Western's damages. Western cross-appealed, contending that if the statute of limitations does apply, the district court erred by not

1. Eventually, Western had to dedicate a repair department, with as many as ten technicians, exclusively for repairing (free of charge) the delamination problems. In total, Western has had, or will have, to repair more than 20 percent of the Filon-sided RVs that it laminated with Adhesive.

requiring Swift to demonstrate how much, if any, of the lost-profit damages are attributable to the limitations period.[6]

### II.

We first address the related statute of limitations and damages issues. The transactions between Swift and Western constituted a sale of goods sufficient to trigger application of Washington's version of the Uniform Commercial Code. As a result, UCC section 2-725's four-year statute of limitations applies to Western's action:

> (1) An action for breach of any contract for sale must be commenced within four years after the cause of action has accrued. . . .
> (2) A cause of action accrues when the breach occurs, regardless of the aggrieved party's lack of knowledge of the breach. *A breach of warranty occurs when tender of delivery is made, except that where a warranty explicitly extends to future performance of the goods and discovery must await the time of such performance the cause of action accrues when the breach is or should have been discovered.*

*Id.* §2-725 (emphasis added). Western discovered the Filon problems in 1987 and filed suit against Swift on January 17, 1990. As a result, section 2-725 bars all claims arising from Adhesive delivered prior to January 17, 1986, unless Swift made a warranty of future performance within the meaning of the statute, in which case all of Western's claims survive.

The district court held that Swift had in fact warranted the future performance of Adhesive. In so holding, the court refused to apply the majority rule requiring future performance warranties to refer *explicitly* to specific temporal periods:

> This Court doesn't read or feel the need to read "explicit" to require a temporal fix of months or years. The word means to the Court the clear and unequivocal understanding by the parties—and it seems to the Court that all of the attendant circumstances which are repleat [sic] in the record and which this Court has alluded to on a number of occasions—are such that without a word being said, just a silent thumbs-up from Swift—would have been sufficient—sufficiently clear and unequivocal to advise [Western] that [it] should go ahead and use this in the future and that it would be all right for future use. . . .
>
> This Court doesn't see certainty as a goal more important in the law than justice. To substitute in this, or any other contract, a requirement of a certain period of months in place of the natural and normal meaning of an explicit reference does, in the view of this Court—and would in this case—foster injustice.

The court also held that, alternatively, Swift had in fact referred to a specific time period by promising that Adhesive would work as well on Filon as on aluminum siding: "The aluminum had been bonded by this glue for five years. It had provided absolutely satisfactory suitability for a period of five years. So

---

6. The only part of the opinion being reproduced here deals with the applicability of the statute of limitations—Ed.

if a warranty of explicit reference to the future requires a fix in time, it seems to this Court that [Western] was given it."

A.

Swift does not challenge the district court's factual finding that it expressly warranted Adhesive to work as well on Filon as on aluminum. Instead, Swift contends the court erred by concluding that the warranty "explicitly extends to future performance" within the meaning of section 2-725.

Washington courts have not yet considered the scope of section 2-725's "future performance" exception. We therefore must predict how the Washington Supreme Court would decide the issue. *E.g., General Motors Corp. v. Doupnik,* 1 F.3d 862, 865 (9th Cir. 1993). The overwhelming majority of out-of-state cases, which provide the best guidance for making such a prediction, interpret the exception very narrowly:

> Most courts have been very harsh in determining whether a warranty explicitly extends to future performance. Emphasizing the word "explicitly," they have ruled that there must be specific reference to a future time in the warranty. As a result of this harsh construction, most express warranties cannot meet the test and no implied warranties can since, by their very nature, they never "explicitly extend to future performance."

*Standard Alliance Indus. v. Black Clawson Co.,* 587 F.2d 813, 820 (6th Cir. 1978), *cert. denied,* 441 U.S. 923, 99 S. Ct. 2032, 60 L. Ed. 2d 396 (1979). Under this majority rule, therefore, courts construe "the term 'explicit' [to mean] that the warranty of future performance must be unambiguous, clearly stated, or distinctly set forth." *R.W. Murray Co. v. Shatterproof Glass Corp.,* 697 F.2d 818, 822 (8th Cir. 1983).

The rationale underlying the rule is fulfillment of statutory purpose. Section 2-725 "serve[s] the important function of providing a point of finality for businesses after which they c[an] destroy their business records without the fear of a subsequent breach of contract for sale or breach of warranty suit arising to haunt them." *Ontario Hydro v. Zallea Sys.,* 569 F. Supp. 1261, 1266 (D. Del. 1983).

> It is clear that a buyer and a seller can freely negotiate to extend liability into the future; that is why specific allowance was made for warranties "explicitly" extending to future performance. In the absence of specific agreement, however, UCC section 725(2), reflecting the drafters' intention to establish a reasonable period of time, four years, beyond which business persons need not worry about stale warranty claims[,] is applicable. This policy consideration underlying section 2-725 makes it acceptable to bar implied warranty claims brought more than a specified number of years after the sale; otherwise merchants could be forever liable for breach of warranty on any goods which they sold. Similarly, an express warranty which makes no reference at all to any future date should not be allowed to extend past the limitations period.

*Standard Alliance,* 587 F.2d at 820 (citations omitted).

Applying the majority rule to cases with facts analogous to this case, several courts have declined to find a warranty of future performance. The Third Circuit, for example, found no future performance warranty in sales literature boasting that, "[o]n the record, [the seller] can cite many asbestos roofs that, today, are still performing satisfactorily after more than forty (40) years of exposure to heat, cold, water, air and even fire." *Jones & Laughlin,* 626 F.2d at 291. According to the court, such representations did not satisfy section 2-725's rigorous inquiry:

> The statements . . . may not reasonably be relied on by [the buyer] as *explicit* extensions of any warranty to cover the future performance of the product, as is required by section 2-725(2). Nor does knowledge by [the seller] of [the buyer]'s expectations, or the possible reliance by [the buyer] on [the seller]'s expertise, transform these representations regarding the performance of existing products, advanced in advertising brochures, into explicit warranties of future performance.

*Id.*

Similarly, in a case particularly on point, the Vermont Supreme Court refused to apply the future performance exception to a warranty promising that the "product 'would last as long as the built-up roofing would last,' that it 'would do as good a job as the roofing material originally specified with the built-up roof of 20 years,' that it performed satisfactorily in other situations, and that it was suitable for Vermont climatic conditions." *South Burlington,* 410 A.2d at 1366. The court held this warranty insufficiently explicit to trigger the exception:

> To the extent that these representations spoke to the future, it cannot be said that they constitute the *explicit* warranty of future performance. . . . [W]here, as here, the words alleged to extend a warranty to future performance are so unclearly stated and are so set forth that there is doubt as to their meaning[,] a court should not infer that more than a warranty of present characteristics, design or condition was intended. . . . [T]he fact that [the buyer] expected a durable and adequate roof, or that it relied on [the seller]'s expertise, [is not] sufficient to raise these representations of present characteristics to explicit warranties of future performance.

*Id.*

Rather than follow the majority rule, the district court relied on *Mittasch v. Seal Lock Burial Vault,* 42 A.D.2d 573, 344 N.Y.S.2d 101 (1973), and *Iowa Mfg. Co. v. Joy Mfg. Co.,* 206 Mont. 26, 669 P.2d 1057 (1983). In *Mittasch,* a New York appellate court held, without analysis, that a promise that a burial vault "will give satisfactory service at all times" constituted an explicit warranty of future performance. *Mittasch,* 42 A.D.2d 573, 344 N.Y.S.2d at 102. In *Iowa Manufacturing,* the Montana Supreme Court concluded, without analysis, that an assurance that an asphalt mixing plant "would meet the state of Montana Air Pollution Standards" satisfied the section 2-725 exception. *Iowa Mfg.,* 669 P.2d at 1059.

The district court relied on these cases, which loosely interpreted section 2-725's "explicitly extends" requirement, because it felt that the majority rule "perpetuates a fraud." This reliance was misplaced. There is no reason to believe that Washington courts would abandon the overwhelming majority rule to prevent a purported "fraud" which is, in reality, the commonplace running of a statute of limitations. "Any harshness [that results from the statute] is directly attributable to the restrictive language of the Code which leaves courts with no alternative but to render a narrow decision." *Poppenheimer,* 658 S.W.2d at 111. Presumably, Washington courts would, like most others, be "reluctant . . . to waive the specific eligibility requirements established by the legislature [in section 2-725] for what, it must be remembered, is an *exception* to the general limitations rule. . . . [I]f there is to be an exception to the . . . exception, it should be up to . . . lawmakers to design it." *Wilson,* 850 F.2d at 5-6.

Particularly in this case, where the only representations were Swift's oral statements that Adhesive would work as well on Filon as on aluminum, "[t]o find that th[e] warranty was covered by section []2-725(2) would require an entirely strained and unrealistic interpretation of the phrase 'future performance of the goods.' Moreover, such a result would also require that we completely ignore the Code drafter's command that the warranty be explicit." *Poppenheimer,* 658 S.W.2d at 111. We therefore hold that Swift did not make an explicit warranty of future performance within the meaning of section 2-725(2) and that, as a result, Western may not recover damages resulting from Adhesive delivered prior to January 17, 1986.

## QUESTION AND PROBLEMS

1. If the adhesive had worked on aluminum for five years and if the seller promised the buyer that it would work just as well on Filon, how is it fair to permit the statute of limitations to run before the veracity of the warranty could be determined?

***Problem 7-14.*** In a contract for the sale of a mobile home, the warranty states that the manufacturer promises to repair or replace any defective parts for 12 months from the date of purchase. The mobile home is sold in 1988. The buyers allegedly discover in 1995 that the roof was defectively manufactured. The buyers file a lawsuit against the seller in 1997. Has the statute of limitations run? Did the seller give the buyer a "warranty" as defined in section 2-313?

***Problem 7-15.*** Buyers purchase paintings purported to be by the famous artist Salvador Dali. The seller provides a certificate indicating that the paintings are "authentic." The seller provides a new certificate to the buyers every year for five years. Seven years after purchasing the painting, buyers discover that the painting was a forgery and sue. Has the UCC statute of limitations run? *See Balog v. Center Art Gallery—Hawaii,* 745 F. Supp. 1556 (D. Hawaii 1990).

***Problem 7-16.*** Buyer purchases a painting from Seller in 2006. In 2011, Buyer discovers that the painting had been stolen and the rightful owner successfully sues to obtain possession. Has the statute of limitations on the warranty of title run on an action between Buyer and Seller? See UCC §2-725(2).

***Problem 7-17.*** Buyer purchases a car from Seller. The car is defective, and Seller makes numerous attempts to fix it. Seller continues to assure Buyer that the problem will be fixed. Finally, when the statute of limitations has expired, Seller refuses to continue to attempt repair. Is Buyer's action against Seller for breach of warranty barred? See Annot., *Promises or Attempts by Seller to Repair Goods as Tolling Statute of Limitations for Breach of Warranty,* 68 A.L.R.3d 1277 (1976).

## Kohl's Department Stores v. Target Stores

United States District Court, E.D. Virginia

290 F. Supp. 2d 674 (2003)

This consolidated action involves claims for damages to the buildings that make up the Chesterfield Crossing Shopping Center ("the Project"), a retail shopping establishment located in Chesterfield County, Virginia. The four buildings that make up the Project have sustained significant structural damage, which began to appear shortly after construction. The owners of three of the four buildings each filed actions against Target Stores, Inc. ("Target"), the developer/owner of the Project, seeking contractual indemnification for the damage to their respective buildings. Target filed a third-party complaint against the site contractor on the same theory. A number of third-party indemnity claims ensued. The parties allege that Xtra Fill, a synthetic fill material consisting principally of fly ash sold by ReUse Technologies, Inc. ("ReUse"), caused this damage. ReUse has moved for partial summary judgment on several of the third-party claims pending against it, asserting that those claims based on negligence theories are time-barred under Virginia Code section 8.01-250, a statute of repose protecting improvers of real property, and that the indemnity claims sounding in warranty are time-barred under Virginia Code section 8.2-725, the statute of limitations contained in the Virginia Uniform Commercial Code ("UCC").[7]

### Statement of Facts

At some point before May 1997, Target and Ukrop's Supermarkets, Inc. ("Ukrop's") purchased land at a site later developed as the Project. In May 1997, Kohl's Department Stores, Inc. ("Kohl's") and Ukrop's, along with Chesterfield Crossing Shopping Center, L.L.C. ("CCSC"), entered into a site development agreement with Target. Under this agreement, Target agreed to convey a portion of its land to CCSC and to perform all of the site development on the Project for CCSC, Kohl's, and Ukrop's.

Target contracted the site development work to the general contracting firm of Williams Company of Orlando, Inc. ("Williams"). Williams, in turn, contracted with various subcontractors; one of which was S.W. Rodgers Co., Inc. ("Rodgers"), which Williams retained to perform various earth-moving services. Rodgers, in turn, purchased the Xtra Fill from ReUse.

After the Project was completed, the buildings owned by Target, Kohl's, Ukrop's, and CCSC began to experience cracks in the floors and walls. All parties but ReUse assert that the damage to the buildings is the result of the expansion of the Xtra Fill. The cause, says ReUse, is not the expansion of the Xtra Fill, but instead is the result of the failure properly to prepare the subsoil on which the Xtra Fill was placed. ReUse contends that this failure caused soil settlement which, in turn, caused the damage to the buildings.

Kohl's filed a complaint against Target (the "Kohl's action"). Upon receipt of this complaint, Target impleaded Williams which then filed a fourth-party

7. Only the part of the opinion relating to the UCC warranty claim is presented here—Ed.

complaint against, inter alia, Rodgers. Rodgers then filed a fifth-party complaint against ReUse seeking indemnity for any sums it was required to pay by virtue of Williams' indemnity action against Rodgers. Rodgers' various indemnity claims against ReUse are grounded in theories of both negligence and breach of warranty.

CCSC filed a complaint against Kohl's (the "CCSC action") which, in turn, filed a third-party complaint against Target, predicated on a contractual indemnity provision. Target filed a third-party complaint against Williams, which, in turn, impleaded Rodgers. Rodgers then filed a sixth-party complaint against ReUse seeking indemnity against all sums that Rodgers was required to pay to Williams. As in the Kohl's action, the Rodgers' indemnity claims are founded in both negligence and breach of warranty theories.

The actions filed by Kohl's, Ukrop's, and CCSC were consolidated. ReUse has moved for summary judgment on Rodgers' allegations that sound, in whole or in part, in tort, relying on Virginia Code section 8.01-250, a statute of repose protecting certain improvers of real property. ReUse also has moved for summary judgment on all of Rodgers' claims that sound, in whole or in part, in warranty, contending that those claims are time-barred by the statute of limitations set forth in the UCC, Virginia Code section 8.2-725. For the reasons that follow, ReUse's motions for summary judgment on Rodgers' negligence-based indemnity claims are granted and its motions for summary judgment on Rodgers' warranty-based indemnity claims are denied.

**Discussion**

ReUse argues that, because Rodgers commenced its action against it more than four years after delivery of the last sale of Xtra Fill to Rodgers, the indemnity claims asserted by Rodgers (several of which, as presented by the parties seeking indemnity, sound in warranty) are barred by the Virginia UCC's statute of limitations applicable to warranty claims. UCC §2-725.

Pointing to Rodgers' response to ReUse's request for admission number 13, ReUse states that it is an undisputed fact that its last delivery of Xtra Fill to Rodgers for use on the Project was in July 1997. It is not disputed that Rodgers' indemnity claims against ReUse were commenced in the fall and winter of 2002, more than four years after July 1997. Hence, ReUse asserts that, because Rodgers' indemnity claims originated as breach of warranty claims, the indemnity claims are time-barred by the statute of limitations contained in the UCC.

Rodgers contends that section 2-725 simply does not apply here because its claim against ReUse is for indemnification and that, therefore, the relevant statute of limitations is Virginia Code section 8.01-249(5), not the statute of limitations contained in the UCC. In pertinent part, section 8.01-249.5 provides that:

> The cause of action in the actions herein listed shall be deemed to accrue as follows:
>
> .....
>
> In actions for contribution or indemnification, when the contributee or the indemnitee has paid or discharged the obligation. A third-party claim permitted

> by subsection A of section 8.01-281 and the Rules of Court may be asserted before such cause of action is deemed to accrue hereunder.

Va. Code Ann. §8.01-249(5). Because its underlying claim is for property damage, Rodgers asserts that a five-year statute of limitations applies, see Va. Code Ann. §8.01-243, and that a proper application of section 8.01-249(5) mandates that this five-year period begins to run on the date that it pays or discharges its obligation to the third parties (i.e., Williams, Kohl's, Target, etc.).

The Supreme Court of Virginia has not decided directly whether the claim of a thirty-party plaintiff who impleads a third party for indemnification based on a warranty theory is time-barred because section 2-725 would bar a direct action by that third-party plaintiff against that third-party defendant. Thus, it is necessary to "predict what course the highest court in the state would take," *Byelick,* 79 F. Supp. 2d at 623, using as guideposts "canons of construction . . . recent pronouncements of general rules or policies by the state's highest court, well considered dicta, and the state's trial court decisions." *Wells,* 186 F.3d at 528. The proper analysis here leads to the prediction that the Supreme Court of Virginia would hold that UCC section 2-725 would not apply to bar Rodgers' claims for indemnification.

At common law, it was well-settled that an action for indemnification did not accrue until the plaintiff suffered an injury; that is, until the plaintiff paid out money to a third party. *See Nationwide Mut. Ins. Co. v. Jewel Tea Co.,* 202 Va. 527, 118 S.E.2d 646, 649 (1961). The General Assembly codified this common law rule when it enacted section 8.01-249(5). ReUse seeks to escape the necessary consequences of section 8.01-249(5) by arguing that, because it was more recently enacted, the UCC controls this issue.

There is a split of authority respecting the interplay between a UCC statute of limitations and the common law (and often statutory) rule that a cause of action for indemnification sounding in warranty does not arise until the indemnitee has paid the obligation. See generally Comment, Paul J. Wilkinson, *An Ind. Run around the U.C.C.: The Use (or Abuse?) of Indemnity,* 20 Pepp. L. Rev. 1407 (1993) (summarizing split of authority). ReUse concedes that the authority in a slight majority of states is inconsistent with its position but it argues that, if presented directly with the issue, the Supreme Court of Virginia would hold that the UCC statute of limitations prevails over section 8.01-249(5) and thus bars Rodgers' claim.

To begin, it is quite clear that, if Rodgers, on its own behalf, had sued ReUse directly for breach of warranty, UCC section 2-725 would have applied. Thus, a direct claim for breach of warranty would be barred unless initiated within four years of delivery of the product sold by ReUse.

However, the Supreme Court of Virginia has held that a third-party plaintiff may maintain a claim in indemnification based on a warranty theory against a third-party defendant where section 2-725 would prevent the original plaintiff from suing the third party directly. In *Gemco-Ware, Inc. v. Rongene Mold & Plastics Corp.,* 234 Va. 54, 360 S.E.2d 342 (1987), a consumer suffered burns when the handle of a teakettle separated from the kettle causing boiling water to spill on her leg. The consumer filed an action against Gemco-Ware, Inc. ("Gemco"), the manufacturer of the kettle, but not against Rongene Mold and Plastics Co. ("Rongene"), which had manufactured the handle. Gemco later filed a third-party motion for judgment seeking contribution and indemnity against Rongene. In response, Rongene filed a demurrer asserting that, because the statute of limitations had expired as to any cause of action that the consumer may have had against Rongene, Gemco could not maintain an action in indemnity or contribution arising from the same suit. *Gemco-Ware, Inc.,* 360 S.E.2d at 343. The Supreme Court of Virginia rejected Rongene's argument and held that Gemco's claim for contribution and indemnification against Rongene was not time-barred even though the statute of limitations had run on the consumer's claim against Rongene. *Id.* at 345.

The precise issue presented here, however, is slightly different than that presented in *Gemco-Ware, Inc.* The issue in this action is whether Rodgers can sue ReUse for indemnification based on warranty theories even though section 2-725 would bar a direct claim for breach of warranty by Rodgers against ReUse. Thus, although the decision in *Gemco-Ware, Inc.* holds that a third-party claimant may maintain an indemnity claim sounding in warranty against a third party in a situation where section 8.2-725 would prevent the original plaintiff from suing the third party, the Supreme Court of Virginia has not decided whether a third-party plaintiff who impleads a third party for indemnification based on a warranty theory is time-barred because section 8.2-725 would bar a direct suit by the third-party plaintiff against that third party.

Nonetheless, this action and *Gemco-Ware, Inc.* share a common underlying circumstance. Both cases involve a party with an underlying claim that would be time-barred under UCC section 2-725. And, there is no reason to believe that the Supreme Court of Virginia would not apply in this action the crux of its decision in *Gemco-Ware, Inc.* that the statute of limitations for indemnification and contribution begins to run upon payment and is not controlled by the statute of limitations applicable to the underlying warranty theory. The right of action to recover indemnification "arises upon discharge of the common obligation and the statute of limitations begins to run at that time." *Gemco-Ware, Inc.,* 360 S.E.2d at 345. In other words, the rationale upon which *Gemco-Ware, Inc.* was decided discloses no reason for not applying the same principles here, notwithstanding the factual difference between this action and *Gemco-Ware, Inc.*

For the foregoing reasons, the motion for partial summary judgment on Rodgers' indemnity claims sounding in warranty are DENIED.

## QUESTION

Is the decision consistent with the policy of finality discussed in *Western Recreational Vehicles*?

## CHAPTER 7 REVIEW PROBLEM

Seller guaranteed Buyer that a piece of equipment it sold to Buyer for use in Buyer's manufacturing process would be defect-free for three years. The purchase price of the equipment was $50,000. Shortly before the end of the three-year period, the equipment became defective, slowing Buyer's manufacturing process. Buyer immediately wrote Seller a letter, complaining that the equipment was not working well. Seller ignored the letter. Buyer attempted to fix the equipment itself, and was able to get the equipment to work for a while until it broke again. Buyer made a couple of additional attempts at repair, which again were successful for short periods of time. Finally, Buyer wrote a letter to Seller attempting to revoke acceptance of the equipment. Seller again ignored the letter. Buyer then purchased substitute equipment that cost $10,000 more than the equipment it had purchased from Seller. Buyer claims that its costs in attempting to repair the equipment were $5,000 and that it lost $20,000 in profits because of the delays in the manufacturing process caused by the defective equipment. Five years after it had purchased the equipment from Seller, Buyer sued, claiming (a) the $50,000 it had paid; (b) the $10,000 extra it had to pay for the substitute equipment; (c) the $5,000 it had paid in trying to repair the equipment; and (d) the $20,000 in lost profits. Will Buyer be successful? Please analyze under both the UCC and the CISG. The relevant UCC sections are 2-507, 2-602, 2-608, 2-711, 2-712, 2-714, 2-715 and 2-725. The relevant CISG Articles are 25, 26, 39, 45, 74 and 75.

CHAPTER 8

# SELLER'S REMEDIES

## A. SELLER'S REMEDIES UNDER THE UCC

As is the case with buyer's remedies, the policy of the UCC according to section 1-305 is to put the injured party in the position that it would have been in if the contract had been performed. It is not the goal of the UCC to punish breaching parties beyond what it takes to make the injured party whole. The provisions governing seller's remedies to a great extent mirror those governing buyer's remedies, distinguishing cases in which the goods have not been delivered from those in which the goods have been delivered and accepted.

### 1. GOODS NOT DELIVERED DUE TO BUYER'S BREACH AND GOODS WRONGFULLY REJECTED

#### (a) Right to Refuse Delivery

Section 2-703 provides, among other options, that if the buyer fails to make a payment when due or wrongfully rejects or revokes acceptance of goods, the seller may withhold delivery of goods, stop delivery by a carrier or other bailee pursuant to section 2-705, resell the goods and recover the difference between the contract price and the resale price, or recover damages under a contract/market formula similar to the one previously discussed under buyer's remedies. The seller may also refuse delivery except for cash if the seller discovers that the buyer is insolvent. UCC Section 2-702(1).

GOLDSTEIN V. STAINLESS PROCESSING CO.

United States Court of Appeals, Seventh Circuit

465 F.2d 392 (1972)

This is an appeal from a judgment entered following the direction of a verdict for the defendant (Stainless) in a diversity action in which the plaintiff (Goldstein) sought to recover damages arising out of an alleged breach of contract for the delivery of nickel cathodes.

The parties were dealers in metals. Neither had dealt with the other prior to the transaction in question. The facts support the premise that neither reposed any confidence in the other.

As a result of telephonic conversations, Goldstein agreed to buy and Stainless agreed to sell 20,000 pounds of nickel cathodes at a price of $4.60 per pound, FOB Chicago. During the conversations, Stainless had asked that some money be sent on account, which request Goldstein had declined. Variations on the request were proposed with equally negative responses. Finally, Stainless suggested that Goldstein send a $20,000 check that Stainless would hold in escrow.

Goldstein's version of the conversation, which we accept for the purposes of considering the propriety of directing a verdict, is that "he would do that provided that they would hold the check until the time he would come to Chicago to verify the material, then they would return the check to Goldstein at the time of delivery, and he would pay the entire amount due in full by a single certified check."

Stainless sent its confirmation of sale, dated August 27, 1969, which specified as "Terms" the following: "$20,000.00 deposit. Balance by certified check at time of pickup." No reference was made to any escrow arrangement.

On August 28, 1969, Goldstein, not yet having received the confirmation, sent a letter to Stainless confirming the telephone conversation of the previous day by outlining the terms and provisions of the oral agreement. The letter concluded as follows:

> We are enclosing our check in the amount of $20,000.00 as a good faith deposit. This check is to be held in escrow. When we get to Chicago and the entire shipment is weighed and verified, we will issue one check to cover the full amount. Please sign and return the enclosed copy of this letter for our files.

Stainless signed and returned to Goldstein a copy of this letter about September 5, 1969. However, prior to the 5th the following significant incidents occurred. On the same day that Goldstein mailed the "good faith deposit" check, he went to his bank and stopped payment on it. This apparently had no connection with an insufficiency of funds as his bank balance showed substantially more than the amount of the check. Further, Stainless, unaware of the stop-payment order, upon receipt of the check went to its bank and deposited the "in escrow" check in its account.

On September 2, 1969, Goldstein wrote Stainless in part as follows:

> We acknowledge receipt of your sales Contract No. 2633 and note that it varies slightly from our understanding as stated in our contract letter of August 28, 1969; namely, you mentioned on the telephone that you would like to have a $20,000.00 check to be held in escrow. We have sent you this check. (Underlining emphasis in original.)

The check traveled in banking channels without incident until its confrontation with the stop-payment order. Upon its arrival back at its point of embarkation, or shortly thereafter, a telegram was dispatched by Stainless to Goldstein as follows:

THIS IS TO ADVISE THAT WE ARE CANCELING HEREWITH OUR SALES ORDER 1633 FOR 10,000 DEPOSIT AND FAILURE TO ACKNOWLEDGE OUR SALES CONFIRMATION. YOUR CHECK WILL BE RETURNED PROMPTLY.

The telegram followed by two days another Goldstein letter of September 10 to Stainless, which referred to the acceptance of the September 2 (escrow) amendment and to a conversation of the 10th extending delivery date from September 15 to the 25th. In the correspondence to the time of this letter, Goldstein had refrained from mentioning that he had stopped payment and Stainless likewise failed to mention that it had attempted to reduce the check to cash.

Stainless in subsequent correspondence declined to elaborate on its telegram as to its reasons for cancellation.

The only remaining fact of significance, and which probably is not of surprise status, is that the market price of nickel cathodes had risen by September 16 from $4.60 to $5.75 per pound. Goldstein purchased the metal elsewhere and sought to recover the resultant $23,000 additional sum he was required to pay.

At the conclusion of the plaintiff's evidence, the motion for directed verdict was sustained and this appeal followed.

While some fringe issues are asserted, the basic issue is correctly phrased by Goldstein, "[i]f Goldstein's stop-payment order was a material breach sufficient to justify cancellation of the contract, then the verdict in the trial court should be sustained."

In our opinion, the question posed may be answered quite simply. Stainless bargained for and had every right to expect that it would receive a valid check. The check at the time of receipt was not valid as it was subject to a stop-payment order. Stainless did not get what it bargained for and had a right to expect. It, therefore, under the Uniform Commercial Code as adopted in Illinois, had the right to cancel the contract. UCC §§2-610, 2-703.

The fact that it might well not have chosen to do so if the price of the metal had gone down instead of up is immaterial.

What is material is that if the price had gone down, the holding of a valid check would have been salutary in its ability to aid Stainless in any attempt it might make to hold Goldstein to his bargain.

Nor do we attach significance to the fact that Stainless may have had other remedies under the Uniform Commercial Code. The remedy chosen was cancellation.

We do not condone the action of Stainless in attempting to cash the check, but we do not find that Goldstein is in a position in the present action for breach of contract to assert lack of clean hands. Further, while Stainless did violate what appears to be its clear obligation to continue to hold the check, we do note that if the check had cleared, Goldstein would certainly have been in a position to hold Stainless to its contract or in the alternative to recover his damages.

Affirmed.

## NOTE, QUESTIONS, AND PROBLEM

The UCC rejects the doctrine of election of remedies. UCC §2-703, Comment 1. This means that the seller could terminate the contract and also seek damages for breach. In the foregoing case, there were no damages since the market price of the goods had increased in the meantime. Official Comment 1 to section 2-703 does suggest that pursuit of one remedy by a seller may in some situations preclude pursuit of another. When might that be the case? Keep in mind the UCC policy of giving the injured party sufficient recovery to place that person in the position that it would have been if the contract had been performed, without otherwise penalizing the breaching party. In the foregoing case, is it unduly punitive to permit the seller to terminate the contract when the buyer failed to give the seller a good check since the buyer was not supposed to deposit the check anyway? Does the contract even require that the buyer give the seller a good check? Why shouldn't the buyer be given an opportunity to cure?

***Problem 8-1.*** Hiross Industries manufactured truck bodies and toolboxes, which it sold to Morrison Industries. Morrison in turn resold the goods to its customers. Morrison would periodically place orders with Hiross and would then either instruct Hiross to ship the goods directly to Morrison's customer or to hold the goods for future disposition. The parties did business on credit, and approximately $190,000 was owed by Morrison to Hiross. Hiross had in its possession $100,000 worth of completed truck bodies that were being held for shipment to Morrison's customers. Assume that Morrison is insolvent. UCC §1-201(b)(23). Can Hiross refuse to deliver the goods that it is holding for Morrison? UCC §2-702(1). Can Hiross stop delivery of any goods that it has shipped by carrier to one of Morrison's customers? UCC §2-705, Official Comment 2. See *In re Morrison Industries*, 175 B.R. 5 (W.D.N.Y. 1994).

### (b) Seller's Resale Remedy

In cases in which the seller has justifiably canceled the contract before delivery due to breach by the buyer, the seller is allowed to identify goods to the contract that have not been identified if they are in the seller's possession or control, and may also treat unfinished goods as the subject of resale if the goods "have demonstrably been intended for the particular contract." UCC §2-704(1). In addition, the seller may decide to either scrap or finish unfinished goods "in the exercise of reasonable commercial judgment for the purposes of avoiding loss and effective realization." UCC §2-704(2). Official Comment 1 to section 2-704 states that "the seller is given express power to complete manufacture or procurement of goods for the contract unless the exercise of reasonable commercial judgment as to the facts as they appear at the time he learns of the breach makes it clear that such action will result in a material increase in damages." The comment goes on to say that the burden is on the breaching buyer to show that the seller acted unreasonably. Section 2-704 and its comment codify the common law requirement that the injured party take reasonable steps to mitigate damages, with the burden being placed on the breaching party to show failure to mitigate.

In the event that the seller properly completes and identifies the goods for resale, and in cases in which the buyer has breached by improperly rejecting the goods or revoking acceptance, the seller may resell them and hold the buyer responsible for the difference between the contract price and the resale price. UCC §§2-703, 2-706. In order to take advantage of this remedy, the seller must normally notify the breaching buyer prior to the resale, must act in good faith, and must conduct the resale in a commercially reasonable manner.

## Smith v. Paoli Popcorn Co.

Supreme Court of Nebraska

260 Neb. 460, 618 N.W.2d 452 (2000)

In March 1994, Smith and Paoli entered into a contract in which Paoli agreed to purchase popcorn grown by Smith during the 1994 growing season for ten cents per pound. Smith harvested the popcorn in late September or early October 1994. During the harvest, it began to mist, and Smith's son Steve Smith noticed that smut[1] had attached to one of the loads of popcorn.

Tom Harmon, an agent of Paoli's, visited the grain bins to which the popcorn was delivered on the day of the harvest. Harmon took two samples of the popcorn, one about a foot below the surface of the bin and the second at a greater depth. In the process of taking those samples, Harmon noticed smut attached to the kernels. It was Harmon's belief that the smut could not be cleaned off and that, therefore, the popcorn would be difficult to market. While at the site, Harmon had a discussion with Rob Smith, another of Smith's sons. Although Harmon expressed concerns with the quality of the popcorn, he did not reject the popcorn at that time. Instead, Harmon conveyed that he intended to try to market the popcorn as best he could.

From the time the popcorn was harvested until early April 1995, the parties had several discussions regarding its marketability. On April 4, 1995, Harmon called Smith and rejected the popcorn. Two days later, the rejection was formalized by a letter from Paoli to Smith.

After Smith received the letter of rejection, he and Steve Smith attempted to resell the popcorn. Steve Smith testified that he contacted several popcorn companies that were likely to be in the market for popcorn. If a company showed any interest at all, Steve Smith sent them a sample of the popcorn and requested a bid. He sent these companies the worst part of the popcorn because "[t]hey weren't interested in seeing what the best [was], they wanted to know what the worst was." When the samples were sent, Steve Smith also informed the companies that most of the popcorn was fine.

Bids of five cents per pound were obtained from three separate companies. These five-cent bids were communicated to Paoli, which responded with a bid of 5.25 cents per pound. Smith relayed Paoli's 5.25-cent offer to the three companies, but only Colorado Cereal, Inc., showed further interest by offering six cents per pound. This offer was communicated to Paoli, which offered 6.25 cents per pound. Smith agreed to accept this offer if he could retain the right to collect the difference between the contract price of ten cents per pound and the current bid of 6.25 cents and if Paoli would pay the balance by certified

1. Dirt or fungus—Ed.

check. Paoli refused, and in May 1995, Smith sold the popcorn to Colorado Cereal for six cents per pound.

Smith sued Paoli for wrongful rejection of the popcorn, seeking damages for the reduced price of the popcorn, storage fees, and interest.

In the first trial, the court granted summary judgment for Smith on the issue of liability, finding that Paoli had ineffectively rejected the goods. The court subsequently granted a directed verdict in the amount of $28,542.37. We reversed the judgment and remanded the cause for further proceedings, finding that a genuine issue of material fact as to whether Paoli rejected the goods within a reasonable time precluded summary judgment.

On remand, the trial court granted Smith's motion for directed verdict on the issue of the commercial reasonableness of the resale. The jury subsequently returned a verdict in favor of Smith in the amount of $31,175.19, and Paoli appeals.

**Analysis**

On appeal, Paoli first argues that the trial court erred in directing a verdict that Smith resold the popcorn in a commercially reasonable manner. A trial court should direct a verdict as a matter of law only when the facts are conceded, undisputed, or such that reasonable minds can draw but one conclusion therefrom.

Paoli contends that Smith did not act in a commercially reasonable manner because Smith (1) sent samples of the "worst part" of the popcorn to potential buyers, (2) denied Paoli an independent sampling of the popcorn after Paoli's rejection, (3) refused Paoli's offer of 6.25 cents per pound, (4) sold the popcorn for six cents per pound, and (5) asked one of the potential buyers for a bid for "low-quality-type popcorn" in order to give Smith leverage in dealing with Paoli.

The phrase "commercially reasonable" is not specifically defined in UCC section 2-706. Assuming a buyer has wrongfully rejected goods, section 2-706 provides that where resale is made in good faith and in a commercially reasonable manner, the seller may recover the difference between the resale price and the contract price together with any incidental damages allowed. Section 2-706(2) requires that every aspect of the sale, including the method, manner, time, place, and terms, must be commercially reasonable.

We conclude that the trial court did not err when it determined as a matter of law that Smith resold the popcorn in a commercially reasonable manner.

With regard to the method and manner used by Smith to resell the popcorn, Harmon stated that if he were a farmer selling popcorn, he would call different popcorn companies to see if they were bidding. If they were, he would provide samples and would then get bids and negotiate for the best price. This method was similar to the one used by Smith in negotiating the sale to Colorado Cereal. Harmon also testified that short of directly marketing the popcorn, there was nothing else a farmer could do to sell the product.

With regard to the price ultimately obtained by Smith, Bernard Blach, an agent for Colorado Cereal, testified that six cents per pound was a fair value for Smith's popcorn and that the price paid to Smith ended up being more than Colorado Cereal had paid other producers for popcorn in the same time period.

He also testified that the transaction between Smith and Colorado Cereal was made in good faith and in a commercially reasonable manner. Furthermore, Dennis Kunnemann, who had been involved in selling and processing popcorn in the Imperial, Nebraska, area for 13 to 14 years, stated that the market price for popcorn in the area during the summer of 1995 was six to seven cents per pound. Even Paoli's agent, Harmon, testified that if there had been a market for less than premium popcorn in the fall of 1994 through the winter of 1995, the price would have been three to four cents per pound. In addition, a letter from the president of Paoli to Smith dated April 18, 1995, indicated that eight cents per pound was substantially more than the market price.

Paoli also argues that Steve Smith did not act in a commercially reasonable manner by sending potential buyers samples of the "worst part" of the popcorn. Steve Smith testified that this was the part of the crop the companies wanted to see. He also told the companies that the sample reflected one truckload placed on the top of the bin and that the rest of the popcorn was fine.

Paoli further contends that Smith's asking for a bid for "low-quality-type popcorn" was not commercially reasonable. It is undisputed that this bid was conveyed to Paoli, which then submitted another bid.

Giving every reasonable inference to Paoli, we conclude as a matter of law that Smith's actions in reselling the popcorn were commercially reasonable and that the trial court did not err in directing a verdict on this issue.

## QUESTION AND PROBLEM

1. Are questions of "commercial reasonableness" of a resale more appropriately left for the judge or for the jury?

***Problem 8-2.*** Apex Oil Company contracted to sell heating oil to The Belcher Company. When the oil was delivered by ship on February 9, 1982, Belcher improperly rejected it, wrongfully claiming that it had improper sulfur content. Apex then took the rejected oil and delivered it to another customer that it already had under contract. Apex and Belcher negotiated for several weeks regarding shipment of substitute oil. In early March, The Belcher Company repudiated its obligation to accept delivery. Apex notified Belcher that if it would not accept delivery, Apex would identify oil to the contract and sell it to a third party and hold Belcher responsible for the difference between what Belcher had agreed to pay and what the third party paid. When Belcher refused to take delivery, Apex sold in April the quantity of oil due to be purchased by Belcher for 13.45 cents per gallon less than the Apex/Belcher contract price. The price the third party, Gill & Duffus Co., agreed to pay was the market price in April. At the time that the oil was delivered to Belcher in February, the difference between the contract price and the market price was approximately two cents per gallon; prices had been falling during the entire period. In addition, during the period between February 9 and April, Apex had sold oil to other buyers at prices between what Belcher had agreed to pay and what Gill & Duffus paid for the April delivery. Can Apex sue Belcher under UCC section 2-706 for the difference between the contract price and the price it obtained on the sale to Gill & Duffus? Is it necessary that the exact same oil be resold in order to use section 2-706? Did the sale to Gill & Duffus occur sufficiently proximate to the breach? *See Apex Oil Co. v. The Belcher Co.*, 855 F.2d 997 (2d Cir. 1988).

### (c) Seller's Contract/Market Formula

Similar to the buyer's rights under UCC section 2-713 when the buyer does not cover, the seller is allowed to obtain the difference between the market price and the contract price for goods that the buyer wrongfully refuses to accept. UCC §2-708(1). The next case deals with how the market price is determined.

### B & R Textile Corporation v. Paul Rothman Industries Ltd.

New York County Civil Court

101 Misc. 2d 98, 420 N.Y.S.2d 609 (1979)

Plaintiff originally brought this action to recover damages sustained when defendant failed to accept approximately 36,000 yards of fabric out of a total shipment of 74,077 yards.

In its decision herein the court awarded damages to the plaintiff in the sum of $4,584.50, and applied the measure of damages set forth in UCC section 2-708(1).

The major thrust of defendant's argument is that the plaintiff did not give the defendant notice of its intention to resell the repudiated goods as required by UCC section 2-706 (where the resale is made privately and not by public auction) and therefore the plaintiff was not entitled to recover the difference between the contract price and the resale price.

The defendant apparently based its argument on the erroneous assumption that, in the course of the trial, plaintiff did not prove market price but instead relied solely on the resale price of $.925 per yard.

The seller has the burden of proof with respect to market price or market value. A seller cannot avail itself of the benefit of section 2-708 when it has not presented evidence of market price or market value.

While market value may usually be proved by a resale of the goods where the seller has taken proper measures to secure as fair and reasonable a sale as possible, the price realized on resale is not necessarily conclusive.

During the trial of this action, not only was there testimony to the effect that in an effort to mitigate damages, plaintiff sold the bulk of the remaining goods to Dorfler Turk Textiles, Inc. at a price of $.925 per yard, but there was further evidence adduced that a portion of the rejected goods were sold to others at similar prices. There was sufficient evidence adduced to permit the court to find that the market value of the unaccepted goods was $.925 per yard.

Having determined that the resale of the goods accurately reflected the market price since there was an available market for the goods, the court's application of section 2-708(1) as the measure of damages was correct.

Once the court determined that $.925 per yard was the market value and applied that sum as the measure of damages pursuant to section 2-708, it became of no consequence that the plaintiff did not give the defendant notice of the resale as required by section 2-706.

Accordingly, defendant's motion to set aside the judgment herein is denied.

## QUESTION AND PROBLEM

1. UCC sections 2-723 and 2-724 deal with the question of proof of market price. Does the court's decision give proper weight to the requirement that the seller's resale be made in good faith and in a commercially reasonable manner?

***Problem 8-3.*** In a contract for the sale of oil at $1 per gallon, Buyer wrongfully repudiates its obligation to take delivery. At the time and place of tender, the market price of the oil is $0.70 per gallon. Seller sells the oil, without giving notice to Buyer, for $0.80 per gallon. Should Seller's damages be calculated under UCC section 2-706 or section 2-708(1)? See UCC §2-703, Official Comment 1. Compare UCC §2-711 and §2-713, Official Comment 5.

### (d) Lost Profits

Both UCC sections 2-706 and 2-708(1) assume that a seller has a finished good that can be resold. Application of those sections will make the seller whole if the contract of sale contemplates sale of an existing good that can be resold if the buyer breaches the contract. For example, if I contract to sell my television set to someone, and that person breaches the contract, I can sell the television to somebody else. Section 2-706 will make me whole in awarding me the difference between the contract price and the resale price. If I do not choose to follow the procedures of 2-706, section 2-708(1) will give me the hypothetical resale remedy, assuming that I resold the television for the prevailing market price.

Sections 2-706 and 2-708(1) arguably do not work well if the seller loses a sale as a result of the breach or if the seller does not have an existing, completed good to resell when the buyer breaches. For example, in the earlier hypothetical I can be made whole when I resell my television by awarding me the difference between the contract price and the resale price. But if a buyer breaches a contract with a television store, the store is arguably not made whole by awarding the difference between the contract price and the price the store receives when it sells the television to another buyer because the store will argue that it could have made two sales rather than one. It may have sufficient inventory to permit a sale both to the breaching buyer and to the second buyer. It is in situations such as this, the "lost volume" situation, where section 2-708(2) may have application. Other injured sellers who might argue for damages under section 2-708(2) include the manufacturer who has not completed manufacture at the time the buyer repudiates the contract and the middleperson who has not as yet procured the goods that are the subject matter of the contract at the time of repudiation. The reason those sellers might not be made whole under sections 2-706 and 2-708(1) is that they do not have a completed good to resell at the time of repudiation. They can be made whole by giving them the profit that they would have made if the breaching buyer had performed.

Sometimes it may not be clear that a seller has lost a sale. Would the seller have been in position to make the second sale if the buyer had not breached? It may not always be clear that sufficient inventory exists or that a second sale would have been profitable. The reason a second sale might not be profitable is that the costs involved in a second sale might be higher than the proceeds received from the sale. For example, assume that a manufacturer is operating at capacity in producing the products that it sells. If it were to manufacture one more product, it would need to hire additional employees or move into a larger plant. The cost of the additional employees or the additional rent might far exceed the proceeds received from one additional sale, so the manufacturer would choose not to make the second sale. It can thus be a difficult factual question sometimes as to (a) whether a seller would have made the second sale, and (b) what profits would have been obtained from such a sale. The next case and problem explore these issues.

## Lake Erie Boat Sales, Inc. v. Johnson

Ohio Court of Appeals

11 Ohio App. 3d 55, 463 N.E.2d 70 (1983)

Appellant Lake Erie Boat Sales, Inc., initiated an action in the Municipal Court of Cleveland, seeking damages alleged to be due from James E. Johnson et al., the appellees herein, for breach of a purchase sales agreement. This action proceeded to trial and judgment was rendered in favor of the appellees.

On July 11, 1981, appellees entered into a written sales contract with appellant for the purchase of a 1981 Mark Twain boat. The purchase price, under the terms of this agreement, was $15,233. Appellees provided a $200 down payment upon execution of this contract of sale.

Thereafter, on July 13, 1981, appellees sought a repudiation of the purchase agreement explaining that the necessity for such a renunciation was due to appellee James Johnson's heart problems.

At some point subsequent to appellees' July 13, 1981, renunciation of the purchase contract, the Mark Twain boat was sold to a third party for the same purchase price as that agreed to by appellees.

Upon trial of this matter before the lower court, appellant was found to have failed to present evidence establishing its position as a volume seller, thereby entitling appellant to lost profit damages.

The concept of lost profits, as it applies to volume sellers, has been statutorily codified in Ohio, pursuant to UCC section 2-708(2).

Section 2-708(2) applies principally in two situations: (1) when a volume seller has unlimited access to goods and easily available substitute buyers; and (2) when a manufacturer produces goods to order for a breaching buyer, and substitute buyers are unlikely to be found.

Under section 2-708(1), the measure of damages is the difference between the unpaid contract price and the market price. In applying that section to the case sub judice, because the boat and equipment were sold to a third party for the same amount as that contracted for by appellees, no damages would therefore be recoverable. However, had appellees performed, theoretically, the appellant as a volume seller would have been entitled to the proceeds of two sales: one with the appellee James Johnson, and the other with the third-party "resale purchaser." It is in such instances that the damage provisions of section 2-708(2) become applicable.

The controlling issue regarding appellant's assertion of an entitlement to lost profits is whether the appellant sufficiently established its status as a volume seller.

In an action very similar to the case at bar, this reviewing court held the following evidence to be sufficient in establishing the status of a volume seller:

> Plaintiff's president testified that plaintiff is a franchised dealer of Bayliner Marine Corporation products and Bayliner has never refused to deliver any of plaintiff's orders.

However, in the instant action the lower court had only the testimony of Mr. A. Leslie, a salesman of appellant company, to consider. Though Leslie testified that *to his knowledge* appellant had an unlimited supply of the same type of boat and equipment as purchased by appellees, there exists no other evidence in the record to substantiate Leslie's testimony. Further, Johnson's testimony directly conflicts with that provided by Leslie, appellee stating that he had been informed by Leslie that the boat under dispute was the only one available.

The question before the trial court became one of witness credibility. The weight to be given the evidence and the credibility of the witnesses are primarily for the trier of fact. We therefore must conclude that appellant failed to adequately establish its status as a volume seller. In so holding, we find that appellant was not entitled to the lost profit provisions of section 2-708.

*Judgment affirmed.*

## QUESTIONS AND PROBLEMS

Why didn't section 2-708(2) apply in the preceding case? What would the seller have had to prove in order to obtain damages under that section?

***Problem 8-4.*** Buyer agrees to purchase a complex electronic good for $20,000. Seller manufactures the good to order. The cost of the components is $6,000. The rent for the factory is $10,000 per year. Seller normally sells about 1,000 of these goods per year. If 1,000 units are manufactured, the labor cost per product manufactured is $4,000, which includes employees who service the product under warranty after it is sold. When the product is finished, Buyer wrongfully refuses to take delivery or pay for the good. Seller is able to resell the good to another buyer for the same price, $20,000. Seller contends that it could have manufactured another one of these goods for the second buyer and thus claims to have lost a sale. Seller contends it could do this without hiring any additional employees or moving to a larger plant. How can this be determined one way or the other? How would damages be calculated under section 2-708(2)? *See Teradyne, Inc. v. Teledyne Industries, Inc.*, 676 F.2d 865

(1982); Gillette & Walt, *Sales Law: Domestic and International* 343-349 (rev. ed.).

***Problem 8-5.*** Copymate Marketing had an option from a supplier to purchase 3,000 photocopiers that had been in storage for nine years for $50,000. It entered into a contract with Modern Merchandising to sell them the copiers for $150,000. Copymate agreed to spend $50,000 on an advertising program to assist Modern Merchandising in the marketing of the copiers. Without justification, Modern Merchandising repudiated the contract. Believing that there was no other market for the copiers at any price greater than the acquisition price, Copymate decided not to exercise its option to purchase them from its supplier. It sues Modern Merchandising for breach of contract, and seeks to recover its lost profits under UCC section 2-708(2). Should Copymate be entitled to recover under that section? See UCC §2-704. If so, how should the lost profits be calculated? *See Copymate Marketing, Ltd. v. Modern Marketing, Inc.,* 34 Wash. App. 300, 660 P.2d 332 (1983).

### (e) Action for the Price

In situations in which the buyer refuses to accept delivery of goods under the contract, section 2-709 permits the seller to sue for the price if "the seller is unable after reasonable efforts to resell them at a reasonable price or the circumstances reasonably indicate that such effort will be unavailing." Section 2-709(2) requires that in this event, the seller must hold the goods for the buyer and, if resale becomes possible before collection of the judgment, must credit the buyer with the proceeds of any resale. Is there any safeguard to protect the buyer in cases like this from commercially unreasonable resales? Compare UCC §2-706.

## Foxco Industries, Ltd. v. Fabric World, Inc.

United States Court of Appeals, Fifth Circuit

595 F.2d 976 (1979)

Foxco is in the business of manufacturing knitted fabrics for sale to retail fabric stores and the garment industry. Fabric World is engaged in the retail fabric business and operates a chain of stores in a number of states.

There are two seasons in the fabric industry, a spring season and a fall season. Before the beginning of each season Foxco displays for customers samples of the line of fabrics it will manufacture that season. Customer orders are accepted only from the fabric shown on display. Foxco's manufacturing operation is limited to filling these orders; no fabrics are manufactured merely to be held as inventory. There was some conflict in the testimony as to whether fabric specially knit for one customer, such as Fabric World, could be resold to another customer.

On October 21, 1974, Feller (Foxco's sales manager) returned to Huntsville to show Jameson (Fabric World's president) the line for the following spring season. He gave Feller a new order, in writing, for 12,000 yards of first-quality fabric, at a price of $36,705, to be delivered by January 15, 1975.

A few weeks after the October 21 order was placed, the textile industry began to experience a precipitous decline in the price of yarn. Because of a drop in the price of finished goods, Fabric World wrote Foxco on November 15, 1974, and canceled its October 21 order. Foxco immediately replied, stating that the manufacture of the order was substantially completed and that it could not accept the cancellation. On November 27, 1974, Foxco's attorney wrote Fabric World that if the goods were not accepted they would be finished and sold and Fabric World sued for the difference between the contract price and the sales price received by Foxco. On December 3, 1974, Fabric World agreed to accept the order but threatened to return the entire shipment if it contained one flaw. Foxco, believing that it was impossible to produce an order of this magnitude without a single flaw, decided it would not ship the order (which was completed a short time later).

Fabric World established that in December 1974 the fair market value of the October order was approximately 20 percent less than the contract price. However, Foxco made no attempt to sell the goods from the time Fabric World canceled the order until September 1975, when the goods had dropped 50 per cent in value. In that month Foxco sold at a private sale, without notice to Fabric World, approximately 7,000 yards from the order for an average price of between $1.50 and $1.75 per yard, a total consideration of $10,119.50. By the time of trial in April 1976, Foxco had on hand about 5,000 yards of the order, worth between $1.25 and $1 per yard, or about $6,250.

The court instructed the jury that, if it found that Fabric World was liable to Foxco, it was free to calculate Foxco's damages under either section 2-708 or 2-709 of the Uniform Commercial Code. Fabric World objected, asserting that section 2-709 is inapplicable in this case, and that the $26,000 verdict awarded to Foxco cannot be supported.

As Fabric World correctly argues, Foxco cannot invoke section 2-706 in this case because, following Fabric World's breach, Foxco privately sold some of the goods without notice to Fabric World. Thus, Foxco is limited to its remedies under either section 2-708 or 2-709. The district court charged the jury under both of these latter provisions, leaving to the jury the determination of which was more appropriately applicable under the facts developed at trial. Since Fabric World properly concedes that a section 2-708 instruction was warranted on the state of the record before the trial judge, we may reverse only if the evidence was insufficient for the jury to invoke section 2-709 as a measure of Foxco's damages.

The jury was appropriately instructed, and Foxco's damages awarded must be approved.

When Fabric World canceled its October 1974 order on November 15, 1974, Foxco had not yet fully completed the manufacture of the contracted-for fabric. The jury obviously decided that Foxco acted in a commercially reasonable manner when it decided to process to a conclusion the manufacture of the already substantially completed Fabric World order. Foxco was then entitled to the appropriate seller's breach of contract remedy.

The evidence at trial clearly established that all of Foxco's goods were specially manufactured for the customer who ordered them and that it was difficult for Foxco to resell fabric manufactured for one purchaser to another buyer. Further, it was normally very difficult to sell Foxco's spring fabric after the spring buying season had ended; the precipitous decline of the knitted fabric market presented an additional barrier to resale. It was not until the next spring buying season returned that Foxco, in September 1975, finally sold a portion of the goods identified to Fabric World's October 1974 order.

Fabric World argues that Foxco made no effort whatsoever to resell the goods during the months that intervened (between the contract breach and Foxco's eventual disposition of the fabric in September 1975) despite the presence of some market for the goods in that interim period. Thus, Fabric World concludes, the requisites of section 2-709(1)(b) were not satisfied. Under section 2-709(1)(b), however, Foxco was required only to use reasonable efforts to resell its goods at a *reasonable* price. From the time of Fabric World's breach to September, 1975, there was a 50 percent decline in the market price of this material. We cannot say that the jury was precluded from finding that Foxco acted reasonably under the circumstances or that there was no reasonable price at which Foxco could sell the goods. Fabric World breached its contract with Foxco, and the jury was entitled to a charge which gave Foxco the full benefit of its original bargain.

## QUESTIONS

Why did the court (and jury) think that resale was not reasonably available here? Was this finding consistent with the (apparently uncontradicted) testimony that "in December 1974, the fair market value of the October order was approximately 20 percent less than the contract price"? With the fact that Foxco *did* eventually resell some of the goods?

## 2. GOODS DELIVERED

The parties may agree that the buyer is not required to pay for the goods until some time after the goods have been delivered. Or the parties may agree that the buyer can pay for the goods by personal check. In such a case, where the buyer fails to pay when payment is due or if the check tendered for the goods is dishonored ("bounced"), the seller will be interested either in suing the buyer to obtain the price of the goods or perhaps in trying to reclaim the goods themselves.

When the seller has either delivered the goods to a carrier for delivery to a buyer or has delivered the goods to the buyer directly, the seller's reclamation rights to the goods themselves are limited. When we talked earlier about title to goods, we discussed the seller's right to reclaim goods within a reasonable time of delivery in the event that a buyer pays with a check which is subsequently dishonored. See UCC §§2-507, 2-511. We learned, however, that the right to reclamation is lost if the goods are resold to a good faith purchaser for value. See UCC §2-507, Official Comment 3; Problem 4-1, *supra*.

As discussed at the beginning of this chapter, the seller may stop delivery of goods in possession of a carrier or other bailee if the seller discovers that the buyer is insolvent. UCC §2-705. If a seller has delivered goods to a buyer on credit and discovers that the buyer was insolvent when the goods were delivered, the seller may reclaim the goods under the circumstances specified in section 2-702. The right to reclaim the goods is lost if the goods are sold to a good faith purchaser for value. In addition, successful reclamation of goods precludes the seller from seeking other remedies. UCC §2-702(3).

In practice, the best way for a seller to retain a right to reclaim goods if the buyer does not pay for them is to reserve a security interest in the goods. For the definition of "security interest," see UCC section 1-201(b)(35). When the seller takes a security interest, the seller is contractually obtaining a right to recover the goods upon default in payment, and is then permitted to resell the goods to pay off what is owed by the breaching buyer. For example, you may have purchased a car on credit, allowing the seller of the car or a bank financing the transaction to keep the certificate of title ("pink slip") until you have paid the price. In such a case, the creditor (i.e., the seller or the bank) has a security interest in the car and may foreclose upon it if you fail to make payments. The relationship of the Article 2 rights to reclaim to the rights of secured parties is better explored in a course covering secured transactions in personal property.

The more likely remedy for the seller to follow if the seller does not have a security interest in the goods is to sue for the price in the event that the buyer accepts the goods but does not pay for them. Section 2-709(1)(a) permits the seller to sue for the price "of goods accepted or of conforming goods lost or damaged within a commercially reasonable time after risk of their loss has passed to the buyer."

### F&P Builders v. Lowe's of Texas, Inc.

Court of Appeals of Texas

786 S.W.2d 502 (1990)

The sole issue in this sworn account case is whether, subsequent to delivery and acceptance of goods by a buyer, the seller has the duty to mitigate its damages by accepting a return of the goods upon the buyer's request. We hold that it does not.

F&P Builders ordered construction products from Lowe's. Lowe's delivered the products, and F&P accepted them. F&P was unable to pay for them and requested that Lowe's return to the delivery sites and pick up the goods. Lowe's refused to do so. F&P argues that the goods were in the same condition as delivered and that it would take minimal effort and expense for Lowe's to comply. The trial court granted Lowe's motion for summary judgment upon its sworn account.

F&P judicially admitted that the goods were delivered and accepted. Its only contention is that there is a fact question in this case as to the seller's duty to mitigate damages.

F&P claims that notwithstanding UCC section 2-709, the Code does not abrogate the common law duty to mitigate damages. We acknowledge that the Code may not displace the common law in every case. We assume but do not decide that there is a common law duty upon the seller to mitigate damages for goods delivered and accepted. However, in our view, section 2-709(1)(a) supplants any duty upon the seller to mitigate damages for goods delivered and accepted. We hold that Lowe's was entitled to a summary judgment as a matter of law, and we affirm the trial court's judgment.

## NOTES AND QUESTIONS

1. Is the seller entitled to the price in all cases in which goods have been accepted by the buyer? If so, what is the meaning of section 2-709(3), which indicates that at times a seller may not be entitled to the price in the event of a wrongful revocation of acceptance? Is *Smith v. Paoli Popcorn*, page 239, *supra*, a case in which the court uses a remedy other than awarding the price where goods have been accepted (buyer failed to reject within a reasonable time, which constitutes "acceptance" under UCC §2-606(1)(b)).
2. Is the seller entitled to consequential damages? Compare UCC §2-710 to UCC §2-715. Why would the UCC distinguish between the buyer's right to consequential damages and the seller's right? Under what circumstances might a seller be legitimately entitled to consequential damages? *See Cherwell-Ralli, Inc. v. Rytman Grain Co., Inc.*, Chapter 6, *supra*.

## 3. LIQUIDATED DAMAGES AND BREACHING BUYER'S RIGHT TO RESTITUTION

As we have previously discussed, the parties to a contract for sale may craft their own remedies in the contract. One thing the parties may do is liquidate damages. One question that needs to be asked is whether the contractual provision liquidating damages is optional, or is the exclusive remedy. Section 2-719(1)(b) indicates that resort to a contractually provided remedy is optional unless the contract expressly provides that it is to be exclusive. Another question is whether the liquidated damage provision is enforceable or is an unlawful penalty? You probably remember from your contracts class that liquidated damages provisions are suspect, as the law does not permit clauses that call for the payment of a penalty in the event of a breach. In addition, even a breaching party is entitled to restitution in the event that it has conferred a benefit on the other party in excess of damages caused by breach. UCC section 2-718 deals with both the enforceability of liquidated damages clauses and the breaching buyer's right to restitution.

### KVASSAY v. MURRAY

Court of Appeals of Kansas

15 Kan. App. 2d 426, 808 P.2d 896 (1991)

Plaintiff Michael Kvassay, d/b/a Kvassay Exotic Food, appeals the trial court's finding that a liquidated damages clause was unenforceable and from the court's finding that damages for lost profits were not recoverable. Kvassay contends these damages occurred when Great American Foods, Inc. (Great American) breached a contract for the purchase of baklava.

On February 22, 1984, Kvassay, who had been an independent insurance adjuster, contracted to sell 24,000 cases of baklava to Great American at $19.00 per case. Under the contract, the sales were to occur over a one-year period and Great American was to be Kvassay's only customer. The contract included a clause which provided: "If Buyer refuses to accept or repudiates delivery of the goods sold to him, under this Agreement, Seller shall be entitled to damages, at the rate of $5.00 per case, for each case remaining to be delivered under this Contract."

Problems arose early in this contractual relationship with checks issued by Great American being dishonored for insufficient funds. After producing approximately 3,000 cases, Kvassay stopped producing the baklava because Great American refused to purchase any more of the product.

In April 1985, Kvassay filed suit for damages arising from the collapse of his baklava baking business. The court conducted bench hearings on the validity of the liquidated damages clause and ruled that liquidated damages could not be recovered.

Kvassay claimed $105,000 in losses under the liquidated damages clause of the contract, representing $5 per case for the approximately 21,000 cases of baklava that he was not able to deliver. The trial court determined that Kvassay's use of expected profits to formulate liquidated damages was improper because the business enterprise lacked duration, permanency, and recognition. The court then compared Kvassay's previous yearly income (about $20,000) with the claim for liquidated damages ($105,000) and found "the disparity becomes so great as to make the clause unenforceable."

Since the contract involved the sale of goods between merchants, the Uniform Commercial Code governs.[2] See UCC §2-102. "The Code does not change the pre-Code rule that the question of the propriety of liquidated damages is a question of law for the court." 4 Anderson, *Uniform Commercial Code* §2-718:6, p. 572 (3d ed. 1983).

[The court quotes from UCC section 2-718.]

To date, the appellate courts have not interpreted this section of the UCC in light of facts similar to those presented in this case. In ruling on this issue, the trial court relied on rules governing liquidated damages as expressed in *U.S.D. No. 315 v. DeWerff,* 6 Kan. App. 2d 77, 626 P.2d 1206 (1981). *DeWerff,* however, involved a teacher's breach of an employment contract and was not governed by the UCC. Thus, the rules expressed in that case should be given no effect if they differ from the rules expressed in section 2-718.

In *DeWerff,* this court held a "stipulation for damages upon a future breach of contract is valid as a liquidated damages clause if the set amount is determined to be reasonable and the amount of damages is difficult to ascertain." 6 Kan. App. 2d at 78, 626 P.2d 1206. This is clearly a two-step test: Damages must be reasonable and they must be difficult to ascertain. Under the UCC, however, reasonableness is the only test. UCC §2-718. Section 2-718 provides three criteria by which to measure reasonableness of liquidated damages

2. Is the UCC limited only to sales of goods by merchants?—Ed.

clauses: (1) anticipated or actual harm caused by breach; (2) difficulty of proving loss; and (3) difficulty of obtaining an adequate remedy.

In its ruling, the trial court found the liquidated damages clause was unreasonable in light of Kvassay's income before he entered into the manufacturing contract with Great American. There is no basis in section 2-718 for contrasting income under a previous unrelated employment arrangement with liquidated damages sought under a manufacturing contract. Indeed, the traditional goal of the law in cases where a buyer breaches a manufacturing contract is to place the seller "in the same position he would have occupied if the vendee had performed his contract." *Outcault Adv. Co. v. Citizens Nat'l Bank,* 118 Kan. 328, 330-331, 234 P. 988 (1925). Thus, liquidated damages under the contract in this case must be measured against the anticipated or actual loss under the baklava contract as required by section 2-718. The trial court erred in using Kvassay's previous income as a yardstick.

Was the trial court correct when it invalidated the liquidated damages clause, notwithstanding the use of an incorrect test? If so, we must uphold the decision even though the trial court relied on a wrong ground or assigned an erroneous reason for its decision. To answer this question, we must look closer at the first criteria for reasonableness under section 2-718—anticipated or actual harm done by the breach.

Kvassay produced evidence of anticipated damages at the bench trial showing that, before the contract was signed between Kvassay and Great American, Kvassay's accountant had calculated the baklava production costs. The resulting figure showed that, if each case sold for $19, Kvassay would earn a net profit of $3.55 per case after paying himself for time and labor. If he did not pay himself, the projected profit was $4.29 per case. Nevertheless, the parties set the liquidated damages figure at $5 per case. In comparing the anticipated damages of $3.55 per case in lost net profit with the liquidated damages of $5 per case, it is evident that Kvassay would collect $1.45 per case, or about 41 percent, over projected profits if Great American breached the contract. If the $4.29 profit figure is used, a $5 liquidated damages award would allow Kvassay to collect 71 cents per case or about 16.5 percent over projected profits if Great American breached the contract.

An examination of these precontract comparisons alone might well lead to the conclusion that the $5 liquidated damages clause is unreasonable because enforcing it would result in a windfall for Kvassay and serve as a penalty for Great American. A term fixing unreasonably large liquidated damages is void as a penalty under section 2-718.

A better measure of the validity of the liquidated damages clause in this case would be obtained if the actual lost profits caused by the breach were compared to the $5 per case amount set by the clause. However, no attempt was made by Kvassay during the bench trial to prove actual profits or actual costs of production. Thus, the trial court could not compare the $5 liquidated damages clause in the contract with the actual profits lost by the breach. It was not until the jury trial that Kvassay attempted to prove his actual profits lost as part of his damages. Given the trial court's ruling that lost profits were not recoverable and could not be presented to the jury,[3] it is questionable whether the court would have permitted evidence concerning lost profits at the bench trial.

The trial court utilized an impermissible factor to issue its ruling on the liquidated damages clause and the correct statutory factors were not directly addressed. We reverse the trial court on this issue and remand for further consideration of the reasonableness of the liquidated damages clause in light of the three criteria set out in UCC section 2-718.

## NOTES, QUESTIONS, AND PROBLEMS

1. If the seller in this case is required to prove the actual damages that were suffered in order to justify the liquidated damages provision, then what is the point of the provision at all? When, if ever, should the actual damages be relevant in assessing the enforceability of a liquidated damages provision? *See Harty v. Bye*, 258 Ore. 398, 483 P.2d 458 (1971). Why should courts regulate liquidated damages provisions? Should liquidated damages provisions that are too low be invalidated? See UCC §2-302.

***Problem 8-6.*** In a long-term contract for the sale of natural gas, buyer agrees to purchase and seller agrees to deliver a minimum quantity of gas during a specified period at a specified price. In the event that buyer fails to take delivery of the minimum quantity during the specified period, the buyer is nevertheless required to pay for that quantity. The buyer is permitted to demand delivery of the gas that was paid for but not taken in a future period. For example, if only seventy-five percent of the minimum quantity was taken in January but was paid for, buyer would be entitled to the remaining twenty-five percent in the next month on top of the maximum quantity for that month. Often, however, it is not practical for the buyer to take sufficient quantity in future months to make up for the gas not taken in prior months. This means that sellers can resell the gas not taken to others. These types of provisions are called "take or pay" provisions. Should these provisions be considered liquidated damages provisions under UCC section 2-718? If the buyer refuses to take the minimum quantity and pays only for the gas that it does take, should the buyer be liable to pay under the terms of the contract or should the seller be entitled to the difference between the contract price and the market price under section 2-708(1) for the difference between the minimum quantity and the amount actually taken by the buyer? See Coffee, *Fairness Is in the Eye of the Beholder: The Conflicting Interpretations of the Correct Measure of Damages for Breaches of Natural Gas Contract Containing Take-or-Pay Provisions*, 14 BYU J. Pub. Law 151 (1999); Brooke, *Great Expectations: Assessing the Contract Damages of the Take-or-Pay Producer*, 70 Tex. L. Rev. 1469 (1992).

---

3. The trial court had held that evidence of lost profits would not be admissible because the evidence was too speculative. In another part of the opinion, the court holds that the evidence should have been admissible and that it is apparently also relevant on the issue of the reasonableness of the liquidated damages provision.—Ed.

***Problem 8-7.*** Buyer gives Seller a $1,000 deposit payment for the purchase of a car. The total purchase price is $10,000. Buyer has a change of heart, and notifies Seller that Buyer will not take delivery of the car. Seller is able to sell the car to someone else, and can show damages of $300 under section 2-708(2). How much, if any amount, is Buyer entitled to recover in restitution under UCC sections 2-718(2) and (3)?

## B. SELLER'S REMEDIES UNDER THE CISG

The seller's options in the event of breach of contract by the buyer are spelled out in Article 61. As is the case with buyer's remedies, the CISG rejects the doctrine of election of remedies in that the seller may both avoid the contract and seek damages under it. Article 62 does provide, however, that the seller may not seek specific performance if the seller has resorted to an inconsistent remedy; for example, if the seller has resold the goods to somebody else. Sellers' remedies under the CISG will be explored through the problems posed after the following hypothetical, which is to some extent based on a case that was decided in 1992 by the International Chamber of Commerce Court of Arbitration in Paris, France, case number 7585/1992, *http://cisgw3.law.pace.edu/cases/927585i1.html* (accessed Oct. 2011).

> Buyer and Seller entered into a contract for the sale of machinery to be used on a production line. Seller was located in Italy and Buyer was located in the United States. The contract expressly states that the CISG is to apply. The contract price was to be paid in U.S. dollars (the official currency of Italy is the euro). The contract provided that upon favorable inspection of the goods, Buyer was to establish a letter of credit in favor of Seller so as to insure that Seller would be paid once the goods were shipped. The date of inspection was November 28. Although the inspection was favorable, no letter of credit was established due to Buyer's financial difficulties. Seller was aware of these difficulties, and waited until March 10 before declaring the contract avoided. Before giving notice of avoidance on March 10, Seller never gave Buyer a formal notice that Buyer had until March 10 to establish the letter of credit or otherwise to make the payment. The contract provided that "if the agreement is terminated by fault of the supplier before the goods have been delivered, the purchaser will be returned any sum he has previously transferred to the supplier as down payment, without interest. If the agreement is terminated by fault or request of the purchaser—including force majeure—the supplier is entitled to a compensation fee of 30 percent of the price." Following avoidance, Seller resold the goods to another purchaser at a reduced price.

Assume that during this time, the interest rate for judgments in Italy was 15 percent and 10 percent in the United States. Assume also that the prime rate of interest for loans in Italy was 10 percent and in the United States it was 5 percent. Seller generally maintained liquid funds in a bank account that paid 3 percent. The London Inter-Bank Offered Rate (LIBOR) for U.S. dollar–denominated international loans between banks was 2 percent.

## PROBLEMS

***Problem 8-8.*** Was Seller within its rights in declaring the contract avoided? Was the period between November 28 and March 10 "an additional period of time of reasonable length," thus triggering avoidance rights under Article 64(1)(b)? If not, was the delay in establishing the letter of credit a "fundamental breach" under Article 25? See CISG Articles 54 and 59.

***Problem 8-9.*** Could Seller have sued Buyer for specific performance rather than avoiding the contract? CISG Articles 62 and 28.

***Problem 8-10.*** Is Seller entitled to the difference between the contract price and the resale price? CISG Article 75. Should Seller also be entitled to recover the cost of storing the goods during the time it was waiting for the Buyer to pay? CISG Article 74.

***Problem 8-11.*** Is the "compensation fee" enforceable, and can it be recovered in addition to the damages calculated under Articles 74 and 75? See CISG Articles 4(a) and 8. See also Mattei, *The Comparative Law and Economics of Penalty Clauses in Contracts*, 43 Am. J. Comp. Law 427 (1995).

***Problem 8-12.*** Is Seller entitled to interest on the amounts owing from Buyer? What interest rate should be used in calculating any interest due? See CISG Article 74 and 78. See also UNIDROIT Principles of International Commercial Contracts Article 7.4.9, *www.cisg.law.pace.edu/cisg/principles/uni78.html*. When is it appropriate to use the UNIDROIT principles in CISG cases?

## CHAPTER 8 REVIEW PROBLEM

A buyer contracts to purchase a specially manufactured "double-spindle stud driver" for a price of $12,377. Three months after ordering it and with it costing only $360 more to complete the machine, the buyer calls the seller and tells the seller it does not want the machine. The specially manufactured machine required a number of design changes, differentiating this machine from the typical machine sold by the seller. The scrap value of the machine in its unfinished condition is $1,500. What are the options available to the seller? See UCC §2-704. If the seller decides to finish the machine, should the seller be entitled to sue for the price if the good cannot be resold because of its special condition? UCC §2-709. Should the seller be limited to the difference between the contract price and the market price? If the seller gave proper notice to the breaching buyer and sold the machine for $5,000, could it recover the difference between the contract price and the resale price? If the machine is scrapped, how should the seller's damages be calculated? See UCC §§2-706 and 2-708. *See Detroit Power Screwdriver Co. v. Ladney*, 25 Mich. App. 478, 181 N.W.2d 828 (1970). If at the time of repudiation it would cost the seller $10,000 more to complete the machine, would the analysis be different? Please also analyze these questions under the CISG. The relevant CISG Articles are 28, 62, and 74-77.

CHAPTER 9

# THIRD PARTIES INVOLVED IN THE SALES TRANSACTION

In many sales transactions, especially international sales, third parties will have important roles in the transaction. When the buyer and the seller reside many miles apart, carriers, such as trucking companies or airlines, will be used to transport the goods from the seller's place of business to the buyer's place. In addition, the seller may not trust the creditworthiness of the buyer and may ask the buyer to obtain a bank's undertaking to pay for the goods or to agree to make certain that the buyer pays before the goods are delivered. In this chapter, we consider the duties of banks and carriers in the sales transaction.

## A. THE DOCUMENTARY SALE—DOCUMENTS OF TITLE

When goods are shipped by a seller to a buyer by using a common carrier (i.e., a shipping company) the carrier will issue a "bill of lading" to the seller. The "bill of lading" represents a receipt for the goods and is also the contract between the seller and the carrier. The bill of lading describes the goods that are being shipped, names the person to whom the goods are to be delivered (the "consignee"), and may also spell out the limitations of liability for the carrier in the event that the goods are lost or damaged in transit. The bill of lading is defined in the UCC as a "document of title" because it evidences the person entitled to receive and dispose of the goods covered by the bill. See UCC §1-201(b)(16). Documents of title are covered by UCC Article 7, which was most recently revised in 2003.[1] Bills of lading used in interstate commerce are covered by the Federal Bill of Lading Act, 49 USC §80101, et. seq. The differences between the Federal Bill of Lading Act and UCC Article 7 are not great.

1. The revisions mostly accommodate the creation of electronic documents of title and modernize the terminology of Article 7.

Sometimes goods that are located in a warehouse will be sold without being moved. In these cases, the warehouse operator will issue a "warehouse receipt" to the owner of the goods who stores the goods in the warehouse. The warehouse receipt is also a document of title covered by Article 7 of the UCC. The title to the goods may be transferred by transferring possession of the document of title rather than physically transferring possession of the goods themselves. Use of this mechanism can facilitate commerce when the goods are bulky and thus difficult to move.

Documents of title can be either negotiable or nonnegotiable. A document of title that states that the goods are to be delivered to the bearer of the document or to the order of the named person is negotiable, unless it states that it is "nonnegotiable." UCC §7-104, 49 USC §80103. Other documents of title are nonnegotiable—they simply state to whom the goods are to be delivered, the consignee, without indicating that the consignee may instruct the warehouse or carrier to deliver the goods to anyone else. A nonnegotiable bill of lading is often referred to as a "straight" bill of lading because delivery is to be straight to the consignee (without intervening holders of the bill).

The effect of a document of title being negotiable is that proper negotiation of the document gives the holder of the document title to the document and also title to the goods, at least if the person who first obtained the document of title covering the goods had title at the time the document was issued. UCC §7-502, 49 USC §80105. The document of title is negotiated by delivery to the transferee with the signature (indorsement) of the transferor. You can think of indorsement of documents of title in the same way that you think of indorsement of a check—you typically sign on the back of a check payable to you before you deposit the check into your bank account. Thus, if a negotiable warehouse receipt indicated that delivery was to be "to Party *A* or to order," Party *A* could transfer title to the document and to the goods by signing the bill (indorsing it) and handing it to the transferee. This might be done, for example, if Party *A* wanted to obtain financing from a bank and the bank wanted to hold title to the goods as security for repayment of the loan.[2] The document could be negotiated to the bank, which then would have a right to direct delivery of the goods until the bank was paid, after which it would transfer the document back to Party *A*.

The warehouse operator or the carrier is obligated to deliver the goods only to the consignee of the nonnegotiable document of title or the holder of the negotiable document. UCC §7-403, 49 USC §80110. On a nonnegotiable bill of lading, the shipper (consignor) of the goods, normally the seller, may divert delivery of the goods until they have been delivered to the consignee. UCC §7-303, 49 USC §80111(a)(2). If a buyer fails to make payments when due, repudiates, or appears insolvent, the seller may stop delivery of the goods. UCC §2-705. So if the goods have not yet been delivered, and the seller learns that the buyer is insolvent or has not made a payment that is due, the seller may stop delivery and ask that the goods be shipped someplace else.

In a documentary sale, the seller may thus prevent the buyer from taking delivery of the goods until payment is made. The buyer needs the documents

2. This type of transaction would be subject to UCC Article 9. See UCC §9-313.

to take delivery of the goods, and the seller is issued the documents by the carrier. The buyer and seller in their contract may require that payment be made by the buyer as a condition to the buyer's receipt of the documents and thus receipt of the goods. As the following materials point out, the parties may use the banking system for the purpose of delivering the documents from the seller to the buyer and for assuring that payment is made before the buyer can take possession of the goods.

## B. BANK OBLIGATIONS UNDER LETTERS OF CREDIT

Documents of title may be used in connection with letters of credit. In a letter of credit, a bank agrees to pay a seller for the goods; the seller is the "beneficiary" under the letter of credit. Under this type of arrangement, the buyer will arrange for a bank essentially to step in for the buyer and make payment upon proof that the goods have been shipped. The buyer is referred to as the "applicant" for the letter of credit. The letter of credit will provide that the seller must present specified documents to the bank issuing the letter of credit (called the "issuer") in order to be paid. Typically, the documents may include a bill of lading issued by the carrier showing that the goods have been handed to the carrier and are being shipped to the buyer, invoices, a certificate of inspection, and certificates of insurance. If the documents on their face comply with the requirements of the letter of credit, the bank is required to make payment to the seller. This payment must be made even if it turns out that the goods do not conform to the contract of sale, in which case the buyer must seek recourse from the seller. The seller is thus assured that it will be paid even if the buyer is insolvent or dissatisfied with the goods. This type of letter of credit is called a "commercial" letter of credit.

Another type of letter of credit is called the "standby" letter of credit, pursuant to which the bank agrees to pay a specified sum of money upon certification that one of the parties has failed to perform. These types of letters of credit are often seen in construction contracts, in which the owner of the project may require a contractor to post a standby letter of credit naming the owner as the beneficiary in the event that the contractor does not complete the project in a timely fashion. In a sale of goods transaction, a buyer might require a seller to post a standby letter in the event that the seller does not deliver the goods on time. The standby letter of credit requires that the issuing bank pay the beneficiary upon certification, perhaps by the beneficiary itself, that the event triggering payment has occurred (for example, the goods have not been delivered by the specified date). The bank has no obligation to determine whether the triggering event has in fact occurred; it is obligated to pay upon being presented with the demand for payment specified by the letter of credit.

Other banks besides the bank issuing the letter of credit may also be involved in the transaction. If the seller prefers to deal with a bank other than the bank that is issuing the letter of credit, perhaps because the issuer is located overseas, the seller may ask to have a local bank "confirm" the letter of credit. This means that the "confirming bank" will agree to pay the letter of credit as if it were the issuer, and the issuer will agree to reimburse the confirming bank if it pays the beneficiary in accordance with the terms of the letter of credit. A bank may also be asked by the issuer or the confirmer to advise the beneficiary regarding the terms of the letter of credit. If the bank agrees to so advise, it is called an advising bank and is not required to honor the letter of credit. It is only required to accurately advise the beneficiary regarding its terms. For example, the bank used by the seller in its business transactions may not be willing to confirm the letter of credit but it may be willing to advise its customer, the seller, regarding its terms.[3]

Letters of credit are similar to guarantees in that a third party is essentially guaranteeing payment on behalf of the principal obligor. There is a very significant difference between guarantees and letters of credit, however, in that the issuing bank's obligation to pay does not depend on performance of the underlying contract. The bank's obligation is independent of the underlying contract. This is the so-called "independence principle" of letters of credit. The bank is contractually obligated to pay the beneficiary upon presentation of the documents called for by the letter of credit. The documents may be false and the goods may be nonconforming, but the bank's obligation is based on whether the documents conform on their face. Defenses that are typically available to guarantors are not available to banks liable on letters of credit.

The law governing letters of credit in the United States is Article 5 of the Uniform Commercial Code. Article 5 was last revised in 1995; unless otherwise indicated, these materials cite to the 1995 revision. In addition and of equal or more importance, many letters of credit are governed by the Uniform Customs and Practice for Documentary Credits ("UCP"), which is a compendium of bank practices (trade usages) in dealing with letters of credit. The UCP is promulgated by the International Chamber of Commerce, and its current edition is referred to as UCP 600 (effective July 1, 2007). The UCP is not "law" and only applies if the parties agree to be bound by their rules. Letters of credit will often state that they are to be governed by the UCP. The UCP contains rules regarding how banks will determine if documents presented comply with the terms of the letter of credit. See UCP 600 Article 14. The UCP and Article 5 are largely complementary, but to the extent that they conflict the UCC generally yields to the UCP. UCC §5-116(c).

Standby letters of credit may also be subject to the UCP, but the International Chamber of Commerce has also promulgated rules that are particularly suited to those types of letters of credit, the International Standby Practices (ISP 98), effective January 1, 1999. For international standby letters of credit, UNCITRAL has promulgated the Convention on Independent Guarantees and Standby Letters of Credit. As of the time of this writing (fall 2011), this Convention has been ratified by eight nations and has been signed, but not yet ratified, by the United States.[4] This Convention will apply if two parties to the overall letter of credit transaction have places of business in different countries. In addition, the country in which the issuer is located must have acceded to the Convention, or the rules of private international law must lead to the application of the law of a nation that has acceded to the Convention. See Convention on International Guarantees and Standby Letters of Credit at Article 4.

---

3. See UCC §5-107 for the duties of advising and confirming banks.

4. For the list of countries ratifying or signing the Convention, see the UNCITRAL Web site at *www.uncitral.org/uncitral/en/uncitral_texts/payments/1995Convention_guarantees_status.html* (accessed Oct. 2011).

## 1. HAS A LETTER OF CREDIT BEEN ISSUED?

The first question that must be analyzed is whether a letter of credit has in fact been issued. In analyzing this issue, please look at UCC sections 5-102(a)(10), 5-103, and 5-104. The following case demonstrates the different treatment of a letter of credit as compared to a guarantee.

### Wichita Eagle & Beacon Publishing Co. v. Pacific Nat'l Bank of San Francisco

United States District Court, N.D. California

343 F. Supp. 332 (1971)

This action arises from a complaint filed herein on May 4, 1965, by the Wichita Eagle and Beacon Publishing Company, Inc. ("Wichita Eagle") against the Pacific National Bank of San Francisco ("Bank").

**Facts**

Beginning in 1962, Wichita Eagle had been a lessee of certain property ("Property") located in downtown Wichita, Kansas, upon which were three buildings used by the Wichita Eagle for its publication business. In 1960, the then–Wichita Eagle had purchased the assets of a rival newspaper, the Wichita Beacon, and had proceeded to merge the Wichita Beacon into the Wichita Eagle. Among the assets purchased by the Wichita Eagle was a new publishing plant owned by the Wichita Beacon. The Wichita Eagle decided to move its operations to this new plant after the merger and thus freed the Property, upon which its old plant remained, for other development.

Following a period of negotiations, on February 28, 1962, Marcellus M. Murdock and others, lessors of the Property ("Lessors"), entered into a 99-year lease ("Lease") with Circular Ramp Garages, Inc. ("Circular Ramp") of the Property. By subsequent amendment the date of the Lease was changed to April 28, 1962.

Paragraph IV(a) of the Lease required Circular Ramp to exercise due diligence to obtain necessary permits and to commence and complete construction on the Property of a parking garage in accordance with a specified time schedule and having a minimum value of $500,000.

Paragraph IV(b) of the Lease required Circular Ramp to deposit cash or government bonds in the amount of $250,000 in a Kansas bank or provide a surety bond, letter of credit, or other form of guaranty in the same amount to guarantee Circular Ramp's performance of paragraph IV(a) of the Lease. Pursuant to this provision, Circular Ramp arranged for the Bank to issue to the Lessors and the Wichita Eagle as beneficiaries an instrument (hereinafter sometimes "instrument") dated May 9, 1962, and designated "Letter of Credit No. 17084" (see Appendix hereto for full text of the Instrument). The Bank made and received its usual letter of credit charge for issuing the Instrument.

[The court determines that Circular Ramp did not exercise due diligence under Paragraph IV(a) of the Lease. No parking garage was ever built by Circular Ramp.]

Because of the defalcation of Circular Ramp, the Lessors executed a new lease of the Property to Macy's on October 30, 1964, the term of which was to start on November 1, 1964. The Macy's lease was for a 30-year period with renewal options to be available for six ten-year periods with contemplated renegotiations of the rental provisions. Also on October 30, 1964, the Lessors and Wichita Eagle executed a "Termination Agreement" and an assignment to the Wichita Eagle of all rights under the letter of credit. During the period from November 1, 1962, to October 30, 1964, Wichita Eagle as lessee of the Property had paid to the Lessors rent in the amount of $226,000 before credit of $37,500.03.

On March 17, 1965, counsel for the Wichita Eagle wrote the Bank and enclosed notices sent to Circular Ramp and Pacific Company pursuant to the enforcement provisions of the Instrument. Counsel for the Wichita Eagle indicated that the Wichita Eagle proposed to draw a draft pursuant to the Instrument within a few weeks from that date.

On May 3, 1965, Wichita Eagle, as the assignee of the Lessors, presented to the Bank a $250,000 draft drawn upon the "Letter of Credit No. 17084" together with documents specified therein. The Bank refused payment.

In a joint pretrial order filed herein on December 9, 1969, and approved by another judge of this court, said judge ruled as a matter of law that the "Letter of Credit No. 17084" was not a letter of credit at all, but was in fact a performance bond or surety agreement subject to the law of performance bonds and surety agreements. Upon transfer of this case to the undersigned for trial, however, the issue of the nature of the "Letter of Credit No. 17084" was reopened and the ruling of the transferor judge was vacated. Upon reopening the Bank offered expert testimony concerning the nature of the Instrument, and the parties submitted additional written authorities in support of their respective positions.

A letter of credit may be broadly defined as an engagement by a bank or other person at the request of a customer that the issuer will honor drafts or other demands for payment upon compliance with the conditions specified in the credit.

While in a sense every letter of credit is a form of guaranty, the letter of credit differs from the classical surety undertaking in that it is a primary obligation between the issuer and the beneficiary. The issuer of the credit is not concerned with the arrangements existing between the beneficiary and issuer's account party.

The Bank contends that the Instrument is not a letter of credit but is instead a performance bond, surety agreement, or other such guaranty. The Bank argues that there can be only two types of letters of credit: "clean" and "documentary." A clean letter of credit requires only the submission of a draft (or drafts) for payment, while a documentary letter of credit requires specified accompanying documents as well. The Instrument here, however, is neither clean nor documentary, the Bank claims, since at least two of its three stated conditions are not documentary. The Bank's approach is, however, too parochial and exalts formalism over commercial reality and usage.

The authorities are uniform, for example, that a letter of credit need be in no particular form. Although letters of credit have been most commonly used in sales transactions, they are certainly not unknown in the context of a construction contract, as here.

One of the reasons behind the growth and spread of the letter of credit as a commercial tool has been the willingness of the courts to align case law with progressive and current commercial practice. The very type of letter of credit being questioned here by the Bank as a radical departure from traditional usage is but another example of the commercial community pouring old wines into new flasks.

In finding the Instrument to be a letter of credit this court gives respect to one of the oldest canons of contractual construction, namely giving effect wherever possible to the intent of the contracting parties. Here the parties intended to enter into a letter of credit arrangement; said letter was drafted by an attorney who was counsel for the Pacific Company and later for Circular Ramp and approved by both the Wichita Eagle and the Bank; the Bank charged and received its usual letter of credit charge; and the letter clearly and conspicuously calls itself a letter of credit.

Although the question is not free from doubt, the Instrument denominated "Letter of Credit No. 17084" should be treated as a letter of credit and be subject to the law respecting letters of credit to the extent applicable and appropriate.

The letter of credit listed three conditions precedent to the payment of any sight drafts presented against the letter: First, that Circular Ramp had failed to perform the terms and conditions of paragraph IV(a) of the Lease; second, that the payee have sent a written notice to the Pacific Company and Circular Ramp specifying how Circular Ramp had failed to perform the terms and conditions of said paragraph IV(a) of the Lease, and have delivered to the signatories for the Bank an affidavit signed by Marcellus M. Murdock stating that the written notices required were sent to the Pacific Company and Circular Ramp, such notices to have been sent more than 30 days prior to the date the draft is drawn; and third, that either Circular Ramp or the Pacific Company had failed during the 30 days following the delivery of the notices to them to cure any actual default existing under the terms of said paragraph IV(a) of the Lease as so specified in the written notices.

The Wichita Eagle complied with all the conditions precedent sufficient to require that the Bank have honored its $250,000 draft drawn against the letter of credit.

[In the balance of the opinion, the court calculates the damages that should be awarded for the wrongful refusal to pay the letter of credit and determines that, due to mitigation of damages, Wichita Eagle should only be entitled to recover $163,000 in damages.]

**Appendix**

Pacific National Bank of San Francisco

International Department
May 9, 1962

Marcellus M. Murdock; Victor Delano; Katherine M. Henderson; Marsh Murdock and Victoria Neff, as the Trustees of the Pearl Jane Murdock Trust; Wichita Eagle, Inc.; and the Prairie Improvement Company, Inc.

Gentlemen:

We hereby establish our Letter of Credit No. 17084 in your favor on the terms and conditions herein set forth for the account of Circular Ramp Garages, Inc. for the total sum of $250,000.00, available by drafts drawn at sight on the Pacific National Bank providing that all of the following conditions exist at the time said draft is received by the undersigned:

1. That Circular Ramp Garages, Inc., has failed to perform the terms and conditions of paragraph IV(a) of the lease dated February 28, 1962, as amended to April 28, 1962, between all of you as Lessor and Circular Ramp Garages, Inc., as Lessee, a copy of which lease is attached hereto.
2. That you have sent by registered United States mail, return receipt requested, with all postage and registration fees prepaid, a written notice to Circular Ramp Garage, Inc., at 343 Sansome Street, San Francisco 4, California, and to The Pacific Company Engineers and Builders at 801 Cedar Street, Berkeley, California, specifying how Circular Ramp Garages, Inc., has failed to perform the terms and conditions of said paragraph IV(a) of said lease and further that you have delivered to the undersigned an affidavit signed by Marcellus M. Murdock stating that he sent said written notice in such manner to the above Circular Ramp Garages, Inc., and The Pacific Company Engineers and Builders, to which affidavit shall be attached the return receipt from said registered mail delivery, which affidavit and any attached return receipt shall show that said notice was delivered to said Circular Ramp Garages, Inc., and The Pacific Company Engineers and Builders more than 30 days prior to the date the draft is drawn by you against this Letter of Credit.
3. That either Circular Ramp Garages, Inc., of The Pacific Company Engineers and Builders has failed during said 30 days following the delivery of said notice to them to cure any actual default existing under the terms of said paragraph IV(a) of said lease as so specified in said written notice.

The credit extended under this lease shall terminate at the time and upon the happening of any of the following:

a. At the time that the City of Wichita, Kansas, refuses to issue a permit to construct a circular ramp parking garage building in accordance with plans and specifications submitted by Circular Ramp Garages, Inc., or its engineer or architect, on the property subject to said lease and fails to issue said permit to either Circular Ramp Garages, Inc., or the contractor hired to construct said building, provided, however, that said refusal is accepted as a final refusal by Circular Ramp Garages, Inc., or by said contractor. However, if Circular Ramp Garages, Inc., or said contractor has been unable to obtain such a permit by October 28, 1962, and either of them wishes to continue trying to obtain said permit, this Letter of Credit shall be automatically reduced at said date to a principal sum of $50,000.00 until terminated by any of the following conditions or events.

b. At the time that the contractor who is to construct said building obtains a performance bond from a surety company licensed to conduct a bonding business in Kansas insuring that said building will be completed in accordance with the plans and specifications therefore within three years after Circular Ramp Garages, Inc., is obligated to take possession of said premises or April 28, 1965, whichever date shall first occur.
c. At the time after such permit from the City of Wichita, Kansas, is obtained that no construction loan or takeout loan to finance the construction of said building is obtainable, if the reason that said loan is not obtainable is due to some provision in said lease between you and Circular Ramp Garages, Inc., which you refuse to amend pursuant to the requirements of said Lease. For the purposes of this paragraph it will be deemed that no such construction loan or takeout loan is obtainable if such has not been obtained after application to three lending companies which have theretofore made loans in Kansas for the purpose of constructing buildings or amortizing the cost thereof, if Circular Ramp Garages, Inc., then elects not to apply to any other lending company.
d. At the time that Circular Ramp Garages, Inc., has performed or caused to be performed the terms of said paragraph IV(a) of said lease.
e. At the end of three years from the date of this letter.

Upon termination of the credit established under this letter you are to return the letter to the Pacific National Bank.

This Letter of Credit shall be irrevocable from its date providing that you accept the same within ten days from said date. Your acceptance is to be shown by the receipt by the undersigned of a copy of this letter with your acceptance shown by signing below.

PACIFIC NATIONAL BANK OF SAN FRANCISCO

/s/ A. G. Cinelli
A. G. Cinelli Vice President
/s/ D. Bannatyne
D. BANNATYNE for Cashier
The terms of the above Letter of Credit are accepted.

Dated May 17, 1962.

/s/ Marcellus M. Murdock
MARCELLUS M. MURDOCK

### Wichita Eagle & Beacon Publishing Co. v. Pacific Nat'l Bank of San Francisco

United States Court of Appeals, Ninth Circuit

493 F.2d 1285 (1974)

We do not agree with the district court that the instrument sued upon is a letter of credit, though it is so labeled. Rather, the instrument is an ordinary guaranty contract, obliging the defendant bank to pay whatever the lessee Circular Ramp Garages, Inc., owed on the underlying lease, up to the face amount of the guaranty. Since the underlying lease clearly contemplated the payment of $250,000 in case of default, and since this provision appears to be a valid liquidated damages clause, the judgment below must be modified to award the plaintiff $250,000 plus interest.

We do not base our holding that the instrument is not a letter of credit on the fact that payment was triggered by default rather than performance or on the fact that the instrument was written in a lease context, for we recognize that the commercial use of letters of credit has expanded far beyond the international sales context in which it originally developed.

The instrument involved here strays too far from the basic purpose of letters of credit; namely, providing a means of assuring payment cheaply by eliminating the need for the issuer to police the underlying contract. The instrument neither evidences an intent that payment be made merely on presentation on a draft nor specifies the documents required for termination or payment. To the contrary, it requires the actual existence in fact of most of the conditions specified: for termination or reduction, that the city have refused a building permit; for payment, that the lessee have failed to perform the terms of the lease and have failed to correct that default, in addition to an affidavit of notice.

True, in the text of the instrument itself the instrument is referred to as a "letter of credit," and we should, as the district court notes, "give effect wherever possible to the intent of the contracting parties." 343 F. Supp. at 338. But the relevant intent is manifested by the terms of the agreement, not by its label. And where, as here, the substantive provisions require the issuer to deal not simply in documents alone, but in facts relating to the performance of a separate contract (the lease, in this case), all distinction between a letter of credit and an ordinary guaranty contract would be obliterated by regarding the instrument as a letter of credit.

It would hamper rather than advance the extension of the letter of credit concept to new situations if an instrument such as this were held to be a letter of credit. The loose terms of this instrument invited the very evil that letters of credit are meant to avoid—protracted, expensive litigation. If the letter of credit concept is to have value in new situations, the instrument must be tightly drawn to strictly and clearly limit the responsibility of the issuer.

The bank contends that whatever the nature of the instrument, by its terms it had either reduced to $50,000 or terminated entirely by the time the draft was drawn. But the district court found that the lessee "failed to use due diligence to obtain the necessary building permits," and the lease provides that the lessee must "use due diligence to obtain all permits necessary." Since the instrument is a guaranty rather than a letter of credit, the bank should not be able to interpose a defense not available to the lessee unless such an intent is clear in the instrument. Therefore, we interpret the termination provisions to be subject to the duty of due diligence imposed by the lease. Since the lessee did not proceed with due diligence, it was not entitled to regard the building permit as refused, and the bank was not entitled to terminate the instrument because of the lessee's representations to that effect.

Since the instrument is not a letter of credit, the amount due depends upon what the lessee owes for the admitted breach. The underlying lease contemplates forfeiture of the entire $250,000 security in the event of total breach. The issue is whether the forfeiture clause is a valid provision for liquidated damages, or provides for a penalty and is therefore unenforceable.

The district court found that the lessor's damages "might well have been the face amount of the draft presented, $250,000." We take this to be a finding that the amount of actual damages that would flow from a total breach was uncertain and that the amount set was a reasonable forecast of such damages. Indeed, the defendant bank seems to concede that these two criteria for enforceable stipulated damages have been met; it argues only that no "intent" to liquidate damages was proven. Brief for Appellee and Cross-Appellant at 23-30.

But "intent" to liquidate damages, as opposed to intent to provide a penalty for breach, does not appear to be an independent element for enforcement of liquidation clauses in either Kansas or California. Although the California courts sometimes talk in terms of intent, in fact the cases turn solely on the reasonableness of the estimate and the difficulty of determining actual damages.

The district court's fact finding on the necessary prerequisites for enforcing a stipulated damages clause is supported by the evidence. We therefore hold the stipulated damages clause to be valid, and plaintiff is entitled to judgment for the amount stipulated. And since the claim is for a liquidated amount, plaintiff is also entitled to an award of interest from the date of the bank's refusal to honor the draft.

Reversed and remanded, with directions to enter judgment for plaintiff and against defendant in the amount of $250,000 together with interest thereon at the legal rate from and after May 3, 1965.

## NOTES, QUESTIONS, AND PROBLEM

1. The result by the Ninth Circuit Court of Appeals was approved by the drafters of Revised Article 5. See UCC §5-102, Official Comment 6.
2. If the bank's undertaking was to pay $250,000 upon receipt of a certification by the beneficiary that Circular Ramp Garages, Inc., had failed to comply with paragraph IV(a) of the lease rather than being conditioned on whether there had in fact been a failure to comply, would the undertaking be a "letter of credit" as defined in UCC section 5-102(a)(10)? Would the bank be required to pay even if there was no default under the lease? UCC §5-108(a). If the undertaking is a letter of credit, does it matter if the $250,000 was a reasonable liquidated damages amount, or can the policy against penalty clauses in contracts be circumvented via a letter of credit? See McLaughlin, *Standby Letters of Credit and Penalty Clauses: An Unexpected Synergy*, 43 Ohio St. L.J. 1 (1982).

***Problem 9-1.*** A bank's undertaking states that the bank is to pay the beneficiary upon presentation of bills of lading showing the shipment of goods by sea. The undertaking also indicates that shipment is not to be on ships that are over 15 years old. The beneficiary presents bills of lading showing that the goods have, indeed, been shipped. The buyer calls the issuer to complain that the goods have been shipped on a 20-year-old freighter. Is the undertaking a letter of credit? If so, what is the distinction between this hypothetical and *Wichita Eagle*? Should the bank pay? See UCC §5-102, Official Comment 6. See also UCC §5-108(a) and (g), Official Comment 9.

## 2. HAS THE DOCUMENTARY PRESENTATION COMPLIED WITH THE TERMS OF THE LETTER OF CREDIT?

UCC section 5-108 describes the issuer's duties when presented with a demand to pay under a letter of credit. The issuer is required to use standard banking practices in examining the documents presented and must determine whether they strictly comply with the terms of the letter of credit. If they do comply, the issuer is generally required to honor the presentation and pay. The issuer is then entitled to reimbursement from the applicant; that is, the party who requested the issuance of the letter of credit (e.g., a buyer of goods). If the documents do not comply, the issuer should not pay unless the applicant waives any discrepancies. If the issuer pays on a noncomplying presentation, the issuer may not be entitled to reimbursement. The following case demonstrates the principle of "strict compliance."

### Courtaulds North America, Inc. v. North Carolina Nat'l Bank

United States Court of Appeals, Fourth Circuit

528 F.2d 802 (1975)

A letter of credit with the date of March 21, 1973, was issued by the North Carolina National Bank at the request of and for the account of its customer, Adastra Knitting Mills, Inc. It made available upon the drafts of Courtaulds North America, Inc., "up to" $135,000.00 (later increased by $135,000.00) at "60 days date" to cover Adastra's purchases of acrylic yarn from Courtaulds. The life of the credit was extended in June to allow the drafts to be "drawn and negotiated on or before August 15, 1973."

Bank refused to honor a draft for $67,346.77 dated August 13, 1973, for yarn sold and delivered to Adastra. Courtaulds brought this action to recover this sum from Bank.

The defendant denied liability chiefly on the assertion that the draft did not agree with the letter's conditions, viz., that the draft be accompanied by a "commercial invoice in triplicate stating (inter alia) that it covers . . . 100% acrylic yarn" ; instead, the accompanying invoices stated that the goods were "Imported Acrylic Yarn."

Upon cross motions for summary judgment on affidavits and a stipulation of facts, the district court held defendant Bank liable to Courtaulds for the amount of the draft, interest, and costs. It concluded that the draft complied with the letter of credit when each invoice is read together with the packing lists stapled to it, for the lists stated on their faces: "Cartons marked: — 100% Acrylic." After considering the insistent rigidity of the law and usage of bank credits and acceptances, we must differ with the district judge and uphold Bank's position.

The letter of credit prescribed the terms of the drafts as follows:

> Drafts to be dated same as Bills of Lading. Draft(s) to be accompanied by:
> 1. Commercial invoice in triplicate stating that it covers 100,000 lbs. 100% Acrylic Yarn, Package Dyed at $1.35 per lb., FOB Buyers Plant, Greensboro, North Carolina Land Duty Paid.
> 2. Certificate stating goods will be delivered to buyer's plant land duty paid.
> 3. Inland Bill of Lading consigned to Adastra Knitting Mills, Inc. evidencing shipment from East Coast Port to Adastra Knitting Mills, Inc., Greensboro, North Carolina.

The shipment (the last) with which this case is concerned was made on or about August 8, 1973. On direction of Courtaulds bills of lading of that date were prepared for the consignment to Adastra from a bonded warehouse by motor carrier. The yarn was packaged in cartons and a packing list referring to its bill of lading accompanied each carton. After the yarn was delivered to the carrier, each bill of lading with the packing list was sent to Courtaulds. There, invoices for the sales were made out, and the invoices and packing lists stapled together. At the same time, Courtaulds wrote up the certificate, credit memorandum, and draft called for in the letter of credit. The draft was dated August 13, 1973, and drawn on Bank by Courtaulds payable to itself.

All of these documents — the draft, the invoices and the packing lists — were sent by Courtaulds to its correspondent in Mobile for presentation to Bank and collection of the draft which for the purpose had been endorsed to the correspondent.

This was the procedure pursued on each of the prior drafts and always the draft had been honored by Bank save in the present instance. Here the draft, endorsed to Bank, and the other papers were sent to Bank on August 14. Bank received them on Thursday, August 16. Upon processing, Bank found these discrepancies between the drafts with accompanying documents and the letter of credit: (1) that the invoice did not state "100% Acrylic Yarn" but described it as "Imported Acrylic Yarn" ; and (2) "Draft not drawn as per terms of (letter of credit), Date (August 13) not same as Bill of Lading (August 8) and not drawn 60 days after date" (but 60 days from Bill of Lading date 8/8/73). Finding of Fact 24. Since decision of this controversy is put on the first discrepancy we do not discuss the others.

On Monday, August 20, Bank called Adastra and asked if it would waive the discrepancies and thus allow Bank to honor the draft. In response, the president of Adastra informed Bank that it could not waive any discrepancies because a trustee in bankruptcy had been appointed for Adastra and Adastra could not do so alone. Upon word of these circumstances, Courtaulds on August 27 sent amended invoices to Bank, which were received by Bank on August 27. They referred to the consignment as "100% Acrylic Yarn," and thus would have conformed to the letter of credit had it not expired. On August 29 Bank wired Courtaulds that the draft remained unaccepted because of the expiration of the letter of credit on August 15. Consequently the draft with all the original documents was returned by Bank.

During the life of the letter of credit some drafts had not been of even dates with the bills of lading, and among the large number of invoices transmitted during this period, several did not describe the goods as "100% Acrylic Yarn." As to all of these deficiencies Bank called Adastra for and received approval before paying the drafts. Every draft save the one in suit was accepted.

### Conclusion on Law

The factual outline related is not in dispute, and the issue becomes one of law. It is well phrased by the district judge in his "Discussion" in this way:

> The only issue presented by the facts of this case is whether the documents tendered by the beneficiary to the issuer were in conformity with the terms of the letter of credit.

The letter of credit provided:

> Except as otherwise expressly stated herein, this credit is subject to the "Uniform Customs and Practice for Documentary Credits (1962 revision), the International Chamber of Commerce, Brochure No. 222." Finding of Fact 6.

Of particular pertinence, with accents added, are these injunctions of the Uniform Customs:

> Article 7. Banks must examine all documents with reasonable care to ascertain that they appear on their face to be in accordance with the terms and conditions of the credit.

> Article 8. In documentary credit operations all parties concerned deal in documents and not in goods.
>
> If, upon receipt of the documents, the issuing bank considers that they appear on their face not to be in accordance with the terms and conditions of the credit, that bank must determine, on the basis of the documents alone, whether to claim that payment, acceptance or negotiation was not effected in accordance with the terms and conditions of the credit.

> Article 9. Banks . . . do (not) assume any liability or responsibility for the description, . . . quality, . . . of the goods represented thereby. . . .
>
> The description of the goods in the commercial invoice must correspond with the description in the credit. In the remaining documents the goods may be described in general terms.

Also to be looked to are the North Carolina statutes, because in a diversity action, the federal courts apply the same law as would the courts of the state of adjudication. Here applicable would be Article 5 of the Uniform Commercial Code. [The court quotes from prerevision section 5-109, the provisions of which appear in current UCC section 5-108.]

In utilizing the rules of construction embodied in the letter of credit—the Uniform Customs and State statute—one must constantly recall that the drawee bank is not to be embroiled in disputes between the buyer and the seller, the beneficiary of the credit. The drawee is involved only with documents, not with merchandise. Its involvement is altogether separate and apart from the transaction between the buyer and seller; its duties and liability are governed exclusively by the terms of the letter, not the terms of the parties' contract with each other. Moreover, as the predominant authorities unequivocally declare, the beneficiary must meet the terms of the credit—and precisely—if it is to exact performance of the issuer. Failing such compliance there can be no recovery from the drawee. That is the specific failure of Courtaulds here.

Free of ineptness in wording the letter of credit dictated that each invoice express on its face that it covered 100 percent acrylic yarn. Nothing less is shown to be tolerated in the trade. No substitution and no equivalent, through interpretation or logic, will serve. Harfield, *Bank Credits and Acceptances* (5th ed. 1974), at p.73, commends and quotes aptly from an English case: "There is no room for documents which are almost the same, or which will do just as well." *Equitable Trust Co. of N.Y. v. Dawson Partners, Ltd.*, 27 Lloyd's List Law Rpts. 49, 52 (1926). Although no pertinent North Carolina decision has been laid before us, in many cases elsewhere, especially in New York, we find the tenet of Harfield to be unshaken.

At trial Courtaulds prevailed on the contention that the invoices in actuality met the specifications of the letter of credit in that the packing lists attached to the invoices disclosed on their faces that the packages contained "cartons marked: —100% acrylic." On this premise it was urged that the lists were a part of the invoice since they were appended to it, and the invoices should be read as one with the lists, allowing the lists to detail the invoices. But this argument cannot be accepted. In this connection it is well to revert to the distinction made in *Uniform Customs, supra,* between the "invoice" and the "remaining documents," emphasizing that in the latter the description may be in general terms while in the invoice the goods must be described in conformity with the credit letter.

The district judge's pat statement adeptly puts an end to this contention of Courtaulds:

> In dealing with letters of credit, it is a custom and practice of the banking trade for a bank to only treat a document as an invoice which clearly is marked on its face as "invoice." Finding of Fact 46.

This is not a pharisaical or doctrinaire persistence in the principle, but is altogether realistic in the environs of this case; it is plainly the fair and equitable measure. (The defect in description was not superficial but occurred in the statement of the quality of the yarn, not a frivolous concern.) The obligation of the drawee bank was graven in the credit. Indeed, there could be no departure from its words. Bank was not expected to scrutinize the collateral papers, such as the packing lists. Nor was it permitted to read into the instrument the contemplation or intention of the seller and buyer. Adherence to this rule was not only legally commanded, but it was factually ordered also, as will immediately appear.

Had Bank deviated from the stipulation of the letter and honored the draft, then at once it might have been confronted with the not improbable risk of the bankruptcy trustee's charge of liability for unwarrantably paying the draft moneys to the seller, Courtaulds, and refusal to reimburse Bank for the outlay. Contrarily, it might face a Courtaulds claim that since it had depended upon

Bank's assurance of credit in shipping yarn to Adastra, Bank was responsible for the loss. In this situation Bank cannot be condemned for sticking to the letter of the letter.

Nor is this conclusion affected by the amended or substituted invoices that Courtaulds sent to Bank after the refusal of the draft. No precedent is cited to justify retroactive amendment of the invoices or extension of the credit beyond the August 15 expiration of the letter.

Finally, the trial court found that although in its prior practices Bank had pursued a strict constructionist attitude, it had nevertheless on occasion honored drafts not within the verbatim terms of the credit letter. But it also found that in each of these instances Bank had first procured the authorization of Adastra to overlook the deficiencies. This truth is verified by the district court in its Findings of Fact:

> 42. It is a standard practice and procedure of the banking industry and trade for a bank to attempt to obtain a waiver of discrepancies from its customer in a letter of credit transaction. This custom and practice was followed by NCNB in connection with the draft and documents received from Courtaulds.
>
> 43. Following this practice, NCNB had checked all previous discrepancies it discovered in Courtaulds' documents with its customer Adastra to see if Adastra would waive those discrepancies noted by NCNB. Except for the transaction in question, Adastra waived all discrepancies noted by NCNB.
>
> 44. It is not normal or customary for NCNB, nor is it the custom and practice in the banking trade, for a bank to notify a beneficiary or the presenter of the documents that there were any deficiencies in the draft or documents if they are waived by the customer.

This endeavor had been fruitless on the last draft because of the inability of Adastra to give its consent. Obviously, the previous acceptances of truant invoices cannot be construed as a waiver in the present incident.

For these reasons, we must vacate the decision of the trial court, despite the evident close reasoning and research of the district judge, *Courtaulds North America, Inc. v. North Carolina N.B.*, 387 F. Supp. 92 (M.D.N.C. 1975). Entry of judgment in favor of the appellant Bank on its summary motion is necessary.

Reversed and remanded for final judgment.

## NOTES, QUESTIONS, AND PROBLEMS

1. The court's reasoning in this case was approved by the drafters of Revised Article 5. See UCC §5-108, Official Comment 6.
2. UCC section 5-108(e) requires the issuer to use standard practices of financial institutions in reviewing documents presented under a letter of credit. The question of whether the issuer observed such standards is one for the court to decide. Why should a court decide such a fundamental question? See UCC §5-108, Official Comment 1. Doesn't this rule effectively deny the parties to litigation over a letter of credit the right to a jury trial?

***Problem 9-2.*** How "strict" does "strict compliance" have to be? Assume that the letter of credit requires that drafts drawn under it make reference to "Letter of Credit No. 95-922." The draft presented makes reference to "Letter of Credit No. 95-9222." The bank's letter of credit numbering system does not go higher than 95-999. Is the beneficiary entitled to payment? See UCC §5-108(a) and (e), Official Comment 1. If the bank wishes to dishonor the letter of credit, how soon must it do so and what must it tell the beneficiary regarding its reasons for dishonor? UCC §5-108(b) and (c). Note that if the letter of credit is subject to UCP 600, the maximum period of time the bank has to examine it is five banking days. UCP 600 Art. 14.b.

***Problem 9-3.*** The letter of credit calls for invoices describing shipment of "blue widgets." In the widget industry "blue widgets" and "red widgets" are interchangeable, and a contract calling for the shipment of blue widgets can be performed by shipping red widgets. Both buyer and seller are aware of this trade usage. The seller and beneficiary under the letter of credit ships red widgets, and the invoice describes the goods being shipped as "red widgets." When the invoices are presented to the issuing bank, is it required to pay under the letter of credit? UCC §5-108(f)(3), Official Comment 10. Would the bank have a statutory right of reimbursement if it paid the buyer? UCC §5-108(i). See also UCC §5-117(a). Would the seller have recourse against the buyer if the buyer refuses to accept the red widgets?

***Problem 9-4.*** The documents presented to the issuing bank did not comply with the terms of the letter of credit. The bank contacted the applicant and asked if the discrepancies would be waived. The applicant responded that it would try to work things out with the beneficiary, but that for now it would not waive the discrepancies. The original presentation was thus properly dishonored. Subsequently, the applicant sent a letter to the issuing bank stating that if the beneficiary signed a letter, a copy of which was provided to the bank, the applicant would waive the discrepancies. The beneficiary then presented the documents again, along with a signed copy of the letter. The issuing bank contacted the applicant again, and was now told that the applicant would not waive the discrepancies. The bank thus dishonored the presentation and the letter of credit expired before a conforming presentation could be made. Did the bank properly dishonor the presentation? *Marsala International Trading Co. v. Comerica Bank*, 976 P.2d 275, 39 UCC Rep. Serv. 2d 217 (Colo. App. 1998).

***Problem 9-5.*** Buyer contracts to purchase shirts. Bank *X* issued a letter of credit in favor of Seller, which was confirmed by Bank *Y*. The letter of credit required, among other documents, that Seller present a sworn "Statement of Beneficiary" to the effect that the goods conformed to the contract of sale. The goods were shipped and Seller made a presentation of documents to Bank *Y*. Bank *Y* overlooked the missing Statement of Beneficiary and paid Seller. The goods were delivered to Buyer, who was unhappy with the quality of the goods. When the documents were presented to Bank *X* by Bank *Y*, Buyer contacted Bank *X* and asked it not to pay until it resolved its dispute with Seller regarding the quality of the goods. Bank *Y* agreed to the delay, provided it received interest on the money it had paid to Seller. Neither Buyer nor Bank *X* noticed the missing Statement of Beneficiary. Six months later, Buyer and Seller resolved their differences regarding the shirts, with Buyer receiving some credit off of the purchase price. Bank *X* then noticed the missing Statement of Beneficiary and refused to pay under the letter of credit. Does Bank *Y* have recourse against Bank *X*? If Bank *X* pays Bank *Y*, does it have recourse against Buyer? See UCC §§5-107(a), 5-108(b), (c) and (i)(1), Official Comment 5, 5-111, Official Comment 2 and 5-117. *See also Petra Int'l Banking Corp. v. First American Bank of Virginia,* 758 F. Supp. 1120 (E.D. Va. 1991).

## 3. FRAUD

As previously noted, the obligation of the issuer to pay under the letter of credit is independent of the underlying contract. If the documents comply on their face, it doesn't matter if the goods that are shipped are nonconforming. The issuer is required to pay, and the buyer's recourse is against the seller. What happens, however, if the buyer learns before the letter of credit is honored that the seller has forged the necessary documents or has shipped empty boxes? Should the bank pay any attention to the buyer's allegations of fraud? The following case deals with this issue.

### United Bank Limited v. Cambridge Sporting Goods

Court of Appeals of New York

41 N.Y.2d 254, 360 N.E.2d 943, 392 N.Y.S.2d 265 (1976)

On this appeal, we must decide whether fraud on the part of a seller-beneficiary of an irrevocable letter of credit may be successfully asserted as a defense against holders of drafts drawn by the seller pursuant to the credit. If we conclude that this defense may be interposed by the buyer who procured the letter of credit, we must also determine whether the courts below improperly imposed upon appellant buyer the burden of proving that respondent banks to whom the drafts were made payable by the seller-beneficiary of the letter of credit were not holders in due course. The issues presented raise important questions concerning the application of the law of letters of credit and the rules governing proof of holder in due course status set forth in Article 3 of the Uniform Commercial Code.

In April 1971, appellant Cambridge Sporting Goods Corporation (Cambridge) entered into a contract for the manufacture and sale of boxing gloves with Duke Sports (Duke), a Pakistani corporation. Duke committed itself to the manufacture of 27,936 pairs of boxing gloves at a sale price of $42,576.80; and arranged with its Pakistani bankers, United Bank Limited (United) and The Muslim Commercial Bank (Muslim), for the financing of the sale. Cambridge was requested by these banks to cover payment of the purchase price by opening an irrevocable letter of credit with its bank in New York, Manufacturers Hanover Trust Company (Manufacturers). Manufacturers issued an irrevocable letter of credit obligating it, upon the receipt of certain documents indicating shipment of the merchandise pursuant to the contract, to accept and pay, 90 days after acceptance, drafts drawn upon Manufacturers for the purchase price of the gloves.

Following confirmation of the opening of the letter of credit, Duke informed Cambridge that it would be impossible to manufacture and deliver the merchandise within the time period required by the contract, and sought an extension of time for performance until September 15, 1971, and a continuation of the letter of credit, which was due to expire on August 11. Cambridge replied on June 18 that it would not agree to a postponement of the manufacture and delivery of the gloves because of its resale commitments and, hence, it promptly advised Duke that the contract was canceled and the letter of credit should be returned. Cambridge simultaneously notified United of the contract cancellation.

Despite the cancellation of the contract, Cambridge was informed on July 17, 1971, that documents had been received at Manufacturers from United purporting to evidence a shipment of the boxing gloves under the terms of the canceled contract. The documents were accompanied by a draft, dated July 16, 1971, drawn by Duke upon Manufacturers and made payable to United, for the amount of $21,288.40, one half of the contract price of the boxing gloves. A second set of documents was received by Manufacturers from Muslim, also accompanied by a draft, dated August 20, and drawn upon Manufacturers by Duke for the remaining amount of the contract price.

An inspection of the shipments upon their arrival revealed that Duke had shipped old, unpadded, ripped, and mildewed gloves rather than the new gloves to be manufactured as agreed upon. Cambridge then commenced an action against Duke in Supreme Court, New York County, joining Manufacturers as a party, and obtained a preliminary injunction prohibiting the latter from paying drafts drawn under the letter of credit; subsequently, in November 1971, Cambridge levied on the funds subject to the letter of credit and the draft, which were delivered by Manufacturers to the sheriff in compliance therewith. Duke ultimately defaulted in the action and judgment against it was entered in the amount of the drafts in March 1972.

The present proceeding was instituted by the Pakistani banks to vacate the levy made by Cambridge and to obtain payment of the drafts on the letter of credit. The banks asserted that they were holders in due course of the drafts that had been made payable to them by Duke and, thus, were entitled to the proceeds thereof irrespective of any defenses that Cambridge had established against their transferor, Duke, in the prior action, which had terminated in a default judgment. The banks' motion for summary judgment on this claim was denied and the request by Cambridge for a jury trial was granted. Cambridge sought to depose the petitioning banks, but its request was denied and, as an alternative, written interrogatories were served on the Pakistani banks to learn the circumstances surrounding the transfer of the drafts to them. At trial, the banks introduced no evidence other than answers to several of the written interrogatories, which were received over objection by Cambridge to the effect that the answers were conclusory, self-serving, and otherwise inadmissible. Cambridge presented evidence of its dealings with Duke including the cancellation of the contract and uncontested proof of the subsequent shipment of essentially worthless merchandise.

The trial court concluded that the burden of proving that the banks were not holders in due course lay with Cambridge, and directed a verdict in favor of the banks on the ground that Cambridge had not met that burden; the court stated that Cambridge failed to demonstrate that the banks themselves had participated in the seller's acts of fraud, proof of which was concededly present in the record. The appellate division affirmed, agreeing that while there was proof tending to establish the defenses against the seller, Cambridge had not shown that the seller's acts were "connected to the petitioners (banks) in any manner."

We reverse and hold that it was improper to direct a verdict in favor of the petitioning Pakistani banks. We conclude that the defense of fraud in the transaction was established and in that circumstance the burden shifted to petitioners to prove that they were holders in due course and took the drafts for value, in good faith and without notice of any fraud on the part of Duke. UCC §3-302. Additionally, we think it was improper for the trial court to permit petitioners to introduce into evidence answers to Cambridge's interrogatories to demonstrate their holder in due course status.

This case does not come before us in the typical posture of a lawsuit between the bank issuing the letter of credit and presenters of drafts drawn under the credit seeking payment. Because Cambridge obtained an injunction against payment of the drafts and has levied against the proceeds of the drafts, it stands in the same position as the issuer, and, thus, the law of letters of credit governs the liability of Cambridge to the Pakistani banks. Article 5 of the Uniform Commercial Code, dealing with letters of credit, and the Uniform Customs and Practice for Documentary Credits promulgated by the International Chamber of Commerce set forth the duties and obligations of the issuer of a letter of credit. A letter of credit is a commitment on the part of the issuing bank that it will pay a draft presented to it under the terms of the credit, and if it is a documentary draft, upon presentation of the required documents of title. Banks issuing letters of credit deal in documents and not in goods and are not responsible for any breach of warranty or nonconformity of the goods involved in the underlying sales contract. Subdivision (2) of section 5-114,[5] however, indicates certain limited circumstances in which an issuer may properly refuse to honor a draft drawn under a letter of credit or a customer may enjoin an issuer from honoring such a draft.[3] Thus, where "fraud in the transaction" has been shown and the holder has not taken the draft in circumstances that would make it a holder in due course, the customer may apply to enjoin the issuer from paying drafts drawn under the letter of credit. See 1955 Report of N.Y. Law Rev. Comm., vol. 3, pp. 1554-1559. This rule

---

5. Note that this case is being decided under the prerevised version of UCC Article 5. The counterpart in current Article 5 to §5-114 is current §5-109. As will be discussed following the case, current §5-109 is similar but not identical to §5-114—Ed.

3. Subsection (2) of §5-114 provides that:

> (u)nless otherwise agreed when documents appear on their face to comply with the terms of a credit but . . . there is fraud in the transaction (a) the issuer must honor the draft or demand for payment if honor is demanded by a . . . holder of the draft . . . which has taken the draft . . . under the credit and under circumstances which would make it a holder in due course (§3-302) . . .; and
>
> (b) in all other cases as against its customer, an issuer acting in good faith may honor the draft . . . despite notification from the customer of fraud, forgery or other defect not apparent on the face of the documents but a court of appropriate jurisdiction may enjoin such honor.

represents a codification of precode case law most eminently articulated in the landmark case of *Sztejn v. Schroder Banking Corp.*, 177 Misc. 719, 31 N.Y.S.2d 631, Shientag, J., where it was held that the shipment of cowhair in place of bristles amounted to more than mere breach of warranty, but to fraud sufficient to constitute grounds for enjoining payment of drafts to one not a holder in due course.

The history of the dispute between the various parties involved in this case reveals that Cambridge had in a prior, separate proceeding successfully enjoined Manufacturers from paying the drafts and has attached the proceeds of the drafts. It should be noted that the question of the availability and the propriety of this relief is not before us on this appeal. The petitioning banks do not dispute the validity of the prior injunction nor do they dispute the delivery of worthless merchandise. Rather, on this appeal they contend that as holders in due course they are entitled to the proceeds of the drafts irrespective of any fraud on the part of Duke. Although precisely speaking there was no specific finding of fraud in the transaction by either of the courts below, their determinations were based on that assumption. The evidentiary facts are not disputed and we hold upon the facts as established, that the shipment of old, unpadded, ripped, and mildewed gloves rather than the new boxing gloves as ordered by Cambridge constituted fraud in the transaction within the meaning of subdivision (2) of section 5-114. It should be noted that the drafters of section 5-114, in their attempt to codify the *Sztejn* case and in utilizing the term "fraud in the transaction," have eschewed a dogmatic approach and adopted a flexible standard to be applied as the circumstances of a particular situation mandate. It can be difficult to draw a precise line between cases involving breach of warranty (or a difference of opinion as to the quality of goods) and outright fraudulent practice on the part of the seller. To the extent, however, that Cambridge established that Duke was guilty of fraud in shipping, not merely nonconforming merchandise but worthless fragments of boxing gloves, this case is similar to *Sztejn*.

If the petitioning banks are holders in due course they are entitled to recover the proceeds of the drafts, but if such status cannot be demonstrated their petition must fail. The parties are in agreement that section 3-307 of the Code (Revised UCC section 3-308) governs the pleading and proof of holder in due course status. [Court quotes from what is now Revised UCC section 3-308.]

Even though [Revised UCC section 3-308] is contained in Article 3 of the code dealing with negotiable instruments rather than letters of credit, we agree that its provisions should control in the instant case. Thus, a presenter of drafts drawn under a letter of credit must prove that it took the drafts for value, in good faith, and without notice of the underlying fraud in the transaction. UCC §3-302.

It was error for the trial court to direct a verdict in favor of the Pakistani banks because this determination rested upon a misallocation of the burden of proof; and we conclude that the banks have not satisfied the burden of proving that they qualified in all respects as holders in due course by any affirmative proof. The only evidence introduced by the banks consisted of conclusory answers to the interrogatories. The failure of the banks to meet their burden is fatal to their claim for recovery of the proceeds of the drafts and their petition must therefore be dismissed.

## NOTES AND PROBLEMS

The Official Commentary to UCC section 5-109 explains what the drafters had in mind when they require "material fraud" as a requirement for an injunction against payment. As to materiality, Comment 1 notes that if a contract calls for 1,000 barrels of salad oil but the seller knowingly ships only 998 barrels, the fraud may nonetheless be immaterial and the letter of credit should be honored if the documents comply on their face. The comment goes on to state: "Material fraud by the beneficiary occurs only when the beneficiary has no colorable right to expect honor and where there is no basis in fact to support such a right to honor."

In the prior case, it does not appear that there was any issue but that the beneficiary under the letter of credit was engaging in "material fraud." The issue was whether the issuer (in this case the buyer was standing in the shoes of the issuer because it had taken over the proceeds of the letter of credit from the issuing bank) had to pay anyway because the parties claiming a right to payment were "holders in due course."

A holder in due course is basically a bona fide purchaser of a negotiable instrument. Negotiable instruments are covered by Article 3 of the Uniform Commercial Code, and include most promissory notes and checks. In this case, United Bank and Muslim Commercial Bank were claiming that they were holders in due course of "drafts" issued by the seller (Duke) and drawn on the issuer of the letter of credit (Manufacturer).

You can think of a "draft" as being like a check. When you draw a check from your bank account, you are ordering the bank to pay to the order of the person you name as the payee. In the documentary sales transaction, the seller will draw a draft ordering the buyer or the bank issuing the letter of credit to pay the seller, or somebody else designated by the seller. The buyer or issuer of the letter of credit is thus like the bank in the check example, and is referred to as the "drawee" of the draft. See UCC §3-103(a)(2). The seller is the "drawer." UCC §3-103(a)(3). One of the drafts in the preceding case might have looked something like this:

> [Date]
>
> At 90 days deferred from acceptance, pay to the order of United Bank $[amount] and charge to account of Cambridge Sporting Goods Corporation.
>
> To: Manufacturers Hanover Trust Co./s/ Duke Sports
>
> [Address] Duke Sports

Assuming that the documents required under the letter of credit are in order, the issuer, in this case Manufacturers Hanover Trust Co., will "accept" the draft by signing it and dating it. Acceptance of a draft simply means that the person accepting is agreeing to pay it. UCC §3-409(a).

In cases such as this one, the seller may need money immediately and does not want to wait 90 days for payment. It may then sell the draft at a discount to another financial institution. This appears to have occurred in this case, with United Bank and Muslim Commercial Bank providing the financing. It does not appear in this case, however, that Manufacturers Hanover accepted the drafts — the injunction appears to have prevented it. Under Revised UCC section 5-109(a)(1)(iii), it would not matter then whether the presenting banks were holders in due course because Revised Article 5 only protects holders in due course who purchase drafts after acceptance. Why should holders in due course be protected at all when the party selling the draft engaged in fraud? Why should they only be protected after the issuer has accepted the draft?

***Problem 9-6.*** Assume the same facts as in the preceding case, except that United Bank was a confirming bank under the letter of credit. United Bank was not aware that the seller was shipping worthless goods. The beneficiary, Duke, presented documents to United Bank that conformed on their face with the terms of the letter of credit. United Bank honored the presentation. Before the documents were presented to Manufacturers Hanover, the applicant, Cambridge Sporting Goods, learned of the fraud. Can Cambridge obtain an injunction prohibiting Manufacturers Hanover from paying under the letter of credit? See UCC §5-109(a)(1)(ii) and (b)(4).

***Problem 9-7.*** If the issuing bank is told by the applicant of a fraud, either in terms of forgery of the documents or similar to the situation described in the preceding case, what are its options if the documents comply on their face and the applicant does not obtain an injunction? See UCC §5-109. What is the bank's exposure in the event that it dishonors the presentation and it turns out that the applicant was lying? Can the bank be liable for consequential damages or attorney's fees? UCC §5-111.

***Problem 9-8.*** Assume that a bank wrongfully dishonors a presentation under a letter of credit and returns the documents to the seller. The seller is able to stop delivery of the goods to the buyer. Is the seller required to resell the goods and thus reduce the issuing bank's liability? If the seller does resell the goods, is the bank's liability reduced? UCC §5-111(a).

## C. BANK COLLECTION OF DOCUMENTARY DRAFTS

In some situations, the parties may decide to forego a letter of credit and instead condition delivery of the document of title to the buyer upon the buyer's payment for the goods. The banking system may be used in these cases to transmit the documents from the seller's place of business to the buyer's place of business. At that location, the buyer will inspect the documents and if they are in order, make payment. The presenting bank will then give the documents to the buyer, enabling the buyer to take delivery of the goods.

In this transaction, the seller of goods will draw up a document ordering the buyer to pay for the goods. This document is called a "draft," and it is a negotiable instrument if it orders the buyer to pay to the order of the seller or some other named person. It is covered by Articles 3 and 4 of the UCC. Drafts are discussed in the immediately preceding section of this book, pages 278-279, *supra*.

The draft, the bill of lading, and any other documents required by the sales contract, such as inspection certificates, will then be forwarded by the seller through the banking system to a bank located near the buyer. The buyer will be notified that the documents have arrived, and will go to the bank to inspect them. If the documents are in order, the buyer will pay the draft and receive possession of the documents if the draft is immediately payable. If the parties have decided to do business on credit, meaning that the buyer has more than three days to make payment after presentment of the draft, the buyer is required to "accept" the draft, meaning that the buyer acknowledges liability. See UCC §4-503(1). "Acceptance" occurs by the buyer simply signing the draft. UCC §3-409. If the buyer refuses to accept or pay, the presenting bank is required to give notification to the seller of dishonor, and await instructions regarding disposition of the goods. UCC §§4-501 and 4-503.

As is the case with the letter of credit transaction, when the buyer agrees to pay against presentation of documents, the buyer is generally forfeiting the right to inspect the goods before payment. UCC §2-513(3)(b). The buyer still has a right to inspect the goods before accepting them, but if the buyer decides to reject, the buyer will be forced to sue the seller to obtain a refund of the price.

In payment against documents situations, the buyer must rely on the descriptions of the goods found in the bills of lading and other documents that are tendered. The carrier issuing a bill of lading owes a duty to a consignee of a nonnegotiable bill of lading who has given value and acted in good faith and to a holder of a negotiable bill to whom the bill has been duly negotiated that the description of the goods and the date of the bill of lading are accurate. UCC §7-301 and 49 USC §80113. The carrier can generally avoid liability for misdescription of goods that were packaged by the shipper by providing a disclaimer such as "shipper's weight, load, and count," provided that the carrier is not aware of the misdescription. A common carrier is required, however, to count the number of packages and determine the kind and quantity of bulk freight. This obligation cannot be disclaimed. The bank presenting the documents only warrants that it is acting in good faith and with proper authority. UCC §7-508.

## Rheinberg-Kellerei GmbH v. Vineyard Wine Co.

North Carolina Court of Appeals

53 N.C. App. 560, 281 S.E.2d 425 (1981)

Plaintiff, a West German wine producer and exporter, instituted this action to recover the purchase price of a shipment of wine sold to defendant and lost at sea en route between Germany and the United States. Subsequent to a hearing, the court, sitting without a jury, made the following findings of fact.

Plaintiff is a West German corporation engaged in the business of producing, selling, and exporting wine. Defendant, a North Carolina corporation, is a distributor of wine, buying and selling foreign and domestic wines at wholesale. Frank Sutton, d/b/a Frank Sutton & Company and d/b/a The Empress Importing Company, and other names, of Miami Beach, Florida, is a licensed importer and seller of wines. During 1978 and 1979 Sutton served as an agent for plaintiff and was authorized to sell and solicit orders for plaintiff's wine in the United States. During 1978 and early 1979, Randall F. Switzer, then of Raleigh, North Carolina, was a broker soliciting orders of wine on behalf of several producers and brokers, including Sutton, on a commission basis.

[Defendant contracted through Switzer and Frank Sutton to purchase 620 cases of plaintiff's wines.]

On or about November 27, 1978, plaintiff issued notice to Sutton giving the date of the shipment, port of origin, vessel, estimated date of arrival, and port of arrival. Sutton did not give any of such information to defendant or to Switzer and did not notify defendant of anything. There was never any communication of any kind between plaintiff and defendant, and defendant was not aware of the details of the shipment.

Plaintiff delivered the wine ordered by defendant, consolidated in a container with the other wine, to a shipping line on November 29, 1978, for shipment from Rotterdam to Wilmington, North Carolina, on board the MS Munchen. Defendant did not request the plaintiff to deliver the wine ordered to any particular destination, and plaintiff and its agent, Sutton, selected the port of Wilmington for the port of entry into the United States. The entire container of wine was consigned by plaintiff to defendant, with freight payable at destination by defendant.

After delivering the wine to the ocean vessel for shipment, plaintiff forwarded the invoice for the entire container, certificate of origin, and bill of lading to its bank in West Germany, which forwarded the documents to Wachovia Bank and Trust Company, N.A., in Charlotte, North Carolina. The documents were received by Wachovia on December 27, 1978. The method of payment for the sale was for plaintiff's bank in West Germany to send the invoice, certificate of origin, and bill of lading to Wachovia, whereupon defendant was to pay the purchase price to Wachovia and obtain the shipping documents. Wachovia then would forward payment to plaintiff's bank, and defendant could present the shipping documents to the carrier to obtain possession.

Wachovia mailed to defendant on December 29, 1978, a notice requesting payment for the entire consolidated shipment by sight draft in exchange for documents. The notice was not returned by the post office to the sender.

On or about January 24, 1979, defendant first learned that the container of wine had left Germany in early December 1978 aboard the MS Munchen, which was lost in the North Atlantic with all hands and cargo aboard between December 12 and 22, 1978.

Defendant did not receive any wine from plaintiff and did not pay Wachovia for the lost shipment. Plaintiff released the sight draft documents to Frank Sutton. Defendant was not furnished with any copy of said documents until receiving some in March and April 1979 and the others through discovery after this action was filed.

The order and "Special Instructions," mailed by Sutton to plaintiff, but not to defendant, provided inter alia: (1) "Insurance to be covered by purchaser"; (2) "Send a 'Notice of Arrival' to both the customer and to Frank Sutton & Company"; and (3) "Payment may be deferred until the merchandise has arrived at the port of entry."

From judgment in favor of the defendant, dismissing plaintiff's action, both plaintiff and defendant have appealed.

WELLS, Judge.

The first question presented by plaintiff's appeal is whether the trial court was correct in its conclusion that the risk of loss for the wine never passed from plaintiff to defendant due to the failure of plaintiff to give prompt notice of the shipment to defendant. Plaintiff made no exceptions to the findings of fact contained in the judgment and does not contend that the facts found were unsupported by the evidence.

All parties agree that the contract in question was a "shipment" contract; that is, one not requiring delivery of the wine at any particular destination. The Uniform Commercial Code, as adopted in North Carolina, dictates when the transfer of risk of loss occurs in this situation. [The court quotes from UCC section 2-509(1)(a).]

Before a seller will be deemed to have "duly delivered" the goods to the carrier, however, he must fulfill certain duties owed to the buyer. In the absence of any agreement to the contrary, these responsibilities, set out in UCC section 2-504, are as follows:

[The court quotes section 2-504.]

The trial court concluded that the plaintiff's failure to notify the defendant of the shipment until after the sailing of the ship and the ensuing loss, was not "prompt notice" within the meaning of UCC section 2-504, and therefore, the risk of loss did not pass to defendant upon the delivery of the wine to the carrier pursuant to the provisions of UCC section 2-509(1)(a). We hold that the conclusions of the trial court were correct. The seller is burdened with special responsibilities under a shipment contract because of the nature of the risk of loss being transferred. Where the buyer, upon shipment by seller, assumes the perils involved in carriage, he must have a reasonable opportunity to guard against these risks by independent arrangements with the carrier. The requirement of prompt notification by the seller, as used in UCC section 2-504(c), must be construed as taking into consideration the need of a buyer to be informed of the shipment in sufficient time for him to take action to protect himself from the risk of damage to or loss of the goods while in transit. It would not be practical or desirable, however, for the courts to attempt to engraft onto section 2-504 of the UCC a rigid definition of prompt notice. Given the myriad factual situations which arise in business dealings, and keeping in mind the commercial realities, whether notification has been "prompt" within the meaning of UCC will have to be determined on a case-by-case basis, under all the circumstances.

In the case at hand, the shipment of wine was lost at sea sometime between December 12 and 22, 1978. Although plaintiff did notify its agent, Frank Sutton, regarding pertinent details of the shipment on or about November 27, 1978, this information was not passed along to defendant. The shipping documents were not received by defendant's bank for forwarding to defendant until December 27, 1978, days after the loss had already been incurred. Since the defendant was never notified directly or by the forwarding of shipping documents within the time in which its interest could have been protected by insurance or otherwise, defendant was entitled to reject the shipment pursuant to the term of UCC section 2-504(c).

Affirmed.

## NOTES AND QUESTIONS

1. Please read Official Comment 5 to UCC section 2-504. Was the foregoing case properly decided in light of that comment?
2. How would this case be decided under the CISG? See CISG Articles 31, 32, 34, and 67.
3. What are the duties of the presenting bank in a documentary draft transaction? See UCC §§4-501 through 4-504 and the following case.

### Rheinberg-Kellerei GmbH v. Brooksfield National Bank of Commerce

United States Court of Appeals, Fifth Circuit

901 F.2d 481 (1990)

American bank did not notify German bank of difficulty in payment on international collection order that came due on arrival of goods in Houston; the collection order was eventually dishonored. The district court held that the American bank did not know, and had no duty to inquire, whether goods had arrived, and entered take-nothing judgment. Because we find that the American bank was on notice of the possibility of dishonor and should have told the German bank of the problem in collection, we REVERSE.

#### Facts

In January 1986, J&J Wine, an American company, ordered a shipment of wine from a German firm, Rheinberg Kellerei GmbH, through an importer, Frank Sutton & Co.[1] Payment was to be made through an international letter of collection handled by Edekabank ("Edeka") in Germany and Brooksfield National Bank of Commerce Bank in San Antonio ("NBC Bank").[2] On March 27, NBC Bank received the letter of collection, bill of lading, and invoices from Edeka. The letter of collection noted that payment was due "on arrival of goods in Houston harbor," and called for NBC Bank to notify Sutton "in

1. The "GmbH" designation means "Gesellschaft mit beschrankter Haftung," or "company with limited liability." GmbH is a common form of corporate organization in Germany and is similar to the "Inc." designation in the American corporate system.

2. In a case like this one, international letters of collection are issued by the seller's bank (Edeka) and sent to the buyer's bank (NBC Bank), which in turn presents the letter and its documents to the buyer. To receive the documents and collect the goods, the buyer pays the amount due to its bank, which then forwards the funds to the seller's bank. Enforcement of these letters is governed by the International Chamber of Commerce's International Rules for Collection.

case of any difficulty of lack payment." The invoices noted an estimated time of arrival: April 2, 1986. NBC Bank then presented the documents to J&J Wine on March 27.

There is some dispute as to what, exactly, J&J Wine told NBC Bank about its financial situation at the time, but it is sure that J&J Wine did not pay the amount due, and instead asked NBC Bank to hold the letter for a time while J&J Wine worked to raise the money for payment. NBC Bank did not notify Edeka or Sutton of J&J Wine's failure to pay on presentment. In fact, NBC Bank did nothing further until early May, when Sutton informed them that the wine was still at the Houston port and NBC Bank cabled Edeka for further instructions.

The wine had arrived in Houston on March 31, but NBC Bank did not receive notice of that. Because J&J Wine had not taken delivery of it, the wine sat, exposed, at Houston harbor in metal containers until it had deteriorated completely. U.S. Customs agents eventually sold it at auction.[4] J&J Wine subsequently went out of business, and Rheinberg Kellerei was never paid for the wine.

Rheinberg Kellerei then brought this suit, alleging that NBC Bank had negligently failed to inform it of J&J Wine's failure to pay, and that because of that negligence, the wine had spoiled at Houston harbor. After a bench trial, the district court entered a take-nothing judgment for NBC Bank. The court reasoned that, because payment was not due until the wine's arrival, and NBC Bank had no notice of that arrival and no duty to inquire further, NBC Bank had no knowledge that J&J Wine was in breach of the payment terms. For that reason, the district court held that NBC Bank could not be held liable for failure to inform Edeka of J&J Wine's default.

Complaining that the district court improperly applied the requirements of the International Rules for Collection (the "Rules") and erred in construing the letter of collection itself, Rheinberg Kellerei brought this appeal.

## Discussion

### I. Duty to Inform

NBC Bank presented the letter of collection and the other documents to J&J Wine for payment on March 27, 1986, before the wine had arrived and before the payment was due. Rheinberg Kellerei argues that, regardless of whether NBC Bank knew when the wine had arrived, once NBC Bank presented the documents, it had a duty to inform Edeka of any problem in collecting J&J Wine's payment. We agree. That duty arises both from the Rules and the collection letter itself.

#### A. Letter of Collection

The letter, which is the primary source of responsibility in this case, instructs NBC Bank to notify Sutton "in case of any difficulty of lack payment." The district court found that section demanded notice only if there were a "lack of

4. There is no evidence in the record as to the price paid at auction, or whether that amount was more than the customs and wharfage fees.

payment or failure to pay." Likewise, NBC Bank emphasizes that the trigger for notice is a *lack* of payment.

What the court below and NBC Bank ignore is the word "difficulty." The letter did not instruct NBC Bank to notify Sutton only if there were a default, or a failure to pay, or a lack of payment. Rather, NBC Bank was called on to act also if there were any *difficulty* in collecting payment. And the request that NBC Bank hold the letter while J&J Wine sought financing certainly posed a difficulty in collection. Once NBC Bank knew that J&J Wine had asked for time to come up with the money, it should have notified Sutton in accordance with the letter's instructions.

The Rules specify that any special instructions posted on a letter of collection should be "complete and precise." General Provisions, §C. While the instructions given on this letter could have been in clearer language, they are sufficiently precise to make NBC Bank aware of its duty to notify Sutton once difficulty arose in the collection.

B. International Rules for Collection

Article 20(iii)(c) of the Rules provides that the "collecting bank [NBC Bank] must send without delay advice of nonpayment or advice of nonacceptance to the bank from whom the collecting order was received [Edeka]." The court below and NBC Bank submit that section called on NBC Bank to notify Edeka if J&J Wine had not paid on the letter at the time it came due—on arrival of the goods in Houston harbor. And, they argue, since NBC Bank had no actual notice of the arrival of the goods, it did not breach that duty to notify.

The issue, it seems, is the definition of "nonpayment" as it is used in Article 20(iii)(c). Does it refer to a failure to pay on presentment? Does it require an affirmative statement of intent not to pay? Must the due date have arrived? No court has yet defined the term and its attendant duties, so we must look for guidance elsewhere.

The Rules were adopted to aid in "defining, simplifying, and harmonizing the practices and terminology used in international banking." I.C.C. Banking Commission, Statement of Services to Business. They serve, for the international banking community, the same function as the Uniform Commercial Code does for domestic players. There is no reason, then, to ignore the UCC as an advisory source.

Section 4-502 of the UCC governs payment of "on arrival" drafts, such as were presented in our case. Under that section, a bank such as NBC Bank may, but need not, present the documents to the buyer before the goods arrive. But if the buyer does not pay at that time, the bank must notify the seller's bank: "Refusal to pay or accept because the goods have not arrived is not dishonor; *the bank must notify its transferor of such refusal* but need not present the draft again. . . ." UCC §4-502 (emphasis added). The UCC imposes on the presenting bank a duty to notify the seller's bank of any delay or failure to pay on presentment of an "on arrival" draft, *whether or not the draft is yet due.*

If section 4-502 were applied to our case, NBC Bank would have a duty to notify Edeka of J&J Wine's failure to pay the letter of collection when it was presented on March 27, even though the goods were not yet in Houston harbor and the payment was not yet due. This is not to say that J&J Wine was in default at that time or had dishonored the letter. Rather, the notice is an act of prudence, an exercise in due care. And, as the aims of the Rules and the UCC are more than consistent, and both demand the exercise of due care, we find that the Rules impose the same duty. NBC Bank should have notified Edeka of J&J Wine's failure to pay at presentment, as that failure constituted a "nonpayment" under Article 20(iii)(c).

NBC Bank and the court below rely heavily on the fact that NBC Bank had no actual knowledge of the wine's arrival in Houston, and had no duty to inquire further. We agree with those premises, but do not feel they affect NBC Bank's duty to notify. That duty arose—under both the Rules and the letter itself—when J&J Wine failed to pay on presentment and asked for time. Arrival of the wine did not trigger it. And NBC Bank cannot avoid liability by hiding from knowledge of arrival and claiming that ignorance as a defense.

II. Damages

State law governs the measure of damages in a case such as this one. UCC section 2-709 gives the relevant standard: "[T]he seller may recover, together with any incidental damages under the next section, the price (1) of goods accepted or of conforming goods lost or damaged . . . after risk of their loss has passed to the buyer." Risk of loss had passed to J&J Wine when the goods arrived at Houston harbor and were available for J&J Wine to take delivery. UCC §2-509(1)(b). The district court found that because the wine was exposed for such a long period in Houston harbor, it was "'overcooked' and had deteriorated, lost its original flavor, freshness, was flat and should not be sold into the market that it was intended." Since the goods were so damaged, Rheinberg Kellerei is entitled to the contract price plus the unpaid freight costs, as provided in UCC section 2-709(1)(a).

NBC Bank is entitled to a credit for the net proceeds of any resale of the damaged wine. Customs agents sold the wine at auction, but we have no evidence before us of the price paid or the net amount remaining after customs fees, wharfage, and the costs of the auction were paid. For that reason, we remand this case to the district court for the limited purpose of calculating that net amount. After finding that net amount, the district court should enter judgment for Rheinberg Kellerei for the contract price plus freight charges, less the net proceeds of the customs auction.

**Conclusion**

NBC Bank had a duty to notify Edeka or Sutton, which was triggered when J&J Wine failed to pay the letter of collection on presentment and asked for more time. That duty arose from two sources: the Rules and the letter itself. Though payment was not due until the wine arrived in Houston harbor, that arrival was not a triggering event for the duty to arise, and lack of knowledge of it is no defense. The judgment of the district court is, therefore, REVERSED, and this cause is REMANDED for calculation of damages.

It is so ordered.

## PROBLEM

***Problem 9-9.*** Assume that a contract for sale of wine calls for payment against documents with the documents to be presented through banks. The documents are expected to arrive before the wine. The negotiable bill of lading states, "Shipper's weight, load, and count." The bill of lading states "32 cases of wine," which was consistent with the terms of the contract for sale. Is buyer allowed to inspect the shipment before paying? See UCC §2-513. Assume that the buyer pays the presenting bank and receives the bill of lading. The buyer then takes delivery of the goods. The buyer learns that only 31 cases of wine were shipped and delivered. In addition, one of the cases is filled with bottles of vinegar rather than wine. (Note: The bottles were vinegar before they were shipped; not bad wine that turned into vinegar!) May the buyer reject the goods? See UCC §§2-602, 2-605(2) and its Official Comment 4. Is the carrier liable for the misdescription? See UCC §7-301(1) and (2); 49 USC §80113. Is the presenting bank liable for the misdescription? See UCC §7-508.

# D. OBLIGATIONS OF CARRIERS

The carrier is obligated to deliver goods to the holder of a negotiable bill of lading or the consignee of a nonnegotiable (straight) bill of lading. This section deals with the liability of carriers if (a) goods are delivered to the wrong person, or (b) goods are lost or destroyed in transit. The carrier's liability for misdescription of the goods in the bill of lading is discussed on page 280.

## 1. MISDELIVERY

In determining the obligation of a carrier to deliver, one must ascertain whether the bill of lading is negotiable or nonnegotiable. As previously noted, a document of title that states that the goods are to be delivered to the bearer of the document or to the order of the named person is negotiable, unless it states that it is "nonnegotiable." UCC §7-104, 49 USC §80103. Other documents of title are nonnegotiable—they simply state to whom the goods are to be delivered, the consignee, without indicating that the consignee may instruct the warehouse or carrier to deliver the goods to anyone else. A nonnegotiable bill of lading is often referred to as a "straight" bill of lading because delivery is to be straight to the consignee (without intervening holders of the bill).

Bills of lading may also have other titles. Bills of lading issued by air carriers are called "air bills." A "through" bill of lading means that some of the delivery will be undertaken by parties other than the issuer—under the "through" bill the issuer of the bill of lading is responsible for the actions of those third parties. See UCC §7-302. "Waybills" are issued by one carrier to another. "Freight forwarder bills" are issued by companies that consolidate shipments into carloads. "Destination bills" are issued at the destination of the goods to an agent of the shipper.[6]

---

6. *See generally* White & Summers, *Uniform Commercial Code* §21-2 (2d ed.).

The following case discusses the problem of misdelivery.

### C-Art, Ltd. v. Hong Kong Island Lines America

United States Court of Appeals, Ninth Circuit

940 F.3d 530 (1991)

This case involves a shipment of goods by an ocean carrier from Hong Kong to California. C-ART, Ltd. ("C-ART"), an exporter of goods based in Hong Kong, had a contract with the New York Merchandising Company ("NYMCO"), a New York importing company, for the purchase of goods from manufacturers in Hong Kong. The goods were shipped by Hong Kong Islands Line America, S.A. ("HKIL"), an ocean carrier, from Hong Kong to California.

Between January and March 1986, C-ART purchased goods from various Hong Kong manufacturers and arranged for their shipment to NYMCO in California. Upon delivery of each shipment of goods to HKIL in Hong Kong, HKIL issued to C-ART a bill of lading, which C-ART would in turn present to a bank to exchange for payment from NYMCO. Under the scenario contemplated by the express terms of the bill of lading, NYMCO would ultimately receive the original bills of lading in exchange for its proper payment to C-ART for the goods. NYMCO would then present these bills of lading to HKIL upon the arrival of its ship in California in order to take possession of the goods.

Under the parties' prior course of dealing in this case, however, rather than waiting to receive the bills of lading to release the goods, HKIL would instead release the goods upon NYMCO's presentment of a "bank guarantee," which in effect would absolve HKIL of liability for any claim of misdelivery of the goods without a properly endorsed original bill of lading. The shipments at issue here, however, were released by HKIL to NYMCO upon the presentment of a mere NYMCO "corporate guarantee," which contained no security guarantee from a bank.

Shortly after HKIL's release of the goods to NYMCO based solely on the corporate guarantee but before C-ART had been paid, NYMCO filed for bankruptcy under Chapter 11 of the Bankruptcy Code. After unsuccessfully attempting to recover payment for the goods from NYMCO, C-ART filed the present suit against HKIL for misdelivery of the goods without a properly endorsed bill of lading. The district court ruled in favor of C-ART and entered judgment for $185,997.65. HKIL appeals and we affirm.

C-ART claims it is entitled to recovery because HKIL's misdelivery of the goods constitutes a breach of a contract between C-ART and HKIL for shipment of the goods. Specifically, C-ART's argument is premised on HKIL's issuance of a bill of lading to C-ART upon C-ART's delivery of the goods to HKIL's vessel. The bill of lading issued by HKIL designated goods as consigned "to order of shipper" and its express terms required the goods to only be delivered "upon surrender of the original, properly endorsed bill of lading."

#### A.

We agree with other circuits that have held that bills of lading constitute "contracts of carriage" between a shipper and carrier and, as contracts of adhesion, are strictly construed against the carrier. Absent a valid agreement to the contrary, the carrier, the issuer of the bill of lading, is responsible for releasing the cargo only to the party who presents the original bill of lading.

In this case, it is undisputed that the terms of the bill of lading required HKIL to obtain from NYMCO the original, properly endorsed bill of lading prior to delivery of the goods. It is also undisputed that HKIL delivered the goods without the bill of lading, instead relying on NYMCO's corporate guaranty. We therefore conclude that HKIL is liable to C-ART for its misdelivery of the goods.

**B.**

In its defense, HKIL argues that misdelivery could not have occurred because NYMCO had title to the goods from the time the goods were delivered to the ship in Hong Kong and therefore had the exclusive and immediate right to possession of the goods upon arrival of the ship in California. This argument is inimical to the express provisions of the bill of lading. Although the goods were shipped "FOB Hong Kong," with NYMCO consequently bearing the risk of loss from the time the goods were delivered to HKIL's ship in Hong Kong, it is undisputed that NYMCO never paid C-ART for the goods. In this case, therefore, the bill of lading controls.

The district court's judgment in favor of C-ART is AFFIRMED.

## PROBLEM

***Problem 9-10.*** A contract for the shipment of wine from a California winery to a large beverage retailer in Chicago calls for delivery to be "FOB San Francisco." Payment is to be made 30 days after delivery. The carrier issues the seller a straight bill of lading, naming the buyer as consignee. The shipment is by rail, so delivery is not anticipated for several days. The day after the goods have been delivered to the carrier, seller learns that buyer is insolvent. What can seller do? Does the buyer have any rights against the carrier if the carrier follows the seller's instructions not to deliver? Under what circumstances may the carrier not follow the seller's instructions? If the bill of lading had been a negotiable bill and had been transmitted to the buyer, could the seller have stopped delivery? See UCC §§2-705 and 7-403.

## 2. DAMAGE TO GOODS AND DELAYS IN DELIVERY

The general common law rule regarding damage to goods during shipment is that the carrier is absolutely liable, subject to exceptions for act of God, act of public enemy, act of shipper, act of public authority, or loss due to the inherent vice or nature of the goods. This rule has basically been codified.[7] Carriers are thus placed in the position of being insurers of the goods. Carriers are able to limit their liability by requiring that the shipper state a value of the

7. *See* 49 USC §§11706, 14706; UCC §7-309; White & Summers, *Uniform Commercial Code* §21-1 (2d ed.); 8A Am. Jur. 2d Aviation §75.

goods being transported.[8] Different rates may be charged depending on the value of the goods. In addition, for international shipments by air and sea, the Warsaw Convention and the Carriage of Goods by Sea Act limit the liability of carriers.[9]

On the question of damages caused by delay in delivery, the case law holds that the carrier is only responsible to use due diligence in making delivery. A duty is imposed on the carrier to notify the shipper of any known reasons why delivery might be delayed, if such information is not known by the shipper.[10]

The following case demonstrates application of the Warsaw Convention.

### Motorola, Inc. v. Federal Express Corp.

United States Court of Appeals, Ninth Circuit

308 F.2d 995 (2002)

In this appeal, Kuehne & Nagel, Inc. ("K&N") challenges the district court's award of $244,080 and prejudgment interest to Motorola, Inc. Motorola brought claims under the Warsaw Convention arising out of damage to cargo sustained during transit from Texas to Japan after it hired K&N to transport the cargo. K&N principally contends that the district court erred in determining the liability limitation based on the weight of the entire shipment rather than only on the weight of the damaged component; that, in any event, the damaged portion of the shipment did not affect the value of the remainder of the shipment; and that prejudgment interest is not allowable under the Warsaw Convention. We disagree. We hold that Article 22 of the Warsaw Convention provides for liability limitation based on the entire weight of the shipment where, as here, the damaged portion of the cargo affects the value of the entire shipment. Additionally, we hold that prejudgment interest is available under the Warsaw Convention and that the district court properly awarded such interest to make full restitution to the injured party.

#### Factual and Procedural History

Motorola, an electronics equipment manufacturer, hired K&N, an indirect carrier and freight forwarder, to transport a cellular telephone base station system, valued at almost five million dollars, from Dallas, Texas, to Tokyo, Japan. Motorola hired another company, Relocation Services, Inc., to package the cargo into approximately 20 crates for shipping. K&N then arranged for

---

8. *See, e.g.,* UCC §7-309(2).

9. *See* 46 App. USC §1300 *et seq.*; 49 USC §40105 (note following statute reprints Warsaw Convention). The Carriage of Goods by Sea Act largely follows the 1924 Brussels Convention, which has been ratified by most of the significant commercial countries. The United Nations Convention on the Carriage of Goods by Sea was finalized in Hamburg in 1978, and is in force in 34 countries at the time of this writing (fall 2011). For a list of countries adopting the "Hamburg Rules," visit *www.uncitral.org/uncitral/en/uncitral_texts/transport_goods/Hamburg_status.html* (accessed Oct. 2011). In 2008, the United Nations Convention on Contracts for the International Carriage of Goods Wholly or Partly by Sea was finalized in Rotterdam. At the time of this writing, the "Rotterdam Rules" have not yet entered into force. For the current status of the Rotterdam Rules, see *www.uncitral.org/uncitral/en/uncitral_texts/transport_goods/2008rotterdam_rules.html* (accessed Oct. 2011) .

10. *See Gold Star Meat Co. v. Union Pac. R.R. Co.,* 438 F.2d 1270 (10th Cir. 1971).

Federal Express ("FedEx"), a direct air carrier, actually to transport the cargo via airplane to Tokyo. Between July 10 and 15, 1997, FedEx transported the cargo in a series of six flights. K&N issued a single air waybill covering the entire shipment and stating that there was no apparent damage to the cargo prior to transport. When the cargo arrived at the airport in Tokyo, K&N noted that a portion of the cargo was damaged. Upon receipt of the cargo, Motorola found that the damaged crate contained the system's cabinet-like common control frame, which consisted of printed circuit board cards and wiring. Motorola was forced to replace the equipment at a cost of $459,330.70, and waited six weeks for the replacement's arrival. The total weight of the shipment was 12,204 kilograms. The weight of the damaged crate was approximately 680 kilograms.

Motorola and Fireman's Fund Insurance Company, Motorola's insurance carrier, subsequently filed suit in California state court against K&N and FedEx, alleging breach of contract and negligence. The court granted partial summary judgment for K&N, finding the cargo suffered at least some damage while in FedEx's custody. Additionally, the court ruled that, under the Warsaw Convention, the liability limitation would be calculated according to the weight of the entire shipment — and not just that of the damaged portion — if Motorola proved at trial that the damaged portion of the cargo affected the value of the entire shipment. The court left for trial the questions of whether the overall shipment was affected and the extent of damage done to the property.

The district court conducted a two-day bench trial. After Motorola presented its case, K&N rested without presenting any evidence. The court found in favor of Motorola and awarded damages of $244,080, based on the weight of the entire shipment, and subsequently awarded Motorola prejudgment interest. On appeal, K&N challenges both damages and the award of prejudgment interest. We affirm on all counts.

## Discussion

### I. Liability Limitations

### A. Affected Weight Standard

The parties agree that this action falls within the parameters of the Warsaw Convention, an international treaty governing the liability that arises from the "international transportation of persons, baggage, or goods performed by an aircraft for hire." See Warsaw Convention for the Unification of Certain Rules relating to International Transportation by Air, October 12, 1929, Article 1, 49 Stat. 3000, T.S. No. 876 (1934), reprinted in note following 49 USC §40105. "The Convention creates a presumption of air carrier liability but, in turn, substantially limits that liability." *Ins. Co. of N. Am. v. Fed. Express Corp.,* 189 F.3d 914, 917 (9th Cir. 1999); *see Dazo v. Globe Airport Sec. Svcs.,* 295 F.3d 934, 937-938 (9th Cir. 2002). The Convention sets forth uniform rules of liability for loss, damage, or delay of international shipments by air, and embodies a tradeoff between the interests of carriers and shippers. Among its provisions is the rule that cargo carriers are entitled to a limitation of liability based on the weight of the shipment, presently set at $20 per kilogram. *See Trans World Airlines, Inc. v. Franklin Mint Corp.,* 466 U.S. 243, 255, 104 S. Ct. 1776, 80 L. Ed.

2d 273 (1984); Warsaw Convention Article 22. The relevant section of Article 22 provides:

> In the transportation of checked baggage and of goods, the liability of the carrier shall be limited to a sum of 250 francs ($20) per kilogram, unless the consignor has made, at the time when the package was handed over to the carrier, a special declaration of the value at delivery and has paid a supplementary sum if the case so requires. In that case the carrier will be liable to pay a sum not exceeding the declared sum, unless he proves that that sum is greater than the actual value to the consignor at delivery.

Article 22(3). The Convention preempts state and federal claims falling within its scope. See *id.* at Article 24 (stating that claims for personal injuries, for damage to, or loss of, baggage or goods, and for damages occasioned by travel delays, "however founded, can only be brought subject to the conditions and limits set out in this convention.").

K&N argues that the liability limitation should be calculated based only on the weight of the damaged portion of the shipment. Motorola maintains, and the district court agreed, that the defendants' liability limitation under the Convention should be calculated based on the weight of the entire shipment, approximately 12,204 kilograms, and not simply the weight of the damaged crate, approximately 680 kilograms. The text and drafting history of the Warsaw Convention are silent on this question. Accordingly, we may look to, among other things, evidence of the postratification understanding of the Convention's contracting parties to determine whether the Convention includes the "affected weight standard." *El Al Israel Airlines, Ltd. v. Tseng,* 525 U.S. 155, 167, 119 S. Ct. 662, 142 L. Ed. 2d 576 (1999); *Chan v. Korean Air Lines, Ltd.,* 490 U.S. 122, 134, 109 S. Ct. 1676, 104 L. Ed. 2d 113 (1989); *Hosaka v. United Airlines,* 305 F.3d 989, 993-994 (9th Cir. 2002).

Under the 1955 Hague Protocol, which amended the Warsaw Convention, the affected weight standard is made an explicit part of Article 22.[6] It states:

> In the case of loss, damage or delay of part of registered baggage or cargo, or of any object contained therein, the weight to be taken into consideration in determining the amount to which the carrier's liability is limited shall be only the total weight of the package or packages concerned. Nevertheless, *when the loss, damage or delay of a part of the registered baggage or cargo, or of an object contained therein, affects the value of other packages covered by the same baggage check or the same air waybill, the total weight of such package or packages shall also be taken into consideration in determining the limit of liability.*

Article 22(2)(b) (emphasis added).

The evidence suggests that the parties to the Hague Protocol understood the incorporation of the affected weight standard as a mere clarification of the

6. The treaty is formally known as the Protocol to Amend the Convention for the Unification of Certain Rules Relating to International Carriage by Air signed at Warsaw on 12 October 1929, Sept. 28, 1955, 478 U.N.T.S. 371. The Hague Protocol did not enter into force for the United States until the Montreal Protocol No. 4 was ratified by the Senate on Sept. 28, 1998, and became effective on March 4, 1999—after the shipment at issue here. Accordingly, the Hague Protocol does not govern here, but we look to it as an amendment to the Warsaw Convention that may provide insight into the shared understanding of the Warsaw Convention's contracting parties.

Warsaw Convention or, at any rate, that they understood the new language to be no less advantageous to the shipper than existing Warsaw Convention language. The minutes of the Hague Protocol say nothing to suggest that the new language expressly articulating use of the affected weight standard substantively changed the Convention. The carriers' own representative, the International Air Traffic Association, did not argue that the amended version substantively changed Article 22 by increasing the carriers' liability, only that it "had reached the conclusion that there was ambiguity in the present Convention as to problems of settlement for partial loss." See International Conference on Private Air Law: Vol. I, Minutes of Twentieth Meeting, Sept. 19, 1995 at p.252. Moreover, the U.S. delegation opposed the amended version and voiced its preference for the unamended version, because it believed the new version reflected a *decrease* in carriers' liability under Article 22. The delegation interpreted the unamended version to "[m]ean that when a passenger or shipper lost one of a number of articles being carried, he would think that he had available to him the entire liability of the carrier as determined by the total weight of the articles." *Id.* In hearings before the United States Senate Foreign Trade Committee on the Hague Protocol, the Federal Aviation Administration's acting administrator for International Aviation Affairs testified that with respect to changes in liability limitation, "there isn't any change between . . . the Warsaw Convention and the Hague Protocol with respect to rates of recovery." *See* Hague Protocol to Warsaw Convention: Hearings Before the Senate Comm. on Foreign Relations, 86th Cong., 1st Sess. 22 (1965). Given this history, we conclude that the additional language created by the Hague Protocol only clarified, and certainly did not expand, carrier liability with respect to the affected weight standard. The Hague proceedings evince that the contracting parties to the Warsaw Convention understood in 1955 that existing Article 22 incorporated—or, at the very least, was not hostile to—the affected weight standard.

We think this understanding is sound. In light of the view of the Warsaw Convention reflected by the Hague Protocol and the rulings of other courts, we hold that, when a portion of a shipment is damaged in transit, the liability limitation under the Convention is based on the weight only of the damaged portion; but when the damaged portion affects the value and usability of other parts of the shipment, the liability limitation is based on the weight of all affected items in the shipment.

B. Standard as Applied to this Case

Here, the district court found that the cellular base station "could not function at all" without the damaged control frame, concluding that the damaged component rendered the system "inoperable, useless, and of diminished value." The court further found that little or no assembly could begin until the damaged control frame was replaced because it constituted the "heart and soul of the overall system and had a critical and central role in the overall system." Acknowledging that there was no direct evidence that the six-week delay in obtaining the replacement actually delayed the timetable for installation of the entire system, the court nevertheless determined that "a legitimate and reasonable inference can be drawn . . . that the actual assembly was, in fact, delayed in this case by the length of time it took to get the replacement, meaning six weeks." K&N argues that the district court clearly erred in finding that the damaged control frame caused a delay in the installation of the station and thereby affected the value of the entire shipment. K&N contends that Motorola presented no evidence that the damage and resulting delay in construction in any way lowered the system's value and asserts that the proper liability limitation should therefore be based on the weight only of the control frame.

In making its factual findings, the district court relied on the testimony of Motorola project manager and engineer Gary Koepke. Koepke testified that it was not possible to construct the remainder of the station while awaiting the arrival of the replacement control board: "In some cases that's possible, but not with this one because this is one of the fundamental pieces. We have to start out with this one and before others at the very beginning and get that installed. . . . We can't do it later. It's the foundation for the rest of it." He stated that although "a couple of other frames" could be assembled, that process would take only one or two days "and then, you would have to stop and wait [for the control frame]." Koepke testified that a six-week delay in receiving the component—although a "quick" time frame in which to obtain a replacement—normally would delay installation of the entire system by six weeks. K&N offered no evidence to refute Koepke's testimony. The district court did not clearly err in relying on Koepke's expert testimony and finding that the damage to the control frame affected the value and operation of the entire base station. Accordingly, the court properly determined that the liability limitation here must be based on the weight of the entire cellular base station, not only on that of the damaged control frame.

### C. K&N's Other Arguments

K&N offers two other reasons for avoiding or limiting its liability, neither of which is persuasive. First, we do not accept K&N's argument that by contracting with FedEx to transport the cargo, K&N effectively carried out its duty to take all necessary measures to avoid damage as required by Article 20 of the Convention. Forwarders such as K&N assume the responsibility of a carrier, who actually executes the transport, even though the forwarder does not carry the merchandise itself. "Article 20 requires of defendant proof . . . of an undertaking embracing all precautions that in sum are appropriate to the risk." *Mfr. Hanover Trust Co. v. Alitalia Airlines,* 429 F. Supp. 964, 967 (S.D.N.Y. 1977). The record does not contain any evidence that K&N took all necessary measures to avoid damage to the cargo. In fact, K&N failed to even offer any such proof at trial.

Second, K&N argues that its air waybill, which serves as the bill of lading for goods transported by air, prescribed the amount of damages available to Motorola. K&N's air waybill included the following provision: "In cases of loss, damage, or delay of part of the consignment, the weight to be taken into account in determining carrier's limit of liability shall be only the weight of the package or packages concerned." Although Article 33 of the Convention allows carriers to make "regulations which do not conflict with the provisions of this convention," Article 23 specifically states that "[a]ny provision tending to relieve the carrier of liability or to fix a lower limit than that which is laid down in this convention shall be null and void." To the extent that K&N's air waybill provision may fix a lower liability limit here, where the damaged portion affected the entire shipment, the provision conflicts with and is null and void under Article 23.

II. Prejudgment Interest

The district court awarded Motorola prejudgment interest in addition to the liability damages. The combined dollar amount of the award including such interest thus exceeded the liability limitation allowable under the Convention. The Convention does not discuss prejudgment interest and provides only for an amount calculated by multiplying the weight of the cargo by the dollar-per-unit-of-weight multiple. We have not previously addressed the availability of a prejudgment interest award under the Convention. We conclude, however, that the award of prejudgment interest is consistent with the purposes of the Warsaw Convention and with postratification understandings of the treaty's contracting parties. [The court goes on to discuss the split of authority that exists with respect to this issue.]

The Convention was intended to balance the interests of shippers seeking recovery for lost, delayed or damaged goods, and the interests of air carriers seeking to limit potential liability. The award of prejudgment interest simply assures that the limited damages available to the successful claimant will not be eroded by the defendant's actions in delaying a prompt resolution of the claim. Such interest does not convert a damage award into full compensation to the plaintiff because the carrier's damage liability remains fixed and limited by the Convention's weight-based formula. Rather, prejudgment interest is a mechanism by which the court, in an appropriate case, may assure that the plaintiff receives the full value of his limited damages.

We affirm the district court's award of $244,080 and prejudgment interest to Motorola.

AFFIRMED.

## PROBLEM

***Problem 9-11.*** A contract for the sale of oranges to a grocery store in Iowa calls for delivery to be "FOB Los Angeles." The oranges were to be sold at retail in the stores. Ordinarily, delivery would occur three days after shipment. In this case, due to lack of ordinary care on the part of the carrier, delivery did not occur for six days. The oranges were still saleable. During the three-day delay, the wholesale price of oranges in Iowa rose by $0.25 per pound. The buyer did not purchase any additional oranges during that period. Does the buyer have any recourse against either the seller or the carrier? How should damages be measured? Should the carrier be able to limit liability for consequential damages due to delays in delivery? *See Great Atlantic & Pac. Tea Co. v. Atchison, T. & S.F. Ry. Co.*, 333 F.2d 705 (7th Cir. 1964); UCC §§2-509 and 7-309.

## E. OBLIGATIONS OF WAREHOUSE OPERATORS

Sometimes the goods that are being sold will be located in a warehouse operated by someone who is neither controlled by the seller or the buyer. The goods will not be moved after the sale—the warehouse operator will now be holding the goods for the benefit of the buyer rather than the seller. This section discusses the obligations of such a warehouse operator.

When goods are delivered to a warehouse operator, the owner of the goods is a bailor and the warehouse operator is a bailee. The warehouse operator will sometimes deliver a warehouse receipt to the bailor, which is a document of title. As is the case with bills of lading, the warehouse receipt can be either negotiable or nonnegotiable. A warehouse receipt is negotiable if it states that the goods covered by it are to be delivered to bearer or to order of a named person. See UCC §7-104. Negotiable warehouse receipts will normally be marked "NEGOTIABLE" while nonnegotiable warehouse receipts will be marked "NONNEGOTIABLE."

Required terms for a warehouse receipt are provided in UCC section 7-202. The warehouse receipt constitutes a contract between the bailor and the bailee, and also indicates to whom the goods are to be delivered. The warehouse receipt will typically indicate the storage charges and will reserve a lien against the goods to secure payment of the charges. The receipt will describe the goods that are being stored.

The warehouse operator is responsible to deliver the goods to the holder of a negotiable warehouse receipt or to the person to whom delivery is to be made according to the terms of a nonnegotiable warehouse receipt. A person is a "holder" of a negotiable warehouse receipt if it indicates that goods are to be delivered to bearer or to the order of that person. UCC §1-201(b)(21). The initial holder of the warehouse receipt may "negotiate" it to somebody else so that the recipient becomes a holder. This is accomplished by signing the receipt and handing it to the recipient, similar to how one would negotiate a check. If the initial holder negotiates it simply by signing her or his name and not indicating to whom the document is being negotiated, the goods are then deliverable to the bearer of the document.

One can see that negotiable documents are dangerous in that if they indicate that delivery of the goods is to be to bearer, there is a danger that the document will be lost or stolen and that the goods will wind up in the hands of someone who otherwise would not have good title to them. But negotiable documents may be useful in obtaining bank financing against the goods in that the bank may take possession of the document to secure its right to payment. It is easier to transfer possession of the document than of the goods themselves.

The warehouse operator is responsible to a good faith purchaser for value of a warehouse receipt for misdescription or nonreceipt of goods listed in the receipt. The warehouse operator may avoid liability by conspicuous disclaimers to the effect that it is unknown whether the goods described were ever received; for example, "contents, condition and quality unknown." See UCC §7-203.

Unlike a carrier, the liability of the warehouse operator for damage done to the goods while in the operator's possession is not absolute. The warehouse operator is responsible for any damage to the goods caused by negligence. UCC §7-204. The warehouse operator may further limit liability by establishing a limit with respect to each article being stored. UCC §7-204(b).

One of the greatest financial scandals in American financial history, the "Great Salad Oil Scandal" of 1963, involved the issuance of warehouse receipts that were used as collateral to procure loans based on the salad oil that was represented by the receipts. Through various means, the unscrupulous vegetable oil dealer, Allied Crude Vegetable Oil Company, shipped and stored vegetable oil in ways that made it look like there was more oil than actually existed. For example, since oil floats, vegetable oil was stored on top of water. If the tanks were inspected from the top, a tank would appear to be full of vegetable oil when in fact it contained mostly water. When the fraud was discovered, in 1963, $175 million in salad oil was missing. The owners of the field warehouses issuing the receipts had a lot of explaining to do! American Express, which through subsidiaries issued warehouse receipts in the scandal, lost approximately $58 million.[11]

## Fischer v. Herman

Civil Court, City of New York

63 Misc. 2d 44, 310 N.Y.S.2d 270 (1970)

In this suit for damages for breach of a bailment contract it is undisputed that defendant accepted from plaintiff's wife a fur coat for storage in May 1966, and that the coat was missing when demanded in October 1966.

Two principal defenses were presented at the trial. First, that the coat had been stolen during a burglary, and that the defendant had exercised due care to safeguard the property against loss from that or any other cause. Second, that in any event recovery should be limited to $100, that being the value placed on the coat in a receipt mailed to plaintiff's wife some time after the defendant accepted the coat.

The latter contention has little merit. In *Abend v. Haberman*, 281 App. Div. 262, 264, 119 N.Y.S.2d 488, 490-491 (1st Dept. 1953), the appellate division squarely held that the mailing of such a document after formation of the bailment contract on delivery of the property is not effective to alter the original arrangement in the absence of actual consent.

No such consent was established here. It is true that the defense alleged a routine under which the mailing of the receipt would be preceded by a telephone call to the bailor, who would be told of the $100 value if the property were insured. Even assuming that such a conversation took place, which plaintiff's wife flatly denied, it would fall far short of establishing a meaningful consent to the valuation.

11. For more information, read Miller, *The Great Salad Oil Scandal* (1965); *see also Proctor & Gamble Distributing Co. v. Lawrence Ware Corp.*, 16 N.Y.2d 344, 266 N.Y.S.2d 735, 213 N.E. 2d 873 (1966).

The basic relevant rule with regard to the kind of bailment presented is that the bailee assumes a duty of care, that the failure to return the bailed property creates a presumption of negligence, that the burden then shifts to the bailee to show how the loss occurred, and if that burden is then met, the plaintiff must prove actual negligence. *Proctor & Gamble Distributing Co. v. Lawrence Ware Corp.*, 16 N.Y.S.2d 344, 266 N.Y.S.2d 785, 213 N.E.2d 873 (1966), N.Y.Juris., Bailments, Secs. 54, 56-59.

The defense here failed wholly to present any legally admissible evidence to explain the disappearance of the coat. The defendant, who was his only witness, was not even in New York when the alleged burglary occurred, and relied wholly on what he was told by an employee who did not testify and whose failure to testify was not explained.

Indeed, even the hearsay account raises more questions than it answers, since it was indicated that an elaborate network of alarms was somehow not triggered, and that entrance was gained without any indication of a break.

In any event, I find that the evidence established actual negligence by the defendant.

Quite apart from the failure of the defendant to send the coat to its normal storage facilities, for reasons that were sharply disputed, the defendant's negligence is clearly established by the fact that they kept the plaintiff's coat on the rack in their factory together with other coats held for storage while their own manufactured coats were kept in a vault. I find wholly inadequate the defendant's explanation for the striking difference in care between coats defendant owned and coats defendant held as a bailee.

On the question of value, I accept the testimony of the defendant—the only expert called on the question—that the coat was worth 30 percent of market value.

Since the coat was bought for $3,800 some three years before, I find for the plaintiff in the sum of $1,140 with interest from December 1966.

## PROBLEMS

***Problem 9-12.*** Buyer contracts to purchase furniture inventory that is located at a warehouse. The furniture is covered by a nonnegotiable warehouse receipt. Buyer receives the nonnegotiable warehouse receipt together with written instructions from Seller addressed to the warehouse operator instructing the operator to transfer title to Buyer. The next day, and before Buyer had a chance to present the instructions to the warehouse operator, the warehouse was destroyed by fire through no fault of anyone. Who has the risk of loss with respect to the goods? Would the result be different if a negotiable warehouse receipt had been transferred to Buyer? UCC §§2-503(4), 2-509(2), and §7-204.

***Problem 9-13.*** Thief stole a valuable painting from Owner and stored it in a warehouse, obtaining a negotiable warehouse receipt indicating that delivery was to be to the bearer of the receipt. Thief then sold the painting to a good faith purchaser for value, delivering the warehouse receipt to the purchaser. As between Owner and the good faith purchaser, who has good title to the painting? Would the result be different if Owner had entrusted the painting to Thief for safekeeping? Is Owner liable for the warehouse operator's charges? See UCC §§7-209, 7-502, and 7-503.

## CHAPTER 9 REVIEW PROBLEM

Buyer Department Store contracted to buy men's suits from Seller Clothing Manufacturers, Inc. Buyer was required to post an irrevocable letter of credit naming Seller as beneficiary. The letter of credit was duly issued by the Bank of America, and stated that it was governed by UCP No. 500. The letter of credit provided that the bank would honor drafts drawn on it if accompanied by an invoice indicating the shipment of "100 men's suits, 100% wool" and a bill of lading showing that cartons were similarly marked.

Seller erroneously shipped 50 women's suits along with 50 men's suits, but the invoice read "100 men's suits, 100% wool." The bill of lading indicated "cartons marked 100 men's suits, 100% wool," and also indicated "shipper's weight, load, and count."

The bill of lading and invoice were duly presented to the bank. Accompanying the invoice was a packing list that simply stated "clothing." The bank officer looked over the documents, not paying attention to the packing list, and honored the letter of credit by paying Seller.

Meanwhile, due to mechanical problems on the carrier's truck, delivery of the clothing was delayed by one week. Buyer was told of the problem when the mechanical problem arose. When the goods arrived, Buyer was upset to see that women's suits were shipped along with men's suits. Buyer was also upset by the delay in shipment, because Buyer had publicized a big sale and did not have sufficient inventory to satisfy the customers who had come in. Does Buyer have any recourse against the Bank of America or the carrier? Note that UCP No. 500 provides that documents not stipulated in the letter of credit need not be examined by the bank, and also indicates that the description of the goods in the commercial invoice must correspond with the description in the letter of credit, but that in other documents, the goods may be described in general terms not inconsistent with the description of the goods in the credit. See UCC §§5-108, 7-301, and pages 268-272, *supra*.

PART 2

# LEASES OF GOODS AND LICENSES OF INFORMATION

# CHAPTER 10
# LEASES OF GOODS

A party may prefer to lease goods rather than purchase them. "Lease" is defined in UCC section 2A-103 as "a transfer of the right of possession and use of goods for a term in return for consideration. . . ." A party may need the goods for only a short time, in which case leasing the goods is preferable to purchasing them. Many people prefer to lease automobiles rather than purchase them, especially if they frequently wish to change to more updated models. Parties may also prefer to lease goods rather than purchase them for tax or accounting reasons. For example, a purchase of goods on credit may result in a liability on the balance sheet of the purchaser while a lease of the goods might not.[1]

Uniform Commercial Code Article 2A, added in 1987, deals with lease transactions. It was revised in 1990, and has been adopted in some form by every state except Louisiana. For international transactions, the International Institute for the Unification of Private Law (UNIDROIT) approved the Convention on International Financial Leasing in 1988. At the time of this writing (fall 2011), it is in force in ten nations.[2] The United States has signed the Convention, but it has not yet been ratified and is not in force. In this chapter, we will only cover UCC Article 2A. Our focus will be on areas where the law differs from UCC Article 2 because of particular problems posed by leases.

## A. IS THE TRANSACTION A LEASE OR A SALE?

As noted above, some tax laws and accounting rules may treat sales differently from leases. Under the UCC, sales in which the seller retains title to the goods until the price is paid in full, so-called "conditional sales," are covered both by Article 2 and Article 9. UCC Article 9 deals with secured transactions, in which personal property is used as collateral for loans. In the conditional sale, the goods being sold are considered collateral securing the obligation of the buyer to pay the price.

---

1. *See* White & Summers, *Uniform Commercial Code* §21.3 (5th ed.).

2. For the current status of the Unidroit Convention on International Financial Leasing, *see* *www.unidroit.org/english/implement/i-88-l.pdf* (accessed Oct. 2011).

UCC Article 9 generally requires creditors taking collateral to take steps to notify others of their interest in collateral. This requirement is similar to the requirement that somebody taking real estate as collateral record a mortgage or deed of trust to perfect their interest against third parties. Under Article 9, creditors will often file a document called a "financing statement" in the relevant state's secretary of state's office to perfect their interest in personal property. By contrast, UCC Article 2A does not require a lessor to file any documents putting others on notice of its interest in goods.

Because of a desire to obtain favorable accounting or tax treatment, parties may label their transaction a lease when in fact it is a conditional sale. For example, a lease may provide that the lessee is obligated to make payments on goods for five years and at the end of the lease term may purchase the goods for $1. Is that really a lease, or is it instead a disguised conditional sale? The UCC looks at the economic realities of the transaction and would label this transaction as a disguised sale, with the lessor really being a seller who holds a security interest in the goods to secure payment of the price. See UCC §1-203. The seller would be required to follow UCC Article 9 to perfect its security interest in the goods.

What are the consequences of a court finding that a transaction is a sale instead of a lease? If the lessor/conditional seller has not complied with Article 9, the seller will be considered to have an unperfected security interest in the goods. This means that buyers of the goods and other creditors with claims to the goods may be able to take priority over the seller in the event that the buyer defaults or goes into bankruptcy. See UCC §9-317. If the buyer goes into bankruptcy, the bankruptcy trustee will take priority over the seller. See Bankruptcy Code §544. Even if the seller has complied with Article 9, leases are generally given more favorable treatment under the Bankruptcy Code, meaning that the lessor has a better chance of being paid in full or getting back the leased goods.[3]

The nominal consideration cases, where the lessee may own the goods at the end of the lease term by paying $1 or some other nominal sum, are easy cases and are considered sales under the UCC, at least if the lessee cannot legally terminate the lease during the lease term. UCC §1-203. Parties are generally not so crude, however, as to mischaracterize such a transaction as a lease. Transactions called leases might combine characteristics of both sales and leases. UCC section1-203 provides some complicated guidance to courts in trying to classify these transactions.

Think for a minute about what things you might expect to find in a lease transaction as compared to a sale. You might expect that at the end of the lease term, something of value will go back to the lessor. If there is an option to purchase the goods at the end of the lease term, one might expect that it will reflect a price approximating the value of the goods at the end of the term and the rational lessee might either decide to exercise the option or not. If you see a contract in which it is contemplated that there will be nothing of value to return to the lessor at the end of the lease term or where no rational lessee

3. A lease would be considered an executory contract and the bankruptcy trustee would be compelled to either assume or reject the lease. *See In re Architectural Millwork of Virginia, Inc.*, 226 B.R. 551, 39 UCC Rep. Serv. 2d 36 (1998). An Article 9 secured party may be subjected to a "cram-down," meaning that the bankruptcy estate can retain the goods by paying fair market value rather than the amount owed under the contract. *See* White & Summers, *Uniform Commercial Code* §21-3 (5th ed.).

would elect not to exercise the option to purchase at the end, then you should probably strongly consider the possibility that this contract represents a sale rather than a lease. The following case shows a court's analysis under the UCC as to whether a lease was really a disguised sale.

### In Re Hoskins

United States Bankruptcy Court, W.D. Missouri

266 B.R. 154, 45 UCC Rep. Serv. 2d 1025 (2001)

In the matter presently under consideration, the court must determine whether an agreement between Ford Motor Credit Company, as assignee, and Charles and Sylvia Hoskins is a true lease or security for a conditional sales contract. For the following reasons, the court determines that the agreement is a true lease, and rules in favor of Ford Motor Credit Company in this adversary proceeding.

#### Factual Background

On November 8, 1997, Charles and Sylvia Hoskins entered into a written contract with Southtown Ford, Inc., titled "Motor Vehicle Lease Agreement" to lease a new 1998 Ford Windstar for a period of 24 months. Charles and Sylvia Hoskins were designated as "Lessee" and "Co-Lessee" in the contract, and Southtown Ford, Inc., was designated as "Lessor." After execution, Southtown Ford, Inc., assigned this contract to Ford. The contract stated that "'Ford Credit' is Ford Motor Credit Company. The 'Holder' is FMCC and its assigns. By signing 'You' (Lessee and Co-Lessee) agree to lease this Vehicle according to the terms on the front and back of this lease."

The contract obligated the Hoskinses to make payments in the amount of $596.58 per month for 24 months. A portion of each monthly payment was designated as "rent charge" in the total amount of $4,010.48 for the 24-month term. Over the 24-month period the Hoskinses were obligated to pay Ford the total amount of $9,420.00, which was designated as depreciation for the vehicle's decline in value through normal use. The agreed-upon value of the vehicle on the date of execution of the contract was $26,434.48. After payment of all amounts due under the contract, the residual value of the vehicle would be $15,013.60 at the end of the 24-month term. The contract provided that at the end of the "Lease Term" the Hoskinses had the option to purchase the vehicle for $15,263.60, plus official fees and taxes, as long as they had not defaulted or terminated the lease early.

The contract further provided that the vehicle was covered by a standard new vehicle warranty; placed the responsibility for maintenance of the vehicle and repairing damage to the vehicle upon the Hoskinses; required the Hoskinses to pay all license, title, and registration costs; and obligated the Hoskinses to insure the vehicle during the lease term. The contract provided for early termination of the lease term; however, in the event of early termination, the Hoskinses still would be required to pay the remaining sums due under the lease (the amount due depended upon several factors), plus a $200.00 early termination fee. The contract provided that, among other things, the Hoskinses would be in default if they failed to make any of the payments when due. Pursuant to the terms of the contract, if the Hoskinses defaulted, Ford could cancel the lease, repossess the vehicle, and sell it at a public or private sale. The contract was silent regarding Ford's obligation to notify the Hoskinses of any proposed sale of the vehicle following default and repossession. Upon default, the Hoskinses would also be liable to pay the remaining sums due under the lease (again, the amount due depended upon several factors), plus other expenses incurred by Ford and reasonable attorney's fees. Finally, the contract provided that the vehicle would be titled in the name of Ford.

The Hoskinses ceased making payments after March 18, 1999, and on May 28, 1999, they voluntarily surrendered the vehicle to Southtown Ford, Inc. On June 3, 1999, Sylvia Hoskins signed a Voluntary Surrender form in which she acknowledged that she was voluntarily surrendering possession of the 1998 Ford Windstar to Ford and that she understood that Ford would sell the vehicle. The Voluntary Surrender form also provided that Sylvia Hoskins agreed to pay Ford for any deficiency resulting from the sale. On or about June 1, 1999, Ford sent Sylvia Hoskins a Red Carpet Lease Notice of Private Sale informing her that the vehicle would be sold by Ford at a private sale. This Notice of Private Sale again informed Sylvia Hoskins that she might be held liable if a deficiency resulted from the sale. Ford did not notify Charles Hoskins of the pending sale. On June 23, 1999, Ford sold the vehicle through a private sale. After crediting the Hoskinses' account with the proceeds of the sale, a deficiency balance remained due in the amount of $3,653.81. On August 24, 2000, Ford filed a lawsuit in the Jackson County, Missouri, circuit court against the Hoskinses seeking to recover this deficiency. The Hoskinses filed an answer in which they contended, in relevant part, that Ford was not entitled to recover the deficiency balance remaining after the sale of the vehicle, alleging that Ford had violated UCC section 9-504 (Revised UCC section 9-611) by failing to properly notify Charles Hoskins of the pending sale of the vehicle. The Hoskinses also filed a counterclaim in which they asserted that because Ford had failed to properly notify Charles Hoskins of the pending sale of the vehicle, they were entitled to recover damages from Ford in the amount of $4,952.48 pursuant to UCC section 9-507 (Revised UCC section 9-625). In their response to Ford's motion for summary judgment, the Hoskinses conceded that Ford had properly notified Sylvia Hoskins of the pending sale of the vehicle, but asserted that any recovery against her was subject to discharge under the Chapter 13 proceedings.

### Discussion

The Hoskinses do not dispute that a deficiency balance in the amount of $3,653.81 remained after Ford sold the 1998 Ford Windstar. The determinative question is whether the written agreement between the Hoskinses and Ford, as assignee, is a true lease or security for a conditional sales contract. If the agreement constitutes a true lease then Article 2A of the Missouri Uniform Commercial Code governs, and Article 2A does not require that notice of a pending sale of leased property be sent by the lessor to the lessee upon the lessee's default. *See* UCC §§2A-501 and 2A-502. Further, the parties' contract does not provide for notice of sale to the Hoskinses in the event of default. Accordingly, Ford would be entitled to a judgment against the Hoskinses for the deficiency balance, and allowed to pursue recovery of same from the Hoskinses to the extent permitted by the Bankruptcy Code. If, on the other hand, the agreement constitutes security for a conditional sales contract, then Article 9 of the Missouri Uniform Commercial Code governs, and Ford was required to follow the procedures set forth in UCC Article 9 following the Hoskinses' default, or face the consequences of its noncompliance, including an award of damages in favor of the Hoskinses, and denial of recovery of the deficiency balance. *See In re Huffman,* 204 B.R. 562, 563-564 (Bankr. W.D. Mo. 1997); *McKesson Corp. v. Colman's Grant Village, Inc.,* 938 S.W.2d 631, 633 (Mo. App. 1997).

"To determine a debtor's property rights, such as an interest in a lease, the bankruptcy court is required to look to state law." *Brown v. Kempker (In re Kempker),* 104 B.R. 196, 202 (Bankr. W.D. Mo. 1989) (quoting *Johnson v. First Nat. Bank of Montevideo, Minn.,* 719 F.2d 270, 273 (8th Cir. 1983)). UCC section 2A-103(1)(j) defines "lease" to mean "a transfer of the right to possession and use of goods for a term in return for consideration, but a . . . retention or creation of a security interest is not a lease." [Revised UCC section 9-109(a)(1) applies to "a transaction, regardless of its form, that creates a security interest in personal property or fixtures by contract." ] The term "security interest" is defined in UCC section 1-201(37) (Revised UCC section 1-203):

[The court quotes from former UCC section 1-201(37), section 1-203 in Revised Article 1]

The Comment to UCC section 1-201(37) explains that the amendment was adopted because:

> Prior to this amendment, section 1-201(37) provided that whether a lease was intended as security (i.e., a security interest disguised as a lease) was to be determined from the facts of each case; however, (a) the inclusion of an option to purchase did not itself make the lease one intended for security, and (b) an agreement that upon compliance with the terms of the lease the lessee would become, or had the option to become, the owner of the property for no additional consideration, or for a nominal consideration, did make the lease one intended for security.
>
> Reference to the intent of the parties to create a lease or security interest has led to unfortunate results. In discovering intent, courts have relied upon factors that were thought to be more consistent with sales or loans than leases. Most of these criteria, however, are as applicable to true leases as to security interests. Examples include the typical net lease provisions, a purported lessor's lack of storage facilities or its character as a financing party rather than a dealer in goods. Accordingly, amended section 1-201(37) deletes all reference to the parties' intent.

In *Banterra Bank v. Subway Equip. Leasing Corp. (In re Taylor),* 209 B.R. 482 (Bankr. S.D. Ill. 1997), a dispute arose over whether an equipment lease was a true lease or a disguised security agreement. In ruling that the contract at issue was a security agreement, the bankruptcy court applied Illinois law and opined:

> In any analysis under section 1-201(37), the intent of the parties is no longer the primary consideration. Rather, the focus is on the "economic realities" of the transaction. . . . Under this approach, the lease will be construed as a security interest as a matter of law if the debtor cannot terminate the lease *and* one of the enumerated requirements is satisfied. . . . If the court determines that the transaction is not a disguised security agreement per se, it must then

> look at the specific facts of the case to determine whether the "economics of the transaction" suggest such a result. . . .

*Id.* at 484-485 (citations omitted; emphasis in original).

In *In re Owen,* 221 B.R. 56, 60-61 (Bankr. N.D.N.Y. 1998), the bankruptcy court applying New York law explained that the first paragraph of section 1-201(37):

> set[s] out a bright line test whereby, as a matter of law, a transaction creates a security interest. Thus, if the Debtors do not have a right to terminate the purported lease prior to the expiration of its term, then the Court is to examine whether any of the four other enumerated conditions have been met which would establish that the parties entered into a security agreement. . . .

The court further interpreted section 1-201(37) to mean that if the debtor can terminate the lease, then the court need not consider the four factors in order to find that as a matter of law the parties' agreement does not create a security interest, however, the four factors are relevant in the court's continuing examination of the facts of the particular case to determine whether the contract constitutes a security agreement. *Id.* at 61.

Applying the foregoing analysis to this case, this court first must determine whether the Hoskinses had a right to terminate the agreement with Ford. The court finds that although the contract provides a means by which the Hoskinses could terminate the lease early, the Hoskinses could not simply return the vehicle to Ford and then walk away from the transaction with no further future financial responsibility. Upon early termination and return of the vehicle, the Hoskinses were still liable to Ford for the balance of the remaining payments that were due under the lease; the final amount due and owing depended on variable factors. The court concludes that a termination provision in a contract, which provides that a lessee remains financially liable to the lessor after termination of the lease for payments that become due after the date the lease is terminated, does not constitute "termination" within the meaning of section 1-201(37). The court finds that the Hoskinses could not terminate the agreement with Ford, which satisfies the first criteria for finding a security agreement as a matter of law.

Next, the court must determine whether any of the four enumerated conditions set forth in section 400.1-201(37) have been satisfied. Relevant here is whether the option price required to purchase the 1998 Ford Windstar at the expiration of the lease term constituted nominal consideration. In *Banterra Bank v. Subway Equip. Leasing Corp. (In re Taylor)*, the bankruptcy court opined:

> Section 1-201(37)(x) of the Illinois Uniform Commercial Code provides, in pertinent part, that additional consideration is nominal if "it is less than the lessee's reasonably predictable cost of performing under the lease agreement if the option is not exercised." . . . This codification of what has traditionally been referred to as the "economic realities" test focuses on whether the lessee has, in light of all of the facts and circumstances, no sensible alternative but to exercise the purchase option. . . . Under this test, if only a fool would fail to exercise the purchase option, the option price is generally considered nominal and the transaction characterized as a disguised security agreement.

In this case, the contract provided that the agreed-upon value of the vehicle on the date of execution of the contract was $26,434.48. The agreement further provided that at the expiration of the 24-month term of the contract, the Hoskinses had the option to purchase the vehicle for $15,263.60. The court finds that the purchase option price of $15,263.60 does not constitute nominal consideration. Because neither of the four factors is satisfied, the document at issue herein is not a security agreement as a matter of law.

However, the court's inquiry does not end. Although the contract does not constitute a security agreement as a matter of law, the court must examine the specific facts of this case to determine whether the "economics of the transaction" suggest such a result. Guiding this court's decision are a consideration of the four factors enumerated in UCC section 1-201(37) along with the additional guidelines set out in the statute.

In *Commercial Credit Equip. Corp. v. Parsons,* 820 S.W.2d 315, 319 (Mo. App. 1991), the Missouri Court of Appeals opined that "the true character and intention of the agreement is determined not from random phrases or formal designations—such as 'lease,''lessor,''lessee'—but from the economic reality of the agreement, whatever the disguise of the terminology." Under Missouri law, the pivotal factor in determining whether an instrument is a true lease or a security agreement is whether or not the lessee has an absolute obligation to purchase the rental property.

Here, the Hoskinses did have an option to purchase the 1998 Ford Windstar at the expiration of the lease term provided they were not in default and had not terminated the lease early. However, they did not have an absolute obligation to purchase the vehicle. If the Hoskinses had fulfilled their contractual obligations under the agreement, whether they purchased the vehicle at the end of the lease term was entirely up to them. Further, as discussed above, the purchase option price of $15,263.60 was not nominal consideration. Accordingly, based on the facts of this case, the court finds that the agreement in question constitutes a true lease and not a disguised security agreement. In accordance with the guidelines established in amended section 400.1-201(37), the court determines that the Hoskinses' obligation to insure the vehicle during the lease term; maintain and repair the vehicle; and pay all license, title, and registration costs does not transform the lease into security for a conditional sales contract. In sum, the court finds that the agreement in question constitutes a true lease.

### Conclusion

Based on the above discussion, the court determines that the motor vehicle lease agreement entered into between Charles and Sylvia Hoskins and Ford Motor Credit Company, as assignee, is a true lease and is not security for a conditional sales contract. Accordingly, Ford Motor Credit Company is entitled to a judgment against Charles and Sylvia Hoskins in the amount of $3,653.81 for the deficiency balance remaining after the sale of the 1998 Ford Windstar. Ford Motor Credit Company may pursue recovery of same to the extent permitted by the Bankruptcy Code.

## NOTES, QUESTIONS, AND PROBLEM

1. In the foregoing case, were there any aspects of the contract that were more consistent with a sale as compared to a lease? Who normally bears the risk of loss in a lease transaction? See UCC §2A-219. Why were the factors favoring a lease more compelling than the factors favoring a sale?
2. If the transaction is considered a lease, UCC Article 2A applies to the transaction. Article 2A has many similarities to Article 2 on the questions of contract formation and enforcement. For example, section 2A-204 on formation is very similar to section 2-204. There is a statute of frauds under Article 2A, section 2A-201, which is triggered for leases of $1,000 or more (as compared to $500 in section 2-201). There is nothing in Article 2A comparable to UCC section 2-207, reflecting the view that lease contracts are not typically formed through a "battle of the forms." There also are warranty provisions in Article 2A similar to the warranties given under Article 2. As noted in the next section, however, these warranties are not given by lessors in "finance lease" situations.

***Problem 10-1.*** XYZ Leasing Company enters into a "Lease Agreement" with ABC Manufacturing pursuant to which ABC will lease some computer equipment for five years. The estimated useful life for the equipment is seven years. At the time the agreement is entered into, it is estimated that the equipment will be worth $50,000 at the end of the lease term. The contract provides that ABC may purchase it for $30,000 at the end of the term. Under the agreement, ABC is responsible for insuring the equipment and for all maintenance expenses that may arise during the term. Is this agreement a true lease or a disguised conditional sale? See UCC §1-203 and its Official Comments. If XYZ is concerned about possibly being treated as a conditional seller under UCC Article 9, what can it do to protect itself? See UCC §9-505.

## B. IS THE LEASE A "FINANCE LEASE"?

In some cases, a third party will be involved in facilitating the lease transaction. The party interested in obtaining possession of the goods wishes to lease the goods rather than purchase them, and the supplier of the goods is not interested in a lease or a credit transaction. In such a case, a leasing company may come into the picture which will technically purchase the goods from the supplier and will then lease the goods to the party interested in obtaining possession. This type of lease may fall within the definition of a "finance lease" in UCC section 2A-103(1)(g). Two fundamental characteristics of a "finance lease" under that section are (1) the lessor does not select the goods, and (2) the lessor acquires the goods in connection with the lease.

Finance leases are given special treatment under Article 2A. The main advantage of the nonconsumer finance lease from the lessor's perspective is that the lessee's promise to pay rent under the lease becomes irrevocable upon the lessee's acceptance of the goods, no matter whether the goods prove to be defective. See UCC §2A-407. Article 2A thus codifies the "hell or high water" clause existing in leases that requires the lessee to pay the rent no matter what happens to the goods subject to the lease. See UCC §2A-407, Official Comment 1. This rule makes sense in situations in which the lessor does nothing more than finance the transaction. Remember that in a finance lease it is the lessee who selects the goods from the supplier; the finance lessor does not have any control over whether the goods will be suitable to the lessee's purposes or not. The lessee is given the benefit of any warranties given by the supplier of the goods under section 2A-209, so the lessee can sue the supplier in the event that the goods do not conform to any express or implied warranties given in the sale of the goods to the lessor. The following case demonstrates the obligations of the lessee under a finance lease.

## AT&T Credit Corp. v. Transglobal Telecom Alliance

United States District Court, District of New Jersey

966 F. Supp. 299, 33 UCC Rep. Serv. 2d 492 (1997)

This matter comes before the court on the motion of plaintiff AT&T Credit Corporation ("AT&T Credit") for summary judgment against defendants Transglobal Telecom Alliance ("Transglobal") and James Carraway ("Carraway") (collectively referred to as "defendants") seeking a determination that defendants breached the terms of a lease agreement and guaranty between AT&T Credit and the defendants. AT&T Credit also seeks an award of damages and a determination that it is entitled to possession of the equipment it leased to Transglobal. Defendants brought a cross-claim to compel discovery responses.

Oral argument was heard in this matter on February 24, 1997. Based upon a review of the record and the arguments of counsel, and as more fully set forth below, AT&T Credit's motion for summary judgment is GRANTED. The court, however, declines to certify the judgment as final due to the remaining claims in the case between defendants and AT&T Corporation, a third-party defendant.

### Statement of Facts

On or about July 19, 1994, defendant Transglobal executed a Master Equipment Lease Agreement ("Agreement") which was accepted by plaintiff AT&T Credit on August 5, 1994. Pursuant to this Agreement, AT&T Credit agreed to lease AT&T Corp. telephone equipment to Transglobal. At the same time, Transglobal executed Master Equipment Lease Agreement Schedule 00010 ("Schedule 00010"). According to Schedule 00010, AT&T Credit leased to Transglobal an AT&T Corp. Conversant Communications System and other related equipment ("the Leased Equipment") for a lease term of 48 months, commencing August 31, 1994, with monthly rental payments of $4,537.41.

On or about July 19, 1994, Transglobal executed a document acknowledging that the Agreement, Schedule 00010, and all other agreements constituted the entire agreement between Transglobal and AT&T Credit relating to the Leased Equipment. Transglobal also executed a Master Equipment Lease Agreement Commencement Certificate ("Commencement Certificate"), in which Transglobal acknowledged delivery, acceptance, and proper working condition of the Leased Equipment.

Also on or about that same day, defendant Carraway executed a Master Equipment Lease Agreement Guaranty ("Guaranty"), personally guaranteeing to AT&T Credit the full and prompt payment, observance, and performance when due of all obligations of Transglobal under the lease.

Soon after the lease commenced on August 31, 1994, Transglobal's account became delinquent with AT&T Credit. Transglobal made its November 1994 payment, but made no further payments. The Agreement and Schedule 00010 (collectively referred to as "the Lease") provide for a series of specific remedies to AT&T Credit in the event of Transglobal's default. If Transglobal fails to make any monthly payment within ten days of the due date, Transglobal is obligated to pay AT&T Credit a late charge of 5 percent of the monthly payment. It also obligates Transglobal to pay AT&T Credit interest at a rate of 1.5 percent per month.

Paragraph 20 of the Agreement is a liquidated damages provision, which provides that if default occurs, AT&T Credit has the right to recover damages in the amount of the Lessor's Return, which is defined as the sum of the following amounts:

(a) the aggregate amount of delinquent rental payments (including late fees and interest); plus
(b) the present value of all rental payments due for the remaining term of the lease, discounted at 5 percent; plus
(c) the present value (discounted at 5 percent) of the casualty value of the equipment.

As of May 2, 1996, AT&T Credit calculated that amount as $250,658.58. The Agreement also provides for the payment of costs to AT&T Credit, and allows AT&T Credit to take possession of or render unusable the Leased Equipment.

Defendants deny that they are in default in performing their obligations under the Lease documents and that any payments are due to AT&T Credit. Defendants allege that the reason they had to discontinue their operations was that AT&T Corp. breached its agreement with Transglobal. AT&T Corp. and Transglobal had entered into an agreement that provided that AT&T Corp. would provide equipment, lines, and minutes to Transglobal to start up its call turnaround ("CTA") business.[2]

Transglobal joined AT&T Corp. as a third-party defendant in this matter for breach of this agreement. There are several allegations against AT&T, with one being that AT&T Corp. continued amending the agreement after Transglobal had begun operations at an agreed-upon rate. Most simply put, Transglobal contends that the equipment lease with AT&T Credit was merely a component

2. CTA exploits the differential between the lower rates charged for international and domestic long distance telephone service provided by major U.S. telecommunications carriers and the substantially higher rates charged for such service by the government-controlled foreign telephone administrations or postal, telephone, or telegraph authorities. CTA technology allows a telephone customer in a foreign country to place an international or domestic long distance call at a rate available from a CTA provider by using international outbound service to call an established CTA telephone number in the United States.

of a complex business arrangement with AT&T Corp., and that Transglobal and Carraway have valid defenses to the enforcement of the Agreement and the Guaranty.

**Discussion**

In order for AT&T Credit to prevail, it must show that a contractual relationship existed between it and Transglobal, that Transglobal breached the contract, and that AT&T Credit suffered damages.

It is undisputed that Trangslobal entered into the Lease, as Transglobal admits in its Answer, and the terms of the Lease are the embodiment of the parties' agreement.

Additionally, Transglobal has failed to make any payments under the Lease since November 1994. Transglobal has not pointed to any fact to show that it made any payments. The Agreement provides that the lessee "agrees that it has an unconditional obligation to pay all rental payments and other amounts when due." Agreement, ¶14. Furthermore, pursuant to the Agreement, the lessee is not entitled to "recoupments, cross-claims, counterclaims or any other defenses to any rental payments or other amounts due hereunder, whether those defenses arise out of claims by lessee against lessor, seller, this agreement, any schedule, or otherwise." Agreement, ¶12.

Transglobal contends that summary judgment is inappropriate based on the claims pending against AT&T Corp. However, those claims are independent of the claims by AT&T Credit. No allegation in Transglobal's third-party complaint against AT&T Corp. claims that AT&T Credit committed any wrongdoing. The Agreement provides that "lessor shall not be bound by, or liable for, any representation or promise made by seller (even if lessor is affiliated with seller)." *Id.*

New Jersey law governs this dispute, as stated by the express provisions of the Lease. Under New Jersey law, a promise to make all requisite payments and not to assert any defenses to payment are valid and enforceable. The New Jersey Uniform Commercial Code ("NJUCC") provides: [The court quotes from UCC section 2A-407.]

The controlling question in this matter is whether the Lease is in fact a finance lease as defined under UCC section 2A-103(1)(g):

> (g) "Finance lease" means a lease with respect to which:
> (i) the lessor does not select, manufacture, or supply the goods;
> (ii) the lessor acquires the goods or the right to possession and use of the goods in connection with the lease; and
> (iii) one of the following occurs:

[inapplicable subsections deleted]

> (D) if the lease is not a consumer lease, the lessor, before the lessee signs the lease contract, informs the lessee in writing (a) of the identity of the person supplying the goods to the lessor . . . ; (b) that the lessee is entitled under this chapter to the promises and warranties, including those of any third party, provided to the

> lessor by the person supplying the goods in connection with or as part of the contract by which the lessor acquired the goods or the right to possession and use of the goods; and (c) that the lessee may communicate with the person supplying the goods to the lessor and receive an accurate and complete statement of those promises and warranties, including any disclaimers and limitations of them or of remedies.

The first two conditions are satisfied in that AT&T Credit did not select, manufacture, or supply the Leased Equipment, and it acquired the equipment in connection with the Lease.

Subsection (g)(iii)(D), the third condition, is also satisfied. Transglobal clearly had possession of the Lease documents before signing, and therefore was provided with the requirements enunciated by subsection (g)(iii)(D). Transglobal was made aware of the warranties and representations in the Lease documents and that Transglobal had a right to pursue the seller (AT&T Corp.) for "any and all claims and warranties relating to the equipment." Agreement, ¶15, "Lessor Disclaimers; Limitation of Remedies."

Comment (g) to NJUCC section 2A-103 is instructive in this matter. The Comment provides in part:

> Due to the limited function usually performed by the lessor, the lessee looks almost entirely to the supplier for representations, covenants and warranties. If a manufacturer's warranty carries through, the lessee may also look to that. Yet, this definition does not restrict the lessor's function solely to the supply of funds; if the lessor undertakes or performs other functions, then express warranties, covenants, and the common law will protect the lessee.

N.J.S.A. 12A:2A-103, Comment (g) (West Supp. 1997). Here, AT&T Credit merely provided the vehicle necessary for Transglobal to finance the equipment. AT&T Credit performed no other function. Its disclaimers were prominent in the Lease, and the Lease provided that Transglobal had a right of action as to AT&T Corp. for any warranties, representations, etc.

Transglobal argues that the "close connection" between AT&T Credit and AT&T Corp. gives it defenses not otherwise available for a finance lease. This argument is without merit. The UCC "creates no special rule where the lessor is an affiliate of the supplier; whether the transaction qualifies as a finance lease will be determined by the facts of each case." *Id.*

The terms of the Lease are clear and unambiguous. Transglobal discontinued making its monthly payments while in possession of the Leased Equipment. Therefore, this court finds that the Lease in this matter between AT&T Credit and Transglobal is a finance lease and that Transglobal breached the Lease. Consequently, summary judgment is appropriate as to Transglobal.

[The court also holds that the guarantor is liable.]

## PROBLEM

***Problem 10-2.*** A consumer leases a Mercedes-Benz automobile. The lessee selected the car from the Mercedes dealership. The dealership uses a form prepared by Mercedes-Benz Credit Corporation (MBCC), the financing arm of the manufacturer. The contract is prepared showing the dealership as the lessor, but provides that the lease will be immediately assigned to MBCC. It contains the following provisions:

> **6. VEHICLE WARRANTIES AND DISCLAIMERS**
> To the extent they are assignable, you [lessor] agree to assign to me [lessee] all your rights and remedies under the manufacturer's standard written warranties applicable to the vehicle. I acknowledge that you make no express warranties regarding the vehicle as to its condition, merchantability, or fitness for use, that you disclaim any implied warranties and that I am leasing it from you "as is."
>
> **19. ABATEMENT**
> The monthly rent shall be paid for the full term of the lease . . . without setoff, counterclaim, reduction, abatement, suspension, deferment, or any other defense because of . . . unsatisfactory performance of the vehicle or for any other reason whatever including, but not limited to, mechanical or warranty problems. . . .

The car was sold to MBCC along with the assignment of the lease and the lessee made payments to it. During this time, the lessee was dissatisfied with the performance of the car and took it back numerous times to the dealership. The lessee never complained to MBCC, believing that the dealership and MBCC were the same entity (although they were not). Finally, lessee stopped making payments and surrendered the car. MBCC sued for the amount due under the lease, and lessee sought to defend by asserting breach of warranty of quality. Is this a finance lease? See UCC §2A-103(1)(g). Has MBCC given any warranties of quality in this case? See UCC §2A-211 through 2A-213. Is the lessee bound by the "hell or high water" clause? How is this problem distinguishable from the immediately preceding case? See UCC §2A-407, Official Comments 2 and 6; *Mercedes-Benz Credit Corp. v. Lotito*, 306 N.J. Super. 25, 703 A.2d 288, 34 UCC Rep. Serv. 2d 1 (App. Div. 1997).

## C. RIGHTS OBTAINED BY LESSEE

Just as the buyer of goods generally obtains no better title than the seller had, the lessee of goods generally obtains no greater rights in the goods than the lessor had. See UCC §2-403 and §2A-304, Official Comment 1. There are some situations in which the lessor has voidable title and can actually convey greater rights than the lessor had. The next two problems explore the rights obtained by buyers and lessees in situations in which the seller-lessor had less than clear title to the goods.

### PROBLEMS

***Problem 10-3.*** Computers `R Us sells a computer to Mom & Pop Manufacturing Company. Because Mom & Pop do not have much storage space, the parties agree that Computers `R Us will store the computer until needed by Mom & Pop. Computers `R Us then unlawfully leases the computer to PDQ Delivery Service. When Mom & Pop find out what has happened, it wants to obtain possession of the computer from PDQ. What rights does Mom & Pop have in this situation? See UCC §2-403, §2A-304, Comment 3, §2A-305, and §2A-307.

***Problem 10-4.*** Dull Computers leases a computer to High Tech Retailers. High Tech is in the business of selling computers to the public. The leased computer is to be used as equipment by High Tech and is not for resale. Nevertheless, High Tech decides to sell the computer to an innocent purchaser for value. Does the purchaser take free of the lease? If the computer were leased by High Tech to an innocent lessee, would the lessee take free of the lease between Dull and High Tech? See UCC §2-403, §2A-305.

## D. PERFORMANCE, BREACH, AND REMEDIES UNDER A LEASE CONTRACT

The rules dealing with performance and breach under Article 2A are very similar to the corresponding rules under UCC Article 2. The lessor is required to deliver goods that conform to the warranties given under the lease contract. Similar to Article 2, Article 2A distinguishes between cases in which leased goods are to be delivered in installments and cases in which the goods are delivered in a single tender. In a noninstallment sale, the "perfect tender rule" applies, and the lessee may reject goods that do not in any respect conform to the lease contract, subject to the lessor's right to cure that is similar to UCC section 2-508. See UCC §§2A-509 and 2A-513. In an installment sale, the lessee is only allowed to reject if a nonconformity substantially impairs the value of the installment and cannot be cured. The contract may be canceled only if the nonconformity or default with respect to one or more installments substantially impairs the value of the contract as a whole. UCC §2A-510.

The lessee has a right to revoke acceptance under UCC section 2A-517 similar to the right afforded buyers under UCC section 2-608. Except in finance lease cases, the lessee may revoke acceptance if a nonconformity substantially impairs the value of the goods to the lessee and (i) the goods were accepted on the reasonable assumption that the nonconformity would be cured and the lessor does not reasonably cure; or (ii) if it was difficult to discover the nonconformity before acceptance. Even in finance lease cases, the lessee may also revoke acceptance if a nonconformity substantially impairs the value of the goods to the lessee and the lessee's acceptance was reasonably induced by the lessor's assurances. Remember that in finance lease cases, the lessor is generally not responsible for the quality of the goods. It will be a rare case where a finance lessor makes assurances to the lessee regarding the quality of the goods since the lessee selects the goods from a third-party supplier.

The lessor's rights upon a lessee's default are similar to the rights of a seller under Article 2 if the buyer defaults. Article 2A distinguishes between installment leases and noninstallment leases, permitting cancellation of an installment lease only if the buyer's default substantially impairs the value of the whole lease contract. Otherwise, if the lessee wrongfully rejects or revokes acceptance of goods, fails to make a payment when due, or repudiates, the lessor is given a number of options, including cancellation of the lease, withholding delivery in some cases and disposing of the goods and recovering damages. See UCC §2A-523.

There is an additional remedy given to a lessor that reflects the lessor's retention of title in the goods. If the lessee fails to make payments, the lessor may repossess the goods. In addition, if the lessee otherwise breaches the lease contract, the lessor may repossess if permitted under the lease contract or if the default substantially impairs the value of the lease contract. UCC §§2A-523(3) and 2A-523(5).

In terms of damages, Article 2A, like Article 2, allows the injured party to "cover" or to recover damages under a contract/market formula. See UCC §§2A-518, 2A-519, 2A-527, and 2A-528. Lost-volume lessors may try to argue for lost profits under section 2A-528. Since lease contracts are long-term as compared to sales, it is necessary to make present value calculations when doing a contract market analysis or when comparing the value of a breached lease contract with the value of a substitute lease contract. For example, assume that on the date that goods are repossessed by the lessor, the rent under the lease is $1,000 per month while the market rent at that time is $750 per month. If there are five years left on the lease, the court needs to do a present-value analysis, factoring in an appropriate interest rate, to determine the difference in the value of the leases at that time. "Present value" is defined in UCC section 2A-103(1)(u) as "the amount as of a date certain of one or more sums payable in the future, discounted to the date certain." That section also permits the parties in the contract to set the interest rate that will be used, provided it is not manifestly unreasonable at the time of the contract. Otherwise, it is a commercially reasonable rate. See Official Comment (u) to section 2A-103 for a discussion of this definition.

Similar to Article 2's different treatment of buyers and sellers, Article 2A permits lessees to obtain consequential damages and incidental damages in appropriate cases but permits lessors to obtain only incidental damages. See UCC §§2A-520 and 2A-530.

Lessors are given the right to sue for the rent under the lease contract in situations similar to those that give the seller the right to sue for the price under Article 2. See UCC §2A-529. The lessee's right to specific performance of the lease contract is similar to the right of a buyer to specific performance in a sale of goods case—basically, that the goods are sufficiently unique that the lessee cannot obtain reasonable substitute goods. See UCC §2A-521.

## The Corner, Inc. v. Pinnacle, Inc.

Supreme Court of Wyoming

907 P.2d 1281, 31 UCC Rep. Serv. 2d 455 (1995)

The sole issue in this case is the proper method of computing damages for the breach of a contract to lease coin-operated machines. The Corner, Inc., d/b/a The Other Corner (The Corner) leased a jukebox, a pool table, an electronic dartboard, and two vending machines from Pinnacle, Inc., d/b/a Games Plus (Pinnacle) but, within a few days, The Corner repudiated the lease agreement. The breach of the lease agreement was conceded, and the sole issue at trial was the proper amount of damages.

The Corner's business is a cocktail lounge and a package liquor store in which entertainment is provided for patrons in the form of music and games. Pinnacle's business is providing coin-operated vending machines to businesses like The Corner. On September 9, 1993, The Corner and Pinnacle executed a contract (Agreement) pursuant to which Pinnacle leased to The Corner a compact disc jukebox, a pool table, an electronic dartboard, a new cigarette/candy vending machine, and one used cigarette vending machine. The term of the Agreement was three years and gave Pinnacle "the exclusive right to maintain and operate coin-operated equipment" at The Corner. The Agreement was to become effective upon installation of the equipment which, subject to availability, was to be installed no later than 14 days after the Agreement was signed.

The consideration for the jukebox furnished by Pinnacle was $65 per week. The consideration for the pool table was a down payment of $400 and a payment of $250 per month to Pinnacle for 12 months. It then provided that The Corner would have the option of purchasing the pool table for $1 after the first 12 months of the lease, and then would pay $75 per month for a "Maintenance, League Service agreement" with Pinnacle. The consideration for the dartboard was an equal division of the proceeds, and for the cigarette machines the consideration provided for ten percent of the gross income to The Corner with the balance to Pinnacle.

On September 13, 1993, The Corner advised Pinnacle it did not intend to continue with the Agreement. The principals met on September 14, 1993, to discuss this repudiation, but later that day The Corner advised Pinnacle that it intended to persist in its repudiation. Pinnacle was able to place the dartboard in another location, but was unsuccessful in finding locations for any of the other equipment. Some three months later, Pinnacle brought this action against The Corner in which it alleged breach of contract and damages under paragraph six of the Agreement for lost profits, reasonable attorney fees and costs, all consequential damages, and other relief the court might deem proper. The Corner admitted breach of the contract and contested only damages.

At trial, The Corner elicited testimony with respect to certain aspects of Pinnacle's costs and the mitigation of its damages. Pinnacle did return the pool table and the jukebox to its supplier, but it was assessed a restocking fee of $650. Pinnacle did not have to pay the $1,850 price of the pool table nor the $4,500 price of the jukebox. It did place the electronic dartboard, costing $1,850, at a different location. Pinnacle canceled the order for the new cigarette machine prior to shipment, and it incurred no costs with respect to that machine. The Corner presented no evidence about revenues and expenses, but it did assert the damages claimed were unfair and unreasonable.

The essential premise for the argument The Corner presents is the usual rule that the remedy for breach of contract is the award of damages sufficient to place the plaintiff in the same position as he would have attained had the contract been fully performed, less any proper deductions. The Corner's contention is that Pinnacle is placed in a better position than it would have attained had the Agreement been performed because Pinnacle was allowed to recover costs and expenses it did not incur. The Corner contends that, in effect, it was penalized because it repudiated the Agreement.

[The Corner argues] that the damages awarded did not reflect Pinnacle's true losses because Pinnacle calculated depreciation for the jukebox and the pool table for the three-year period of the Agreement. The Corner contends Pinnacle should have deducted the cost of the jukebox and pool table as expenses because those machines were returned to their supplier and Pinnacle was credited with that amount less the restocking fee. Because of the manner in which the damages for the pool table were calculated, we hold that Pinnacle should have deducted the cost of the pool table rather than depreciation, but we sustain the trial court's judgment in all other respects.

We conclude that the proper measure of damages here is the difference between the contract price and the cost of performing the first contract, as the court apparently held below. In the case of realty, which (unlike the jukebox) is specific and not to be duplicated on the market, the lessor could not properly lease it to another for the same period unless the first lease were broken or terminated. In such a case the lessor should not be awarded two profits merely because of the first lessee's default.

So in general we may say that gains made by a lessor on a lease entered into after the breach are not to be deducted from his damages unless the breach enabled him to make the gains. The recoverable damages in the case of a contract are such as may reasonably be within the contemplation of the parties at the time of the contract ***; and with that in view, we should not in the present case deny lessor the benefit of his bargain.

The essential formula adopted for the measure of damages is the difference between the contract price and the imputed direct costs of performing that contract.

Article 2 on sales generally provides the model for the provisions of Article 2A relating to remedies. [The court quotes from UCC sections 2A-523, 2A-527, and 2A-528, emphasizing section 2A-528(2).]

We find this pertinent statement as to when profit is the measure of damages in 3A William D. Hawkland & Frederick H. Miller, *Uniform Commercial Code Series* §2A-528:03, at 1102-1103 (1993) (footnotes omitted, emphasis added):

> The principal measure of recovery provided by section 2A-528 is the difference between the market rent and the contract rent together with incidental damages. This measure is designed to result in a recovery that approximates the value of the lessor's bargain. Sometimes, however, this formula, which subtracts the market rent from the contract rent, does not afford an adequate basis upon which to measure the value of the lessor's bargain. In these cases, the lessor is permitted to compute damages for qualified defaults by proving loss of expected profits.
>
> A simple illustration of a situation in which damages based upon the difference between the market and contract rent do not make the lessor whole is one in which the subject of the lease involves goods that lease under a standard lease contract. For example, suppose that an automobile dealer leases

> a car to a lessee for $7,500, which is the standard lease offered by this dealer for this car; that the lessee repudiates the deal and refuses to take possession of the car, or pay; and that the lessor then releases the same car to another customer for $7,500. In this case, the lessor would not want to use the rule of section 2A-527 to measure damages, because there is no difference between the release rent and the contract rent. Nor would the dealer want to use the rule for damages stated in section 2A-528(1), for there also would seem to be no difference between the market and contract rents. This might suggest that the lessor has not been injured by the repudiation, but the lessor has lost a profit because of the default if another car could have been leased to the second customer; that is, if the lessee had not defaulted, the lessor would have leased two cars instead of one. Stated differently, if it is assumed that the lessor has an unlimited supply of cars, the lessee's default costs the lessor a lease, because no matter how many cars the lessor may lease in a given period, the lessor would have leased one more had the lessee not defaulted. This arguably should be equally true if the dealer could have sold another car to the second customer, because the recovery is not for the profit on the second transaction; that profit exists. The point is that the second transaction should not be made possible by the lessee's default; the absence of that circumstance is what demonstrates a loss to the lessor. See Comment 2 to section 2A-529. Any economic consequence resulting from a dissimilarity in the transactions can be adjusted by due credit as provided in section 2A-528(2).

This case fits that analysis. Pinnacle produced evidence that "there are a limited number of locations versus a virtually unlimited amount of equipment." The analogy to the example concerning the leasing of cars is clear. Any other transactions or mitigation, including re-leasing, by Pinnacle, would fit because those transactions might have occurred if The Corner had performed. The Corner's repudiation did not make those transactions possible. We hold that, in an instance such as this, the lessor has no duty to endeavor to mitigate damages by re-leasing the equipment because its damages remain the same. It still loses the benefit of its bargain under the lease.

We turn to The Corner's argument that Pinnacle is required to deduct as expenses the full costs of the jukebox, $4,500, and the pool table, $1,850, rather than as calculated depreciation for the Agreement's three-year period. Pinnacle's evidence established it had applied a useful life of 20 years to the jukebox and the pool table, and that it deducted as expenses depreciation of $675 on the jukebox and $277.50 on the pool table. We perceive the useful life Pinnacle applied to the jukebox was indeed generous as far as The Corner was concerned, and we find no error in that computation.

We are satisfied, however, that Pinnacle should have deducted the cost of the pool table in arriving at its damages. The damages for the pool table were computed as though the option to purchase at the end of the first 12 months had been exercised by The Corner. The damages for the second and third years of the lease were reduced to $75 per month for the maintenance and league servicing contract. Since the damages were computed in that way, the cost of the pool table ($1,850) should have been credited against these damages rather than the smaller amount of depreciation ($277.50). This adjustment would increase the damages for the lease of the pool table by $277.50 and decrease those damages by $1,850. This leaves a net loss of profits for the pool table of

$1,670 instead of the $3,242.50 reflected in Exhibit C. We will remand the case for the trial court to effect that adjustment in the amount of damages to be reduced to the present value.

The Corner contends Pinnacle also should be required to deduct overhead expenses it did not incur. The language of our statutes is clear, and it provides, "the measure of damages is the present value of the profit, including reasonable overhead * * *." UCC §2A-528(2)(emphasis added). The provision is so stated because the drafters of the UCC recognize a difference between the effect of fixed and variable costs.

In 1 Roy Ryden Anderson, *Damages Under the Uniform Commercial Code* §2:10, at 20-21 (1992) (footnote omitted, emphasis added), relating to the recovery of overhead under the profit formula of the sales provision of UCC section 2-708(2), the concept is explained in this way:

> The profit formula of section 2-708(2) includes a dichotomy of expenses. The formula provides for a recovery by the seller of overhead expenses but requires the seller to account to the buyer for "expenses saved." The distinction is between fixed expenses or "overhead," which are by definition not saved by the breach (e.g., utilities, management salaries, and other fixed costs of doing business), and expenses which are "variable" in that they are attributable only to the breached contract and may be saved if not incurred prior to the breach (e.g., labor, materials, and expenses of transportation attributable to the breached contract).
>
> Clearly, if the expenses are saved the defendant buyer should be credited with the savings; otherwise the seller will receive a windfall. The important point is that overhead expenses, which by definition are fixed and do not vary from contract to contract, are not saved when a buyer breaches. That an aggrieved party, whether or not his action is governed by the Code, is entitled to recover such fixed expenses is now well settled by the cases. The clearest discussion of the proposition remains that of Judge Staley in *Vitex Mfg. Corp., Ltd. v. Carbitex*[sic]*Corp.*[377 F.2d 795 (3d Cir. 1967)]. If a seller were not allowed to recover from the buyer the percentage of the fixed overhead expenditures attributable to the breached contract, the profitability of the seller's remaining sales transactions would be unfairly reduced. Assume, to borrow Judge Staley's example, that the seller has a fixed overhead of $10,000 and five sales contracts. Each contract then bears $2,000 of the overhead expense. If one of the contracts is breached and the seller is not allowed to recover the $2,000 overhead, each of the remaining contracts will be forced to bear $2,500 of the overhead, and the seller's profitability on these remaining contracts will be reduced accordingly.
>
> At trial, the most effective way to prove profit plus reasonable overhead under section 2-708(2) is to establish the unpaid price of the breached contract and to deduct only the variable expenses attributable to it. The resulting figure would then include both profit and fixed overhead expenses. The courts have uniformly approved this procedure. This technique will avoid the near impossibility of proving every item of a seller's overhead and the tedium of having opposing counsel object time and again as to the unreasonableness of each and every item.

We hold that the damages were correctly established under the UCC. The Corner was not penalized by the calculation of damages by the trial court, which correctly applied UCC section 2A-528(2) providing for lost profits as the measure of damages. The damages for the lease of the pool table must be adjusted by deducting the cost of the pool table and adding the amount allowed for depreciation. That has the effect of reducing the total damages by $1,572.50. We affirm the judgment entered by the trial court, but we remand the case for the entry of a corrected judgment in favor of Pinnacle.

## QUESTIONS AND PROBLEMS

1. Why is the cost of the pool table subtracted from damages rather than depreciation? Is the pool table transaction a "lease" or is it a "sale" ? What kinds of expenses should be subtracted under the maintenance part of the pool table contract?

***Problem 10-5.*** A lease contract provides that in the event of default by the lessee, the lessor's damages will be the sum of lease payments that are past due, plus the present value of future lease payments at the time of default discounted at an interest rate of 3 percent, plus the estimated residual value of the goods at the end of the lease ($25,000), minus the value of the goods at the time of default. You may assume that the discount rate is reasonable. The value of the goods at the time of default is determined by subtracting from the initial value of the goods depreciation for the time the goods are held by the lessee. The contract provides that the initial value of the goods is $50,000 and the depreciation per year is $5,000. These are reasonable estimates at the time the parties contract. The lessee defaults two years into the five-year lease. After taking possession, the lessor is immediately able to resell the goods for $43,000. Is the provision in the contract calculating damages enforceable? See UCC §2A-504(1). Would it be enforceable under UCC section 2-718? See the Official Comment to UCC §2A-504.

***Problem 10-6.*** Lessor wrongfully fails to deliver goods under a lease contract. At the time of default, the present value of lease payments due under the lease is $50,000. The present value of market rent for comparable goods with a comparable lease term is $60,000. Rather than lease substitute goods, the lessee decides to hire an additional employee who will do the work that was supposed to be done by the goods that were going to be leased. For the term of the lease, the employee's wages and benefits will be $200,000. How should the lessee's damages be calculated? See UCC §§2A-519 and 2A-520.

## CHAPTER 10 REVIEW PROBLEM

Sanitation Company ("Lessee") needed a new garbage truck, and decided for accounting reasons that it made sense for it to lease the truck instead of buying it. Lessee found a truck that it liked from Truck Dealers, Inc. ("Seller"), but Seller was not interested in entering into a leasing transaction. Lessee then turned to Friendly Finance Company ("Lessor"), which agreed to finance the transaction. Lessor frequently engaged in these types of transactions involving commercial trucks. Lessee and Lessor entered into an agreement whereby Lessor agreed to purchase the truck that Lessee wanted and then lease the truck to Lessee for five years. The lease was not revocable, and no express warranty of quality regarding the truck was given by Lessor. The truck was covered by a five-year warranty given by Seller. The predicted useful life of the truck was ten years. The monthly payments made by Lessee over the terms of the lease in the aggregate would exceed by approximately 10 percent the cash value of the truck. At the end of the five-year period, Lessee had the option of purchasing the truck for $30,000. It was estimated that the fair market value of the truck would be $50,000 at the end of the lease period. Lessee was responsible for risk of loss with respect to the goods and had to pay all costs of registration of the truck.

The lease had a liquidated damages provision, which provided that if default occurred, Lessor had the right to recover the following amounts:

(a) the aggregate amount of delinquent rental payments (including late fees and interest); plus
(b) the present value of future lease payments discounted at a rate of 3 percent; plus
(c) the estimated residual value of the goods at the end of the lease ($50,000) minus
(d) the value of the goods at the time of repossession, which is calculated at the cash price for the goods ($100,000) minus depreciation of $10,000 per year.

The prime rate of interest at the time of the lease was around 5 percent, meaning that the present value calculated under the lease will be greater than if it was calculated under the prime rate by several thousand dollars.

After a couple of years, Lessee started to have problems with the truck. Lessee took the truck back to Seller numerous times, but Seller was unable to make proper repairs. At the end of the second year Lessee gave notice to Lessor that it wished to revoke the lease and stopped making payments. Lessor then seized the truck, managed to get it repaired, and then sold it for $90,000. It paid $2,000 for the repairs. The depreciation value of the truck was $80,000 at the time Lessor took possession. Is the transaction between Lessor and Lessee a true lease, or is it instead the financing of a sale? UCC §1-203. Assuming it is a lease, does Lessee have any recourse against Lessor for the defective truck? UCC §§2A-103(1)(g), 2A-212, 2A-407, and 2A-508. Assuming it is a lease, does Lessee have any recourse against Seller? UCC §2A-209. Lastly, assuming a lease, is the damages formula in the lease agreement likely to be enforceable? UCC §§2A-103(1)(u) and 2A-504.

CHAPTER 11

# LICENSES OF INFORMATION

As the economy becomes more reliant on computer software and computerized informational databases, licenses of rights in technology and of access to information have become more commonplace. When you purchase software either in a store or over the Internet, you are likely to be confronted with a license agreement which you will have to accept by clicking on a button on a computer screen in order to use the software. You are not technically buying the software; you are purchasing the right to use it according to the terms of the license. Likewise, when you access an informational database, such as Westlaw or LEXIS, you will be doing so pursuant to the terms of a license.

What is a "license" in a transaction involving software or other computer technology? The Uniform Computer Information Transactions Act ("UCITA") defines "license" as "a contract that authorizes access to, or use, distribution, performance, modification, or reproduction of, information or informational rights, but expressly limits the access or uses authorized or expressly grants fewer than all rights in the information. . . ." UCITA §102(a)(41). "Information" is defined by UCITA as including computer programs. UCITA §102(a)(35). The definition of license can be contrasted to the definition of a "sale," in that a sale involves the transfer of title for a price. UCC §2-106(1). Under a license, the licensee has permission to use information but does not obtain title to that information.

The law governing licenses is not as well developed as the law governing sales and leases of goods. Because of the paucity of statutory or case law, courts have often used UCC Article 2 in determining the rights and obligations of parties to a software license. *See Specht v. Netscape Communications Corp.*, page 328 *infra*. The National Conference on Uniform State Laws ("NCCUSL") has sponsored UCITA in an attempt to fill the statutory void.

UCITA applies to a "computer information transaction," which is defined as "an agreement or the performance of it to create, modify, transfer, or license computer information or informational rights in computer information." UCITA §§102(a)(11) and 103. Because "computer information" is a very broad term as defined in section 102(a)(10), there are a number of exclusions from UCITA's scope spelled out in section 103(c), such as financial service transactions, insurance service transactions, and agreements to distribute motion pictures or audio or visual programming, other than in a mass-market transaction.

There has been much opposition to UCITA by consumer advocates and by other organizations because of the view that UCITA favors software developers in largely upholding their license agreements.[1] At the time of this writing (summer 2011), UCITA has been adopted in only Maryland and Virginia. Because of the heavy opposition, NCCUSL has decided not to expend any additional resources in trying to have UCITA adopted by the states, although it is still available for legislatures to adopt and for courts to use.[2]

Even if UCITA does not become widely enacted, it may nevertheless be important for lawyers to be aware of it. Until some codification of licensing law occurs, courts may be tempted to look to UCITA as persuasive authority in cases of first impression in their jurisdictions. Parties may contractually attempt to have UCITA be the governing law by choosing the law of a state that has adopted it, although at least one state has adopted a so-called "bomb shelter" statute that protects its citizens from choice-of-law clauses adopting UCITA.[3] In addition, parties may look to UCITA for guidance in drafting contractual provisions for their licenses. This may be true in international as well as domestic transactions, as international licensing law is also not well developed.

Another source of rules is the *Principles of the Law of Software Contracts* finalized by the American Law Institute in 2010. The *Principles* can be found on Westlaw in the "ALI-SOFTWARE" database. The *Principles* were promulgated by experts in contract law and indicate that they are intended to be a guide to courts in resolving issues arising out of software licensing transactions. The "Introduction" to the *Principles* states that because the law is fairly unsettled in the area, it is inappropriate to call the *Principles* a *Restatement*. It is possible that the *Principles* will be persuasive authority to courts, but their influence has yet to be seen. To some extent, the *Principles* draw from comparable provisions in UCITA. In this chapter, a few of the *Principles* will be discussed that vary from UCITA.

## A. SALES COMPARED TO LICENSING TRANSACTIONS

NCCUSL and other supporters of UCITA believe that UCC Article 2 is not an appropriate statutory framework for dealing with licenses of information.[4] The premise of the *Principles of the Law of Software Contracts* is also that Article 2 does not adequately answer all questions raised by software license transactions. Article 2 was designed to deal with contracts involving the passing of title to tangible personal property. Technology licenses involve limited rights in intangible personal property, which are also governed by copyright and

---

1. For a list of objections to the 2000 version of UCITA, see Braucher, *The Uniform Computer Information Transactions Act (UCITA): Objections From a Consumer Perspective, www.ftc.gov/bcp/workshops/warranty/comments/braucherjean.pdf* (accessed Nov., 2011). Some of the objections listed were addressed in the 2002 amendments to UCITA.

2. *See www.library.yale.edu/~llicense/ListArchives/0308/msg00017.html* (accessed July 27, 2011).

3. *See, e.g.,* Iowa Code §554D.125.

4. *See* Nimmer, *Through the Looking Glass: What Courts and UCITA Say about the Scope of Contract Law in the Information Age,* 38 Duq. L. Rev. 255 (2000).

patent law. Contract formation in licensing transactions may involve the use of shrinkwrap or "click through" licenses as compared to the "battle of the forms" in sales transactions. The implied warranty of merchantability in a sales transaction may be inappropriate in a situation in which someone is accessing information. Likewise, the "perfect tender rule" of sales law may not be appropriate in licensing transactions, since there are likely to be small "bugs" in all software. Proposed amendments to UCC Article 2 would have excluded pure "information" transactions from the scope of Article 2, including pure software licensing transactions. Those amendments did not become law, however, and were ultimately withdrawn from the official text of the UCC by the Uniform Law Commission and American Law Institute in 2011.

As goods become increasingly complex, many goods will contain computer information that will enable the goods to operate. The sale of such goods may also include a license to use the computer information contained in the goods. In such a transaction, does Article 2 apply, UCITA (if enacted), or both? The following problem explores this issue.

### PROBLEM

***Problem 11-1.*** A buyer purchases a digital camera. The digital camera has embedded software that allows it to operate, and the sale includes a license to use the software. The camera does not perform to the buyer's satisfaction. Would Article 2 or UCITA apply in determining if the buyer has any right to return the camera or obtain damages from the seller? Is the digital camera a "computer" as defined in UCITA? See UCITA §102(a)(9) and UCITA §103, Official Comment 4.[5] See also Koopman and Kaner, *The Problem of Embedded Software in UCITA and Drafts of Revised Article 2, www.badsoftware.com/embedd1 .htm* (commenting on 2000 drafts of UCITA and Revised Article 2). See also the *Principles of the Law of Software Contracts* §§1.07 and 1.08.

## B. CONTRACT FORMATION IN LICENSING TRANSACTIONS

When you purchase software, you have probably encountered either a "shrinkwrap" or "click through" license. A shrinkwrap license, so called because it is found in fine print in the wrapping around the disk containing the software, may provide that the mere opening of the package indicates an assent to the terms of the license. A click-through license displays the terms of the license on the computer screen and requires the user to click "I accept" before using the software, indicating assent to the terms of the license.

Should the terms in the shrinkwrap or click-through license be enforceable, especially if the licensee has already paid for the licensed software before the terms were disclosed? What limits, if any, should be placed on the power

5. If the statutory supplement used for your class does not contain UCITA or its Official Comments, the 2002 Final Act including Comments can be found at the NCCUSL archives, on the Internet at *www.law.upenn.edu/bll/archives/ulc/ucita/2002final.htm* (accessed July 27, 2011).

of the licensor to dictate terms in this way? The following case deals with the enforceability of a license formed over the Internet.

### Specht v. Netscape Communications Corp.

United States Court of Appeals, Second Circuit

306 F.2d 17, 48 UCC Rep. Serv. 2d 761 (2002)

This is an appeal from a judgment of the Southern District of New York denying a motion by defendants-appellants Netscape Communications Corporation and its corporate parent, America Online, Inc. (collectively, "defendants" or "Netscape"), to compel arbitration and to stay court proceedings. In order to resolve the central question of arbitrability presented here, we must address issues of contract formation in cyberspace. Principally, we are asked to determine whether plaintiffs-appellees ("plaintiffs"), by acting upon defendants' invitation to download free software made available on defendants' Web page, agreed to be bound by the software's license terms (which included the arbitration clause at issue), even though plaintiffs could not have learned of the existence of those terms unless, prior to executing the download, they had scrolled down the Web page to a screen located below the download button. We agree with the district court that a reasonably prudent Internet user in circumstances such as these would not have known or learned of the existence of the license terms before responding to defendants' invitation to download the free software, and that defendants therefore did not provide reasonable notice of the license terms. In consequence, plaintiffs' bare act of downloading the software did not unambiguously manifest assent to the arbitration provision contained in the license terms.

#### Background

#### I. Facts

In three related putative class actions, plaintiffs alleged that, unknown to them, their use of SmartDownload transmitted to defendants private information about plaintiffs' downloading of files from the Internet, thereby effecting an electronic surveillance of their online activities in violation of two federal statutes, the Electronic Communications Privacy Act, 18 U.S.C. §§2510 et seq., and the Computer Fraud and Abuse Act, 18 U.S.C. §1030.

Specifically, plaintiffs alleged that when they first used Netscape's Communicator—a software program that permits Internet browsing—the program created and stored on each of their computer hard drives a small text file known as a "cookie" that functioned "as a kind of electronic identification tag for future communications" between their computers and Netscape. Plaintiffs further alleged that when they installed SmartDownload—a separate software "plug-in"[2] that served to enhance

2. Netscape's Web site defines "plug-ins" as "software programs that extend the capabilities of the Netscape Browser in a specific way—giving you, for example, the ability to play audio samples or view video movies from within your browser" *http://wp.netscape.com/plugins*. SmartDownload purportedly made it easier for users of browser programs like Communicator to download files from the Internet without losing their progress when they paused to engage in some other task, or if their Internet connection was severed. *See Specht,* 150 F. Supp. 2d at 587.

Communicator's browsing capabilities—SmartDownload created and stored on their computer hard drives another string of characters, known as a "Key," which similarly functioned as an identification tag in future communications with Netscape. According to the complaints in this case, each time a computer user employed Communicator to download a file from the Internet, SmartDownload "assume[d] from Communicator the task of downloading" the file and transmitted to Netscape the address of the file being downloaded together with the cookie created by Communicator and the Key created by SmartDownload. These processes, plaintiffs claim, constituted unlawful "eavesdropping" on users of Netscape's software products as well as on Internet Web sites from which users employing SmartDownload downloaded files.

In the time period relevant to this litigation, Netscape offered on its Web site various software programs, including Communicator and SmartDownload, which visitors to the site were invited to obtain free of charge. It is undisputed that five of the six named plaintiffs—Michael Fagan, John Gibson, Mark Gruber, Sean Kelly, and Sherry Weindorf— downloaded Communicator from the Netscape Web site. These plaintiffs acknowledge that when they proceeded to initiate installation of Communicator, they were automatically shown a scrollable text of that program's license agreement and were not permitted to complete the installation until they had clicked a "Yes" button to indicate that they accepted all the license terms. If a user attempted to install Communicator without clicking "Yes," the installation would be aborted. All five named user plaintiffs expressly agreed to Communicator's license terms by clicking "Yes." The Communicator license agreement that these plaintiffs saw made no mention of SmartDownload or other plug-in programs, and stated that "[t]hese terms apply to Netscape Communicator and Netscape Navigator" and that "all disputes relating to this Agreement (excepting any dispute relating to intellectual property rights)" are subject to "binding arbitration in Santa Clara County, California."

Although Communicator could be obtained independently of SmartDownload, all the named user plaintiffs, except Fagan, downloaded and installed Communicator in connection with downloading SmartDownload. Each of these plaintiffs allegedly arrived at a Netscape Web page captioned "SmartDownload Communicator" that urged them to "Download With Confidence Using SmartDownload!" At or near the bottom of the screen facing plaintiffs was the prompt "Start Download" and a tinted button labeled "Download." By clicking on the button, plaintiffs initiated the download of SmartDownload. Once that process was complete, SmartDownload, as its first plug-in task, permitted plaintiffs to proceed with downloading and installing Communicator, an operation that was accompanied by the clickwrap display of Communicator's license terms described above.

The signal difference between downloading Communicator and downloading SmartDownload was that no clickwrap presentation accompanied the latter operation. Instead, once plaintiffs Gibson, Gruber, Kelly, and Weindorf had clicked on the "Download" button located at or near the bottom of their screen, and the downloading of SmartDownload was complete, these plaintiffs encountered no further information about the plug-in program or the existence of license terms governing its use. The sole reference to SmartDownload's license terms on the "SmartDownload Communicator" Web page was located in text that would have become visible to plaintiffs only if they had scrolled down to the next screen.

Had plaintiffs scrolled down instead of acting on defendants' invitation to click on the "Download" button, they would have encountered the following invitation: "Please review and agree to the terms of the *Netscape SmartDownload software license agreement* before downloading and using the software." Plaintiffs Gibson, Gruber, Kelly, and Weindorf averred in their affidavits that they never saw this reference to the SmartDownload license agreement when they clicked on the "Download" button. They also testified during depositions that they saw no reference to license terms when they clicked to download SmartDownload, although under questioning by defendants' counsel, some plaintiffs added that they could not "remember" or be "sure" whether the screen shots of the SmartDownload page attached to their affidavits reflected precisely what they had seen on their computer screens when they downloaded SmartDownload.

In sum, plaintiffs Gibson, Gruber, Kelly, and Weindorf allege that the process of obtaining SmartDownload contrasted sharply with that of obtaining Communicator. Having selected SmartDownload, they were required neither to express unambiguous assent to that program's license agreement nor even to view the license terms or become aware of their existence before proceeding with the invited download of the free plug-in program. Moreover, once these plaintiffs had initiated the download, the existence of SmartDownload's license terms was not mentioned while the software was running or at any later point in plaintiffs' experience of the product.

Even for a user who, unlike plaintiffs, did happen to scroll down past the download button, SmartDownload's license terms would not have been immediately displayed in the manner of Communicator's clickwrapped terms. Instead, if such a user had seen the notice of SmartDownload's terms and then clicked on the underlined invitation to review and agree to the terms, a hypertext link would have taken the user to a separate Web page titled "License & Support Agreements." The first paragraph on this page read, in pertinent part:

> The use of each Netscape software product is governed by a license agreement. You must read and agree to the license agreement terms BEFORE acquiring a product. Please click on the appropriate link below to review the current license agreement for the product of interest to you before acquisition. For products available for download, you must read and agree to the license agreement terms BEFORE you install the software. If you do not agree to the license terms, do not download, install, or use the software.

Below this paragraph appeared a list of license agreements, the first of which was "*License Agreement for Netscape Navigator and Netscape Communicator Product Family* (Netscape Navigator, Netscape Communicator, and Netscape SmartDownload)." If the user clicked on that link, he or she would be taken to yet another Web page that contained the full text of a license agreement that was identical in every respect to the Communicator license agreement except that it stated that its "terms apply to Netscape Communicator, Netscape

Navigator, and Netscape SmartDownload." The license agreement granted the user a nonexclusive license to use and reproduce the software, subject to certain terms:

> BY CLICKING THE ACCEPTANCE BUTTON OR INSTALLING OR USING NETSCAPE COMMUNICATOR, NETSCAPE NAVIGATOR, OR NETSCAPE SMARTDOWNLOAD SOFTWARE (THE "PRODUCT"), THE INDIVIDUAL OR ENTITY LICENSING THE PRODUCT ("LICENSEE") IS CONSENTING TO BE BOUND BY AND IS BECOMING A PARTY TO THIS AGREEMENT. IF LICENSEE DOES NOT AGREE TO ALL OF THE TERMS OF THIS AGREEMENT, THE BUTTON INDICATING NON-ACCEPTANCE MUST BE SELECTED, AND LICENSEE MUST NOT INSTALL OR USE THE SOFTWARE.

Among the license terms was a provision requiring virtually all disputes relating to the agreement to be submitted to arbitration:

> Unless otherwise agreed in writing, all disputes relating to this Agreement (excepting any dispute relating to intellectual property rights) shall be subject to final and binding arbitration in Santa Clara County, California, under the auspices of JAMS/EndDispute, with the losing party paying all costs of arbitration.

Unlike the four named user plaintiffs who downloaded SmartDownload from the Netscape Web site, the fifth named plaintiff, Michael Fagan, claims to have downloaded the plug-in program from a "shareware" Web site operated by ZDNet, an entity unrelated to Netscape. Shareware sites are Web sites maintained by companies or individuals that contain libraries of free, publicly available software. The pages that a user would have seen while downloading SmartDownload from ZDNet differed from those that he or she would have encountered while downloading SmartDownload from the Netscape Web site. Notably, instead of any kind of notice of the SmartDownload license agreement, the ZDNet pages offered only a hypertext link to "more information" about SmartDownload, which, if clicked on, took the user to a Netscape Web page that, in turn, contained a link to the license agreement. Thus, a visitor to the ZDNet Web site could have obtained SmartDownload, as Fagan avers he did, without ever seeing a reference to that program's license terms, even if he or she had scrolled through all of ZDNet's Web pages.

The sixth named plaintiff, Christopher Specht, never obtained or used SmartDownload, but instead operated a Web site from which visitors could download certain electronic files that permitted them to create an account with an Internet service provider called WhyWeb. Specht alleges that every time a user who had previously installed SmartDownload visited his Web site and downloaded WhyWeb-related files, defendants intercepted this information. Defendants allege that Specht would receive a representative's commission from WhyWeb every time a user who obtained a WhyWeb file from his Web site subsequently subscribed to the WhyWeb service. Thus, argue defendants, because the "Netscape license agreement . . . conferred on each user the right to download and use both Communicator and SmartDownload software," Specht received a benefit under that license agreement in that SmartDownload "assisted in obtaining the WhyWeb file and increased the likelihood of success in the download process." This benefit, defendants claim, was direct enough to require Specht to arbitrate his claims pursuant to Netscape's license terms. Specht, however, maintains that he never received any commissions based on the WhyWeb files available on his Web site.

II. Proceedings Below

In the district court, defendants moved to compel arbitration and to stay court proceedings pursuant to the Federal Arbitration Act ("FAA"), 9 U.S.C. §4, arguing that the disputes reflected in the complaints, like any other dispute relating to the SmartDownload license agreement, are subject to the arbitration clause contained in that agreement. Finding that Netscape's Web page, unlike typical examples of clickwrap, neither adequately alerted users to the existence of SmartDownload's license terms nor required users unambiguously to manifest assent to those terms as a condition of downloading the product, the court held that the user plaintiffs had not entered into the SmartDownload license agreement.

**Discussion**

I. Standard of Review and Applicable Law

The district court properly concluded that in deciding whether parties agreed to arbitrate a certain matter, a court should generally apply state-law principles to the issue of contract formation. Therefore, state law governs the question of whether the parties in the present case entered into an agreement to arbitrate disputes relating to the SmartDownload license agreement. The district court further held that California law governs the question of contract formation here; the parties do not appeal that determination.

II. Whether This Court Should Remand for a Trial on Contract Formation

[Discussion omitted.]

In sum, we conclude that the district court properly decided the question of reasonable notice and objective manifestation of assent as a matter of law on the record before it, and we decline defendants' request to remand for a full trial on that question.

III. Whether the User Plaintiffs Had Reasonable Notice of and Manifested Assent to the SmartDownload License Agreement

Whether governed by the common law or by Article 2 of the Uniform Commercial Code ("UCC"), a transaction, in order to be a contract, requires a manifestation of agreement between the parties.[13] Mutual manifestation of assent, whether by written or spoken word or by conduct, is the touchstone

---

13. The district court concluded that the SmartDownload transactions here should be governed by "California law as it relates to the sale of goods, including the Uniform Commercial Code in effect in California." *Specht,* 150 F. Supp. 2d at 591. It is not obvious, however, that UCC Article 2 ("sales of goods") applies to the licensing of software that is downloadable from the Internet. *Cf. Advent Sys. Ltd. v. Unisys Corp.,* 925 F.2d 670, 675 (3d Cir. 1991) ("The increasing frequency of computer products as subjects of commercial litigation has led to controversy over whether software is a 'good' or intellectual property. The [UCC] does not specifically mention software."); Lorin

of contract. *Cf. Restatement (Second) of Contracts* §19(2) (1981) ("[t]he conduct of a party is not effective as a manifestation of his assent unless he intends to engage in the conduct and knows or has reason to know that the other party may infer from his conduct that he assents"). Although an onlooker observing the disputed transactions in this case would have seen each of the user plaintiffs click on the SmartDownload "Download" button, a consumer's clicking on a download button does not communicate assent to contractual terms if the offer did not make clear to the consumer that clicking on the download button would signify assent those terms. California's common law is clear that "an offeree, regardless of apparent manifestation of his consent, is not bound by inconspicuous contractual provisions of which he is unaware, contained in a document whose contractual nature is not obvious." *Windsor Mills,* 25 Cal. App. 3d at 992, 101 Cal. Rptr. at 351.

Arbitration agreements are no exception to the requirement of manifestation of assent. "This principle of knowing consent applies with particular force to provisions for arbitration." *Windsor Mills,* 101 Cal. Rptr. at 351. Clarity and conspicuousness of arbitration terms are important in securing informed assent. "If a party wishes to bind in writing another to an agreement to arbitrate future disputes, such purpose should be accomplished in a way that each party to the arrangement will fully and clearly comprehend that the agreement to arbitrate exists and binds the parties thereto." *Commercial Factors Corp. v. Kurtzman Bros.,* 131 Cal. App. 2d 133, 134-135, 280 P.2d 146, 147-148

---

Brennan, *Why Article 2 Cannot Apply to Software Transactions,* PLI Patents, Copyrights, Trademarks, & Literary Property Course Handbook Series (Feb.-Mar. 2001) (demonstrating the trend in case law away from application of UCC provisions to software sales and licensing and toward application of intellectual property principles). There is no doubt that a sale of tangible goods over the Internet is governed by Article 2 of the UCC. *See, e.g., Butler v. Beer Across Am.,* 83 F. Supp. 2d 1261, 1263-1264 & n.6 (N.D. Ala. 2000) (applying Article 2 to an Internet sale of bottles of beer). Some courts have also applied Article 2, occasionally with misgivings, to sales of off-the-shelf software in tangible, packaged formats. *See, e.g., ProCD,* 86 F.3d at 1450 ("[W]e treat the [database] licenses as ordinary contracts accompanying the sale of products, and therefore as governed by the common law of contracts and the Uniform Commercial Code. Whether there are legal differences between 'contracts' and 'licenses' (which may matter under the copyright doctrine of first sale) is a subject for another day."); *I.Lan Sys., Inc. v. Nextpoint Networks, Inc.,* 183 F. Supp. 2d 328, 332 (D. Mass. 2002) (stating, in the context of a dispute between business parties, that "Article 2 technically does not, and certainly will not in the future, govern software licenses, but for the time being, the Court will assume that it does").

Downloadable software, however, is scarcely a "tangible" good, and, in part because software may be obtained, copied, or transferred effortlessly at the stroke of a computer key, licensing of such Internet products has assumed a vast importance in recent years. Recognizing that "a body of law based on images of the sale of manufactured goods ill fits licenses and other transactions in computer information," the National Conference of Commissioners on Uniform State Laws has promulgated the Uniform Computer Information Transactions Act ("UCITA"), a code resembling UCC Article 2 in many respects but drafted to reflect emergent practices in the sale and licensing of computer information. UCITA, prefatory note (rev. ed. Aug. 23, 2001) (available at *www.ucita-online.com/ucita.html*). UCITA—originally intended as a new Article 2B to supplement Articles 2 and 2A of the UCC but later proposed as an independent code—has been adopted by two states, Maryland and Virginia. *See* Md. Code Ann. Com. Law §§22-101 *et seq.;* Va. Code Ann. §§59.1-501.1 *et seq.*

We need not decide today whether UCC Article 2 applies to Internet transactions in downloadable products. The district court's analysis and the parties' arguments on appeal show that, for present purposes, there is no essential difference between UCC Article 2 and the common law of contracts. We therefore apply the common law, with exceptions as noted.

(1955) (internal quotation marks omitted). Thus, California contract law measures assent by an objective standard that takes into account both what the offeree said, wrote, or did, and the transactional context in which the offeree verbalized or acted.

### A. The Reasonably Prudent Offeree of Downloadable Software

Defendants argue that plaintiffs must be held to a standard of reasonable prudence and that, because notice of the existence of SmartDownload license terms was on the next scrollable screen, plaintiffs were on "inquiry notice" of those terms. We disagree with the proposition that a reasonably prudent offeree in plaintiffs' position would necessarily have known or learned of the existence of the SmartDownload license agreement prior to acting, so that plaintiffs may be held to have assented to that agreement with constructive notice of its terms. It is true that "[a] party cannot avoid the terms of a contract on the ground that he or she failed to read it before signing." *Marin Storage & Trucking,* 89 Cal. App. 4th at 1049, 107 Cal. Rptr. 2d at 651. But courts are quick to add: "An exception to this general rule exists when the writing does not appear to be a contract and the terms are not called to the attention of the recipient. In such a case, no contract is formed with respect to the undisclosed term." *Id.; cf. Cory v. Golden State Bank,* 95 Cal. App. 3d 360, 364, 157 Cal. Rptr. 538, 541 (1979) ("[T]he provision in question is effectively hidden from the view of money order purchasers until after the transactions are completed. . . . Under these circumstances, it must be concluded that the Bank's money order purchasers are not chargeable with either actual or constructive notice of the service charge provision, and therefore cannot be deemed to have consented to the provision as part of their transaction with the Bank.").

Plaintiffs were responding to an offer that did not carry an immediately visible notice of the existence of license terms or require unambiguous manifestation of assent to those terms. Thus, plaintiffs' "apparent manifestation of . . . consent" was to terms "contained in a document whose contractual nature [was] not obvious." *Windsor Mills,* 25 Cal. App. 3d at 992, 101 Cal. Rptr. at 351. Moreover, the fact that, given the position of the scroll bar on their computer screens, plaintiffs may have been aware that an unexplored portion of the Netscape Web page remained below the download button does not mean that they reasonably should have concluded that this portion contained a notice of license terms. In their deposition testimony, plaintiffs variously stated that they used the scroll bar "[o]nly if there is something that I feel I need to see that is on — that is off the page," or that the elevated position of the scroll bar suggested the presence of "mere[] formalities, standard lower banner links" or "that the page is bigger than what I can see." Plaintiffs testified, and defendants did not refute, that plaintiffs were in fact unaware that defendants intended to attach license terms to the use of SmartDownload.

We conclude that in circumstances such as these, where consumers are urged to download free software at the immediate click of a button, a reference to the existence of license terms on a submerged screen is not sufficient to place consumers on inquiry or constructive notice of those terms. The SmartDownload Web page screen was "printed in such a manner that it tended to conceal the fact that it was an express acceptance of [Netscape's] rules and regulations." *Larrus,* 266 P.2d at 147. Internet users may have, as defendants put it, "as much time as they need[]" to scroll through multiple screens on a Web page, but there is no reason to assume that viewers will scroll down to subsequent screens simply because screens are there. When products are "free" and users are invited to download them in the absence of reasonably conspicuous notice that they are about to bind themselves to contract terms, the transactional circumstances cannot be fully analogized to those in the paper world of arm's-length bargaining. In the next two sections, we discuss case law and other legal authorities that have addressed the circumstances of computer sales, software licensing, and online transacting. Those authorities tend strongly to support our conclusion that plaintiffs did not manifest assent to SmartDownload's license terms.

### B. Shrinkwrap Licensing and Related Practices

Defendants cite certain well-known cases involving shrinkwrap licensing and related commercial practices in support of their contention that plaintiffs became bound by the SmartDownload license terms by virtue of inquiry notice. For example, in *Hill v. Gateway 2000, Inc.,* 105 F.3d 1147 (7th Cir. 1997), the Seventh Circuit held that where a purchaser had ordered a computer over the telephone, received the order in a shipped box containing the computer along with printed contract terms, and did not return the computer within the 30 days required by the terms, the purchaser was bound by the contract. *Id.* at 1148-1149. In *ProCD, Inc. v. Zeidenberg,* the same court held that where an individual purchased software in a box containing license terms which were displayed on the computer screen every time the user executed the software program, the user had sufficient opportunity to review the terms and to return the software, and so was contractually bound after retaining the product. *ProCD,* 86 F.3d at 1452; *cf. Moore v. Microsoft Corp.,* 293 A.D.2d 587, 587, 741 N.Y.S.2d 91, 92 (2d Dep't 2002) (software user was bound by license agreement where terms were prominently displayed on computer screen before software could be installed and where user was required to indicate assent by clicking "I agree"); *Brower v. Gateway 2000, Inc.,* 246 A.D.2d 246, 251, 676 N.Y.S.2d 569, 572 (1st Dep't 1998) (buyer assented to arbitration clause shipped inside box with computer and software by retaining items beyond date specified by license terms); *M.A. Mortenson Co. v. Timberline Software Corp.,* 93 Wash. App. 819, 970 P.2d 803, 809 (1999) (buyer manifested assent to software license terms by installing and using software), *aff'd,* 140 Wash. 2d 568, 998 P.2d 305 (2000); *see also I.Lan Sys.,* 183 F. Supp. 2d at 338 (business entity "explicitly accepted the clickwrap license agreement [contained in purchased software] when it clicked on the box stating 'I agree'").

These cases do not help defendants. To the extent that they hold that the purchaser of a computer or tangible software is contractually bound after failing to object to printed license terms provided with the product, *Hill* and *Brower* do not differ markedly from the cases involving traditional paper contracting discussed in the previous section. Insofar as the purchaser in *ProCD* was confronted with conspicuous, mandatory license terms every time he ran the software on his computer, that case actually undermines defendants' contention that downloading in the absence of conspicuous terms is an act that binds plaintiffs to those terms. In *Mortenson,* the full text of license terms was printed on each sealed disk envelope inside the software box, printed again on the inside cover of the user manual, and notice of the terms appeared on the computer screen every time the purchaser executed the program. *Mortenson,* 970 P.2d at 806. In sum, the foregoing cases are clearly distinguishable from the facts of the present action.

### C. Online Transactions

Cases in which courts have found contracts arising from Internet use do not assist defendants, because in those circumstances there was much clearer notice than in the present case that a user's act would manifest assent to contract terms. *See, e.g., Hotmail Corp. v. Van$ Money Pie Inc.,* 47 U.S.P.Q.2d 1020, 1025 (N.D. Cal. 1998) (granting preliminary injunction based in part on breach of "Terms of Service" agreement, to which defendants had assented); *America Online, Inc. v. Booker,* 781 So. 2d 423, 425 (Fla. Dist. Ct. App. 2001) (upholding forum selection clause in "freely negotiated agreement" contained in online terms of service); *Caspi v. Microsoft Network, L.L.C.,* 323 N.J. Super. 118, 732 A.2d 528, 530, 532-533 (N.J. Super. Ct. App. Div. 1999) (upholding forum selection clause where subscribers to online software were required to review license terms in scrollable window and to click "I Agree" or "I Don't Agree"); *Barnett v. Network Solutions, Inc.,* 38 S.W.3d 200, 203-204 (Tex. App. 2001) (upholding forum selection clause in online contract for registering Internet domain names that required users to scroll through terms before accepting or rejecting them); *cf. Pollstar v. Gigmania, Ltd.,* 170 F. Supp. 2d 974, 981-982 (E.D. Cal. 2000) (expressing concern that notice of license terms had appeared in small gray text on a gray background on a linked Web page, but concluding that it was too early in the case to order dismissal).[17]

---

17. Although the parties here do not refer to it, California's consumer fraud statute, Cal. Bus. & Prof. Code §17538, is one of the few state statutes to regulate online transactions in goods or services. The statute provides that in disclosing information regarding return and refund policies and other vital consumer information, online vendors must legibly display the information either:

> (i) [on] the first screen displayed when the vendor's electronic site is accessed, (ii) on the screen on which goods or services are first offered, (iii) on the screen on which a buyer may place the order for goods or services, (iv) on the screen on which the buyer may enter payment information, such as a credit card account number, or (v) for non-browser-based technologies, in a manner that gives the user a reasonable opportunity to review that information.

*Id.* §17538(d)(2)(A).

The statute's clear purpose is to ensure that consumers engaging in online transactions have relevant information before they can be bound. Although consumer fraud as such is not alleged in the present action, and §17538 protects only California residents, we note that the statute is consistent with the principle of conspicuous notice of the existence of contract terms that is also found in California's common law of contracts.

In addition, the model code, UCITA, discussed above, generally recognizes the importance of conspicuous notice and unambiguous manifestation of assent in online sales and licensing of computer information. For example, §112, which addresses manifestation of assent, provides that a user's opportunity to review online contract terms exists if a "record" (or electronic writing) of the contract terms is "made available in a manner that ought to call it to the attention of a reasonable person and permit review." UCITA, §112(e)(1) (rev. ed. Aug. 23, 2001) (available at *www.ucitaonline.com/ucita.html*). Section 112 also provides, in pertinent part, that "[a] person manifests assent to a record or term if the person, acting with knowledge of, or after having an opportunity

After reviewing the California common law and other relevant legal authority, we conclude that under the circumstances here, plaintiffs' downloading of SmartDownload did not constitute acceptance of defendants' license terms. Reasonably conspicuous notice of the existence of contract terms and unambiguous manifestation of assent to those terms by consumers are essential if electronic bargaining is to have integrity and credibility. We hold that a reasonably prudent offeree in plaintiffs' position would not have known or learned, prior to acting on the invitation to download, of the reference to SmartDownload's license terms hidden below the "Download" button on the next screen. We affirm the district court's conclusion that the user plaintiffs, including Fagan, are not bound by the arbitration clause contained in those terms.[18]

---

to review the record or term or a copy of it . . . intentionally engages in conduct or makes statements with reason to know that the other party or its electronic agent may infer from the conduct or statement that the person assents to the record or term." *Id.* §112(a)(2). In the case of a "mass-market license," a party adopts the terms of the license only by manifesting assent "before or during the party's initial performance or use of or access to the information." *Id.* §209(a).

UCITA §211 sets forth a number of guidelines for "Internet-type" transactions involving the supply of information or software. For example, a licensor should make standard terms "available for review" prior to delivery or obligation to pay (1) by "displaying prominently and in close proximity to a description of the computer information, or to instructions or steps for acquiring it, the standard terms or a reference to an electronic location from which they can be readily obtained," or (2) by "disclosing the availability of the standard terms in a prominent place on the site from which the computer information is offered and promptly furnishing a copy of the standard terms on request before the transfer of the computer information." *Id.* §211(1)(A-B). The commentary to §211 adds: "The intent of the close proximity standard is that the terms or the reference to them would be called to the attention of an ordinary reasonable person." *Id.* §211 Comment 3. The commentary also approves of prominent hypertext links that draw attention to the existence of a standard agreement and allow users to view the terms of the license. *Id.*

We hasten to point out that UCITA, which has been enacted into law only in Maryland and Virginia, does not govern the parties' transactions in the present case, but we nevertheless find that UCITA's provisions offer insight into the evolving online "circumstances" that defendants argue placed plaintiffs on inquiry notice of the existence of the SmartDownload license terms. UCITA has been controversial as a result of the perceived breadth of some of its provisions. *Compare* Margaret Jane Radin, *Humans, Computers, and Binding Commitment*, 75 Ind. L.J. 1125, 1141 (2000) (arguing that "UCITA's definition of manifestation of assent stretches the ordinary concept of consent"), *with* Joseph H. Sommer, *Against Cyberlaw*, 15 Berkeley Tech. L.J. 1145, 1187 (2000) ("There are no new legal developments [in UCITA's assent provisions]. The revolution—if any—occurred with [Karl] Llewellyn's old Article 2, which abandoned most formalisms of contract formation, and sought a contract wherever it could be found."). Nonetheless, UCITA's notice and assent provisions seem to be consistent with well-established principles governing contract formation and enforcement. *See* Robert A. Hillman & Jeffrey J. Rachlinski, *Standard-Form Contracting in the Electronic Age*, 77 N.Y.U. L. Rev. 429, 491 (2002) ("[W]e contend that UCITA maintains the contextual, balanced approach to standard terms that can be found in the paper world.").

18. Because we conclude that the Netscape Web page did not provide reasonable notice of the existence of SmartDownload's license terms, it is irrelevant to our decision whether plaintiff Fagan obtained SmartDownload from that Web page, as defendants contend, or from a shareware Web site that provided less or no notice of that program's license terms, as Fagan maintains. In either case, Fagan could not be bound by the SmartDownload license agreement. Further, because we find that the California common law disposes of the issue of notice and assent, we do not address plaintiffs' arguments based on California's Commercial Code §2207, the UCC Article 2 provision governing the "battle of the forms." Moreover, having determined that the parties did not enter into the SmartDownload license agreement, we do not reach plaintiffs' alternative arguments concerning unconscionability.

## NOTE AND PROBLEMS

If UCITA applies to a transaction, it has many of the contract formational rules found in UCC Article 2. For example, it has a statute of frauds that applies to contracts where the fee is $5,000 or more. UCITA §201. There is also a parol evidence rule. UCITA §301.

UCITA's approach to "shrinkwrap" and "click through" licenses is described in the court's footnote 17 in *Specht v. Netscape*, above.[6] UCITA distinguishes between "mass market" and other licenses. A "mass market" license is one that is marketed to consumers and to the public generally, the type of license a purchaser of most Microsoft software would encounter. UCITA §102(a)(44) and (45). In both "mass market" and other cases, UCITA requires that terms be "made available in a manner that ought to call it to the attention of a reasonable person and permit review." UCITA §113. For "mass market" licenses, a term is only included if the other party assents to it "before or during the party's initial performance or use of or access to the information." UCITA §209.

Where UCITA differs from UCC Article 2 is in its rules that more clearly validate "shrinkwrap" or "click through" licenses, as discussed in the following problems. UCITA expressly approves of the "rolling contract" or "layered contract" theory espoused in such cases as *ProCD v. Zeidenberg* and *Hill v. Gateway*, meaning that terms in a contract can be disclosed to a contracting party after that party has already agreed to pay. UCITA §208. See pages 40-43, *supra*.

The *Principles of the Law of Software Contracts* cover the issue of standard form software licenses in §2.02 and focus on whether a reasonable transferor (the licensor) would believe that the transferee (licensee) intends to be bound to the standard form license. Such a belief would be reasonable if, among other things, the transferee had reasonable access to the license before paying.

***Problem 11-2.*** A small business purchases some accounting software from a retail establishment. When the software first runs, it shows a copy of the license on the screen and requires the operator to scroll to the bottom of the license and to click "I accept" before the software can be used. The employee of the business who uses the software does not read the license carefully and clicks "I accept." Assume that this employee is authorized to act on behalf of the business. Among other things, the license indicates that the governing law will be that of State *X*, which has adopted UCITA. It indicates that any disputes will be litigated in State *A*, the home state of the licensor. The licensee's place of business is in State *B*, which is 3,000 miles from State *A*. Neither State *A* nor State *B* has adopted UCITA. Would UCITA govern this transaction? Would the licensee have to litigate any disputes that it might have regarding the license in State *A*?[7] If the employee had noticed objectionable provisions in the license before clicking "I accept," would the business have been able

---

6. The *Specht* court was commenting on an earlier version of UCITA, so some of the section references do not gibe with the 2002 version.

7. Note that Iowa has adopted a so-called "bomb shelter" provision that protects its residents (including businesses with principal places of business in Iowa) from application of UCITA by voiding a choice of law of a state that has enacted UCITA. Ia. St. §554D.125.

to return the software and get its money back? See UCITA §§109, 110, 112, 113, 208, and 209. Under the *Principles of the Law of Software Contracts* §1.14, a forum selection clause is unenforceable if, among other things, the forum is "unreasonably inconvenient for a party." The commentary to the section indicates that this might be the case if the potential damages to the aggrieved party are small and the party would incur significant expense traveling to the designated forum.

***Problem 11-3.*** Same facts as Problem 11-2. The license also states in bold print, "Except for express warranties stated in the contract, if any, this computer program is provided with all faults, the entire risk as to satisfactory quality, and performance is with the user." The language is in larger type than the surrounding terms of the license, which are not in bold print. The employee for the business does not read the license carefully, does not notice this disclaimer, and clicks "I accept." Under UCITA, would the implied warranties be disclaimed? See UCITA §§102(a)(14), 208, 209, 403 and 406. Would this method of disclaiming warranties, with disclosure of the disclaimer occurring after the goods had been paid for, be effective under UCC Article 2? See pages 83-89, *supra*. Should there be different rules for disclaiming warranties when licenses are involved as compared to the sale of goods? Under the *Principles of the Law of Software Contracts* §3.05, there is a nondisclaimable implied warranty if the licensor receives money or a right to payment in exchange for the license that the licensor is not aware of any hidden material defects in the software.

***Problem 11-4.*** Register.com is an appointed registrar of domain names for the Internet under an agreement with the Internet Corporation for Assigned Names and Numbers ("ICANN"). ICANN is a private, nonprofit public benefit corporation established by various agencies of the United States government to regulate domain names and addresses on the Internet. Under Register's agreement with ICANN, it is required to obtain certain identifying information from anyone seeking to register a domain name, including the name, mailing address, and e-mail address of the registrant (called "WHOIS information"). Under the agreement with ICANN, the WHOIS information must be accessible to the public at no charge. The only restriction that ICANN's agreement permits on use of the WHOIS information is that the holder of the information may forbid its use for the purpose of commercial solicitation via e-mail. The ICANN agreement with Register provides, however, that no third-party beneficiary may sue under the agreement — any complaints that a third party may have should be directed to ICANN.

Verio, Inc., is in the business of selling various Web site–related services, including design and operation. To some extent, it competes with Register .com in that Register also provides Web-related services in addition to being a registrar of domain names. Verio was interested in obtaining the WHOIS information for the purpose of soliciting business. It directed numerous Internet queries through its automated program, called a "robot," to Register .com. Register would respond with the requested information, each time with a legend indicating: "By submitting a WHOIS query, you agree that . . . under no circumstances will you use this data to . . . support the transmission of mass unsolicited . . . advertising or solicitations via direct mail, electronic mail, or by telephone." Should Register be allowed to sue Verio to enforce the solicitation restriction? See UCITA §§112(a)(2), 205, 210; *Restatement (Second) of Contracts* §69(1)(a); *Register.com, Inc. v. Verio, Inc.*, 356 F.3d 393 (2d Cir. 2004).

## C. WARRANTIES AND OTHER CONTRACT TERMS

Similar to UCC Article 2, UCITA provides rules dealing with express warranties and implied warranties of merchantability and fitness. UCITA provides a mechanism for disclaiming implied warranties, covered in Problem 11-3, *supra*. One warranty given in UCITA that does not correspond to warranties given under UCC Article 2 regards informational content. Someone may have a license to refer to a database, for example Westlaw or LEXIS, for information. Is the information contained in that database accurate? UCITA section 404 provides that if a merchant "in a special relationship of reliance with a licensee" provides informational content, there is a warranty that there is no inaccuracy caused by the merchant's failure to perform with reasonable care. There is no warranty with respect to published informational content, meaning information that is available to the general public. See UCITA §102(a)(52).

UCITA also has rules prohibiting contractual provisions that violate public policy and that are unconscionable. UCITA §§105 and 111. It specifically regulates provisions that restrict public comment and reverse engineering of software. UCITA §§105 and 118. For the most part, however, UCITA upholds the ability of the parties to draft whatever contract they like and to vary the terms of UCITA. UCITA §115. In that respect, UCITA is very much like the UCC and the CISG.

Would the following case, dealing with the liability of a party providing inaccurate information under a license, be decided the same way under UCITA section 404?

### DANIEL v. DOW JONES & CO.

Civil Court, City of New York, Special Term

137 Misc. 2d 94, 520 N.Y.S.2d 334 (1987)

With the inexorable march of time has come an age of technology of previously unimagined dimensions. Methods for news delivery have advanced apace with general scientific achievements. While town criers had for centuries informed the local citizenry, general circulation newspapers eventually made criers superfluous. Early in this century, news, transmitted by radio and telephone, became available to subscribers through dedicated news tickers and to the public by "extra" editions of newspapers. Widely available radio and television made news known to the public within minutes of its occurrence. In the past few years, instantaneous news has become available to subscribers with access to a microcomputer and a telephone, even at home.

Do technological advances require rethinking legal principles that have existed for previous modalities? Do modern techniques for delivering the news change the rules applicable to its providers? This case raises the question of whether the providing of a premium service for instantaneous transmission of the news by computer-to-computer linkup places the news service at greater risk to readers than does the providing of the same news by another modality.

The relevant facts in this case are not in dispute. In September 1986, plaintiff, a law student and securities investor, became one of the more than 200,000 subscribers to a service, Dow Jones News/Retrieval, offered by defendant. The service provides what it advertises to be "timely," "accurate" news; it can be accessed from a subscriber's computer. The subscriber telephones defendant's computer. Then, by use of a personal computer and modem, a device that converts computer signals for telephone transmission, the subscriber enters the necessary passwords and access codes to set up an instantaneous, continuous, "interactive" "online" linkage with defendant's computer, thus allowing access to the Dow Jones News Service. The service is "interactive" in that the subscriber describes his or her requests through a home or business computer; defendant's computer responds and, at a charge of $3.00 per minute, searches for the items the subscriber has requested.

Plaintiff asserts that he received a news report from defendant that was false and misleading in that it omitted a material fact. The news item, datelined Calgary, referred to a transaction involving the restructuring of Husky Oil, a Canadian corporation; it did not mention that the prices referred to were in Canadian, not United States, dollars. Plaintiff claims that he relied on the pricing in the report to his detriment.

Defendant, based on affidavits describing the events, moved to dismiss the complaint for failure to state a cause of action. This court provided written notice to both parties of its intention to treat the motion as one for summary judgment. Additional affidavits have been submitted.

The theory of the complaint is that defendant negligently published false and misleading statements. New York has long recognized such a cause of action. Liability exists "only where there is a duty, if one speaks at all, to give the correct information." In addition to knowledge of the possibility of detrimental reliance, "the relationship of the parties, * * * must be such that in morals and good conscience the one has the right to rely upon the other for information, and the other giving the information owes a duty to give it with care." (*International Products Co. v. Erie R.R. Co.,* 244 N.Y. 331, 338, 155 N.E. 662 (1927); *Doyle v. Chatham & Phenix Natl. Bank,* 253 N.Y. 369, 377, 171 N.E. 574 (1930); *see Ultramares Corp. v. Touche,* 255 N.Y. 170, 180-185, 174 N.E. 441 (1931) (an accountant may be liable for a negligent audit opinion but only to a circumscribed class of potential plaintiffs). The cause of action has been severely limited over the years to avoid impinging on basic rights. *Advance Music Corp. v. American Tobacco Co.,* 268 App. Div. 707, 710-711, 53 N.Y.S.2d 337 (1st Dept. 1945), *revd. on other grounds,* 296 N.Y. 79, 70 N.E.2d 401 (1946); *Sacco v. Herald Statesman,* 32 Misc. 2d 739, 223 N.Y.S.2d 329. *Restatement [Second] of Torts,* section 552(2), also supports limiting the class of plaintiffs who may sue for negligent misstatements; liability "is limited to loss suffered (a) by the person or *one of a limited group of persons* for whose benefit and guidance" (emphasis added) the speaker acts. That is, as a matter of public policy, the class of potential plaintiffs must be carefully circumscribed to avoid the potential of unlimited liability.

New York long ago held that a news service is not liable to its readers for negligent false statements. *Jaillet v. Cashman,* 115 Misc. 383, 189 N.Y.S. 743 (Sup. Ct. 1921), *affd.* 202 App. Div. 805, 194 N.Y.S. 947 (1st Dept. 1922), *affd.* 235 N.Y. 511, 139 N.E. 714 (1923). In *Jaillet,* the court held that Dow Jones & Company was not liable to a person who saw an erroneous item on its news ticker in a stockbroker's office. Special Term held that "the relation of the defendant association to the public is the same as that of a publisher of a newspaper, and its duties and obligations are to be measured by the same standard." *Supra,* 115 Misc., at 384, 189 N.Y.S. 743. The court further concluded that, although there was "moral obligation upon everyone to say nothing that is not true," there is no liability unless there is a breach of a specific duty to the injured party. *Supra,* 115 Misc., at 384, 189 N.Y.S. 743. The rationale of the holding was that unless the scope of liability was limited, the publisher of news might become liable to an undefined, infinite class of news readers. "If liability had been upheld, the step would have been a short one to the declaration of a like liability on the part of proprietors of newspapers." *Ultramares Corp. v. Touche, supra,* 255 N.Y. at p.185, 174 N.E. 441.

The rule of *Jaillet* has been consistently followed even after *International Products Co. v. Erie R.R. Co., supra.* In *Courteen Seed Co. v. Hong Kong & Shanghai Banking Corp.,* 245 N.Y. 377, 381, 157 N.E. 272 (1927), the court articulated the principle that "negligent words are not actionable unless they are uttered directly * * * to one to whom the speaker is bound by some relation of duty, arising out of public calling, contract or otherwise, to act with care if he acts at all." More recently, in *Pressler v. Dow Jones & Co.,* 88 A.D.2d 928, 450 N.Y.S.2d 884 (2d Dep't 1982), the court reversed a refusal to dismiss an action for damages based on a negligent misstatement, since "no special relationship existed between the parties." *See Roman v. City of New York,* 110 Misc. 2d 799, 802, 442 N.Y.S.2d 945 (Sup. Ct. Queens Co. 1981) (no liability for misstatements in a text of general circulation).

The federal courts have followed the New York rule requiring a "special relationship" between the parties for liability for negligent misstatements. In *Demuth Dev. Corp. v. Merck & Co.,* 432 F. Supp. 990 (E.D.N.Y. 1977), the court, after surveying New York law, found no cause of action for publishing 276,500 copies of a manual that negligently stated, incorrectly, that plaintiff's chemical was poisonous. The court reasoned that the defendant had no "special" duty which "in morals and good conscience" should make it liable to plaintiff.

The "special relationship" limitation on liability for negligent statements remains despite the weakening of the rule of privity. In *White v. Guarente,* 43 N.Y.2d 356, 361, 401 N.Y.S.2d 474, 372 N.E.2d 315 (1977), the court held that an accountant may be liable to persons of a "known group possessed of vested rights, marked by a definable limit and made up of certain components." *Credit Alliance Corp. v. Arthur Andersen & Co.,* 65 N.Y.2d 536, 548-551, 493 N.Y.S.2d 435, 483 N.E.2d 110 (1985). Even though the duty to make accurate statements is imposed by law, and not by contract or privity, the number of potential plaintiffs remains limited.

Plaintiff here argues that he had a "special relationship" with defendant because he had contracted for its services and, thereby, came within the permitted, limited class of plaintiffs. He also contends that summary judgment should be denied because a finder of facts must determine whether a "special relationship" exists. No trial is needed, however, where the facts do not, and cannot, create liability.

The relationship between the parties here is the same as between any subscriber and a news service; it is functionally identical to that of a purchaser of a newspaper. The advances of technology bring the defendant's service into the home or office of more than 200,000 persons; indeed even nonsubscribers may receive defendant's service through computerized linkages with other database enterprises. There is no functional difference between defendant's service and the distribution of a moderate circulation newspaper or subscription newsletter. The instantaneous, interactive, computerized delivery of defendant's service does not alter the facts: plaintiff purchased defendant's news reports as did thousands of others. The "special relationship" required to allow an action for negligent misstatements must be greater than that between the ordinary buyer and seller. Technological advances must continually be evaluated and their relation to legal rules determined so that antiquated rules are not misapplied in modern settings. "[W]ith new conditions there must be new rules." Cardozo, *The Nature of the Legal Process* 137 (Yale paperbound ed. 1960). Yet, if the substance of a transaction has not changed, new technology does not require a new legal rule merely because of its novelty.

[The court goes on to hold that the negligent publication of nondefamatory information is protected by the United States and New York Constitutions.]

The defendant's motion to dismiss the action is granted.

## NOTE, QUESTIONS, AND PROBLEMS

When does a "special relationship" exist, thus bringing in the implied warranty in UCITA section 404(a)? Official Comment 3A to section 404(a) defines the "special relationship" as being "characterized by the provider's knowledge that the particular licensee plans to rely on the data in its own business and expects that the provider will tailor the information to its needs. The obligation arises only with respect to persons who possess unique or specialized expertise and who are in a special position of confidence and trust with the licensee such that reliance on the inaccurate information is justified and the party has a duty to act with care." The Comment refers the reader to *Murphy v. Kuhn*, 90 N.Y.2d 266, 682 N.E.2d 972 (N.Y. 1997). In that case, the court held that there was no "special relationship" between an insured and his insurance agent that required the agent to tell the insured that he should increase his coverage. The court noted that a special relationship will exist in situations in which someone is relying on professionals, such as accountants, doctors, and lawyers. Such professionals have greater knowledge than their clients, who rely on them to give proper advice. The court held that the insurance agent did not have greater knowledge than the insured regarding his coverage needs.

UCITA Comment 3A also states that the information provided must be specially tailored to the needs of the licensee: "A special relationship does not arise for information made generally available to a group in standardized form even if those who subscribe to the information service believe it is relevant to their commercial needs." That being said, could you safely rely on a legal database's determination as to whether a case has been subsequently overturned?

Even if a warranty is given regarding the accuracy of published informational content, consequential damages for breach of that warranty are not permitted under UCITA unless the contract expressly so provides. UCITA §807(b)(1).

***Problem 11-5.*** A software license has a conspicuous provision forbidding the licensee from publicly commenting on the software in any negative way. A licensee is very dissatisfied with the software, and publishes on a widely read Internet Web site a lengthy comment detailing the negative experiences that the licensee has had, and describes the software as "the lousiest product I have ever purchased." Has the licensee violated an enforceable provision in the license? UCITA §105(c). If UCITA is not the law, would the provision in the license be enforceable? *Cf.* UCC §2-302.

***Problem 11-6.*** HLB Technology developed copyrighted software that engineers could use in making designs. Baystate Technologies developed similar, competing software. Baystate obtained a copy of the HLB software pursuant to a license. The license prohibited reverse engineering, the process by which the licensee could determine the underlying logic and ideas behind the computer program. Reverse engineering has been held to be a "fair use" under the copyright law, provided that it does not result in the ultimate commercial reproduction and sale of the product in a manner that violates the copyright. Copyright law protects the expression of ideas, but not the ideas themselves. There is a public policy favoring the development of new methods of expression; that is, improving technology. *See Atari, Inc. v. JS & A Group, Inc.*, 747 F.2d 1422 (Fed. Cir. 1984).

Baystate violated the contractual prohibition against reverse engineering, and used the information it learned to improve its own software package, rendering the HLB software package uncompetitive with Baystate's. Assume for the sake of the discussion that Baystate's software does not violate HLB's copyright. Could HLB sue Baystate for breach of contract for violating the provision prohibiting reverse engineering? *See Bowers v. Baystate Technologies*, 320 F.3d 1317 (Fed. Cir. 2003). Would it make a difference if Baystate reverse engineered the product for the purpose of making other Baystate software more compatible with it; that is, able to share information with it? See UCITA §§105(b) and 118.

## D. PERFORMANCE, BREACH, AND REMEDIES

In the event of breach of an agreement covered by UCITA, the general rule is that a party may cancel the contract only if the breach is material and has not been cured or if the contract permits cancellation. UCITA §802(a). UCITA is thus in accord with the common law of contracts. See *Restatement (Second) of Contracts* §237. For a discussion of the concept of material breach, see page 154, *supra*. For a nonmaterial breach, the injured party may be entitled to damages but must still perform that party's obligations under the contract. UCITA §701(b).

An exception to this rule exists if the obligation of the breaching party is to provide a single copy of information in a mass-market transaction, which includes consumer contracts. See UCITA §102(a)(44). In such a case, the licensee may reject the copy if it does not conform to the contract, subject to the licensor's right to cure under UCITA section 703. UCITA §704(b). This rule is similar to the "perfect tender rule" under UCC Article 2; see pages 145-146, *supra*. If the licensor is unable or unwilling to cure, the consumer may cancel the contract.

The commentary to section 704 notes that the "perfect tender rule" is a bit of a misnomer—it is more accurately called the "conforming tender rule." The software or other information being licensed need not be perfect—it simply must conform to the terms of the contract, including any express and implied warranties. And with respect to at least some kinds of software, it is reasonable to expect some minor "bugs." See UCITA §403, Official Comment 3A.

The UCITA remedy provisions are largely reflective of common law. There is a goal of giving the injured party the benefit of the bargain, with an obligation on the part of the injured party to reasonably mitigate damages. Speculative damages are not allowed. UCITA §§807, 808, and 809. UCITA does permit parties to contract for specific performance if the performance is other than the payment of money, but the Official Commentary to the section indicates that the court will honor that contractual provision only if the court can administer the remedy and it does not violate a fundamental public policy of the jurisdiction. UCITA §811, Official Comment 2.

One of the most controversial issues considered by the drafters of UCITA was whether licensors should be allowed to use electronic self-help. In the event of a breach by a licensee, a licensor might like to send a signal to the licensee's computer that would disable the licensee from using the licensor's software. Because of concerns that this could seriously harm the business of some licensees, the drafters ultimately decided to prohibit electronic self-help in the event of breach. See UCITA §816. The licensor may also use automatic restraints that would prevent breach, such as including a code that prevents the licensee from making more than the authorized number of copies of the information. UCITA §605. The relationship between electronic regulation of performance and electronic self-help is studied in an upcoming problem.

On an access contract, however, the licensor is permitted to discontinue access upon breach. UCITA §814. "Access contract" is defined as "a contract to obtain by electronic means access to, or information from, an information processing system of another person. . . ." UCITA §102(a)(1). Official Comment 1 to section 102 indicates that an access contract would include a license to obtain information from an online service provider, such as AOL. It could also include a situation in which software is run from the licensor's system rather than being downloaded onto the licensee's system. So while self-help would not be permitted to disable a computer program downloaded onto the licensee's computer, the licensor could discontinue access to the program if the license required the licensee to use it only by accessing it from the licensor's server.

## PROBLEMS

***Problem 11-7.*** A business ("licensee") licenses software from Microhard Technology that is supposed to perform accounting functions. Assume that UCITA applies to the transaction, and that the implied warranty of merchantability under UCITA section 403 has not been disclaimed. The software does not work as well as competing accounting software, but is not completely worthless. The licensee does hire an additional bookkeeper, however, to deal with some accounting issues that should have been more adequately handled by the software. The license is a two-year license, with the licensee having paid $1,000 for the first year and having agreed to pay $1,000 for the second year. The competing accounting software licenses for the same amount. At the end of the first year, the licensee would like to cancel the license. May it do so? If there is a breach of contract by Microhard, how would the licensee's damages be calculated? See UCITA §§601, 701, 801, 802, and 809.

***Problem 11-8.*** Microhard Technology licenses software to businesses that is used to control inventory levels. The license is month-to-month; if payment is received by the beginning of a month, the licensee is allowed to use the software for that month. If payment is not received, Microhard is able to electronically disable the software on the licensee's computer. Is this kind of arrangement lawful? See UCITA §§605, Official Comment 6, and 816.

## CHAPTER 11 REVIEW PROBLEM

A buyer purchases a computer which has software already installed. The buyer is a consumer, and the computer and software are generally marketed to the public. No terms are disclosed at the time that the buyer pays for the computer, and the box containing the computer does not have any language on it alerting the buyer to the terms that are in the box. Inside the box are fine-print licenses giving the buyer the right to use the installed software that indicate that retention of the computer with the software for more than 30 days indicates assent to the terms on the licenses. The licenses and the warranty covering the hardware provide that in the event of any dispute regarding either the hardware or the software, the buyer agrees to arbitration. You may assume that the terms of the arbitration are not unduly burdensome on consumers. See Problem 5-10, supra. The buyer does not pay any attention to the terms on the licenses, and uses the computer for more than 30 days.

The computer is able to do many of the promised functions, but its Internet access works more slowly than it should, because the anti-spyware software has logical errors in it. Spyware is a type of program that merchants and others try to install on computer systems to permit monitoring of the user's Internet habits, either for marketing purposes or for malicious purposes. Spyware can seriously interfere with a computer's operation. This problem is very aggravating to the buyer. The buyer contacts the software provider, which is unable to fix the problem. The buyer would like to return the entire computer system, including both the hardware and the software. You may assume that the relevant jurisdiction has adopted UCITA. Would it apply to the transaction? See UCITA §103(b). If it does apply, what would be the buyer's rights with respect to the computer system? See UCITA §§403, 701, 707, 802, 807, and 809. Would buyer be required to arbitrate any dispute? UCITA §§112, 113, 208, and 209.

If the foregoing case were resolved entirely under UCC Article 2, would the result be any different? See UCC §§2-314, 2-508, 2-601, 2-608, 2-711, 2-714, and 2-715. On the question of arbitration, see UCC section 2-207 and *Hill v. Gateway*, p. 40-43, *supra*.

# TABLE OF CASES

*Principal cases are indicated by italics.*

## D



## E



## F



## G

**H**



**I**



**J**



**K**



**L**



**M**

# UNIFORM COMMERCIAL CODE

# CONTRACTS FOR THE INTERNATIONAL SALE OF GOODS (CISG)

**CISG Article**

# INDEX

**M**

## V



## W